New Theories of

B

New Theories of Discourse
Laclau, Mouffe and Žižek

Jacob Torfing

Copyright © Jacob Torfing 1999

The right of Jacob Torfing to be identified as author of this work has been asserted in accordance with the Copyright, Designs and Patents Act 1988.

First published 1999

Blackwell Publishers Ltd
108 Cowley Road
Oxford OX4 1JF
UK

Blackwell Publishers Inc.
350 Main Street
Malden, Massachusetts 02148
USA

British Library Cataloguing in Publication Data

A CIP catalogue record for this book is available from the British Library.

Library of Congress Cataloging-in-Publication Data

Torfing, Jacob.
New theories of discourse : Laclau, Mouffe, and Žižek / Jacob Torfing.
p.   cm.
Includes bibliographical references and index.
ISBN 0–631–19577–2 (alk. paper). — ISBN 0–631–19558–0 (pbk. : alk. paper)
1. Postmodernism—Social aspects.   2. Postmodernism—Political aspects.
3. Discourse analysis—Social aspects.   4. Discourse analysis—Political aspects.
5. Laclau, Ernesto.   6. Mouffe, Chantal.   7. Žižek, Slavoj.   I. Title.
HM73.T63   1999
300'.1—dc21
98-28667
CIP

Typeset in 10.5 on 12pt Sabon
by G&G Editorial, Brighton
Printed in Great Britain by
TJ International, Padstow, Cornwall

This book is printed on acid-free paper

Contents

Contents

Preface

This book seeks to provide a comprehensive and accessible account of
discourse theory as a reading of the 'postmodern condition' within
social, cultural and political theory. Postmodernity has wide-ranging
implications for the social sciences. There has been much discussion
about the nature of these implications and of how the challenge they
represent can be used to advance our understanding of the world of
today. Discourse theory, as developed by *Ernesto Laclau, Chantal
Mouffe* and *Slavoj Žižek,* draws our attention to the implications of
postmodernity for the way we conceive of the relation between the
political and the social. Postmodernity urges us to take into account
the open and incomplete character of any social totality and to insist
on the primary role of politics in shaping and reshaping social
relations. An insistence upon the contingency of the social and upon
the constitutive role of politics represents a powerful challenge to
traditional social, cultural and political theory and makes thinkable a
whole range of new political projects, of which one of the most
promising and exciting is the development of a radical and plural
democracy.

Unfortunately, no single book has to date provided a comprehensive and accessible account of the new theories of discourse advanced
by Laclau, Mouffe and Žižek. Except for a few review articles and
some rather polemical critiques, the original works of these distinguished contemporary theorists remain the only source for those
wishing to acquaint themselves with this recent development in
discourse theory. As many readers find the works of Laclau, Mouffe
and Žižek challengingly inaccessible, there is a particular need for a
book of this kind.

The structure of the book is as follows: *Part I* (chapters 1–3) explores the theoretical development of the discourse theory of Laclau and Mouffe from a Gramsci-inspired critique of structural Marxism, through a neo-Gramscian theory of discourse, to a new type of post-modern theorizing. The works of Žižek are only considered to the extent that they contribute to this development. Considerations of space prevent the fuller examination that Žižek's work demands; its significance extends far beyond an affinity with the discourse theory of Laclau and Mouffe. *Part II* (chapters 4–6) examines the main arguments of discourse theory in relation to the key concepts of discourse, hegemony and social antagonism. *Part III* (chapters 7–9) aims at directing discourse theory to the study of some central conceptual dyads within social, cultural and political theory: structure/agency, power/authority, universal/particular. *Part IV* (chapters 10–12) illustrates how discourse theory can be applied in more specific studies: to the politics of nationalism and racism, the politics of mass media, and the politics of the modern welfare state. *Part V* (chapters 13–14) discusses the possibility of a radical plural democracy, the development of a new democratic citizenship, and the advancement of a postmodern ethics. In the conclusion I assess the strengths and weaknesses of discourse theory and discuss the prospects for its future development.

The book is intended for advanced undergraduates, postgraduates and professionals within the social sciences. It is divided into relatively short chapters and includes suggestions for further reading and a comprehensive glossary, and is therefore particularly suitable for use in teaching. It is also an ideal introduction for those seeking an accessible point of entry into the fascinating intricacies of discourse theory.

The writing of an introductory textbook necessarily involves a high degree of loyalty to the original sources. Nevertheless, I do not consider myself as merely the mouthpiece for a pre-established truth. Discourse theory firmly rejects the notion that it represents an original doctrine of unquestionable truth; moreover, any attempt to summarize its theoretical insights would be worthless if it failed to engage in critical discussion and elaboration of the argument. Hence I have sought to present the arguments of discourse theory in my own words and, where necessary, to fill the theoretical voids and silences with findings from my own as well as from other people's research. In this way I hope to have succeeded in creating my own version of discourse theory, to be judged in its own right, though with an eye to the family resemblance it bears to the works of Laclau, Mouffe and Žižek.

Acknowledgements

The poststructuralist decentring of the author has long been widely recognized in the field of academic publishing. It is certainly a truism that no book is ever the product of its author alone. This one has been helped into print by a number of people and institutions. Let me first of all express my gratitude to Erik Albæk of the University of Aarhus in Denmark, who in the early 1980s introduced me to the early works of Ernesto Laclau and Chantal Mouffe. Warm thanks go also to my fellow students in the MA and Ph.D. seminars on Ideology and Discourse Analysis at the University of Essex, in the United Kingdom. They created a most stimulating intellectual environment, which has proved invaluable to the development of my understanding of the concepts and arguments of discourse theory. Above all, I am immensely indebted to Ernesto Laclau and Chantal Mouffe, who have been extremely generous with their time in reading through and commenting on earlier versions of this book. They have both done what they could to remove errors and improve the argument. Needless to say, responsibility for any remaining problems is mine alone. My intellectual travelling companion Torben Bech Dyrberg, of the University of Roskilde, Denmark, with whom I have shared an obsessive interest in discourse theory for many years, also commented on the manuscript, and I have benefited greatly from his encouragement and his help in resolving various theoretical problems. The Danish Social Science Research Council has financed parts of my research, and the Centre for Theoretical Studies in the Humanities and Social Sciences, University of Essex, has also provided important resources. I would also like to thank Bob Jessop, of the University of Lancaster, in the United Kingdom, for reading the book prior to its publication. Last but not least my thanks go to Milica Kier-Nielsen, who compiled the references, and to Robin Gable, who took pains to improve my rather imperfect English. Jill Landeryou has proved a supportive and very patient editor. My wife, Eva, and my children, Thomas, Sune and Emil, have suffered from my effort to finish the book, and have helped me to contrast 'the greyness of theory' with 'the greenness of life'. I hope I will be able to repay the debt.

Introduction:
Discourse Theory in Context

The events of *May 1968* spurred the development of a discourse-theoretical approach to social, cultural and political analysis. The struggle against the dominant forms and contents of higher education prompted a closer study of the relation between power and knowledge. The attempt by students to forge an alliance with striking workers, the efforts on the part of various intellectuals to ally with oppressed groups of prisoners, immigrants, and so on, and the failure of the French Communist Party to provide a political and moral-intellectual leadership led to a reformulation of the relation between theory and practice and urged a recasting of Marxism. Finally, the development of the student revolt into a broad struggle against the multiple forms of ideological repression fostered a growing interest in the question of how identity was constructed and transformed.

The epicentre of May 1968 was Paris, but widespread and long-lasting repercussions were felt throughout the western world. In response to the dislocating events, many intellectuals on the left became attracted in due course to the discourse-theoretical approach. The shift among left-wing intellectuals to discourse theory was encouraged by the ever-deepening *crisis of welfare state capitalism,* which was accelerated at the beginning of the 1970s by the oil crisis. For the left, the crisis of the modern welfare state, which had undoubtedly brought the working class considerable benefits, was represented as a triple crisis of its 'classist', 'statist' and 'productivist' legacy. The proliferation of new social movements (for example, the feminist, peace, and green movements, and those involving gays and lesbians), which followed in the wake of the events in May 1968 and gained momentum during the economic crisis, undermined belief in the privileged role of the working class (classism). The failure of the state to

1

restore the conditions for economic growth and social harmony undermined confidence in central state planning (statism). Finally, the
combination of a crisis in the Fordist system of mass production in
Europe and North America and a growing awareness of the threat of
ecological disaster made it increasingly difficult to view continued
economic growth as a goal in itself (productivism).

In a situation where the old political and theoretical scheme was
dying and a new one not yet born, the *structural Marxism* of Althusser
and his associates promised to provide the left with the means to
renew the analysis of modern capitalist societies. The theoretical
advances of structural Marxism can be summarized as follows: an
insistence upon the overdetermined character of social relations and
political struggles which were capable of condensing a multitude of
different meanings into symbolic unities with real effects on social,
cultural and political life; an emphasis on the role of ideology and ideological state apparatuses; a radical decentring of the subject, which
existed only as an articulation of dispersed subject positions; a concern
for the internal contradictions and relative autonomy of the state; and
advocacy of the Gramscian notion of hegemony as a key to understanding the interpenetration of state and economy. This was all very
good, and in the French context it certainly provided a favourable
alternative to both the Stalinist deformation of Marxism and the
humanist response of Sartre (see Benton, 1984). However, the anti-
essentialist credentials of structural Marxism were increasingly
undermined by its fierce attacks on Gramsci's absolute historicism (i.e.
his belief in the primacy of politics), by its insistence on the necessary
class-belonging of ideological elements, and by its dogmatic reassertion of determination in the last instance by the economy. The
structural Marxism of Althusser did not fall apart as a result of its
internal theoretical contradictions – which reflected the ambiguity of
most left-wing intellectuals; rather, it gradually lost its momentum and
strength, thereby leaving the theoretical terrain open to new and more
consequential and consistent efforts to abandon essentialist reasoning
within Marxism, and indeed within social, cultural and political
theory in general. Certain new developments within discourse theory
represented one such effort, and possibly as a consequence it began to
attract a growing number of adherents.

New Theories of Discourse

In 1986 Diane Macdonell published an impressive short volume
entitled *Theories of Discourse*, which was very well received.

Macdonell took the works of writers such as Althusser, Pêcheux, Hindess and Hirst, and Foucault as a starting point for the elaboration of a theory of discourse, which can be summarily characterized as a *constructivist* and *relationalist* perspective on social identity combined with an insistence on the heterogeneity of discourse. Discourse theory abandons the notion of a true or perfect definition together with a conception of social identities as rooted in pregiven essences. Alternatively, discourse theory investigates the ways in which social identities have been constructed historically (Macdonell, 1986: 6). Social identities are constructed as differences within a system of purely negative relations. Saussure's conception of linguistic terms as differential values is preferred to his emphasis on the process of signification whereby a sound-image (the signifier) and a concept (the signified) are joined in a unitary and closed-off sign (1986: 9–10). Social identities are constructed within the relational system of a particular language. Following the break with the conception of such a linguistic system as a closed and centred totality, it has been common to refer to it as a discourse. Contrary to the claim of structuralism there is no general and homogeneous discourse, but rather a plethora of different discourses which together constitute a discursive formation (1986: 11–12).

The main problems and limitations of Macdonell's theory of discourse arise from her attempt to marry post-structuralism with Marxism, and from her rejection of the possibility of developing a theory of the subject. In sharp contrast to this early theory of discourse, I shall in this book introduce and work on the theory of discourse advanced by *Ernesto Laclau* and *Chantal Mouffe*. This particular version of the new theories of discourse has as its explicit ambition the combining of post-structuralism and post-Marxism with a blend of Lacanian subject theory. With regard to the theory of the subject, in particular, the work of the Lacanian political philosopher *Slavoj Žižek* has had a considerable impact on the discourse theory of Laclau and Mouffe. Žižek, a leading figure in the Slovenian Lacanian school, combines Lacanian psychoanalytic theory with an anti-essentialist reading of Hegel and other classical philosophers. Numerous examples drawn from advertising, film and popular culture show the powerful effect of Žižek's cocktail of Lacan and Hegel on the contemporary critique of ideology. An assessment of the theoretical and practical-analytical contribution of Žižek requires a book in its own right. In this volume we must be content with considerably less: the many important insights and arguments advanced by Žižek will be invoked only where they directly contribute to developing the argument of Laclau and Mouffe.

The discourse theory of Laclau and Mouffe in particular and the new theories of discourse in general emerged largely from the breaking up of various theoretical fields of analysis. The structuralist paradigm was problematized by the *post-structuralist* critique of the notion of closed and centred structures. As we shall see later, the growing emphasis on the play of meaning within decentred structures led straight to the notion of discourse. Within the Marxist tradition the destabilization of traditional notions of structure and structural determination, together with the crisis of its Leninist legacy, fostered a surge of interest in the open and undogmatic Marxism of Gramsci. The subsequent elaboration and radicalization of certain of Gramsci's thoughts and ideas contributed to the formation of a theoretical terrain of *post-Marxism*. Both post-structuralist and neo-Gramscian theories focused on the question of the construction of social and political identity. Thereafter, since the idea of a fully constituted and self-enclosed subject had now been abandoned, it was only natural to start drawing on central insights from *Freudian and Lacanian psychoanalysis,* which tend to emphasize the multi-layered and fragmented character of the subject at the level of symbolic signification. Henceforth, Lacan was to be appropriated by many post-structuralists, and numerous articles on post-Marxism and psychoanalysis were written in order to effect a happy marriage between the two. Thus the combination of post-structuralism, post-Marxism and Lacanian psychoanalysis is neither strange nor accidental, as a certain affinity seems to exist between the three theoretical terrains, both in terms of analytical foci and theoretical viewpoints.

Current Challenges

A recent event of enormous consequence is likely to stimulate further the interest in the new theories of discourse. I refer here, of course, to the profound transformations currently taking place in eastern Europe and the former Soviet Union. The *collapse of Communism,* symbolized by the fall of the Berlin Wall in 1989, has had a number of significant effects. Western socialists have generally tended to be somewhat crestfallen: not so much because their 'friends' have been defeated (the new left in western Europe has always criticized the Stalinist regimes, albeit in a somewhat half-hearted way – its critique of 'actually existing socialism' has never matched its fierce critique of the United States), but rather because the 'enemy of their enemy' has lost the battle. For, despite their many faults, the Communist societies provided a platform for criticizing western imperialism, consumerism and inequality. This platform has now gone. However, the fact that since the fall of the Berlin Wall the European left has been forced into a defensive position does not mean that liberalism has won. The first reaction of libertarian intellectuals to the collapse of Communism was to herald the triumphant victory of liberal democracy. According to Fukuyama (1989, 1992), the victory of market-based liberal democracy represents nothing less than the End of History. Yet the second reaction of the libertarians has been a growing confusion and astonishment, arising from the fact that the dismantling of the Communist regimes was not, as was expected, followed by the emergence of liberal-democratic states and thriving market economies. Instead western libertarians were witness to a proliferation of ethnic, nationalist and religious conflicts, which cannot easily be written off as merely a temporal delay of the final victory of universal reason (Mouffe, 1993a: 1). The explosion of particularist conflicts does not constitute a puzzle for discourse theorists, who have abandoned the secular eschatologies of Marxism and liberalism and generally seem much better equipped to analyse the politics of identity that is flourishing, not only in the post-Communist countries in the East but also to a great extent in the liberal-democratic countries in the West.

The discourse theory of Laclau and Mouffe can also be helpful in two other respects. *First,* the collapse of the Communist regimes certainly means that 'the cycle of events which opened with the Russian Revolution has definitively closed, both as a force of irradiation in the collective imaginary of the international left, and in terms of its ability to hegemonize the social and political forces of the societies in which Leninism, in any of its forms, constituted a state doctrine' (Laclau, 1990a: xi). This does not, however, render the ideals of socialism in terms of social justice and economic democracy obsolete. In a world of triumphant liberalism, where social inequality is growing and important economic decisions are taken by a new class of transnational business executive, the goals of socialism are more pertinent than ever. Nevertheless, as the idea of socialism as a completely new social system arising from the ashes of capitalism can no longer be sustained, the goals of socialism must be reinscribed within the framework of a pluralist democracy and articulated with the institutions of political liberalism (Mouffe, 1993b: 90). As we shall see, it is precisely here that the discourse theory of Laclau and Mouffe proves its value. Laclau and Mouffe have persistently aimed to elaborate a perspective that makes it possible to envisage a liberal socialism.

Second, the collapse of Communism also meant that the enemy, which for a long time provided the identity and legitimacy of the liberal

5

democracies in the West, suddenly disappeared. In this situation the meaning and raison d'être of liberal democracy have become blurred. This has in turn made the 'actually existing capitalist liberal democracies' more vulnerable to the communitarian critique of liberal democracy for disregarding the importance of traditional republican values such as community, citizenship and participation. Whereas the communitarians are no doubt right in their critique of liberal democracy, it is essential that communitarian values are rendered compatible with pluralist democracy and political liberalism (Mouffe, 1992a: 3). In this respect, too, the discourse theory of Laclau and Mouffe is of value. For not only do Laclau and Mouffe insist upon grounding pluralist democracy in a political community; they also insist that this community makes room for individuality.

The events following May 1968, the crisis of welfare state capitalism, and the collapse of Communism have contributed to the emergence, development and spread of theories of discourse. Yet, interest in discourse theory is not only stimulated by events in the recent past. The *immediate future* looks set to deliver some major problems, of which discourse theory seems to hold the key, at least at the theoretical level. I shall here mention four of the most urgent problems. The *first* is the rise of fundamentalist movements. These might be nurtured either by the need to fill the gap created by the collapse of the Communist party dictatorships in Eastern Europe and the former Soviet Union (the case with many of the ethnic, nationalist and religious conflicts); by the absence of clear-cut political frontiers in the liberal democracy of the West (the case with particular strands within feminism and ecologism); or by the dissatisfaction felt in many Third World countries with the results of the modernization process promoted by the political projects of socialism or liberalism (the case with of some of the Islamic movements). In a nutshell, fundamentalism involves a more or less militant reassertion of 'non-negotiable moral values and essentialist identities' (Mouffe, 1993a: 6). Fundamentalist reassertion often leads to the denial of the rules of the game of liberal democracy and is often accompanied by a self-sufficient withdrawal from public and communal spaces at the local, national and international levels. As such, we might view fundamentalism as inherently anti-democratic and reactionary. One way to undercut fundamentalist reassertions is to question the whole idea of fundamental values and essential identities. Discourse theory makes an important contribution in this respect as it is radically anti-essentialist. Hence, the discourse theory of Laclau and Mouffe denies the possibility of self-enclosed particularist identities possessing uncontaminated moral values. All identities and all values are constituted by reference to something outside them, which has the character of a subversive margin preventing the possibility of an ultimate fixity.

The *second* and equally important problem lies in the host of threats to our usual way of living that are imposing themselves in the form of ecological disasters, growing poverty, an upsurge of regional wars, and the creation of a global media network controlled by a small, manipulative elite. Although many instances of these threats tend to be presented in far too unambiguous a manner, there is indeed good reason to worry about the future. The apocalyptic tone of the self-professed prophets, though arguably necessary to arouse people's concern about the mounting problems, can be counter-productive, especially if it creates the impression that they are the victim of uncontrollable developments rooted either in 'human nature' or in anonymous 'systems' of capitalism. In order to counter the apocalyptic construction of our common future, we need to emphasize the role of politics and institutionalized meanings, of common responsibility and joint action, and of solutions worked out on the basis of conflictual dialogue. The discourse theory of Laclau and Mouffe emphasizes the ambiguity of social and political phenomena, as well as the primacy of politics, and thereby helps equip us for actually dealing with the urgent problems of our time.

The *third* problem has to do with the unfulfilled potential of liberal democracy. The liberal democratic values of 'freedom and equality for all' have noticeably not swept the world. Many countries are instead sites of authoritarian or even totalitarian rule. Even in those countries where liberal democracy does prevail, it is restricted to the public sphere of the political system and suffers from a lack of active political involvement; the situation is further undermined by the presence of growing social and economic inequality. In the light of this there is no choice but to struggle for a deepening of the 'democratic revolution'. An idea of what could result from such a deepening is provided by Laclau and Mouffe's vision of a radical plural democracy.

The *final* problem, which is somewhat different in character, has to do with growing awareness of the limits of modernity. I shall return to discuss this issue later, so let it suffice here to define briefly the limits of modernity in terms of: (1) recognition of the ambiguity of the constitutive traits of modern society (the tendency within modern societies towards a separation of state and civil society, an ever-deepening social division of labour, and the formation of nation-states has been challenged and to some extent reversed by recent developments); (2) recognition of the contingency of modernity itself, conceived as a philosophical as well as a social and political project that comprises a privileged insight into the true conditions of our being in the world;

(3) recognition of the fact that neither the subject nor reason provides an ultimate starting point for social, cultural or political analysis, since both are constructed in and through unmasterable power strategies taking place within an undecidable discursive terrain. Growing awareness of the limits of modernity makes it increasingly difficult to address the social, cultural and political problems of today from within a modern theoretical perspective. Recent developments in society, the arts, and intellectual life in general urge us towards the adoption of what, in the absence of a better term, might be called a postmodern perspective on social, cultural and political analysis. The discourse theory of Laclau, Mouffe and Žižek gladly accepts this challenge.

Part I

Intellectual Development

Introduction

It is difficult to find an appropriate label for the works of Laclau and Mouffe. To refer to them as '*discourse theory*', as I have done above, runs the risk of conflating them with the works of Habermas (1984–7, 1990 [1985], 1992), who has recently used the term to describe his own project. This is indeed problematic since the works of Laclau and Mouffe in fact constitute the only real response to Habermas and his attempt to ground liberal democracy, modern emancipation and the reconciling power of reason in the ideal of unconstrained communication. As Žižek (1990a: 259) says, the problem with Habermas is not that he fails to recognize that communication is often broken or perverted, but rather that he insists, in spite of this recognition, that reason, ethics and democracy can be grounded in an ideal speech-act situation. By so doing Habermas resorts to an ideological masking of the ultimate failure of the social to constitute an all-encompassing space of representation. Laclau and Mouffe hold quite the opposite position, inasmuch as they assert that the social is structured around an unrepresentable kernel of negativity and thus fails to provide an ultimate grounding for the forms of reason, ethics and democracy associated with modernity. Rather than giving way thereby to irrationality, nihilism and totalitarianism, Laclau and Mouffe assert the openness of the social as the very condition for formulating democratic projects based on contingent forms of reason and ethics hitherto restrained by the rationalist 'dictatorship' of Enlightenment (Laclau, 1990a: 3–4).

This suggests perhaps that we should drop the notion of discourse theory in favour of the alternative label '*discourse analysis*'. But here we run into a new problem, since that label is commonly applied to the linguistic techniques utilized in more or less formal descriptions of the different discursive forms used in communication (Brown and Yule, 1983; Fairclough, 1993). It is true that the works of Laclau and Mouffe may encourage the utilization of such techniques in empirical studies. Nevertheless, it is important to maintain a sharp distinction between formal linguistic techniques and the theoretical propositions of Laclau and Mouffe; this seems to disqualify use of the alternative label 'discourse analysis'.

Confronted with this impasse, it might help to try to determine the status of the theoretical propositions of Laclau and Mouffe. This will inevitably lead to the conclusion that what we are dealing with is neither a theory in the strict sense of a more or less formal set of deductively derived and empirically testable hypotheses, nor a method in the strict sense of an instrument for representing a given field from a point outside it (Torfing, 1991: 51). This does not mean that the works of Laclau and Mouffe are devoid of either theoretical categories or rigorous techniques. What it means is basically two things: first, that the theoretical propositions of Laclau and Mouffe are substantively empty, in the sense that they are not organized around a set of substantiated claims about, say, the development of advanced industrial societies; and second, that we should conceive of ourselves as bricoleurs – willing to use the analytic tools at hand, and prepared to store them for later use if their truth value is seriously questioned (Derrida, 1978 [1967]: 285).

We might therefore view the theoretical propositions of Laclau and Mouffe as constituting a *theoretical analytic* in the Foucauldian sense of a context-dependent, historical and non-objective framework for analysing discursive formations (Dreyfus and Rabinow, 1986 [1982]: 184). Their propositions are context-dependent because they always graft onto other discursive surfaces in terms of theoretical debates in Britain, France and the United States. They are historical not in the sense of an attempt to write a total history, but in the sense of recognizing the unmasterable temporality of the general history into which they are thrown. Finally, they are non-objective since they do not seek to discover a universal truth by shedding light where formerly there was darkness; rather, they aim to unveil certain strictly local truths by questioning the totalizing ideological horizons that deny the contingency of the criteria for truth and falsity.

Viewing the theoretical propositions of Laclau and Mouffe as a theoretical analytics in the Foucauldian sense seems to provide us with an adequate, though rather awkward, label. I shall therefore stick to the label 'discourse theory', which stands as an abbreviation of 'discourse-theoretical analytics'.

Having resolved the problem of labelling, we shall now consider the intellectual development of Laclau and Mouffe's discourse theory. This can best be described in terms of the movement from a *Gramsci-inspired critique of structural Marxism,* via a *neo-Gramscian theory of discourse,* to a *new type of postmodern theorizing.* The three phases of development are neither the result of epistemological ruptures nor the gradual actualization of the theoretical potentials of the first theoretical seeds. Rather, they describe the uneven and partially overlapping steps in the intellectual development of an open-ended research programme, which over time has shifted its point of attack, renewed its vocabulary, and produced new insights. That said, it should be added that the three phases do not successively over-write each other. In fact, there exists a remarkable continuity between them in the sense that together they produce a cumulative set of fairly consistent propositions. However, the writings of Laclau and Mouffe are not 'architectonic' in the sense of providing a coherent set of well-defined concepts, categories and arguments with the character of a unified theoretical system to be used as a manual in concrete studies. Laclau and Mouffe do not share the system-building ambition of, for example, Giddens and Luhmann, but rather develop their theoretical propositions in and through interventions in specific political and theoretical debates. The result of this is that Laclau and Mouffe's works should be seen as providing a guide for postmodern theorizing rather than an all-purpose instrumentarium for social analysis.

In *chapter 1* we shall review Laclau and Mouffe's Gramsci-inspired critique of structural Marxism. This critique was advanced in the period from the mid-1970s to the early 1980s. Its main point of attack is the economistic tendency in the works of Althusser, Balibar and Poulantzas, which deprived the political of its specificity, defined the state in functionalist and instrumentalist terms, and reduced ideological interpellations to their necessary class content. Laclau and Mouffe contrast the theoretical and political shortcomings of the structural Marxist theory of state and ideology with the works of Gramsci. The notions of hegemony, historical bloc, collective will, moral-intellectual reform and national popular ideology, in particular, seem to offer a way out of the problems of structural Marxism. These notions not only help us to understand the political construction of the institutional couplings linking state, economy and civil society; they also open a space for thinking ideological interpellations (nationalist, populist, democratic, etc.) that are not reducible to a particular class content.

In *chapter 2* we take a closer look at Laclau and Mouffe's neo-Gramscian theory of discourse, which was advanced in the mid-1980s. The essentialist remnant in Gramsci, which made him insist on the

13

privileged position of the fundamental classes in hegemonic struggles, is removed, thereby allowing Laclau and Mouffe to reformulate the concept of hegemony. Hegemony is no longer to be conceived of in terms of the unification of political forces around a set of paradigmatic interests that are constituted elsewhere. Rather, hegemony involves the articulation of social identities in the context of social antagonism. As in the work of Derrida, the articulation of identity is taken to be conditioned by the deconstruction of the very notion of structure, which reveals the discursive, and thus the contingent, character of all social identities.

At this stage, however, Laclau and Mouffe fail to distinguish between the subject and its subjectivation in and through different hegemonic practices. Laclau and Mouffe tend to rely on the Althusserian notion of subject positions, and thereby neglect the important task of developing a theory of the subject. This is compensated for in the work from the late 1980s onwards. During this period Laclau and Mouffe advanced a new type of postmodern theorizing, which is discussed in *chapter 3*. Inspired by Lacanian psychoanalysis, they argue that the subject emerges as the empty place of a lack within a dislocated structure, and then seeks to constitute itself as a fully achieved identity within a recomposed social totality. The construction of the identity as well as the recomposition of the dislocated social structure are inherently political, and this makes way for the assertion of the primacy of politics.

1

A Gramsci-Inspired Critique of Structural Marxism

Ernesto Laclau is Argentinean and Chantal Mouffe is Belgian; they are now based in Britain, more precisely in London. Laclau is Professor of Political Theory at the University of Essex and director of the Centre for Theoretical Studies in the Humanities and the Social Sciences. Mouffe is a senior research fellow at the Centre for Studies in Democracy at the University of Westminster. They have in numerous articles and several books worked to develop a discourse-theoretical approach to the study of identity, politics and democracy.

The topical focus of their study and the theoretical content of their approach have been decisively influenced by a series of political events and experiences, and in particular by the attempt to understand *Latin American politics*. Mouffe had a socialist upbringing in Louvain and Paris. During her years at the Université Catholique de Louvain she was active in the Belgian student movement, chief editor of two minor socialist journals, and a member of the left faction of the Socialist Party. In the mid-1960s she moved to Paris, where she attended Althusser's seminar. However, she was not especially interested in Althusser's attempt to provide a theoretical renewal of the French Communist Party (PCF). Hence, she played no part in the activities of the French communists. Instead she became engaged in anti-imperialist struggles and joined several Latin American liberation groups. This interest in Latin American politics encouraged her to go to Colombia, where from 1967 to 1973 she was a lecturer in the Department of Philosophy at the National University. Her concrete experience of the overdetermined political conjuncture in Colombia and in other Latin American countries further stimulated her critical evaluation of the class-reductionist scheme of structural Marxism.

The political trajectory of Laclau was rather different from that of

Chantal Mouffe. Laclau came to Britain in 1969, when he was awarded a scholarship to pursue doctoral studies at St Antony's College in Oxford. In Argentina he had graduated from the University of Buenos Aires in 1964. He was very active in the student movement, having been president of the student union of the Faculty of Philosophy and Arts, and student representative (for the left-wing faction) at the university Senate. In 1966 he obtained a lectureship at the University of Tucuman, which he lost later that year as a result of the military coup. In 1958 he joined the Argentine Socialist Party (PSA) and in 1963 became part of the leadership of the Socialist Party of the National Left (PSIN), one of the splinter groups of the PSA. He was for several years editor of the party's weekly, *Lucha Obrera* (Workers' Struggle). The PSIN was very attentive to the national and democratic aspects of the anti-imperialist struggles. However, its ultimate class-reductionist approach constituted an obstacle to the full understanding of the emerging mass phenomena, whose clearest expression was the rise of Peronism. In increasing disagreement with the politics of the party, Laclau left it in 1968. It was at this time that he began to study Gramsci and Althusser, in whose works he found key concepts such as 'hegemony' and 'overdetermined contradiction'; these helped him to establish an increasing distance from the class-reductionist tendencies dominant in mainstream Marxism.

It is interesting to observe that Laclau and Mouffe seem to have learnt the same lesson from the confrontation of structural Marxism with Latin American politics. Indeed, they both favoured the Althusser of *For Marx* (1979a [1965]), i.e. the Althusser of uneven development and overdetermined contradictions, and rejected the Althusser of *Reading Capital* (1979b [1968]), i.e. the attempt to reconstruct Marxism as an objective science. Thus, their reading of Althusser was from the beginning essentially political and undogmatic, being heavily influenced by their readings of Gramsci.

Some might claim that Laclau's undogmatic stance *vis-à-vis* Marxism was undermined by his critique of Gunder Frank, which was couched in fairly orthodox Marxist terms (Laclau, 1977). However, Laclau never saw his critique of Frank's use of the concept of capitalism as a defence of Marxist orthodoxy. What the critique sets out to do is: (1) to rigorously recover the Marxist content of the concept of capitalism, which Frank insisted on defining in terms of a mode of production rather than of production for the market; and (2) to determine the forms of its articulation into a wider totality, which he conceived in terms of an economic system (1977: 42–3). Laclau was to apply this sort of conceptual analysis on several occasions. In retrospect he contends that 'it was the very act of rigorously limiting certain categories to their Marxist content which enabled me to move towards a theory of articulation and thus of social totalities' (Laclau, 1990a: 202).

Let me conclude this brief biographical introduction by re-emphasizing the important bearing of Laclau's and Mouffe's respective active political engagements had on their intellectual development. First and foremost, their involvement with Latin American politics seems to have had a direct impact on their reading of the works of Althusser, Balibar and Poulantzas. Below we shall examine Laclau and Mouffe's critique of structural Marxism,[1] and discuss the merits and limitations of their own theoretical elaborations, heavily influenced as they are by the works of Gramsci.

The Specificity of the Political

Laclau's book *Politics and Ideology in Marxist Theory* of 1977 includes an earlier essay on the Miliband–Poulantzas debate, which took place in the English journal *New Left Review* in the early 1970s (Poulantzas, 1969; Miliband 1970, 1973). At the beginning of the essay, Laclau (1977: 51) praises Poulantzas (1987 [1968]) for his systematic attempt to theorize the specificity of the political within the theoretical ambit of the 'Althusserian revolution'. Marxist analysis of activities falling under the rubric of the state had tended to rely upon either impressionistic attempts to establish the ultimate correlation between state and economy or the dogmatic assertion of mechanical relations of causality. In the light of this Poulantzas' attempt to develop a regional theory of the capitalist state was most welcome.

Laclau agrees with Poulantzas' *methodological critique* of Miliband's empiricist epistemology, but tends to side with Miliband in his critique of the *structural superdeterminism* of Poulantzas (Laclau, 1977: 59–62, 64–5). According to Miliband (1970: 57), Poulantzas rightly criticizes the instrumentalist account of the state as a simple tool manipulated by the dominant class. However, Poulantzas merely substitutes the notion of objective structures for the notion of dominant class, and thereby ends up with a monocausal relation between the state and the societal structure, which in the last instance is determined by the economy. To make things worse, Poulantzas (1978: 99–100) does in fact retain a somewhat instrumentalist notion of the state, as he wrongly asserts that state power equals class power (Miliband, 1973: 87; Laclau, 1977: 58, 69). In sum, the political, in Poulantzas, hardly has any specificity as it is hollowed out by the reference to the determining effects of objective structures and the attempt of the dominant class to realize its objective interests.

Towards the end of his essay, Laclau (1977: 79) hints at another unfortunate implication of the structural superdeterminism of Poulantzas; his inability to explain, from a theoretical perspective, the process of historical change. Poulantzas shares this problem with Balibar, who has great difficulty explaining the transition from one mode of production to another. In his discussion of the transition from capitalism to socialism, Balibar (1979a: 283) grants that both contradictions and antagonisms are implied by the very structure of capitalism. Yet the problem is that these contradictions and antagonisms, in themselves, can neither determine the limit of capitalism, nor invoke its transgression, since both are intrinsic to the structure of capitalism. According to Balibar (1979a: 290), contradictions and antagonisms are merely local, derivative phenomena, whose effects are predetermined by the structure. This means that in order to explain the possibility of a transition, Balibar must appeal to something extrinsic to the mode of production, which is, nevertheless, still conditioned by the contradictions and antagonisms inherent in the structure of capitalism. Not surprisingly, his choice is class struggle, which he conceives to be the driving force of history (1979a: 292–3). However, it is difficult to see how social classes can possibly play the role of a *deus ex machina*, acting as midwife for the advent of socialism, given that social classes are described as merely the bearers, or supports, of the economic structure of capitalism (1979b: 252–3). Balibar thus seems caught in the trap of structural superdeterminism, which at once requires and negates the existence of a political force that escapes structural determination.

The problem of explaining historical change also arises in Althusser's famous essay on 'Ideology and ideological state apparatuses' (1971 [1969]). The very notion of ideological state apparatuses (the church, the mass media, the educational system, etc.) expands the instrumentalist conception of the state. The exercise of state power is no longer restricted to physical violence, but also includes symbolic violence, carried out by the ideological state apparatuses. Control of the ideological state apparatuses is instrumental for the attempt of the ruling class to impose its ideology on other classes. To stay in power the ruling class must not only exercise economic and political power, but also ideological power in and through the ideological state apparatuses. By exercising its hegemony over and in the ideological state apparatuses the dominance of the ruling class becomes almost total, and the possibility of historical change, therefore, becomes entirely dependent upon class struggle at the level of ideology. However, as

Mouffe notes, 'it is not clear how this struggle could take place, given that Althusser declares that ideology is always inscribed in apparatuses and that these are always state apparatuses which function for the dominant ideology' (Mouffe, 1981: 170). Althusser comes close to asserting the omnipotence of the dominant ideology. Indeed, the only possible way to defeat the dominant ideology seems to be through the destruction of the ideological state apparatuses in a Leninist, or even Maoist, revolution. This reduces politics to the role of realizing the structurally determined interests of the subaltern classes, since the frontal attack on bourgeois ideology leaves no room for a politics of dis- and rearticulation of identity.

The conclusion to all this is that the structural Marxism of Althusser, Balibar and Poulantzas fails to theorize adequately *the specificity of the political*. The state is determined by objective structures and merely reflects the objective interests of the dominant class. Class struggle makes the world go round, but social classes are conceived as mere bearers of the structure, and their political struggle is merely a matter of advancing a pregiven interest.

The Disappearance of Politics

The failure of structural Marxism to account for the specificity of the political comes as no surprise, since there has always been a strong tendency within Marxism to assert that the political – conceived both in terms of the political level of the state, and in terms of a certain advanced form of political class struggle – is determined by something that is not itself political, but rather social, and in the last instance, economic. This tendency is responsible for the creation of the paradox according to which the political theory of Marxism invokes *the disappearance of politics*. This disappearance becomes literal and complete in the Marxist vision of the proletarian revolution, which is the political act to end all politics.

The theoretical scheme underlying the disappearance of politics within Marxism is well established in the literature as *the problem of essentialism*. The general model of essentialism assumes the existence of an underlying essential principle that structures the social totality by delimiting the play of meaning, while itself escaping the process of structuration (Derrida, 1978 [1967]: 278–9). In principle, any force or region within the social totality could be seen as providing the essential principle that makes the social phenomena and their mutual relationships intelligible. Within Marxism, the most frequent form of essentialism is economism, which confers explanatory primacy to the

19

basic contradictions and the endogenous laws of the capitalist economy.

There are two basic, though intimately linked, versions of economism: *epiphenomenalism* and *reductionism* (Mouffe, 1979: 169–70). The general idea of the first is that the form and function of the legal, political and ideological superstructure are determined by the economic base. This determination reduces the superstructure to an epiphenomenon of socioeconomic dynamics; as such, it follows that the superstructure cannot play any independent role in history. The determination of the superstructure by the economic base is sometimes presented as being mediated by various instances and categories. However, although the introduction of elaborate systems of mediation may complicate the theoretical argument about how one moves from the base to the superstructure, it does not prevent the basic relationship being one of simple linear determination. Hence, the philosophical category of mediation leaves that which is mediated unaffected (Laclau and Mouffe, 1987: 93).

The reductionist version of economism is concerned not so much with the role of the superstructural phenomena as with their nature. It is based on the assertion that the complex plurality of these phenomena can be reduced to an expression of a single contradiction within capitalist societies, namely that between the social classes of capital and labour, whose paradigmatic interests are defined by their structural locations in the sphere of material production. The class-reductionist view becomes evident when it is claimed that every legal, political or ideological element – such as nationalism, racism, sexism – has a necessary class character. Thus, although various distinct legal, ideological and political forms appear, they are either perceived as manifestations of a single essence, or discarded as irrelevant contingencies (Laclau and Mouffe, 1985: 21–2).

The structural Marxism of Althusser, Balibar and Poulantzas has struggled against both of these basic forms of essentialism. As we shall see, it made some advances in the struggle against epiphenomenalism, but failed to overcome the problem of class-reductionism.

Epiphenomenalism

Let us begin with the battle against epiphenomenalism. Whereas Lukács (1971 [1923]) aimed to break with epiphenomenalism by making the primacy of class consciousness and the autonomy of the political moment compatible with the notion of objective class interests (Mouffe, 1979: 177), the structural Marxists wanted to justify, theoretically, the *relative autonomy* of the superstructure with respect to the base. The starting point of this exercise is the concept of mode of production, which is defined as the articulation of economic, political and ideological instances into a complexly structured and over-determined whole. The precise articulation of the instances within this whole, which Althusser refers to as the matrix of the mode of production, is determined, in the last instance, by the economic structure. The matrix of the mode of production in turn determines which instance holds the dominant role within a given stage of capitalism (Althusser, 1979b: 97–9; Balibar, 1979c: 224; Poulantzas, 1987: 13–15).

Now, one might think that the notion of structural causality, implicit in the concept of mode of production, makes it impossible to justify the relative autonomy of the capitalist state. This is, indeed, one of the main objections of Miliband, who claims that in Poulantzas 'the structural constraints are so absolutely compelling as to turn those who run the state into the merest functionaries and executants of policies imposed upon them by the "system"' (Miliband, 1970: 57). However, as Laclau (1977: 65) remarks, there is no incompatibility between the insistence upon the structural constraints of the system and assertion of the relative autonomy of the capitalist state, since the latter can be viewed as simply one more structural determination. If this is so, everything seems to depend on Poulantzas' ability to justify the structural determination of the relative autonomy of the capitalist state.

The argument of Poulantzas (1987: 125–30), which is further elaborated by Balibar (1979c: 220–4), draws on Marx's account in *Capital* (1977 [1867–94], vol. III: 790–1) of the difference between social relations in the feudal and the capitalist modes of production. Under capitalism the direct producers are separated both from formal ownership and from actual possession of the means of production, while under feudalism they are separated only from formal ownership of the means of production. In precapitalist societies surplus-labour can therefore be extorted only by means of extra-economic coercion at the level of production. In the capitalist mode of production, where there is unity between labour and surplus-labour, there is no need for extra-economic coercion at the level of production, and this is exactly what allows separation of the political and economic instances, and thereby constitutes them as relatively autonomous spheres.

The argument is clear and simple, but nevertheless invokes a fallacy of equivocation as two entirely different meanings are attributed to the notion of 'the economic' (Laclau, 1977: 74–6). When Balibar and Poulantzas refer to the separation of the political and the economic, they follow Marx in conceiving 'the economic' as another word for production. However, in the reference to extra-economic coercion at the level of production, the notion of 'the economic' obviously cannot refer to production. The reason why extra-economic coercion is needed within precapitalist modes of production is that labour-power has not yet been transformed into a commodity. Hence, the economic in this second sense must necessarily refer to the exchange of commodities within a capitalist market economy. The notion of 'the economic' thus has two different meanings. In the first sense, it refers to material production; in the second sense it refers to capitalist commodity production. The two concepts of 'the economic' belong to different theoretical structures. The first belongs to the general theory of historical materialism, whereas the second is a regional concept belonging to the theory of the capitalist mode of production.

We might 'resolve' the fallacy of equivocation if 'we continue to use the term "*the economic*" for the second meaning, whilst for the first we shall use the term *production*' (Laclau, 1977: 76). A serious problem remains, however, since both Balibar and Poulantzas refer to the economic in their attempt to establish the contrast between the social relations in the feudal and in the capitalist mode of production. Their entire attempt to justify the relative autonomy of the capitalist state, while at the same time insisting that the economic is determinant in the last instance, hinges on a discrimination between economic and non-economic coercion. As 'economic' here refers to capitalist commodity production this discrimination 'projects onto the previous mode of production a type of social rationality existing under capitalism' (Laclau, 1977: 77).

Even if we accepted this anachronistic analysis of the contrast between the feudal and the capitalist modes of production, it is only the relative unity of the capitalist state that is justified. As Laclau (1977: 77) remarks, nothing follows from this relative unity, which is simply the presupposition for conceiving the capitalist state as either relatively autonomous from, or totally determined by, the economic. Poulantzas seems to recognize this decisive distinction between the unity and autonomy of the capitalist state, when he says that 'it presents a relative autonomy *vis-à-vis* the dominant classes and fractions, but [. . .] does this exactly to the extent that it possesses its own peculiar unity [. . .] as a specific level of the CMP' (Poulantzas, 1987: 256). However, he fails to demonstrate that the unity and autonomy of the capitalist state are 'nothing more than two aspects of a single approach' (Poulantzas, 1976: 71). Above all, he fails to show that the unity and autonomy of the capitalist state are linked by a relation of mutual implication.

The attempt by the structural Marxists to combat epiphenome-nalism is not exhausted by the unsuccessful attempt on the part of Balibar and Poulantzas to justify the relative autonomy of the capi-talist state. As Althusser (1971: 135) notes, the index of effectivity of the superstructure has been thought in two ways within the Marxist tradition: as the 'relative autonomy' of the superstructure with respect to the base, and as the 'reciprocal action' of the superstructure on the base. Assuming the relative autonomy of the state, Althusser discusses *the reciprocal action of the state on the base* in his essay on 'Ideology and ideological state apparatuses' (1971).

Althusser begins by asserting that, in order to go on existing, every social formation must reproduce the productive forces and the existing relations of production (1971: 127). With regard to the productive forces, the means of production are in modern capitalist societies reproduced in a 'global procedure' involving the exchange of capital between different departments, branches and firms, while the physical conditions, skills and motivation of the workers are reproduced through consumption, education and submission to the ruling ideology (1971: 130–3). With regard to the relations of production, these are reproduced partly by the production and circulation of capital, and partly through repression and ideology (1971: 148–50). In sum we can conclude that the reproduction of the capitalist social formation depends to a large extent upon something outside the economic sphere, such as the educational system, mass media, and legal-political authorities. This conclusion clearly emphasizes the reproductive role of the superstructure (i.e. state, law and ideology).

According to Althusser, the reproductive function of the super-structure is accomplished 'by the exercise of state power in the state apparatuses, on the one hand the (repressive) state apparatus, on the other the ideological state apparatuses' (1971: 148). Here, as previ-ously mentioned, Althusser adds a new dimension to the traditional Marxist identification of the state with repressive apparatuses of 'prisons and armed men': the so-called ideological state apparatuses. In contrast to the repressive state apparatuses, which are generally united in a single body and which all belong to the public domain, the ideological state apparatuses are plural and often associated with the private sector. If, however, the ideological state apparatuses, in spite of their diversity and private character, can still be conceived as a part of the state, it is because the state stands over and above the legal distinction between the private and the public (1971: 144). Moreover, if the ideological state apparatuses form a coherent whole it is because they are unified by their function of reproducing the ideology of the ruling class (1971: 146).

The latter assertions of Althusser both hinge on a functional definition of the state as a 'factor of cohesion between the levels of a social formation' (Poulantzas, 1987: 44). Hence, the private ideological institutions of society can be conceived as state apparatuses because everything that serves to maintain the cohesion of a social formation forms part of the state. In the same way, the ideological state apparatuses are unified due to their general function of contributing to the maintenance of the cohesion of the social formation. In fact, we might even add that Althusser, by raising the question of the role of the state in the reproduction of capitalist societies, is bound to end up with a functional definition of the state. The problem with this is that a functional definition of the state as a factor of cohesion tends to depict the state as a general dimension of the social fabric. If 'everything which serves to maintain the cohesion of a social formation forms part of the state', then 'the state must simply be a quality which pervades all levels of the social formation' (Laclau, 1977: 69). In that case, however, we can no longer speak of the state as an instance – as in the original formulation of Althusser and Poulantzas. We cannot insist upon the reciprocal action of the superstructural level of the state on the socioeconomic base, and are unable to account for its unity and relative autonomy.

What undermines the attempt of the structural Marxists to combat epiphenomenalism seems, in both cases, to be the underlying assumption that the societal instances and their articulation in the last instance are determined by the economic. It is therefore interesting that Poulantzas in his last book, *State, Power, Socialism* (1980 [1978]), tends to abandon the Althusserian notion of structural determination. According to Poulantzas (1980: 11–20), the state should be conceived neither as a thing-like entity manipulated by the ruling class, nor as a superstructure responding to the needs of the socioeconomic structure. It is not an instrument since political domination is inscribed in the institutional materiality of the state, and it is not a superstructure since the state is always involved in the process of economic reproduction. As such, the state should rather be conceived as a social relation, or more precisely as an institutional condensation of the relations of forces between the social classes and class fractions (1980: 128–9). That is to say, the state is not a monolithic block, but an arena of class struggle.

However, by reducing the scope of structural determination and expanding the scope of class struggle, Poulantzas produces two unfortunate effects (Laclau, 1981: 50). First, Poulantzas seems to lack a concept of the unity of the state, which he ultimately sees, in an entirely instrumentalist manner, as provided by the monopoly fraction of the

24

capitalist class. Second, Poulantzas' abandoning of structuralism seems to open up an untheorized area of indetermination. The notion of structural determination tends to become replaced by a notion of class struggle. The emphasis on class struggle might help Poulantzas to combat epiphenomenalism, but it leaves him open to accusations of being class reductionist – that is to say, at least so long as the question of the formation of non-class subjects has not been dealt with at the theoretical level.

Class Reductionism

Poulantzas' analysis of fascism in *Fascism and Dictatorship* (1979 [1970]) breaks with the reductive analysis of fascism that is characteristic not only of the Comintern but also of theories of totalitarianism (Laclau, 1977: 81–8). Poulantzas captures all the complexity of the ideological crisis from which fascism emerges, and specifies the ideological elements that are fused into the ruptural unity of fascism. Nevertheless, he fails to explain the process by which the various ideological elements are condensed into a ruptural unity (1977: 93). His analysis of the ideological discourse of fascism remains at the purely descriptive level, and the process of condensation is viewed as a simple adding together of the constitutive elements.

The obstacle to the development of a theory about the articulation of ideological elements, through a mutual modification of their identity, lies in Poulantzas' reductionist theory of ideology. This theory revolves around three basic assertions: (1) that all subjects are class subjects; (2) that all ideological elements have a necessary class-belonging; and (3) that all classes have necessary, pure and paradigmatic ideologies (1977: 93–4). It follows that concrete historical ideologies are seen as amalgams of heterogeneous elements, all of which have a necessary class-belonging as they stem from paradigmatic class ideologies. In this perspective the transformation of ideologies cannot result from change in the class-belonging of specific ideological elements, so that, for example, transformed feudal ideology becomes bourgeois ideology. Rather, the transformation of ideologies consists in change in the combination of ideological elements, so that, for example, bourgeois elements become incorporated into an ideology which in its essential elements continues to be feudal (1977: 95–6).

In Althusser, too, theoretical advance was accompanied by theoretical regress. His general theory of ideology in terms of the interpellation (hailing) of individuals as subjects, which is presented at the end of the essay on 'Ideology and ideological state apparatuses', clearly goes beyond the traditional Marxist conception of ideology as false consciousness. According to Althusser (1971: 170–83), the subject can no longer be seen as the source of a conscious (mis)recognition of its objective interests, since it is itself constructed in and by the mechanism of ideological interpellation, which hails individuals as 'consumers', 'citizens', etc., and thereby provides them with points of identification that constitute them as subjects. However, his general theory of ideology remains trapped within class reductionism, and that poses a major obstacle to the development of its full potential (Mouffe, 1981: 169).

The class-reductionist bias in Althusser is fairly explicit. In a postscript to his essay on 'Ideology and ideological state apparatuses', he says that the ideology of the dominant class is realized in the ideological state apparatuses, but that 'it comes from elsewhere', namely 'from the social classes at grips in the class struggle: from their conditions of existence, their practices, their experience of the struggle, etc.' (Althusser, 1971: 185–6). In other words, the ruling ideology, which is realized, but not born, in the ideological state apparatuses, is merely 'the reflection at the ideological level of a certain position within the relations of production at the economic level' (Mouffe, 1981: 171). This implicit assertion clearly undermines Althusser's theory of ideological interpellation, which sought to move beyond the traditional Marxist conception of ideology as a more or less distorted reflection of social reality in consciousness.

Althusser's theory of ideological state apparatuses also suffers from the class-reductionist tendency of his theory of ideology (1981: 169–70). The ideological state apparatuses are seen, first and foremost, as instruments of the dominant class and only to a limited extent as a terrain of struggles for hegemony – as seems to be the view of Gramsci. Hegemony is seen as the result of control over the ideological state apparatuses, following the seizure of state power at the political level, rather than the other way around, as with Gramsci. Finally, the various apparatuses of the state must be smashed rather than rearticulated, as Gramsci recommends. Thus we might conclude that the class-reductionist tendency in Althusser is not only an obstacle to the development of his general theory of ideology; it also sustains a traditional Marxist-Leninist view of state and revolution.

The Path-Breaking Insights of Gramsci

The open and undogmatic Marxism of Gramsci plays a double role in the early works of Laclau and Mouffe. It serves as a yardstick in their critical assessment of the structural Marxism of Althusser, Balibar and Poulantzas, but is also the source of inspiration for their attempt to avoid economism. It is, in particular, the Prison Notebooks, which Gramsci wrote between 1929 and 1935 as a prisoner in Mussolini's jails, that contain path-breaking insights with regard to the theory of state and ideology. It is these insights that Laclau and Mouffe invoke in their attempt to go beyond both epiphenomenalism and class reductionism.

According to Mouffe (1981: 177), Gramsci advances the notion of the *integral state* in order to show that Marxism is capable of accounting for the ethico-political. The integral state 'includes elements which need to be referred back to the notion of civil society (in the sense that one must say that State = political society + civil society, in other words hegemony protected by an armour of coercion)' (Gramsci, 1971 [1948–51]: 263). With this definition, Gramsci expands not only the concept of the state but also the conception of what is political (Mouffe, 1979: 201). One might think that expansion of the concepts of the state and the political reflects the subsumption of civil society under political society. However, this is not Gramsci's intention. 'His project is not a "statification" of civil society, but an indication of the profoundly political character of civil society as a terrain of the struggle for hegemony' (Mouffe, 1981: 178).

Expansion of the concepts of the state and the political leads Gramsci to turn the traditional Marxist hierarchy between the economy and the state upside-down: not in a causal sense whereby it is suddenly the state that determines the economy, but in the sense that the transformation of the ruling class into a state, rather than the seizure of economic power, is seen as the highest moment in the political struggle for hegemony (Gramsci, 1971: 52–3). Hegemony is won when the ruling class has succeeded in eliminating the oppositional forces, and in winning the active, or passive, consent of its allies, and thereby has managed to become a state (1971: 53). Clearly, the expression 'to become a state' does not refer to the state in terms of a repressive apparatus, since as Gramsci contends:

the historical unity of the ruling class is realized in the State, and their history is essentially the history of states and of groups of states. But it would be wrong to think that this unity is simply juridical and political (though such forms of unity do have their importance too, and not only in a purely formal sense); the fundamental historical unity, concretely, results from the organic relations between State or political society and 'civil society'. (1971: 52)

Therefore, the highest moment in the struggle for hegemony is when the state in the narrow sense of political society becomes articulated with civil society within an integral state. The integral state has a formative and educative role in the attempt by the hegemonic force to create a new civilization (1971: 242). The state is an educator both in the positive sense of raising the popular masses to a certain cultural and moral level, and in the negative sense of eliminating certain customs, norms and attitudes and disseminating others (1971: 258–9). The educative and formative functions are also directed towards economic life. The integral state is 'acting essentially on economic forces, reorganizing and developing the apparatus of economic production' (1971: 247). Thus, the economy is far from being depicted as having the privileged role as the ultimate centre of the social totality from where all determination radiates; rather, it is conceived as yet another target for the all-penetrating struggle for hegemony.

Although reversal of the traditional hierarchy between economy and state constitutes a necessary moment in the deconstruction of Marxism, there is no point in substituting one metaphysical hierarchy for another. This does not mean that we should do away with the notion of hierarchy altogether, but rather that we should conceive state, economy and civil society as articulated within a relational totality which has no pregiven centre, and which thus allows for different and shifting relations of dominance between its constituent parts. According to Laclau (1981: 53), such a conception is precisely what Gramsci aims at with his notion of *historical bloc,* which describes a complex, contradictory and only relatively unified ensemble of institutional orders of state, economy and civil society (Gramsci, 1971: 137, 366).

We can approach the concept of historical bloc by way of Gramsci's insistence that, in order to become hegemonic, the ruling class must link its ethico-political struggle with a programme of economic reform (1971: 133). According to Gramsci, 'it is true that conquest of power and achievement of a new productive world are inseparable, and that propaganda for one of them is also propaganda for the other, and [. . .] in reality it is solely in this coincidence that the unity of the dominant class – at once economic and political – resides' (1971: 116). The implicit assertion that the hegemony of the ruling class involves the construction of a tendential unity of state, economy and civil society reveals the political character of the intrasocietal relationships. The political thus comes to the fore, and this is precisely what allows

Gramsci (1971: 412–13, 445–6) to view Marxism as an absolute historicism. The unity of a social formation is not to be found in an abstract logic common to all societies, but rather in a historically specific principle of articulation, which is provided in and by the struggle for hegemony (Laclau, 1981: 55).

Now, Gramsci did not only emphasize the importance of the political superstructures; he also insisted on the *efficacy of ideology*. In fact, Gramsci (1971: 376–7) viewed material forces as well as political subjectivity as constructed in and through ideological practices. However, what is particularly interesting with regard to Gramsci's theory of ideology is that he manages to avoid class reductionism (Mouffe, 1979: 188). As Mouffe (1979: 189–95) has shown, Gramsci (1971: 125–33) opposed the three basic assertions that informed the class-reductionist treatment of ideology in Althusser and Poulantzas. According to Gramsci, the subjects of political action cannot be identified with social classes, since they rather have the form of 'collective wills', which constitute the political expression of hegemonic systems created through ideology. The formation of a collective will is not a consequence of the imposition of the ideology of the dominant class on the other classes. It is, rather, the product of an 'intellectual and moral reform', which breaks up the ideological terrain and rearticulates the ideological elements. With its emphasis on ideological transformation through the rearticulation of existing ideological elements, the notion of intellectual and moral reform is strictly incompatible with the reductionist assertion of the necessary class-belonging of all ideological elements. Finally, as Gramsci repeatedly stresses, intellectual and moral reform should aim to form a collective will with a 'national-popular' character. Articulation of the national-popular elements is what allows a particular class to express the interests of the nation. The national-popular elements can therefore not be discarded as alien elements contaminating the paradigmatic ideology of the working class. On the contrary, in order to be become hegemonic the working class must struggle to appropriate the national-popular. The same goes for the bourgeois class. Thus the idea of paradigmatic class-ideologies must be rejected.

Gramsci's rejection of class reductionism clears the ground for development of an anti-essentialist theory of ideology. Gramsci never presented such a theory in an explicit fashion, but it does exist in a practical state in the way in which he conceived hegemony (Mouffe, 1979: 188). The basic assertion is that the unification of an ideological system is provided by a certain principle of articulation. This principle is advanced in and through the struggle for hegemony. Hegemony is restricted neither to the strategy of the proletariat nor to a political leadership of a class alliance. In Gramsci hegemony is a concept for the practices of the ruling class in general, and it also involves moral-intellectual leadership (Mouffe, 1979: 179). The struggle for hegemony is a struggle within ideology rather than a struggle between ideologies whose origins are located elsewhere. As such, the class character of a particular ideological element will stem from the principle of articulation in operation (1979: 193). In the course of the struggle for hegemony, the narrow class basis of politics will be superseded as a collective will with a national-popular character is formed. The formation of a new collective will requires the development of an organic ideology that can organize the masses and serve as the cement for the articulation of a new historical bloc.

Laclau's Theory of Non-Class Interpellation

As Laclau (1980a: 102–3) notes, structural Marxism always insisted that class contradictions were overdetermined. That is to say, it asserted that class contradictions were either fused with or influenced by other contradictions. In the light of this assertion, it is strange that nobody attempted to develop a theory of non-class contradictions. Laclau's own attempt to do so draws on Althusser's theory of ideology, which as we know focused on the interpellation of individuals to subjects in and through the material practices of ideology. Laclau (1977: 100–4) saw in the theory of ideological interpellation a way of understanding the unity of an ideological system as provided by a privileged interpellation that functions as a symbol for the other interpellations. According to Laclau (1977: 105–8), there are two privileged forms of interpellation: *class antagonisms,* which arise from the relations of exploitation at the level of the mode of production; and *popular-democratic antagonisms,* which arise from the relations of dominance at the level of the social formation. Whereas in the latter case we cannot speak strictly of class struggles, we can nevertheless speak of classes in struggle. However, the subordinate classes are now interpellated as the people.

Having thus opened a space for thinking non-class contradictions, Laclau is at pains to stress that, 'if not every contradiction can be reduced to a class contradiction, every contradiction is overdetermined by class struggle' (1977: 108). The overdetermination of non-class interpellations by class interpellations takes the form of an integration of those interpellations into a particular class discourse (1977: 109). Popular-democratic interpellations constitute a terrain of polyvalent articulations which the social classes struggle to hegemonize. This struggle takes the form of the dis- and re-articulation of ideological elements.

Laclau's Gramsci-inspired theory of non-class interpellations helps him to understand the unity of the 'middle classes' and 'intermediate strata'. These classes and strata are separated from the dominant relations of production in the capitalist society, and their main conflicts with the dominant bloc are therefore posed at the level of political and ideological relations rather than at the level of the dominant relations of production. At the level of political and ideological relations popular-democratic interpellations are much more important than class interpellations. Hence, for the middle classes and intermediate strata 'the identity as *the people* plays a much more important role than the identity as *class*' (1977: 114). This in turn helps Laclau to improve on Poulantzas' understanding of the rise of fascism. Fascism is seen as arising from a dual crisis, and as providing a clear example of the hegemonization of the popular-democratic interpellations by the bourgeoisie (1977: 115–42). As class interpellations only play a secondary role for the middle classes, popular-democratic interpellations can only exist in articulation with the class interpellations of either the bourgeoisie or the proletariat. In prefascist Italy the working class failed to articulate the popular-democratic sentiments due to its sectarian economism. At the same time, the old power bloc failed to articulate popular-democratic antagonisms. Consequently the way was open for more radical, Jacobin attempts to integrate popular-democratic interpellations into the ideological discourse of the dominant fraction of the bourgeoisie.

Socialism is not, as such, the opposite pole to fascism. Both socialism and fascism advance popular political discourses. The important difference is that, whereas the popular discourse of fascism is neutralized and rearticulated by the dominant fraction of the bourgeoisie, the popular discourse of socialism is articulated with the radical anti-capitalism of the working class (1977: 142). This observation finally made it possible for Laclau to develop his theory of non-class interpellations into a general theory of populism. Thus populism involves the articulation of popular-democratic interpellations into class discourse (1977: 164). Yet, not all articulations of non-class interpellations into class discourse qualify as populism, but only those articulations that establish an antagonistic relation to the dominant power bloc (1977: 172–3). This does not, however, mean that populism is always linked to revolutionary movements. A class or class fraction, seeking to transform the power block in order to reassert its hegemony, might try to advance a populist discourse directed against the 'old guard' (1977: 173).

Laclau's theory of non-class interpellation breaks new ground in the field of ideology theory. It is nevertheless haunted by a series of *problems,* which for the most part arise from the fact that Laclau remains a captive of the Althusserian problematic. The first problem has to do with the very notion of *ideological* interpellation. Despite Althusser's recognition of the materiality of ideology, it is an essentially topographical concept designating a certain region within the social. In other words, Laclau's theory of non-class interpellation remains trapped within the architecture of the base–superstructure model. The second problem, which relates to the first, is that class antagonisms at the level of ideology are seen to be directly consequent upon the presence of relations of exploitation at the level of the mode of production. The classes are supposed to constitute themselves in the course of the struggle over the distribution of surplus value. Hence, discursive interventions are not required for the formation of the proletariat into a class. The third problem relates to popular-democratic interpellations, or, more precisely, to the attempt to marry popular and democratic aspects of political struggles in the hyphenated notion of 'popular-democratic'. The two do not logically imply each other, and empirically they are far from always articulated. Indeed, Laclau's claim that both fascism and socialism articulate popular and democratic contradictions is open to question. The fourth and final problem concerns the relation between class interpellations and non-class interpellations. Specifically, it is clearly the case that the notion of popular-democratic interpellations has the status of a supplement in the Derridean sense of the term. That is, the notion is introduced in order to supplement a primordial lack in the concept of class struggle, which consists in the latter's inability to exhaust the field of social contradictions without retreating into an absurd reductionism. One obtains a clear impression of the secondary status of the popular-democratic interpellations, when it is asserted that these can be integrated within different forms of class discourse. The reverse case, the integration of class interpellations within some sort of popular-democratic discourse, is not even considered.

Fortunately these problems are all overcome in Laclau's later writings, which mark the transition from the first to the second phase in the development of Laclau and Mouffe's discourse theory. For example, in his article 'Populist rupture and discourse', Laclau (1980b: 87) notes that as soon as ideologies are considered as discursive constructions, they cease to be superstructures. The reason is that discourse is seen as coextensive with the social. Social identity, whether economic, political or ideological, is constituted in and by discourse. We shall further discuss the concept of discourse in chapter 4. At this point it is sufficient to note that the concept of discourse offers a theoretical perspective that does not involve an a priori commitment to any theoretical position on the articulation of the intrasocietal spheres. In other words, the base–superstructure model is abandoned, and the first problem confronting Laclau's theory of non-class interpellations is thus overcome.

The second problem, relating to the question of the formation of social classes, is also resolved, although it is not addressed directly. For instance, when discussing the rise of peasant revolts in Latin America following the occupation of communal land by the state, Laclau urges us not to confuse the explanation for the rise of antagonisms as such with the explanation for the conditions of possibility: 'it is necessary to explain the discursive construction of the antagonism and not merely the "non-discursive" conditions in which it emerged' (1980b: 90). Notwithstanding the fact that Laclau here makes what he will later consider to be an illegitimate reference to non-discursive, material conditions, the emphasis on the discursive construction of social antagonisms clearly undermines the conception of class interpellations as an immediate response to the extraction of surplus value within the capitalist mode of production.

This brings us to the third problem concerning the relation between the popular and democratic aspect of political struggles. What is new is Laclau's explicit attempt to distinguish between popular and democratic positionalities (1980b: 90–3). A popular positionality exists when society is divided into a dominant and dominated block. The peasants' expansion of a chain of equivalence, which tends to transform all the differential aspects of the antagonist force into symbols of the evil threat of the authoritarian state, leads to a populist rupture. By contrast, the reconversion of the chain of equivalence into a differential system will lead to the formation of a democratic positionality as the distinction between 'us' and 'them' is replaced by a multiplicity of competing political forces. As Laclau concludes, 'a hiatus is thus created between democratic and popular positionalities, a hiatus which makes various types of discursive articulation possible' (1980b: 93). This apparently resolves the problem concerning the a priori fusion of the popular and the democratic. However, Laclau fails to submit the concept of the democratic to closer scrutiny. Had he done so, he would have recognized that the somewhat hasty identification of the democratic with the creation of a differential system is not viable. Democracy is a highly ambiguous term; only when it is articulated within a liberal discourse, which defines democracy in terms of a free competition for the political leadership, can it be identified with the expansion of a differential logic. There is, however, another and

33

more plebiscitary notion of democracy in terms of popular sovereignty, equal rights, and the formation of a *Rechtsstaat*, which tends rather to invoke an equivalential logic. We might therefore conclude that the relation between the popular and the democratic is contingent upon the precise articulation of the democratic (and the popular for that matter). Hence, a premodern conception of democracy as an identity between rulers and ruled will facilitate a fusion between the popular and the democratic, whereas a liberal conception of democracy as elite competition will tend to establish a contradiction between the popular and the democratic.

Last but not least, there is the problem of the supplementary status of popular-democratic interpellations. This problem is not solved at the theoretical level, but only finds a practical-political solution in the concluding remarks in Laclau's article on 'Democratic antagonisms and the capitalist state' (1980a). Towards the end of this article, which discusses the works of Cerroni and Bobbio, Laclau claims that in the post-war period class struggles have taken place on a terrain dominated by democratic antagonisms (1980a: 138). This seems to suggest that the hierarchy between class interpellations and popular-democratic interpellations has been reversed. However, Laclau is careful to stress that the most important task for the left in the years to come is the articulation of the two different forms of antagonism. By thus stating that the future of the left lies in the articulation of socialism and democracy, Laclau not only attempts to think about the two forms of antagonism in a non-hierarchical way but also opens up the way for discussing a new theme, one that will assume prominence in the later works of Laclau and Mouffe.

2

The Advancement of a Neo-Gramscian Theory of Discourse

Laclau and Mouffe both drew extensively on the open and un-dogmatic Marxism of Gramsci in their critical investigation of the structural Marxism of Althusser, Balibar and Poulantzas. They were not alone in their celebration of Gramsci. Indeed, Gramsci served as the main source of inspiration for a whole generation of European Marxists who had become tired of the scholasticism and rigid determinism of Althusserian structuralism. The great attraction of the works of Gramsci was that they offered a way to overcome both epiphenomenalism and class reductionism, whilst remaining true to the Marxist legacy. The many ambiguous concepts, ideas and arguments put forward by Gramsci at once encouraged a theoretical renewal of Marxism and affirmed its general validity as a framework for analysing the historical development of capitalism.

An example will serve to illustrate this last point. Most left-wing intellectuals were stunned by the victory of Margaret Thatcher in the British general election of 1979 (and later in the general elections of 1983 and 1987). The result could not be explained by simple reference to the popular discontent generated by the crisis-management of the former Labour government. The national mood was certainly an important precondition for Thatcher's entry onto the political stage; nevertheless the Thatcher government initially lacked a coherent programme of economic reform to show that it could tackle the economy more successfully than the former Labour administration. Thus, Thatcher's electoral victory was first and foremost a result of the fact that she had won the ideological battle for the hearts and minds of the British people (Hall, 1988; Jessop et al., 1988). This is evidenced by the fact that Thatcher won support not only from middle-class voters but also from a large proportion of working-class voters.

35

In the attempt to analyse the ideological victory of Thatcherism many Marxists turned to Gramsci and his ideas about the formation of hegemony through moral-intellectual reform. The Gramsci-inspired analysis of the ideological discourse of Thatcherism became for many a safe haven, allowing them to change their focus and mode of explanation without risking their reputations as good Marxists.

However, the great attraction of Gramsci to many Marxists hinged on the essentialist residue that prevented Gramsci from developing a completely non-economistic theory of hegemonic articulation. It is a great credit to Laclau and Mouffe that they succeeded in jettisoning this *essentialist remnant,* which was also present in their own earlier, Gramsci-inspired, critique of structural Marxism.

The Last Remnant of Essentialism

As we have already seen, popular-democratic interpellations possess a supplementary status in the early works of Laclau. Likewise, we find in Mouffe (1979: 183; 1981: 172) a straightforward acceptance of Gramsci's somewhat reductionist assertion that only a fundamental class (that is to say, one which occupies one of the two poles in the relations of production of a determinate mode of production) can become hegemonic (Gramsci, 1971 [1948–51]: 161, 182). In fact, towards the end of her essay on 'Hegemony and ideology in Gramsci' Mouffe even claims that Gramsci's insistence on the privileged role of the fundamental classes in the struggles for hegemony brings him into accord with the Althusserian insistence upon determination in the last instance by the economy. What is odd about Mouffe's embrace of this Althusserian insistence is that it appears side by side with her positive appraisal, at the end of the essay, of the contemporary research of Foucault and Derrida, which 'converges with Gramsci's thought' (Mouffe, 1979: 201). For the essentialist remnant that underlies maintenance of the privileged role of the fundamental classes and economic determination in the last instance does not sit comfortably with the completely new conception of politics to be derived from Foucault and Derrida. We shall explore this crucial point in further depth later.

Let us start by clarifying the precise nature of the essentialist remnant in Gramsci, carried over as it is into the early works of Laclau and Mouffe. We can begin by asking the question: *why is it that only the fundamental classes can become hegemonic?* The answer seems to be that they possess an ontological privilege in the struggle for hegemony because the economic laws of motion secure their unification around a set of historical interests decreed by their structural position in the relations of production. Gramsci's analysis of the 'relation of forces' suggests that a fundamental class becomes hegemonic when it succeeds in transcending its corporate interests in order to present itself as the protagonist of other social groups (Gramsci, 1971: 180–2). This hegemonic transcendence is the most purely political phase in the gradual passage from the structure to the superstructure. However, the political transformation of the fundamental class into a hegemonic party presupposes the attainment of a certain degree of homogeneity, self-awareness, organization and class solidarity, which is obtained in a purely economic field. In the last instance, Gramsci claims, 'the level of development of the material forces of production provides a basis for the emergence of the various social classes, each one of which represents a function and has a specific position within production itself' (1971: 180–81). Hence, whilst the hegemonic principle, which unifies political struggles, is formed and operates at a contingent political level, its necessary class character is ensured by the economic structure (Laclau and Mouffe, 1985: 69). In other words, unification of the hegemonic principle around the historical interests of the fundamental classes takes place on a terrain different from that on which the hegemonic articulations take place (1985: 76).

Now, for the economy to play the role of ontological anchorage point for the otherwise contingent struggles for hegemony, the relations of production and the economic laws of motion must 'exclude all indeterminacy resulting from political or other forms of external interventions' (1985: 76). Hence, if the economy was itself political, it would fail to provide an objective grounding for the political. The paradigmatic unity and necessary class character of the hegemonic principle of unification can only be guaranteed exclusively by the economy if the latter provides a homogeneous space governed by its own inner dynamics.

It is exactly this implicit, though strictly necessary, reliance upon a traditional Marxist notion of the economic in terms of a specific logic of market production which constitutes the essentialist remnant in Gramsci and in the early works of Laclau and Mouffe. The essentialist remnant underlies the reductionist insistence upon the privileged ontological capacities of the fundamental classes. But it also explains the insufficiency of the critique of the epiphenomenalist aspect of economism. According to Laclau and Mouffe (1982: 92), the attempt of structural Marxism to limit the effects of economic determination by introducing the notion of the relative autonomy of the superstructure left untouched the traditional conception of the economy. The economy is described merely in terms of the formal combination of certain pregiven elements of production and is thus conceived in total abstraction from concrete economic regimes.

That the *essentialist conception of the economy* is incompatible with the post-structuralist view of politics is evident. Both Foucault and Derrida tend to conceive politics as an all-pervading dimension of the social. Thus, far from constituting a homogeneous social sphere from which all traces of politics have been removed, the economy is a heterogeneous terrain for political struggles. The economy is a site of power and resistance (Foucault); a field penetrated by a pre-ontological undecidability of irrevocable dilemmas and aporias, which provides the condition of possibility for ethico-political decisions about how to organize production, distribution and final consumption (Derrida).

Although Laclau and Mouffe in their early works retained an essentialist conception of the economy, they discarded it in their later writings. What we need, they asserted, is 'a non-economistic understanding of the economy, one which introduces the primacy of politics at the level of the "infrastructure" itself' (1982: 92). In fact, nothing in society is purely infra- or superstructural. State, economy and civil society are interpenetrated, and their precise articulation depends on historical and discursive practices, which are constructed in and through political struggles (Laclau, 1980c: 255).

The reason it took so long to put into question the traditional Marxist notion of the economic is that the political has been conceived as a specific level outside the economic realm (Laclau and Mouffe, 1982: 93). The topographical representation of society in the base–superstructure model prevented an understanding of the political character of the economy. In classical Marxism the economy is seen as a specific societal level governed by its own inner logic. Ultimately, the process of historical development is seen to be driven by the unique contradiction between the forces and relations of production. However, recent studies have shown that the labour process is in fact a locus of domination and thus of political struggles (see Laclau and Mouffe, 1985: 78–80). Bowles and Gintis (1980) argue that labour-power has a capacity for resistance to capitalist control and exploitation and therefore should not be reduced to its commodity form. Marglin (1974) and Stone (1974) claim that the Taylorist fragmentation and specialization of the labour process is not primarily motivated by capital's need for efficiency, but rather by capital's need to exercise domination in the face of workers' resistance. The emphasis on various forms of resistance and domination is also central for writers such as Tronti (1977), Edwards (1979) and Gaudemar (1982), who have all contributed to identifying the political character of the economy.

Certainly, one finds recognition of the *political character of the economy* in Gramsci (Laclau, 1980c: 254). His analysis of the introduction of the Fordist system of mass production and mass consumption clearly depicts the economy as a heterogeneous terrain of political struggle. The introduction of Fordism in Italy relied on 'a skilful combination of force (destruction of working-class trade unions on a territorial basis) and persuasion (high wages, various social benefits, extremely subtle ideological and political propaganda' (Gramsci, 1971: 285). As such, Fordism provides a clear example of a historical situation in which hegemony is 'born in the factory' (1971: 285). Recognition of the political character of the economy provided Gramsci with the theoretical means to elaborate a non-economistic theory of politics and ideology. However, development of the full implications of an anti-economistic understanding of the economy for the theory of hegemony first came with Laclau and Mouffe's attempt to advance a neo-Gramscian theory of discourse.

Towards a Neo-Gramscian Theory of Discourse

In the second phase of their intellectual development, Laclau and Mouffe (1982: 92) came to see the space that traditional Marxism designated 'the economy' as a discursive formation: a terrain for the articulation of discourses of authority and management, technical discourses, discourses of accountancy, discourses of information, etc. Replacement of the traditional Marxist notion of the economy with a theory of the discursive construction of the economic might seem a rather drastic step. Yet the logic of the eradication of the essentialist remnant in Gramsci and the early works of Laclau and Mouffe leads directly to a theory of discourse.

To show the logical nature of this step, we must consider the argument advanced by Derrida in his essay on 'Structure, sign and play in the human sciences' (1978 [1967]). Classical Marxism conceives the economy as the ultimate centre of the social structure. However, according to Derrida (1978: 279), the centre has received many different names throughout the history of western metaphysics. These names all seem to relate to fundamentals such as *eidos, arche, telos*, transcendentality, consciousness, God, man, etc. which tend to invoke the determination of Being as a full presence. The full presence of the centre is reflected in the fact that the notion of centred structure is contradictorily coherent, in the sense that the centre is supposed to govern the structuration of the structure while itself escaping the process of structuration (1978: 279). The centre is supposed to be both within the structure and outside it. This paradox expresses the force of desire. The postulation of an ultimate centre is motivated by the desire to master the anxiety that accompanies a certain mode of being implicated in the process of structuration. Mastery is achieved by suppression of the play of meaning by a privileged centre which is itself beyond play (1978: 279).

According to Derrida (1978: 280), the always unfulfilled desire for a centre gives rise to the endless displacements and substitutions of the centre. However, a centre, which is never itself but is always already displaced and substituted, cannot be thought in terms of a full presence. Henceforth, we must begin thinking about the absence of a centre. The centre is not a fixed locus, but rather a non-locus in which an infinite number of substitutions come into play. This is important since, as Derrida remarks, 'in the absence of a centre or origin, everything becomes discourse' (1978: 280). Discourse is here defined as a system of differences within which the play of signification extends infinitely due to the absence of a transcendental signified. As such, on the basis of Derrida's argument – cited at length by Laclau and Mouffe (1985: 112) – we can conclude that the questioning of the transcendental status of the economy leads directly to the concept of *discourse*. We might even extend our conclusion to include the fact that the problematization of the transcendental status of the economy necessarily takes the form of a questioning of its endogeneity, autonomy and self-identity, or in short its full presence.

The notion of discourse is of central importance to the neo-Gramscian theory of Laclau and Mouffe. As we shall devote three whole chapters to discussion of the concepts of discourse, hegemony and social antagonism, a few preliminary remarks here will suffice. Let us start by invoking Derrida's definition of discourse as a differential system in which the absence of a transcendental signified, in terms of a privileged centre, extends the play of signification infinitely. This definition emphasizes the moment of unfixity in the construction of meaning. Discourse can thus be defined as a decentred structure in which meaning is constantly negotiated and constructed (Laclau, 1988: 254). This broad conception of discourse in terms of an ensemble of signifying sequences allows for the inclusion of both physical objects and social practices as meaningful parts of discourse. Not unlike Wittgenstein's concept of language-games, the concept of discourse in Laclau and Mouffe (1987: 82–3) designates the constitution of a signifying order that is reducible to neither its linguistic nor its extra-linguistic aspects. An example will serve to illustrate the implications of this broad conception of discourse. As reported by Callon (1987), a group of engineers working for the public electricity company in France (the EDF) in the early 1970s aimed at introducing an electric car. Their endeavours were supported by the formation of a discourse which linked a number of diverse elements such as electrons, batteries, social movements, industrial firms, consumer life-styles, and government action. This discourse did more than construct material as well as immaterial elements as meaningful. It also constructed the engineers as representatives of an environmentalist alliance that opposed the manipulation of consumer preferences by the large car industries.

It should be emphasized that the meaning-giving relations of discourse are social as opposed to logical or natural (Laclau and Mouffe, 1982: 98). Whereas Hegelian dialectics views the connections between different notions as a part of the progressive unfolding of Reason, the naturalist scheme – which today dominates large parts of the social sciences – views the relations between different identities as given by nature, i.e. the 'material conditions' of social life. In both cases the presence of a discursive terrain for the social construction of the world is denied. All worldly phenomena are believed to have an essence, which is there for us to discover, although we might not have direct access to it.

In sharp contrast to the essentialist conception of identity, discourse analysis emphasizes the construction of social identity in and through hegemonic practices of articulation,[1] which partially fixes the meaning of social identities by inscribing them in the differential system of a certain discourse. It is interesting to note that '*hegemonic*' here refers neither to the imposition of ruling-class ideology on the other classes, nor to the imposition of the articulatory principle of the fundamental classes on an ensemble of political struggles and social relations (1982: 101). Rather, hegemonic practices are seen as constitutive of all social identity, including class identity. It follows that social classes can no longer be conceived as historical subjects, the identity of which is constituted around transparent and fully defined sets of interests that are determined by the subjects' structural location within capitalist relations of production. The formation of social classes is not a question of establishing relations between different subjects with the same pregiven interests, but rather of articulating different positions within each subject (Laclau, 1983a: 43–4). Hence, the working class, which until recently played a decisive political role in the advanced capitalist societies, was formed by the articulation of a series of subject positions at both the level of production and the level of consumption, housing and education – the latter factors being organized around the central axis constituted by the former (Laclau, 1985: 32). The fact that the workers formerly lived under ghetto-like circumstances, where many

41

subject positions were strongly correlated (i.e. they lived in a well-defined neighbourhood, and formed their own social, cultural and political organizations), provided a favourable condition for the political attempts to transform the proletariat into a class (Laclau, 1987a: 32). Likewise, the fact that the life of the workers at that stage revolved to a large extent around the life of the factories helps to explain the primacy of the relations of production in the articulation of the political identity of the working class (Laclau, 1985: 28). The industrial workers spent most of their day in the factories, and their health, living standard, housing situation, and social and political rights were dependent upon the conditions and struggles at the level of production. In other words, the material conditions were discursively constructed in a way which clearly revealed the over-determination of the various aspects of the life of the workers by the conditions and struggles at the level of production. These relations of overdetermination were re-established at the level of the political identity of the workers. The struggle against capitalist rule was the nodal point for the struggle for the improvement of the social, cultural and political conditions of the workers in the large industrial cities in western Europe. Today these historical conditions have deteriorated to such a degree that the concept of class struggle has become 'totally insufficient as a way of accounting for social conflicts' (Laclau, 1985: 29). Class struggle may continue to play an important role with regard to the distribution of the allocative and authoritative resources of society, but it will cease to provide a primary terrain for political struggle.[2]

The important point here is that the radicalization of the Gramscian notion of hegemony leads to affirmation of the irreducible and constitutive character of difference and thus to the abandoning, once and for all, of the essentialist reduction of difference to identity (Laclau, 1983b: 332–3). The starting point of any analysis of political subjectivity is difference. Identity is a result of the hegemonization of a field of differential subject positions, rather than an embodiment of a pregiven, paradigmatic interest under which a whole lot of other interests and identities can be subsumed. We might conclude, then, that whereas hegemonic practices of articulation constitute discourse, the irreducible play of signification within discourse provides the condition of possibility of hegemonic practices. Hence, within a fully sutured structure where the play of signification is suppressed by the founding centre, there is no room for hegemonic practices of articulation. Articulation presupposes the constitutive unfixity of discourse – an unfixity which stems from the fact that the hegemonic practices of articulation in the absence of a transcendental signified result only in a partial fixation of meaning.

Hegemony and discourse are *mutually conditioned* in the sense that hegemonic practice shapes and reshapes discourse, which in turn provides the conditions of possibility for hegemonic articulation. Yet it remains to be shown that both hegemony and discourse are mutually conditioned by *social antagonisms*. This is readily done since social antagonisms, which are themselves discursively constructed through hegemonic practices of articulation, help to establish the boundaries of discourse and also serve to distinguish hegemonic articulations from other types of articulations. The limits and boundaries of a particular discourse are established by the exclusion of a discursive exteriority that threatens the discourse in question. The exclusion of such an antagonistic force is the *sine qua non* of hegemonic practices of articulation. The unopposed administrative reorganization of a central government agency hardly qualifies as a hegemonic practice, whereas the privatization of a local bus service against the will of the bus drivers will require the combination of force and persuasion that is characteristic of hegemonic practices.

Having thus stressed the central importance of the concept of social antagonism, we shall now take a closer look at its precise meaning. In one of his early essays Laclau (1980b: 88–9) defines social antagonism as a relation of logical contradiction within discourse. He arrives at this definition after a critical evaluation of Colletti's position. Colletti (1975) starts from the Kantian distinction between *real oppositions* and *logical contradictions*. A real opposition involves a clash between two independent physical objects, i.e. a relation of the type A–B, while a logical contradiction involves a mutually affirmative relation between two binarily opposed propositions, i.e. a relation of the type A–nonA. For a materialist like Colletti, who refuses to reduce the real to the concept, social antagonism cannot be understood in terms of a logical contradiction. The notion of negation clearly belongs to the conceptual level of dialectics, and logical contradiction can therefore not serve as a predicate of the relation between social and political forces in the real world. The logical conclusion is therefore to view social antagonism in terms of a real opposition. However, this is a highly unsatisfactory solution since social antagonisms are not relations between physical objects. More generally, the problem with Colletti's solution is that it hinges on a complete separation of thought and reality. Colletti ignores the possibility of the discursive construction of the real world; as soon as this possibility is admitted, social antagonism can be viewed as a relation of logical contradiction within discourse.

However, Laclau and Mouffe (1985: 122–4) later abandon this

definition of social antagonism. First, because it is perfectly possible for two propositions to be contradictory without this contradiction generating any kind of antagonism (e.g. two aspects of a law can be logically contradictory without giving rise to an antagonism). Second, because it is far from always the case that the two poles in an antagonism are logically contradictory (e.g. there is no logical contradiction between Nazism and the Jews).

At this point we might therefore ask why it is impossible to assimilate social antagonism to either real opposition or logical contradiction. Laclau and Mouffe (1985: 124–5) answer that real opposition and logical contradiction both assume that A is fully A, whereas in social antagonism the Other prevents A from being fully A. It is because A is fully A that non-A is in contradiction to A. Likewise, it is because A is fully A that the clash between A and B produces a determinable effect. In the case of social antagonism the situation is entirely different: the identity of A is threatened by the antagonistic force. Hence, what distinguishes social antagonism from both real opposition and logical contradiction is that the latter two are objective relations whereas social antagonism puts into question any objectivity. In the words of Laclau and Mouffe:

real opposition is an objective relation – that is, determinable, definable – among things; contradiction is an equally definable relation among concepts; antagonism constitutes the limits of every objectivity, which is revealed as partial and precarious objectification. (1985: 125)

So if social antagonism helps to establish the boundaries of the discursive formation of society, it also, at the same time, prevents society from constituting an objective, rational and fully intelligible reality. As such, social antagonism is, at once, the condition of possibility and the condition of impossibility of society (1985: 125).

If it seems difficult to provide a clear definition of social antagonism, this is because social antagonism collapses the differential aspect of language. In fact, social antagonism can only exist as a metaphorical disruption of 'natural' language. This is why social scientists are able to explain the conditions of possibility of social antagonism, but fail to account for social antagonism as such. Social antagonism involves a loss of meaning, which cannot be symbolized. In a Wittgensteinian sense, social antagonism cannot be said, but only shown (1985: 124–5). Nevertheless, in place of a clear definition, we can parallel the formulas of real opposition and logical contradiction and simply depict social antagonism in the following way: A–antiA. What we have here is an identity A which is threatened by the antagonistic force

44

anti-A. The result is the subversion of the identity of A. A more concrete example will serve to clarify things: the peasant (A) cannot be a peasant because of the antagonizing force of the landowner (anti-A) who is expelling him from his land. We shall return later to elaborate this diagrammatic depiction of the initial conception of social antagonism, which is nevertheless adequate for our purposes at this stage.

Towards a Non-Idealist Constructivism

Emphasis upon the discursive construction of social identity, in and through hegemonic practices of articulation that always take place in a context of social antagonisms, has led critics such as Geras to accuse Laclau and Mouffe of invoking a 'shamefaced idealism' (Geras, 1987: 65). This accusation is not only ill-founded; it also seems to confuse the *idealism–realism* distinction with the *idealism–materialism* distinction (1987: 65–7). Following Laclau and Mouffe (1987: 86), I shall define *realism* as the assertion of the existence of a world external to thought, and *materialism* as the affirmation of an irreducible distance between thought and reality. Starting from these definitions, I shall aim to show that the radical constructivism of discourse analysis is both realist and materialist.

Let us begin with the realist assertion of the *independent existence of the world*. According to Geras (1987: 66), this independent existence of the world is denied by Laclau and Mouffe, who claim that all objects are given their meaning by virtue of discourse. Geras here makes 'an elementary confusion between the being (*esse*) of an object, which is historical and changing, and the entity (*ens*) of that object which is not' (Laclau and Mouffe, 1987: 84–5). Thus, a spherical object can be a projectile, a source for the extraction of minerals, an object for aesthetic contemplation, etc. It is because it exists that it can be all these things, but none of these states of being follows necessarily from the mere existence of the entity (1987: 85).

Aristotle is right in asserting that *matter* only becomes intelligible when joined with *form*. 'Matter without form is the principle of indefiniteness' (Staten, 1984: 6). However, apart from the fact that he conceives of form in terms of a full presence, the problem with Aristotle is that he conceives every existing reality as a composite of matter and form. The problem is, of course, that the implicit conception of form as something which is always-already joined with matter precludes the development of a constructivist perspective. This problem is removed by Kant, who claims that there is a *radical incompatibility* between what is beyond thought and the cognitive operations with which thought aims to deal with that beyond (1984: 11). The Kantian revolution hinges upon the introduction of a firm distinction between the transcendental subject and the transcendental object. The former possesses a synthetic a priori knowledge about the transcendental forms and categories that provide the condition of possibility for the experience of objects, i.e. for the unification of the disconnected flux of empirical intuitions into forms of knowledge. The experiencing ego has reason to trust the validity of transcendental forms and categories in relation to the experience of things, in so far as it experiences the latter as phenomenal objects; but the ego knows nothing about the things in themselves, independently of their relation to itself. It would therefore be wrong to transfer the properties of the phenomenal object to the thing-in-itself (Lübcke, 1983: 227–34). I shall not here enter the discussion about the precise meaning of Kant's concept of the thing-in-itself, but merely conclude that *there is nothing in the Kantian position which is incompatible with an ultimate realism – even of a constructivist kind*. Kant insists on a clear separation between thought and object, and the fact that he sees the form of phenomenal objects as belonging to thought rather than to the object permits the development of a constructivist perspective wherein meaning is seen to be fabricated rather than found.

It is important to understand that a realist constructivism does not in itself prevent an *idealist reduction of the distance between thought and object*. As the reduction of the distance between thought and reality is what prevents us from reaching a materialist position, we shall briefly examine how this reduction is brought about. The collapse of the distance between thought and object always involves the assertion that some form shows us the essence of the object. The transparent representation of the object by an a priori form is the result of either the predetermination of the experiencing subject by the experienced object (transcendental realism), or the predetermination of the experienced object by the experiencing subject (transcendental idealism) (Staten, 1984: 10).

The first case involves the *essentialization of the object* and thus the reduction of the subject to a passive recipient of an already constituted meaning. For Aristotle form is the ultimate reality of the object, and the world is conceived as a *scala natural* hierarchized from pure matter to God, who is pure form. However, his idealism was not complete as the unassimilable dimension of matter could not ultimately be eliminated. The last step towards a complete idealism is taken by Hegel, whose idealism becomes absolute so far as the dimension of form absorbs the totality of the object. It is in this sense that everything real is also rational. An echo of this Hegelian premise is found in Marx, who stated that historical development is governed by the contradiction between productive forces and relations of production. Hence, the inverted Hegelianism of Marx – who affirmed the causal primacy of the material over the spiritual – does not break with the limits of Hegelianism, but affirms the rationality of the real (Laclau and Mouffe, 1987: 86–91). It is important to realize that these different philosophical positions, in spite of their realistic appearance – or, perhaps, even because of it – are all idealistic as opposed to materialistic. If the world of objects is transparent to thought, it is because it shares something with thought, and that can only be thought itself (Staten, 1984: 7). The result of the implicit assertion of the conceptual character of the object – which finds its highest expression in Hegel's absolute idealism – is that the last residual of matter, which Aristotle defined as that which is irreducible to thought, is eliminated (Laclau and Mouffe, 1987: 87).

The second case, where the experienced object is predetermined by the experiencing subject, involves the *essentialization of the subject* and thus the reduction of the object to an object of thought. The position of Kant is the example *par excellence*. The unity of consciousness is for Kant the condition of possibility for the unification of the manifold intuition into object-representations (Staten, 1984: 11). As such, transcendental idealism involves the assertion of the sovereignty of the subject. In that sense, idealist philosophy is a typical product of modernity. Not only is the philosophy of antiquity not anthropocentric – man, for Aristotle, is just one more ingredient of the cosmos – but the whole idea of an ultimate foundation for the real is also incompatible with ancient thought. Even Plato's demiurge was not the creator of the world, but just the agent who imprinted the world of forms onto pre-existing objects. It is only with Christianity that the idea of absolute creation – *creatio ex nihilo* – arose, and with it the idea of an ultimate ground, out of which the totality of existing things derived. Indeed, the basic turn of modernity consisted in the anthropologization of Christian onto-theology, involving the transference to the human subject of the sovereignty and constitutive powers that until then had been the prerogative of God. This is the turn characteristic of modern transcendental idealism. Its very foundation is the apotheosis of the subject, who becomes the absolute source of the world.

From this brief account of the roots of the idealist reduction of the distance between thought and object, it is clear that a materialist position can only be reached by putting into question the symmetry between object and thought. This is exactly what is involved in a *radical constructivism* that constructs the 'object', because: (1) its

47

meaning is not given to us in a direct and automatic fashion, and (2) we cannot produce the 'object' out of ourselves as an expression of our omnipotence. A non-idealist constructivism thus presupposes the original incompleteness of both the given world and the subject that undertakes the construction of the 'object'. Pragmatism is well aware of this double starting point. The notion of 'thrownness' in the early works of Heidegger points in the same direction. In both constructivism presupposes exactly the opposite of what is traditionally attributed to it: not the production of the object by an omnipotent subject, but the complex interaction between an incomplete subject and an incomplete object.

It is now clear how we move from a constructivist approach to a theory of discourse. Discourse is the articulated meaning-formation resulting from a construction that starts from a situation of radical incompletion. A theory of discourse presupposes the experience of a radical incompletion, i.e. of that which escapes the possibility of symbolization (the 'real' in Lacan and Žižek; and 'undecidability' and 'dislocation' in Derrida and in Laclau and Mouffe). Yet it also requires that this incompletion is somehow transmitted to those discourses that try to master the ultimate lack of meaning. This involves showing their unstable and merely inscribed character, and opening the way to a plurality of conflicting discourses. It is precisely this contingent character of discursive formations that allows us to understand the precise meaning of 'hegemony' and 'social antagonism'.

Beyond Descriptivism and Antidescriptivism

We shall return to discuss the exact meaning of the concept of contingency as soon as we have examined how the discursively constructed forms relate to the external world of objects. This is a crucial question, since post-structuralism is often accused of merely presupposing the external existence of the objects whose meaning is discursively constructed, and thus of failing to provide an account of the role played by these objects in the process of signification. Žižek provides such an account. Inspired by Lacanian psychoanalytic theory, Žižek (1989: 87–129) develops a discourse-theoretical argument that takes us beyond both *descriptivism* and *antidescriptivism*.

The descriptivist account of the relation between the object and its discursively constructed form emphasizes the meaning of the words we use to refer to the external world of objects. Every word (or signifier) has a meaning (or signified), which is defined by a cluster of descriptive features. The word refers to all those objects in reality that

48

possess the properties designated by the cluster of descriptions. By contrast, the antidescriptivist account emphasizes the act of primal baptism that establishes a connection between an object and its name. This link is maintained even if the descriptive features that initially determined the meaning of the word change. For example, we will continue to call what we today identify as gold by that name even if some scientist discovered that we had all been mistaken in our description of gold. Hence, the core of the dispute is that 'descriptivists emphasize the immanent, internal "intentional contents" of a word, while antidescriptivists regard as decisive the external causal link, the way a word has been transmitted from subject to subject in a chain of tradition' (1989: 90).

Having established the differences between the two opposing views, Žižek goes on to show that 'both descriptivism and antidescriptivism *miss the same crucial point* – the radical contingency of naming' (1989: 92). Searle has attempted to defend the descriptivist account of the process of signification against the counter-examples of antidescriptivists like Kripke (1980), who claims that often the only thing we know about an object is that others use a certain name to designate it. According to Searle (1984), such counter-examples are parasitic on the normal functioning of names as names, which logically presupposes that someone knows the descriptive feature linking the name to the object in question. To support his argument Searle invents a primitive hunter–gatherer community in which there is a strict taboo against speaking of the dead. In this primitive tribe the proper name dies together with the person carrying it, and this precludes the possibility of an external causal chain. However, as Žižek points out, not only can it be shown that Searle's myth of a primitive tribe invokes the illusion of a 'transparent community in which referring is not blurred by any absence, by any lack' (Žižek, 1989: 93). It can also be shown that the parasitic use of names is constitutive for every normal use of names in a language which, by definition, cannot be private. As such, descriptivism fails to recognize the circularity of the process of signification that follows from the fact that each name 'refers to a certain object *because this is its name*' (1989: 93). According to Žižek, this tautological character of the process of signification is exactly what is captured by the Lacanian master-signifier, the signifier without signified 'to which things themselves refer to recognize themselves in their unity' (1989: 95–6).

Lacan's notion of *point de capiton* (nodal point) also provides an answer to the basic problem of antidescriptivism, which appears to be obsessed with trying 'to determine what constitutes the identity of the designated object beyond the ever-changing cluster of descriptive features' (1989: 94). To solve this problem antidescriptivism constructs its own myth of an 'omniscient observer of history', who can reconstruct the causal chain all the way back to the act of primal baptism in order to establish the surplus in the object, which stays the same in all counterfactual situations. However, as Žižek remarks, the antidescriptivists search in vain for this objective correlative to the name. There is no permanent, objective features to be named by the name in question as the object only exists as the retroactive effect of the act of naming. Hence, 'it is the name itself, the signifier, which supports the identity of the object' (1989: 95). The signifier, which invokes the retroactive constitution of the object to which it refers, can be nothing other than the Lacanian master-signifier, which, as a pure signifier, a signifier without signified, unifies a given field and constitutes its identity (1989: 95).

Does this dense and abstract argument, which stresses the radical contingency of naming, have any relevance at all to social, cultural or political analysis? By way of giving an affirmative answer, let us consider political scientists' restless search for a minimal definition of democracy. It is widely held that the signifier 'democracy' has many meanings, and can be used as a name for many different political-institutional arrangements. This has generated a strong, and as yet unfulfilled, need to find a minimal definition of democracy that captures the essential features of the object so that we all know precisely what we are talking about. Yet, if the political scientists have failed to determine the positive features of an object against which we can assess the various candidates for a minimal definition of democracy, it is because this object only exists as an objectified void created and maintained by the name which names it. This is reflected in the general feeling that we all know what democracy is, but that it just keeps escaping attempts to define it rigorously. This feeling bears witness to the fact that the object of democracy is nothing but the unrepresentable kernel of the Lacanian real. The object is what cannot be fully conceptualized, and all definitions of democracy will appear, in the absence of a pre-established object, as political constructions.

The Notion of Contingency

To the emphasis on the contingency of discursive formations we have added the idea of the radical contingency of naming. Many more celebrations of contingency could be cited from the works of Laclau and Mouffe, as the notion of contingency became increasingly central to their attempt to advance a neo-Gramscian theory of discourse. We need, in consequence, to give a more precise account of the notion of contingency and of the role that it plays in their theoretical approach.

A first differentiation to be made is that between the '*contingent*' and the '*accidental*'. This differentiation is first made in a precise way by Laclau in *New Reflections on the Social Revolution of Our Time* (1990a). As Laclau (1990a: 18–19) here shows, the accidental, as first conceptualized by Aristotle, is a much broader notion than the contingent. In the *Metaphysics* Aristotle (1975 [1933]: v, xxx) gives two instances of accidental events. The first is the example of somebody who, in digging a hole for a plant, finds treasure. The other is of somebody who arrives in Aegina rather than his intended destination because his ship was carried off-course by a storm. These two examples are fundamentally different: whereas the discovery of the treasure does not interfere with the purposive action of digging a hole for a plant, being carried off-course by a storm makes the purposive action impossible. If Aristotle can treat these two cases as interchangeable examples of the accidental, it is because his only aim is to distinguish the accidental from those permanent features without which a thing would not be what it is.

The contingent, however, presents a very definite characteristic within the general field of the accidental as it involves the notion of finitude. That is to say, it involves not only the impossibility of rendering the object intelligible through the determination of its causes – which is the general denominator of all forms of accidentality – but also the notion of incompletion, as if through the accidental event there was a failure to constitute a full identity. This is the same distinction that we find between empiricity and facticity: whereas the former alludes only to the brute presence of something merely given, the latter shows the given event as the reverse of a full essential constitution that is missing. Contingency, understood in this sense, has its origins in Christianity and the notion of creation as *creatio ex nihilo*. God, as the *ens perfectissimum*, is at an infinite distance from the *ens creatum*. The latter is, as a result, contingent so far as it has, within itself, the traces of its own finitude, of its not having achieved the fullness of its own being (which would only be achieved if its existence was necessary).

Now, if antagonism – as we have seen – is constitutive of social objectivity, the notion of contingency can be generalized, thereby doing away with its theological roots. Let us consider this more carefully. We have seen that contingent is that being whose essence does not involve its existence, who is not *causa sui*. Hence, if antagonism is constitutive of all social identity, if there is always a constitutive outside that is both the condition of possibility and the condition of impossibility of any identity, there is an essential accidentalness that

51

is constitutive of identity. However, if this accidentalness threatens an identity, that identity will be experienced as incomplete, as the vain aspiration to a fullness that will always escape it. This is the dimension of finitude qua incompletion referred earlier.

The Failure of Laclau and Mouffe to Theorize the Subject Before its Subjectivation

As indicated above, Laclau and Mouffe relied on Althusser's theory of *subject positions* in their advancement of a neo-Gramscian theory of discourse. In *Hegemony and Socialist Strategy* Laclau and Mouffe make their position clear when they affirm that, 'whenever we use the category of "subject" in this text, we will do so in the sense of "subject positions" within a discursive structure' (Laclau and Mouffe, 1985: 115). These subject positions are neither totally dispersed nor unified around a transcendental subject, but articulated into relatively unified ensembles in and through hegemonic struggles. *Social antagonism* plays a double role in relation to these relatively unified ensembles: it helps to establish the limits of the different hegemonic projects, and it prevents the articulated subjectivities being what they are by confronting them with an enemy force that negates their identity. Yet, according to Žižek (1990a: 249–54), this argument overlooks the fact that *what is negated in social antagonisms is always-already negated.* It fails to see that the negation invoked by the antagonistic force is always the negation of a negation. Hence, what is negated in a social antagonism is not a fully achieved subjectivity, but rather a split subject who is trying to establish itself as a fully achieved identity through acts of identification.

By not theorizing the constitutive lack of the subject before its subjectivation at the level of subject positions, Laclau and Mouffe blind themselves to the actual working of the ideological illusion that guides the political struggles for emancipation (Žižek, 1990a: 251). The illusion of emancipatory struggles is that after the eventual annihilation of the enemy, whom we hold responsible for the blockage of our full identity, we will finally achieve a full identity. What makes this an illusion is, of course, that the annihilation of our enemy merely confronts us with our own self-blockage. That is, the moment of victory reveals what Hegel calls 'the loss of the loss', i.e. that we never had what we were supposed to have lost (1990a: 252). As we shall see later, the ideological illusion is made possible by the externalization of the constitutive lack of the subject to the antagonistic force that negates us (1990a: 252–3). But where does this constitutive lack come from? From dislocation, seems the obvious answer. From the disruption of the symbolic order by events that cannot be represented or domesticated by that very order.

This answer removes the burden placed on social antagonism since it is not, as previously asserted, social antagonism that makes society impossible, but rather the disruptive force of dislocation. In fact, social antagonism can be seen as a discursive response to societal dislocation (Laclau, 1990a: 5–41). It simplifies the social space by establishing a dichotomous division of society into two camps, and thereby contributes to the stabilization of the social order. However, it does so by introducing a radical negativity, which may or may not provide a new source of dislocation. Take, for example, the impossible attempt by Russian president Boris Yeltsin to establish a centre in Russian politics around which a new social and economic order could be constructed. To do so Yeltsin at one point invoked the danger of Mr Zhirinovsky, whom he described as the personification of the extreme right. Some reports even claimed that Yeltsin had committed electoral fraud in favour of Mr Zhirinovsky and his right-wing party in order to emphasize the pertinence of this danger. By putting Mr Zhirinovsky and the extreme right on the stage, Yeltsin was engaging in a dangerous and highly unpredictable game. That is, there is a constant threat that the extreme right, in the shape of Mr Zhirinovsky or some other demagogue, will grow strong enough to defeat the centrist identity it was supposed to sustain. In sum, we might say that social antagonisms constitute a double-edged sword: they both contribute to the stabilization of a particular discursive formation, and provide a source of destabilization and disruption. Whether the stabilizing or the destabilizing effect will predominate depends on varying historical conditions.

3

Towards a New Type of Postmodern Theorizing

In the advancement of their neo-Gramscian theory of discourse, Laclau and Mouffe relied mainly on two intellectual currents: post-structuralism and post-Marxism. As we have seen, *post-structuralism* puts into question the traditional notion of closed and centred structures (Laclau, 1993a: 433). Social interaction occurs within a context of sedimented structures; however, since these structures lack a privileged centre and do not totalize and exhaust the field of identity, they are constantly changed by the articulations they make possible but fail to master. Post-structuralism thus emphasizes the instability and contingency of the structural context of social interaction. This has, in turn, led to a questioning of the fixed link between the signifier and the signified – elements that are supposedly conjoined in the sign, which has a particular relational position within a linguistic structure (Laclau, 1989: 69). As the play of meaning extends infinitely the unity of the sign is broken. Kristeva (1970), for example, emphasizes the polysemy of the sign, a result of the signifier's simultaneous attachment to different signifieds. The later Barthes (1986 [1970]), for his part, urges us not to privilege denotation over connotation. Denotation is not the first among meanings, but rather the last among connotations, he claims. Finally, Derrida's deconstruction of the metaphysics of presence leads him to observe that 'no element can function as a sign without referring to another element which itself is not simply present' (Derrida, 1981 [1972]: 26). Yet, post-structuralism not only questions the notion of closed and centred structures and the immediacy of the sign; it also confronts the scientific pretensions of structuralism by stressing the element of fictionality in philosophical text (Derrida, 1986a [1972]: 290–7). This insight has led to the development of more playful and diverse modes of writing, the effect

54

of which has been to subvert standard academic conventions and collapse the boundaries between academic disciplines. The overall impact of post-structuralism has thus been the destabilization of all pre-given, self-enclosed unities, be they structures, signs or scientific discourses.

Many post-structuralists included Marxism among the targets of their attack on traditional philosophy. As noted above, the destabilization of essential unities such as the economic structure, together with the crisis of the Leninist legacy, fostered a surge of interest in the open and undogmatic Marxism of Gramsci; the subsequent elaboration and radicalization of some of his thoughts and ideas contributed to the formation of the theoretical terrain of *post-Marxism*. This terrain was not entirely dominated by neo-Gramscian theory, however. Feminists, cultural theorists, and political scientists interested in the rise of new social movements also called upon other sources for inspiration. Nevertheless, many former Marxists now revolted against the dogmas of Marxism. For some this led to its complete abandonment. However, this was never the case with Laclau and Mouffe, who insisted that their post-Marxism was, at once, a *post*-Marxism and a post-*Marxism* (Laclau and Mouffe, 1985: 4). According to Laclau (1989: 72–8), the post-structuralist engagement with Marxism involved a questioning of the myth of origins which governs the Marxist philosophy of history. Such a questioning leads to a weakening of the logic of capital as the foundation of History. As a consequence, the idea of an underlying economic rationality must be abandoned, and therefore also the postulate of an internal relation between the economic structure and a universal class. The destruction of the myth of origins does not result in the rejection of Marxism, however, since such a rejection would wrongly imply that the Marxist tradition constitutes a coherent unity. The result is, rather, a recasting of Marxism and its basic arguments and categories from the perspective of our own problems and present situation. If the kind of arguments and categories we end up with can no longer properly be termed Marxism, it is mainly because they represent something that clearly goes beyond it. Although the new arguments and categories are somehow rooted in the Marxist tradition, they must be advanced under the label of post-Marxism. For 'the danger about passing something off as Marxist when one is clearly moving further is that Marxism ends up being totally unrecognizable' (Laclau, 1990a: 203). The claim that the transcendence of Marxism brings us closer to what Marx 'really wanted to say' undermines the theoretical specificity of the Marxist tradition, thus making any kind of dialogue with Marxism impossible.

It is important to acknowledge that Laclau and Mouffe in their combination of post-structuralism and post-Marxism systematically failed to account for the *subject before its subjectivation*. As observed by Best and Kellner (1992: 20), post-structuralism shares with structuralism the rejection of the autonomous subject. Hence, although post-structuralism stresses the importance of history, power and everyday life in its account of the process of subjectivation (Foucault, 1990 [1976]), it remains within the anti-humanist celebration of the 'death of the subject'. As such, it does not exactly encourage the development of a theory of the subject. The same goes for the various versions of post-Marxism. These tend to fill the empty space left by the abandoning of the idea of a universal class with optimistic references to the proliferation of new social movements in the field of sexual, racial, urban and environmental politics. The focus has therefore been on the formation of new forms of political subjectivity rather than on the elaboration of a theory of the subject.

The absence in the second phase of Laclau and Mouffe's intellectual development of a theoretical account of the subject before its subjectivation can thus be explained, though not excused, by their dependence upon the nexus of post-structuralism and post-Marxism. The absence of a theoretical account of the subject was highly regrettable as it meant that social antagonism was far too readily equated with dislocation. The solution to this problem was inspired by Žižek's (1990a) constructive criticism of *Hegemony and Socialist Strategy*, which served to stimulate Laclau and Mouffe's interest in the psychoanalytical theory of Lacan. Laclau had already in a short article on 'Psychoanalysis and Marxism' (1987b) emphasized the importance of the Lacanian conception of the subject for the development of the theory of hegemony. Yet it was the highly convincing arguments of Žižek, in a number of working papers (subsequently collected in 1989 under the title *The Sublime Object of Ideology*), that were to have an important impact on both Laclau (1990a: 60) and Mouffe (1992a: 11).

Žižek spells out the difference between the Lacanian and post-structuralist positions, the latter shared by many post-Marxists. We are first told that,

In 'post-structuralism', the subject is usually reduced to so-called subjectivation, he is conceived as an effect of a fundamentally non-subjective process: the subject is always caught in, traversed by the pre-subjective process (of 'writing', of 'desire', and so on), and the emphasis is on the individuals' different modes of 'experiencing', 'living' their positions as 'subjects', 'actors', 'agents' of the historical process. (Žižek, 1989: 174)

Žižek then contrasts the post-structuralist and Lacanian notions of the subject. The latter is described in the following way:

> To put it simply: if we make an abstraction, if we subtract all the richness of the different modes of subjectivation, all the fullness of experience present in the way the individuals are 'living' the subject-positions, what remains is an empty place which was filled out with this richness; this original void, this lack of the symbolic structure, is the subject, the subject of the signifier. The *subject* is therefore to be strictly opposed to the effect of *subjectivation:* what the subjectivation masks is not a pre- or trans-subjective process of writing but a lack in the structure, a lack which is the subject. (1989: 175)

The subject is the subject of the signifier. It strives to inscribe itself as a signifier in the symbolic order, but cannot find a signifier which represents it. The subject is therefore penetrated by a constitutive lack. The subject *is* this lack, and the subjectivation of the subject through the identification with different subject positions is merely an attempt to fill it.

We shall return to discuss the subject and its subjectivation through acts of identification in chapter 7. What concerns us here is solely the fact that Laclau and Mouffe's attempt to articulate post-structuralism and post-Marxism with Lacanian psychoanalytic theory provides us with a *new type of postmodern theorizing*. Thus, the third phase in Laclau and Mouffe's intellectual development can in many ways be seen as a theoretical response to the challenge of postmodernity. For some two decades, postmodern debates have dominated the cultural and intellectual scene throughout the western world. However, notwithstanding the many attempts to distinguish between the intellectual trend of postmodernity and the cultural phenomenon of postmodernism, the concept of postmodernity often lacks clear and adequate definition. It is often taken to include everything new under the sun, and is defined in ways which are themselves not without a distinctively modern flavour. In the light of these observations I shall seek to spell out more clearly how the concept of postmodernity is used in the present context.

From Modernity to Postmodernity

Modernity is usually conceived as the age following the classical epoch. The classical epoch was the age of so-called traditional societies. These societies were generally characterized by the absence of socio-institutional cleavages, a low degree of social and technical division of labour, and a general non-correspondence between cultural and political borders. Traditional societies were held together by a common perception of the world as a cosmic order grounded in the absolute authority of God(s). Within this divine cosmos, human beings were characterized by their acceptance of natural and social givens. Hence, nature was seen as an inscrutable, and often rather demanding, condition of everyday life, and the identity of individuals was largely equated with their social role, which in turn was seen as a function of the common good (Kolb, 1986).

Modernity views itself as constituted through a break with the classical age. The break – which started with the Reformation, deepened throughout the period of the Enlightenment, and was more or less completed with the emergence of capitalism – is said to be radical in the literal sense of going to the roots. Modernity swept away the old matrix of society and changed western man's way of thinking about our being in the world. Modern societies brought about an intrasocietal institutional division between civil society and the state, a much greater degree of social and technical division of labour, and the formation of nation-states uniting cultural and political borders. Alongside and partially sustained by these new traits of society there occurred an increasing secularization of social relations. Modernity questioned the idea of the divine grounding of society together with the conception of the world as a cosmic order. Social relations were no longer seen as governed by divine intervention, and world history was stripped of its mythical clothing.

The break with metaphysical foundationalism was seen as the condition of possibility for the emergence of the modern individual. The modern perspective on the world, with its emphasis on the efficacy of its immanent forces and powers, created a distance between human beings and the world they lived in. The worldly surroundings of human beings constituted an unknown, and thus distant, background for what was known by human beings, who were themselves constructed as both subjects and objects of knowledge. The attempt to minimize the perceived distance between human beings and their worldly surroundings spurred the development of increasing human control over the natural and social environment. This was, for example, reflected in growing confidence in the engineering capacity of the social sciences and in the constant improvement of technical skills for mastering physical nature. The break with the political, social and geographical bonds of traditional societies and enhancement of the capacity for exercising control fostered a general feeling of freedom. This feeling in turn made individual self-development within a world of social contingencies and natural laws the main goal of human life. In the perspective of modernity, the individual was no longer a small, insignificant cog in the cyclical movement of society and nature. By contrast, the individual was portrayed as the controller of social life, propelling the linear development of society towards higher states of humanity, in addition to enhancing progressively our protection against the devastating and unpredictable effects of natural forces.

In its own terms modernity was a great achievement for humankind. Not only did it bring us closer to our true conditions of being; it also inaugurated an epoch of social and political liberation and carried with it the promise of a future transcendence of the world of necessity into the world of freedom. However, at the same time, modernity gave rise to a general feeling of despair as individuals recognized that their newly won freedom of self-development was conditioned, not only by their separation from social objectivity but also by the increasing fragmentation apparent within this very objectivity. In the modern age individuals are left alone with the recognition of their finitude, and therefore carry an onerous responsibility for their own development within a largely unknown world in which 'everything solid melts into air'.

This feeling of despair was, however, soon eased as the empty space left by the demolishing of belief in the world's divine grounding was reoccupied by belief in the unlimited reign of Reason (Blumenberg, 1986 [1966]). This reoccupation not only substituted Reason for God(s) but also effected an interiorization of the ground. Reason is internal to the world as it forms the motive force in the progressive development of social institutions and the individuals imbedded in these. Hence Hegel's assertion that the real is rational. The identity between real history and the development of a spiritual rationality made possible the reconciliation of the subject with social objectivity. The distance between subject and object is bridged at the moment the subject identifies with a higher reason and starts transforming society and nature in its image.

Recent developments indicating a crisis, or at least a certain questioning, of the main features of modernity raise the question of whether it is warranted to speak of *postmodernity*. It is nowadays fashionable to create new concepts simply by adding the prefix 'post-' to well-known concepts. In the case of modernity, the addition of the chronological marker 'post-' is often taken to indicate the existence of a limit separating two equally unique and unified epochs, the latter being constituted merely by its negation of the first. In that sense it is totally unwarranted to speak of postmodernity (Laclau, 1989: 63–6; 1993b: 279). *First,* the idea of a limit separating modernity from its equally unified inversion fails to recognize that modernity has for long been subjected to postmodern critiques, for example by thinkers like Nietzsche and Heidegger, and tends to reaffirm the belief in a deep grounding – which supposedly characterized modernity – by merely asserting the pure absence of such a ground. *Second*, despite the radical changes in modern societies and in modes of thinking over the past few decades, there seem to be few signs of an abandonment, or rejection, of modernity. *Third*, the conception of postmodernity as a new era coming after a modern epoch is self-defeating, as it is caught up in modern historiography and its secularized version of the theological eschatologies that describes history as a progressive series of discontinuous epochs. As such, the simple, and unqualified, addition of the temporal prefix 'post-' to the notion of modernity runs the risk of continuing the story modernity used to tell (see Foucault, 1986a: 39).

However, in another sense it seems to be perfectly legitimate to speak about postmodernity, especially if postmodernity is conceived in terms of a movement which at once *splits, radicalizes* and *weakens* modernity. For modernity is increasingly being fissured as the main features of modern societies become still more ambiguous. For example, the line of demarcation between state and civil society continues to figure large in political debates between neo-statists and neo-liberals, while at the same time being blurred by the growing importance of state intervention in the organization of social and economic life. The social division of labour is further deepened as Fordist methods of mass production spread from the productive to the service sector, while the introduction of new post-Fordist methods of flexible and specialized production seems to encourage the re-integration of industrial work processes. Conformity of cultural and political borders in highly exclusive nation-states has become the goal of political elites in eastern Europe, while the sovereignty of western European nation-states is being undermined by the processes of regionalization, internationalization, and perhaps even globalization.

Modernity is radicalized as the modern assertion of the contingency of values, beliefs and ways of life is stretched to include recognition of the contingency of modern metanarratives. Modernity has always presented itself as the final truth about the conditions of our being in the world. However, today, in light of numerous studies of the historical preconditions for the formulation of the project of modernity and with the surge of anti-modern movements in the near Orient, modernity is revealed as simply one among other possible ways of accounting for our conditions of being.

Finally, modernity is weakened in at least two important senses. First, subjectivity is no longer conceived as a unified and self-conscious starting point for the construction of social life, but revealed as a divided and overdetermined subjectivity constructed by unmasterable discursive strategies. Second, rationality fails to provide an ultimate guide for ethico-political judgement and historical development, as it is itself inflicted with aporias that cannot be resolved on logical grounds (e.g. Gödel's theorem, which shows the impossibility of the self-grounding of any logical system). Epistemic reason, for its part, is revealed as simply another form of phronetic reason: it is recognized that scientific knowledge rests on communal rules and values and thus has to renounce all pretence to universality (e.g. Kuhn's notion of scientific paradigms, which emphasizes the formal and informal rules and values governing the research activities of a scientific community).

In sum, we might say that postmodernity describes the emergence of an intellectual climate characterized by *an increasing awareness of the limits of modernity* as a blueprint for the necessary development of society, as a privileged insight into our true conditions of being, and as a subjectivistic and rationalistic reoccupation of the space left by the demolishing of the belief in a divine grounding of the world. Hence, what postmodern philosophy questions is not the legitimacy of modernity and its emancipatory project, but its status as a fundamental ontology. In fact, what is questioned is the very possibility of a fundamental ontology that can provide an ultimate ground able to ensure the intelligibility of a world of objective, social essences.

Some, like Habermas (1984–7), have attempted to counteract postmodernity by trying to restore the intellectual horizon of modernity, its ethics and its rationality, by shifting its grounding from subjectivity to intersubjectivity; while others, like Lyotard (1984 [1979]), have celebrated postmodernity for the anti-totalitarian potentials of the unrestrained plurality of language games it permits now that the so-called metanarratives of modernity have died. Though Lyotard arguably buries the emancipatory values of modernity a little too quickly, his optimistic reaction to Habermas's defence of the reign of reason in power-free speech-acts is commendable. While Lyotard risks losing sight of the glue that binds together the plurality of language games into totalizing – though neither total nor totalitarian – horizons of meaning and action, Habermas ends up fetishizing a communicative rationality which he admits is conditional upon ideal conditions that will never be realized (Habermas, 1992).

61

When the Ground Becomes an Abyss

Laclau and Mouffe's reading of the postmodern condition into social, cultural and political theory leads them to insist on what in Derridean terms could be called the *structural undecidability of the social*. As stated, postmodernity questions the very possibility of a fundamental ontology that provides an ultimate ground for social life. This does not mean that social meaning and action have no ground, but rather that the ground is destabilized, divided and disorganized to such an extent that it ultimately takes the form of an abyss of infinite play, which turns all attempts to ground social identity into provisional and precarious ways of trying to 'naturalize' or 'objectivize' politically constructed identities. It is this abyss of infinite play, which all signification must necessarily presuppose, that Laclau and Mouffe in a deconstructive style refer to as the structural undecidability of the social.

Before we move on to consider the implications of this idea of abyssal grounding for the conception of the role and nature of politics, it is necessary to establish what precisely is meant by structural undecidability. In *New Reflections on the Revolution of Our Time* (1990a) Laclau draws our attention to three different levels of undecidability. The *first level* has to do with the ambiguity of so-called floating signifiers, which stems from the fact that certain signifiers have different meanings in different contexts. Hence the term 'democracy' will acquire one meaning within a socialist discourse and another when articulated by a liberal, conservative, or fascist discourse. It should be noted that we do not have here a polysemic coexistence of different meanings of 'democracy', as the different meanings tend to negate and substitute each other in the course of political struggle. The relation of mutual negation and substitution between a series of signifieds that, one after the other, are attached to the same signifier is captured by Lacan's notion of the sliding of the signifieds under the signifier. The incessant sliding of the signifieds can only be arrested by the intervention of a hegemonic force capable of fixing the meaning of the floating signifier in relation to a greater number of social signifiers organized around a nodal point. The possibility of ultimately fixing the meaning of a certain signifier can, of course, be questioned on empirical grounds by contending that it is not possible for a hegemonic force to impose a complete hegemony. However, this objection tends to maintain as a regulative idea the possibility of a fully transparent society. That is, if an absolute supremacy was empirically attainable, all social identity would finally become completely self-identical.

The possibility of a fully transparent society is ruled out as we reach the *second level* of undecidability, which puts into question the unity and transparency of the hegemonic force itself. This involves asserting that 'the incomplete and contingent nature of the totality would spring not only from the fact that no hegemonic system can be fully imposed, but also from the intrinsic ambiguities of the hegemonic project itself' (1990a: 28). Hence, both within the socialist and the liberalist discourse, we find very different conceptions of democracy – elitist and participatory conceptions of democracy co-exist. It is, of course, possible to imagine that the ambiguity of the hegemonic project is removed as the content of the articulatory principle is clarified. Such a clarification must necessarily take place within a clearly deter-minable context (for example, a particular form of socialism developed within a certain form of capitalist society), and the failure to remove the ambiguity of the hegemonic project will therefore reflect the failure to determine precisely the context of the articulatory prin-ciple. This failure might be seen as resulting from an empirical imperfection on the part of the context which at present is not fully determinable. Yet that would mean that the ideal of a pure contextual transparency is not put into question, but continues its dominance as a regulative idea (1990a: 29).

The ideal of contextual determinacy is undermined as soon as we reach the *third level* of undecidability, which stresses the undecid-ability of the structural context for the clarification of the hegemonic project. In our case, the undecidability of the structural context is present in the form of an inherent dilemma of the social democratic movement in the advanced capitalist societies, which, on the one hand, secures the improvement of the workers' living standards in and through corporatist arrangements that discipline and pacify the workers, but, on the other hand, founds its strength upon the possi-bility of actively mobilizing the working class. The assumption that undecidability is constitutive for the structure forever prevents the removal of ambiguity from the hegemonic project. In fact, the ambi-guity of the hegemonic project is to a large extent something that emanates from the ambiguity of its structural context. The context of the hegemonic principle is itself ambiguous, and an ultimate fixing of the context will necessarily rest upon a political decision.

Laclau invokes Wittgenstein's example of the attempt to continue a numerical series in order to show that the problem 'is not that the coherence of a rule can never be fully realized in empirical reality, but that the rule itself is undecidable' (1990a: 29), because the context of its formulation is undecidable. That is, the fact that a numerical series (1, 2, 3, 4, . . .) can be continued in accordance with a variety of different rules, which all show the first string of numbers to be a fragment of a larger series, points to the absence of super-hard rules in the sense of rules that are founded upon some kind of intrinsic necessity. The structural context of meaning and action contains numerous rules. These are neither rigid nor aprioristic, but flexible, and in the last instance simply an instance of their usage. Nevertheless, they cannot be changed arbitrarily, but have to hegemonize, to a certain extent, the previous instances of usage. As such, we can change the rules of the game in collective wage negotiations in many different ways, but we have to take the pre-existing rules into account and show how they are either compatible or incompatible with the new rules.

Having shown that undecidability cannot be restricted to the exoteric world of speech-acts (i.e. to the level of the signifier and the hegemonic principle) but in fact penetrates deep down to the esoteric structures that provide the context of meaning and action, we should pause briefly in order to consider precisely *what kind of undecidability* we are talking about. Although this is implicit in what is said above about the existence of definite though perfectly negotiable rules, it is important to stress that undecidability has nothing to do with indeterminacy. According to Derrida,

undecidability is always a *determinate* oscillation between possibilities (for example, of meaning, but also of acts). These possibilities are themselves highly determined in strictly *defined* situations (for example, discursive – syntactical or rhetorical – but also political, ethical, etc.). They are *pragmatically* determined. (Derrida, 1988a [1977]: 148)

On the other hand, undecidability 'is not *merely* the oscillation or the tension between determinate decisions' (Derrida, 1992: 24 – emphasis added). It is not reducible to the experience of a play of meaning that resists both strategic calculation and a dialectical *Aufhebung*. In a way that is heterogeneous to both the dialectic and the calculable, undecidability calls for a decision which must necessarily pass through the ordeal of the undecidable, while taking into account the rules of its structural context (Derrida, 1988a: 116; 1992: 24). For instance, when faced with the unique singularity of a case (for example, a case of female circumcision) which within a given discursive context cannot be subsumed under some universal law (the right to privacy, or the right not to be harmed), we still have to take what might seem an impossible decision, and be able to justify it both politically and ethically within a particular hegemonic context (in our case, the liberal democratic discourse of the West).

Having defined undecidability as the impossible decision between two determinate poles, it should be added that the world around us appears for the most part to be rather decided and unambiguous. The fact that we are seldom confronted with the structural undecidability that is constitutive of social, cultural and political phenomena is explained by the impact of the metaphysical tradition on western societies. That is, western philosophy is dominated by metaphysical hierarchies that privilege unity over dispersion, necessity over contingency, presence over absence, etc., and these hierarchies tend to shape the formation of our discursive world with the result that social, cultural and political phenomena appear as self-identical and self-evident essences. Yet, if the metaphysical tradition prevents us from recognizing the structural undecidability of the world, then why not abandon it? The answer is that we cannot. The metaphysical tradition of the West is inescapable, as it constitutes the very principle of Being. How, then, do we ever reach down to the undecidable infrastructure that makes possible the 'violent' inscription of metaphysical hierarchies? How is the undecidable context that permits the formation of decidable texts revealed? The answer is: through deconstruction.

To gain an idea of what deconstruction implies let us start with Derrida's concept of the closure of metaphysics (*la clôture de la metaphysique*), which, with a clear reference to Heidegger, refers to the double rejection of the metaphysical tradition and the idea of its transgression. From here we can proceed to define deconstruction as a 'clotural' reading, i.e. a strategic intervention into metaphysics which attempts to confront metaphysics with its other (Critchley, 1992: 30–1).

Derrida claims in a 'Letter to a Japanese friend' (1988b: 3–4) that deconstruction is not a demolition, not an analysis, not a critique, not a method and not an operation. After all, in itself deconstruction *is* nothing in the sense that all attempts to predicate deconstruction are doomed to failure. Consequently, it should rather be conceived as something which takes place where there *is* something. What takes place is a textual labour (note that, according to Derrida (1976 [1967]: 158), there is nothing outside text) with the form of a double reading (Derrida, 1988a: 21). The first reading is a faithful attempt to follow the dominant interpretation of the text, its presuppositions, its concepts and its arguments. The second reading then consists in tracing the excluded, repressed and inferior interpretation that forms an undercurrent in the text. When the textual hierarchy between the dominant interpretation and its other has been established, it is shown that the dominant interpretation is dependent on what it excludes. Thus, in the case of the non-concept of the supplement, it is shown that if the relation between A and B is more important than A itself, it is because B supplements a primordial lack in A. The emphasis on the constitutive character of what is excluded results in an overturning of the textual hierarchy. What was at first considered to be secondary is suddenly revealed as primary. However, deconstruction is not content with a simple reversal of textual hierarchies, but seeks to account for the undecidable oscillation between the different textual strategies that the inscription of a metaphysical hierarchy must necessarily presuppose.

A final consideration, before moving on to consider the relation between undecidability and politics, concerns Rorty's attack on Gasché's reading of Derrida. In *The Tain of the Mirror* (1986: 177–251) Gasché identifies what he sees as 'a system beyond being' in the works of Derrida. This system beyond being consists of the undecidable infrastructures that according to Derrida are the conditions of possibility for any discursive inscription. However, in *Contingency, Irony and Solidarity* (1989: 122–37) Rorty readily dismisses Gasché's reading of Derrida. According to Rorty, Derrida has no intention of providing a metavocabulary 'which provides a logical space in which to place everything which anybody will ever say' (1989: 125). Rorty denies that Derrida's deconstructions contain any claims to systematicity, and this makes it possible for Rorty to classify the works of Derrida as private, ironic theorizing, which has no public or ethico-political relevance. This in turn makes it possible for Rorty to support a Habermasian universalism at the public and ethico-political level, while sympathizing with Derrida's ironic theorizing at the level of private literary fantasies (1989: 125). If Rorty is right, then there is no reason to consider the implications of deconstruction for the conception of the role and nature of politics. However, Rorty's way of reasoning is arguably illegitimate for two main reasons. The first is that Rorty builds his alternative reading of Derrida only on *Glas* (1986b [1974]) and *The Post Card from Socrates to Freud and Beyond* (1987 [1980]), which, according to Rorty, represent the mature culmination of Derrida's writings. The choice of the two most poetized writings of Derrida is, indeed, far too selective, and makes it impossible to fit in the later and much more political writings of Derrida, such as *Specters of Marx* (1994) or *The Politics of Friendship* (1997). The second reason is that the sharp distinction Rorty maintains between the private and the public is eminently deconstructable. For example, as Rorty (1989: 141–88) himself shows, our private, ironic self-development tends to cause suffering to other people; and this, I would argue, will tend to construct private relations as a site of public political struggles.

The Concept of Politics

Turning finally to the question of the link between deconstruction and politics, it should be emphasized that deconstruction does not recommend any particular ethics or politics. As Derrida says, 'deconstruction is inherently neither "conservative" nor the contrary' (Derrida, 1988a: 141). Deconstruction in the singular cannot be appropriated by the stereotypes of political-institutional discourse. There is nevertheless a close link between deconstruction and politics as the structural undecidability revealed by deconstruction seems to be the very condition for *ethical-political decisions*. As Derrida asserts:

it [undecidability, JT] calls for decision in the order of ethical-political responsibility. It is even its necessary condition. A decision can only come into being in a space that exceeds the calculable program that would destroy all responsibility by transforming it into a programmable effect of determinate causes. There can be no moral or political decision without this trial and this passage by way of the undecidable. (1988a: 116)

If ethical and political decisions are conditioned thus by undecidability, we can initially define politics as the taking of *constitutive decisions* in an undecidable terrain.[1] Given the undecidability of the structure the constitutive decisions must necessarily have a *non-algorithmic* character. That is to say, if the structure is undecidable and thus fails to provide any super-hard rules for our decision-making, the latter will have nothing in common with a mathematical proof where the conclusion is logically derived from a set of axiomatic assumptions. As such, we will never arrive at a situation where the constitutive decisions are, so to speak, taken by the structure and subsequently presented as a *fait accompli*.

The non-algorithmic character of constitutive decisions implies that these become dependent on the creation of a consensus for a certain option among a range of alternative options. The alternative options are actual inasmuch as they serve *de facto* as points of identification for the social agents. The creation of a consensus for a certain option cannot be reduced to simply identifying a shared opinion in the sense of the least common denominator, but rather describes an active process of coming into agreement through *persuasion*. Persuasion involves making somebody, whose beliefs have already been put into crisis, a different set of beliefs by means of quasi-logical argumentation.[2] Thus, persuasion has nothing to do with showing somebody's beliefs to be inconsistent with certain absolute criteria of rationality, since that would reduce persuasion to a formal procedure operating within isolated and limited systems from which any un-decidability has been excluded. Nor has persuasion anything to do with causing somebody to change their beliefs by systematically breaking down their resistance, as in the cases of brainwashing and hypnosis, since clearly this does not involve the provision of motiv-ation through argument. Persuasion, rather, takes the form of an attempt to make somebody give up one set of beliefs in favour of another by offering a more or less thoroughgoing *redescription* of the world which, on a pragmatic basis, presents the new set of beliefs as the more suitable, appropriate or likely (Rorty, 1989: 3–22).

When defined in these terms, persuasion is seen to have little in common with the kind of rational truth-seeking dialogue that Habermas takes as his point of departure in his theory of com-municative action; although persuasive redescriptions might be governed by a set of generally accepted codes of conduct requiring one to speak the truth and be righteous and sincere (Habermas, 1984–7). However, such ethical commitments should not, *pace* Habermas, be conceived as a set of universal and fully realizable demands that lie beneath all discourse and therefore are immune from all critique (May, 1994: 146–7). The ethical codes of conduct to be observed by partic-ipants in a political discussion together constitute an open-ended set of contingent and highly elusive demands which are subject to critical scrutiny and endless negotiation within a discursive framework that is far from power-free. Habermas is not mistaken about the presence of a discourse ethics, but rather about its status.

Although persuasive redescriptions are not guided by the telos of a rational truth, they are likely to provide good reasons and strong moti-vations for someone to adopt a new set of beliefs. However, they could never provide the ultimate ground for a constitutive decision in the sense of linking, in an apodictic way, the belief in that decision with a rational cause, reason or motive which is itself derived from an absolute truth. Hence, in the final analysis, constitutive decisions rest on an ultimately ungrounded choice of A rather than B, C and D. It follows from this that the creation of consensus for a certain option among a range of actual options *always involves repression and force* (Laclau, 1990a: 30; Derrida, 1988a: 149–50). That is, the choice of A always involves the forceful repression of B, C and D. Repression of the alternative options can take a variety of forms. The first possibility is that they are totally annihilated, which is the case when both the alternative options and their historical conditions of existence are destroyed. Second, there is the possibility that they are repressed in a way which tends to restore their potentiality but effectively prevent their actual realization. Finally, it may happen that the alternative options are partially incorporated in the winning option in a modified and subordinate form. Also, the notion of force requires further clarification, since it tends to invoke a suggestion of all kinds of brutal behaviour. As such, it should be noted that physical violence only represents one extreme of a subtle continuum ranging from the exercise of authority and various forms of moral blackmail, to reluctant acceptance of the consequences of majority rule and the use of material and physical sanctions. Yet, no matter how much the concepts of repression and force are modified and relativized, the conclusion remains that the creation of consensus for a certain option among a range of actual options always involves the violent exclusion of alternatives. This does not mean that persuasion can be reduced to the act of forceful repression, since the former involves an element of quasi-logical argumentation, which the latter does not. Rather, the point is that repression and force are structurally inscribed in the process of taking a constitutive decision on the basis of persuasive redescriptions advanced within a terrain of structural undecidability (Laclau, 1990a: 171–4, 1991: 89–90). This conclusion is contrary to the tendency in Gramsci (1971 [1948–51]: 170) to establish a dualism between force and consent, which are taken to be complementary to each other.

What is forcefully repressed can no longer be what it 'is', and as such the constitutive decisions resulting from the creation of consensus through persuasion always involve the subversion of social identity. This is true in a double sense, since the subversion of the alternative options also implies the subversion of the identity of the social agents who identify themselves with these options. This allows us to reformulate our initial definition of politics. Henceforth, *politics is to be defined as, simultaneously, a constitutive and subversive dimension of the social fabric.*

The Primacy of Politics

The conception of politics in terms of a constitutive and subversive decision taken within an undecidable terrain leads to an assertion of *the primacy of politics over the social* (Laclau, 1990a: 33). Not only are social relations shaped and reshaped ultimately by political decisions; but these decisions do not realize some pregiven social rationality, and politics will, therefore, take the form of a radical construction (1990a: 31). Politics is often conceived as derivative of either the rational pursuit of the pregiven interests of individual agents or the reified structures of collective forms of organization.

69

But with the emphasis on the structural undecidability of the social, it is no longer possible to maintain the idea that politics is derived from something which is not itself political. Thus, if the ground of politics is revealed as a bottomless abyss, the decision becomes its own ground.

To insist that politics has primacy over the social is not to say that everything is political. Social relations are shaped in and through political struggles. But they cease to be political when over time they become *sedimented* into an institutional ensemble of rules, norms, values and regularities, which we take for granted in our everyday life. The more the political 'origin' of social relations is forgotten, the more sedimented and institutionalized they will become, and the more they will seem to have a life of their own. In other words, social relations become sedimented in so far as they are not subjected to the ongoing practices of constitution and subversion. The social can therefore be defined as the ensemble of social relations that establishes a horizon for meaning and action, which is recursively validated by the social agents and thus possesses a relatively enduring character. However, we should remember that the political 'origin' of the relatively enduring social institutions is repressed (in the psychoanalytical sense of being kept at another place) and not eliminated. Hence, it can be *re-activated* when these institutions are put into question (Laclau, 1990a: 33–5). Both sedimentation of the politically constructed social relations and the subsequent re-activation of their political 'origin' can be viewed as political processes. Although a minimal degree of codification and routinization is necessary for social orientation and action, the process of sedimentation is most often a part of the political strategies aiming to normalize and naturalize social relations. The effacement of the traces of the act of forceful repression, which constitute the social in one way rather than another, is crucial for the stabilization of a hegemonic project. The subsequent re-activation of the political 'origin' of the social is an effect of resistance to the dominant power strategy. Blumenberg is thus right in claiming that the primacy of politics 'does not consist in the fact that everything is political, but rather in the fact that the determination of what is to be regarded as unpolitical is itself conceived as falling under the competence of the political' (Blumenberg, 1986: 91).

The thesis of the primacy of politics over the social is often unjustly accused of leading to voluntarism and politicism. The charge of *voluntarism* blames the primacy thesis for viewing social relations as constituted by an unrestrained act of will. However, this makes sense only if politics is in some way conceived as radically separate from the social. This is not the case. Politics is neither completely internal nor

70

completely external to the social, but has the status of a hymen in the Derridean sense of something that stands between two extremes without being consumed by either. The undecidability of the social, then, is the condition of possibility of politics, but there will always be a range of sedimented practices conditioning the formulation, realization and transformation of the political strategies responsible for the shaping and reshaping of social relations.

The accusation of *politicism* charges the primacy thesis with simply reversing the Marxist conception of the relation between state and civil society, so that it is now the political level of the state which is in command. However, this understanding is based on a commonplace confusion of politics with the state. What is overlooked is the fact that politics cannot be confined to a particular institutional region of the social, but constitutes an all-pervading dimension of the social fabric. Yet just as politics cannot be subsumed under the category of the state, so the latter cannot be categorized either as a realm of politics or as a social sphere. In fact, the state is both. It is a realm of politics to the extent that it has been constructed as a privileged point of enunciation, permitting the hegemonic forces to speak in the name of society. It is in this role that the state becomes the key target of political struggles, and even the highest form of hegemony. However, the state is also an ensemble of sedimented social institutions (e.g. institutional forms of representation, intervention and internal organization), which live a relatively quiet life, interrupted only by political attempts to reform or even 'overthrow' the state. It is in this second role – that of a sedimented framework for political struggles – that the state can be viewed as a political system.

Rediscovering Politics

Politics has not always been conceived as a constitutive dimension of the social. In fact, if we go back into the history of political philosophy, we will see that, initially, there was not even room for thinking the specificity of the political in the sense of a relatively autonomous political system. *Aristotle,* for instance, saw the political as coextensive with the social. The political level of the city-state was regarded as the last of a series of social associations, each of which was a natural successor of the one before. Thus, marriage and slavery were the basic elements of the family. A number of individual families formed the village. Several villages were united to form the city-state, within which man's pursuit of the good life was fulfilled on the basis of a legal constitution (Aristotle, 1988: 1252b).

Within this schema, which stresses the continuity between the social and the political, the question of the specificity of the political could not even be raised. The collapse of the city-states finally led to a reorganization of western societies around the Christian church, which introduced a certain discontinuity within the social. Hence, *St Augustine* (1988 [1968]) saw the religious order as divided into two distinct realms: the City of God, i.e. the church; and the City of Man, i.e. political society. The secularized City of Man was natural, but was subordinated to the holy City of God. However, the latter was not only implicated in but also largely dependent upon political society, which was considered legitimate to the degree that it promoted peace and stability, encouraged a Christian life, and helped to avoid conflicts between political and religious obligations (Wolin, 1960: 122–5).

The subordination of political society to the church required the political power of the emperor to be sanctioned by the church. But this gradually changed as the holy nature of political power was increasingly seen as emanating directly from God. The fact that the church became less and less involved in the blessing of political power made it possible for *Aquinas* (1989 [1264]) to claim that political society was not necessarily subordinated to the church. Human nature is given by God, but this human nature seems to indicate that Man is a *zoon politicon* (i.e. a political animal) (1989: 240). This Aristotelian addition enables Aquinas to maintain that political society is not 'the city of the devil', but rather a realm of human activity that is completely natural (1989: 280–90). Aquinas goes so far as to claim that whereas all societies necessarily have a *societas humanas*, only some will also have a *societas christianas*. In those societies where there is both a *societas humanas* and a *societas christianas*, reason and faith will tend to fuse into a harmonious whole.

Aquinas's appreciation of the natural character of political society prepared the way for Machiavelli's assertion of its radical autonomy. *Machiavelli*, the first truly modern political philosopher, aimed to furnish the rulers of the Italian city-states with a set of techniques enabling them to win and hold power in the turbulent and conflictual epoch of medieval Europe. His famous dictum that a successful prince should appear, deceitfully, to be lawful and virtuous but, if necessary, know how to be forceful and vicious (Machiavelli, 1988 [1961]: 99–102), announced the emergence of a particular 'state reason', which differed from private morals emphasizing the importance of faith, trust and obligation. The incompatibility between political ethics and private morals establishes a radical discontinuity between the private social sphere and the public political sphere. Hence, politics becomes something in its own right. According to Machiavelli, it includes everything that serves as a means to maintain power within a corrupted world which contains no essential truth. This so-called realistic view of politics shifted the whole problematic about stable rule from divinely grounded political authority to the exertion of mastery by control of an unstable complex of moving forces (Wolin, 1960: 214).

Whereas Machiavelli aimed to interpret the exercise of political power, *Hobbes* wrote his *Leviathan* (1986 [1651]) in order to legitimize the political power of the absolute state (Clegg, 1989: 5). Despite their differing theoretical ambitions – which reflected their different positions *vis-à-vis* state power – both Machiavelli and Hobbes held a modern conception of political power in the sense that it was seen as constitutive of, rather than derived from, the social order. Yet, although they may have been in accord on the role of political power, this was certainly not the case with regard to its nature (1989: 29–38). Machiavelli saw political power as operating within the social, and conceived it in terms of a plethora of practices, strategies and forms of organization. By contrast, Hobbes located political power outside the social, and generally conceived it in terms of the sovereign power of the state. The starting point for Hobbes (1986: chs 13–17) is a genuine doubt regarding the self-regulating capacity of the social. In the counter-factual state of nature everyone is entitled to use all possible means in order to preserve his or her life and to maximize pleasure and avoid pain. The state of nature will therefore take the form of a violent struggle between self-interested and calculative individuals. This war of each against everyone else will bring forth an insecure world of continual fear and permanent danger. In such a miserable state of living nobody will be able to fulfil their desires, and all reasonable men will therefore seek to put an end to the anarchic struggle of life and death by agreeing to hand over their natural rights to a sovereign power. This mortal god will be able to secure peace and defence only by means of concentrating all physical power in the hands of an absolute state. The result is the generation of an all-powerful Leviathan, which constructs the social order from a point outside it. However, it is important to understand that the social order is invented in an act of creation which eliminates all forms of argumentation, dissension and antagonism (Laclau, 1990a: 71). Thus, the artificial construction of Leviathan, which is the antithesis opposite of the state of nature, leads to the eradication of politics in the Machiavellian sense of practice, strategy and organization. Hence, in what seems to be an arch-modern gesture, Hobbes let the political (in the sense of a political system) fill out the space of politics (in the sense of political struggles) that was opened up by Machiavelli's realism.

Locke also was concerned with the relation between the political and the social rather than that between politics and the social. Although, compared with Hobbes, he was much less pessimistic with regard to the self-regulating capacity of the social. Locke envisioned two different contracts: one that establishes a civil society, and one that creates a relation between civil society and the state. The constitution of a civil society within the state of nature has the character of a contract, and as such is characterized not by chaos but by harmony. In civil society everyone has an equal right to unlimited freedom. Everyone is their own master and can do whatever they like so long as they do not thereby harm other people. Everyone can freely utilize their own body and own everything they have produced with it. Nevertheless, despite the self-regulating capacity of civil society, there is a need for a political order so as to guarantee the life and property of the individuals. This leads to the establishment of a new societal contract, which sanctions the formation of a constitutional state that respects the rights of individuals as well as the sovereignty of the people. Given that the emerging bourgeoisie was preoccupied with securing the autonomy of the capitalist market economy and no longer needed a strong absolute monarch in its battle against the old aristocracy, it is perfectly understandable that Locke should emphasize the self-regulating capacity of civil society and see the state as a mere supplement. Thus, the capitalist breakthrough, together with the bourgeois revolutions, invoked an inversion of the Hobbesian hierarchy between state and civil society.

The inversion is repeated in the movement from Hegel to Marx. *Hegel* is often presented as a reactionary thinker who gave prominence to the state at the expense of the individual. Though in Hegel (1967 [1821]) the state is not, in fact, external to the individual but rather the highest form of community, which unifies the particular and the universal and helps individuals to discover this unity in themselves. The ethical state appears as the rational solution to the inherent problems in civil society, which in turn is a rational response to the inherent contradictions in the family. It is interesting how the view that Hegel conceived of the state as the embodiment of the Absolute Spirit came about. Balibar (1985: 6–9) claims that Hegel saw Machiavelli as the very image of politics, but that, in taking Machiavelli on board, he eliminated the important aspects of appearance and deception. In the rationalistic universe of Hegel there is no room for fraud, and politics is therefore reduced to a moment of force which is retroactively justified by the legal constitution of the

74

state. In other words, politics is identified with legitimized violence and, finally, with the legal authority of the state. This is crucial, since the writings of Marx are heavily influenced by Hegel.

The strong tendency in *Marx* to identify politics with the state is particularly manifest in his early essay 'On the Jewish question' (1987a [1843]). Here it is argued that civil society under feudalism had a directly political character. The social structures of civil life, such as the family, the type and manner of work, and the form and amount of property, defined the political relationships of individuals to the state as a whole. The exclusion of the people from the sovereign power of the state took place on the basis of their particular status in the hierarchical order of civil society, which was organically linked to the state through a dense network of contractual relations specifying the rights and obligations of each individual. The political revolutions that followed in the wake of the French Revolution of 1789 severed these feudal bonds and thereby abolished the political character of civil society. As a result the state was constituted as a political sphere of 'common' interest, clearly separated from the scattered realm of civil society (1987a: 55–6). In short, the non-political realm of civil society became opposed to the exclusively political sphere of the bourgeois state.

When Balibar insists that Marx is the 'joker in the pack', it is because he claims to detect a strong Machiavellian, and thus non-Hegelian, aspect in Marx (Balibar, 1985: 11). He supports this claim by referring to the double hypothesis in 'The Communist Manifesto' which says that 'the history of all hitherto existing societies is the history of class struggles', and that 'every class struggle is a political struggle' (Marx, 1987b [1848]: 222, 228). These bold statements indicate that Marx made an effort

> to move above all to a new definition of politics co-extensive over the whole field of class struggle, over the polarized, though not unified, and even less ordered or normalized system of its practices, and thus to a rupture of the equation between politics and the State, which is no more than domination and exploitation under another name. (Balibar, 1985: 10)

Marx's reference to 'proletarian politics' undoubtedly creates an ambiguity in his political theory. For not only is the political class struggle often reduced to a superstructural aspect, but the superstructural level is generally conceived as determined by civil society, the anatomy of which is to be sought in political economy. Thus, the economic structures of civil society not only determine the general forms of state but also the political class struggles fought within concrete state

apparatuses. This double anchoring of the state in the economic structures of civil society fully justifies the claim that Marx asserts the
omnipotence of the latter and relegates the state to the status of a
supplement.

The later works of *Poulantzas* contain the theoretical seeds for a
rediscovery of politics. The early Poulantzas depicted the state as,
simultaneously, a relatively autonomous region within the societal
structure and an all-pervading factor of social cohesion. The theoretical contradiction between these two conceptions of the state reflected
Poulantzas' (Poulantzas, 1987 [1968]: 37) attempt to distinguish
between the political (*le politique*), in the sense of a political superstructure, and politics (*la politique*), in the sense of political class
struggles. This distinction in turn reflected an underlying dualism
between structure and agency, which he could not overcome within
the limits of structural Marxism. However, in his last book Poulantzas
(1980 [1978]) abandons his flirtation with structuralism. Inspired by
Gramsci and Foucault he develops a so-called strategic-relational state
analysis which conceives the state as neither an instrument nor a
subject, but rather as a social relation (1980: 129–31). The state can
be viewed as a social relation in so far as its institutional matrix can
be seen as a material condensation of the relation of forces between
the social classes. With this definition Poulantzas overcomes the
dualism between structure and agency, since the political level of the
state is seen as the sedimentation of social relations constructed in and
through political class struggles. It should immediately be noted that
Poulantzas elegantly avoids a simple reversal of the discursive hierarchy between politics and the political: he assures us that 'the state
apparatus – that special and formidable something – is not exhausted
by state power' (1980: 14). The irreducibility of the state apparatus to
the state power it inscribes, and by which it is always marked, mani-
fests itself in two important ways. First, the institutional matrix of the
state has an independent effect on the realization of different strategies. Information-filtering mechanisms, systematic inaction on certain
issues, contradictory priorities, the uneven implementation of
measures decided by other instances, and the general lack of coordi-
nation – all contribute to advance or obstruct particular fractional or
class interests (1980: 134–59). Second, the specific class affiliations of
state personnel, together with the ideological cement which binds these
personnel together, tend to have a conservative effect. Their conception of their role in society, supported by their place in the social
division of labour, is dominated by a firm belief in the authority of the
state and thus tends to produce a profound distrust in mass initiatives
for self-management or direct democracy (1980: 154–7).

If Poulantzas rediscovers politics in a way that tends to stress the undecidability between politics and the political, he nevertheless fails to account for the specificity of politics. His retreat from structuralism opens up an untheorized and indeterminate field of politics, which is often reduced to its class content. An adequate and non-essentialist mapping of this field requires further elaboration of the key concepts in Laclau and Mouffe's discourse-theoretical analytics.

Part II

Theoretical Concepts

Introduction

The works of Laclau and Mouffe are organized around three basic concepts: discourse, hegemony and social antagonism. Their central importance necessitates further investigation into their meaning and implications. This investigation, which will draw on both the earlier and the later works, will involve defining and explaining a number of associated concepts and claims. The intention is to provide a comprehensive and accessible presentation of the main ideas of discourse theory.

The concepts of discourse, hegemony and social antagonism are not generally found within the standard vocabularies of social, cultural or political theory. Yet, they are not as odd as they seem, for they tend to substitute for the more traditional concepts of structure, politics and conflict, respectively. For example, the complex and deep-seated patterns of social meanings and relations that guide interaction within a social system are often referred to in terms of structures (Giddens, 1979: 59–65). A *structure* is instantiated by the actions of individual actors, but is not reducible to individual action. A structure describes the general properties (rules, norms and procedures) of a social, cultural or political system. The cumulative effect of these deep-seated properties on the flow of social interaction tends to ensure the reproduction of the structure, either directly by permitting what exists to go on existing, or indirectly by requiring the presence of a functional instance. Thus, the concept of structure has an explanatory role. The concept of *discourse* also has an explanatory role since it is assumed that social interaction can only be explained in relation to its discursive context. It does not, however, possess the same determining power as the concept of structure since it has fully dispensed with the idea of an organizing centre that arrests and grounds the play of meaning. As such, we might say that a discourse informs rather than guides social interaction. Also the way in which discourse affects social interaction is different from the way in which structure affects social interaction. Discourse is taken to influence the cognitive scripts, categories and rationalities that are indispensable for social action, whereas structure is merely seen as operating through prescriptive norms of conduct and specific resource allocations – both of which are discursively constructed.

Likewise, *politics* is often conceived in terms of the pursuit of individual or collective interests. Some have insisted on the crucial role of values or beliefs, but politics is still conceived as a matter of choosing a policy option which maximizes or merely satisfies a pregiven hierarchy of preferences. The concept of *hegemony* is just another name for politics, but one which emphasizes the construction of identity, and conceives values and beliefs as an integral part of such an identity. Within this perspective, identity is not the starting point of politics, but rather something that is constructed, maintained or transformed in and through political struggles.

Finally, the fundamental state of society is often purported to be characterized by *conflict* rather than harmony. The absence of a substantive common good and the failure of the mechanisms of normative integration mean that social systems will be penetrated by all kinds of social conflict. Conflict is often conceived merely in terms of an episodic rivalry, which takes the form of dissent, active protest, violence or war. However, this conception tends to miss an important aspect of societal conflicts, namely their central role in constructing the identity of hegemonic discourses. This aspect is captured by the notion of *social antagonism,* which emphasizes the constitutive role of friend–foe divisions.

The following three chapters are devoted to discussion of the three key concepts. *Chapter 4* will look at the different ways of arriving at the concept of discourse, the expansion of its application to the entire field of social relations, and its various logics and operations.

Chapter 5 examines the genealogy of the concept of hegemony, and argues that hegemony is the general form of politics in mass society. The chapter also discusses the different forms of hegemony as well as the function of myth and ideology. The question of whether the concept of hegemony substitutes subjectivism for objectivism is raised and answered, and the relation between deconstruction and hegemony is explained.

Chapter 6 discusses the relation between politics and social antagonism. It closely examines the construction of social antagonisms through the expansion of chains of equivalence, then moves on to consider the unifying and objectifying effects of social antagonism. It finally addresses the crucial question of the relation between dislocation and social antagonism.

4

Discourse

According to Laclau (1993a: 431), the concept of *discourse* has distant roots in *the transcendental turn in western philosophy*. Classical transcendentalism urged us to focus not on the concrete facts, but rather on their conditions of possibility. Kant inquired into the synthetic a priori categories of cause, substance, etc., which he saw as the very condition for the constitution of phenomena. Later, Husserl came to see the intuition of essences, which is constitutive of all 'givenness', as conditional upon certain acts of experience; these in turn are conditional upon the more fundamental acts of experience, which in the last instance are anchored in a transcendental ego. In line with this, discourse theory asserts that 'the very possibility of perception, thought and action depends on the structuration of a certain meaningful field which pre-exists any factual immediacy' (Laclau, 1993a: 431). In other words, our cognitions and speech-acts only become meaningful within a certain pre-established discourse. However, there are two important *differences* between classical transcendentalism and contemporary theories of discourse. First, while classical transcendentalism conceives the conditions of possibility as *ahistorical* and *invariable*, the theories of discourse insist on the *historicity* and *variability* of discourse. That is, the transcendental conditions are not purely transcendental, but continuously changed by empirical events. Second, while classical transcendentalism is still in some sense anchored in an idealist conception of the *subject* as the creator of the world, the theories of discourse rely on a notion of *structure* which has played a key role within Saussurean and post-Saussurean linguistics (1993a: 431). The fundamental claim of discourse theory can now be restated: our cognitions and speech-acts only become meaningful within certain pre-established discourses, which have different structurations that change over time.

The Concept of Discourse

A discourse is a differential ensemble of signifying sequences in which meaning is constantly renegotiated. We can arrive at this concept of discourse in principally two ways: through the deconstruction of the notion of totalizing structures, or through the deconstruction of the notion of atomized social elements.

According to Derrida, 'the notion of structure refers only to space, geometric or morphological space, the order of forms and sites. Structure is first the structure of an organic or artificial work, the internal unity of an assemblage (. . .) governed by a unifying principle' (Derrida, 1978 [1967]: 15). As such, structure is another name for the closure of a topography, a construction, or an architecture, whose internal order is determined by a privileged centre. This traditional conception of structure gives rise to two problems. The first is that, due to its closure, the passage from one structure to another can only be thought of in terms of chance, hazard or catastrophe. The second is that, due to its centredness, morphological changes will be a result of the unfolding of its internal logics (Gasché, 1986: 144–5). Together these problems clearly demonstrate the need for a deconstruction of the concept of structure.

The deconstruction of the concept of structure involves bracketing its figurative connotation of a self-contained space unified by a fixed centre. Thus, we should start by questioning the idea of an ultimate centre, origin, foundation, ground, etc. on which the structure builds. We have already seen how the idea of an ultimate centre is contradictorily coherent, as it is assumed that the centre structures the structure while itself escaping the process of structuration (Derrida, 1978: 279). We have also seen how the desire for a centre gives rise to endless displacements and substitutions which undermine the full presence of the centre. Finally, we have seen how, by giving up the idea of an ultimate centre, which is given in a full presence beyond the reach of the play of meaning, the process of signification within the structure extends infinitely. Together these insights explode the traditional concept of a centred structure. This leads us to the next point, concerning the closure of the structure which results from the structure's attempt to totalize and exhaust the field of identity, leaving no room for a constitutive outside. The idea of closure through totalization can be questioned from an empirical standpoint by reference to the infinite richness of reality, which can never be exhausted by a finite discourse. This classical questioning of closure tends to perceive it as a question of the expansion of a border rather than a question of meaning itself. Closure can also be questioned from the standpoint of the play of meaning. For, as Derrida contends,

> if totalization no longer has any meaning, it is not because the infiniteness of a field cannot be covered by a finite glance or a finite discourse, but because the nature of the field – that is, language and a finite language – excludes totalization. This field is in effect that of *play*, that is to say, a field of infinite substitutions only because it is finite, that is to say, because instead of being an inexhaustible field, as in the classical hypothesis, instead of being too large, there is something missing from it: a centre which arrests and grounds the play of substitutions. (Derrida, 1978: 289)

In other words, if complete totalization, and thus closure, is impossible, it is because the absence of a fixed centre extends the process of signification within the structure infinitely. In the absence of a complete totalization a structure exists only as a field of signification within which an ambiguous and temporary order is established by a multiplicity of mutually substituting centres. The creation of a relative structural order is conditional upon the exclusion of a constitutive outside which threatens the relative order of the structure and prevents an ultimate closure.

Deconstruction of the notion of closed and centred structures brings us directly to the concept of discourse, which can be defined as a differential ensemble of signifying sequences that, in the absence of a fixed centre, fails to invoke a complete closure. Derrida is not alone in questioning the notion of totalizing structures. Hindess and Hirst (Cutler et al., 1977), for example, have suggested that we engage in a logical disaggregation of the notion of totalizing structures. They assert that concrete social formations are composed of various economic, political and cultural elements which interact and combine in relations of 'necessary non-correspondence'. However, their suggestion that there are no necessary relations between the social elements is highly problematic. For the corollary is that, ultimately, the relation between two elements is completely external. There is no way that they can affect or modify each other. The implication is that the discarded notion of a closed and centred totality is repeated in each of the elements, all of which are thus depicted as micro-totalities with no constitutive outside. In short, Hindess and Hirst end up substituting an essentialism of the element for an essentialism of the totality (Laclau and Mouffe, 1985: 101–3; Laclau, 1988: 253). The only way out of this impasse seems to be through the alternative assertion that the relations between the social elements determine their identity. Yet, if this is the case, we are again left with discourse defined as a relational totality of signifying sequences that determine the identity of the social elements, but never succeed in totalizing and exhausting the play of meaning.

From Saussurean Linguistics to Theories of Discourse

The development of the concept of discourse, as defined above, has been closely linked to transformations in the field of linguistics (Laclau, 1993a). Linguistics was originally concerned with *diachronic* analysis of the historical evolution of language. The linguistic theory of Saussure (1981 [1959]: 81), however, focused exclusively on the *synchronic* states of language that confront individual speakers. The synchronic states of language are, according to Saussure (1981: 17–20), to be analysed in terms of a social system of rules for combination and substitution (*la langue*), which is both the instrument and product of actual, individual forms of speech and writing (*la parole*). The unit of analysis in the linguistic theory of synchronic language systems is the *sign*. The sign is a two-sided entity which joins a particular *sound-image* (signifier) with a particular *concept* (signified) (1981: 65–7). One of the basic principles in the analysis of linguistic signs is that *in language there are only differences, with no positive* terms (1981: 120). All identities within the linguistic system of signs are therefore conceived in terms of relational and differential values. For example, the meaning of the term 'socialism' is given only in relation to the meaning of the terms 'feudalism', 'capitalism', etc. Another basic principle states that *language is form and not substance* (1981: 113). The linguistic elements are defined exclusively by the formal rules of their combination and substitution; their substance does not count at all. Thus, we might change the substance of the pieces on a chessboard from, say, marble to wood, but the formal rules governing the movements of the pieces will remain the same (1981: 110).

Saussure builds his novel approach to the study of language on a few basic distinctions and principles, and goes so far as to envisage the future development of his linguistic theory into a semiological science of signs within society (1981: 16, 68). There are, however, two serious limitations on the future development of Saussurean linguistics. The *first* is the problem of isomorphism (Laclau, 1993a: 432). In an entirely differential universe, dominated by purely formal rules, there exists a strict isomorphism: each signifier corresponds to one, and only one, signified. The isomorphism between the order of the signifier and the order of the signified tends to undermine the duality of the linguistic sign. Indeed, the only way to maintain the dual structure of the sign is to reintroduce the distinction between phonic and semantic substances, i.e. between the actual sound-expressions and the meaning-objects. This collapses the linguistic theory of Saussure, as it violates one of its basic principles. More importantly, though, the reference to phonic and semantic substances tied Saussurean linguistics even more closely to the sign, and thereby hindered extension of the application of the principles of linguistic theory to the wider field of social relations.

The *second* limitation has to do with the non-viability of a Saussurean theory of discourse. Saussure defines discourse as a linguistic sequence that is more extended than a single sentence. There can be no systematic theory of discourse because the succession of sentences is entirely governed by the whims of the individual speaker. In fact, the sentence is the limit case for linguistic analysis, since in the syntagmatic combination of words into a sentence there is already 'no clear-cut boundary between the language fact, which is the sign of collective usage, and the fact that belongs to speaking and depends on individual freedom' (Saussure, 1981: 125). In other words, what prevents the advancement of a theory of discourse is the Cartesian assertion of the omnipotence of the subject (Laclau, 1993a: 432). The inscrutable influence of the all-powerful will of the subject bars the development of a systematic analysis of discourse.

The problem of isomorphism was later solved by the glossematic school in Copenhagen. Hjelmslev (1963) reaffirmed the central role of form purged of all phonic and semantic substance,[1] and was therefore forced to resist the temption of distinguishing between the order of the signifier and the order of the signified in terms of their different substances. In order to preserve the difference between the two orders Hjelmslev had to give up the idea that the fundamental linguistic unit was the sign. The sign is instead broken down into lesser units (glossemes). This is done by subdividing the signifier into phonemes and the signified into semes. For example, the signifier 'calf' is made up of three phonemes, /k/, /æ/ and /f/, while the corresponding signified has at least three semantic elements, or semes, /bovine/, /male/ and /young/. According to Ducrot and Todorov, 'it is now clear that the phonic and semantic units thus located can be distinguished from the formal point of view: the combinatorial laws concerning the phonemes of a language and those applying to the semes cannot be shown to correspond to each other' (Ducrot and Todorov, 1981: 22). In other words: if there is no longer any one-to-one relation between signifiers and signifieds, there no longer exists a strict isomorphism.

The solution to the problem of isomorphism is conditional upon a further formalization of linguistics, and this has two important consequences. First, with the formalization of linguistics the general principles of analysis can be expanded to all signifying systems (Laclau, 1993a: 433). That is to say, if linguistic analysis is no longer necessarily attached to a particular phonic or semantic substance and thus becomes an analysis of pure forms, there are no limits to the application of the abstract schemes of linguistic analysis. As the semiological analysis in the pioneering works of Barthes (1987 [1957]) has convincingly demonstrated, not only advertising but also films, exhibitions and cars can be analysed according to the basic principles of structural linguistics. Second, strict formalism also overcomes the above-mentioned obstacle to the development of a theory of discourse (Laclau, 1993a: 433). For, if all identities are to be conceived in terms of formal differences, there is no scope for presupposing the existence of a substantial subject outside the discursive system. The subject is, rather, to be seen as having a particular discursive positionality (what Althusser termed a subject position). The structuralist celebration of the 'death of the subject' aims to capture precisely this change in conception of the subject. What should be emphasized in this connection, however, is that there still exists some notion of a creative subjectivity. Although, 'the way in which the speaker put sentences together could no longer be conceived as the expression of the whims of an entirely autonomous subject but, rather, as largely determined by the way in which institutions are structured, by what is "sayable" in some context, etc.' (1993a: 433). The uncovering of the rules governing the discursive production of meaning was the primary task of the structuralist research programme.

Expansion of the scope of linguistics to include all sorts of discursively constructed social relations led to growing appreciation of the central role of politics in the sense of constitutive and subversive practices. According to Saussure (1981: 71–4), linguistic change is rare and limited due to the fact that language forms a large and complex system of signs which neither the individual speaker nor the community has any interest in transforming. However, things are different when we move from the analysis of language to the analysis of discursive systems of social relations, which are often subject to change due to the impact of social conflict and political struggles. Recognition of the precariousness and instability of discourse fostered an increasing questioning of the notion of closed and centred totalities. The conception of social relations as an open and decentred matrix became fashionable during the 1970s among a large group of post-structuralist theorists, who tended to define their object of analysis in terms of discourse.

The Distinction between the Discursive and the Non-Discursive

The concept of discourse – the product of the theoretical movement from Saussurean linguistics, via Hjelmslev's glossematics and the structuralism of Barthes and Althusser, to the post-structuralist theories advanced by Derrida and others – cuts across the distinction between the discursive and the non-discursive. As Laclau and Mouffe (1985: 107) note, the more we analyse the so-called *non-discursive* complexes – political interventions, technologies, productive organization, etc. – the clearer it becomes that these are relational systems of differential identities, which are not shaped by some objective necessity (God, Nature or Reason) and which can only therefore be conceived as *discursive* articulations.

We should be aware, however, that the distinction between the discursive and the non-discursive was one maintained by Foucault, whose alternative theory of discourse did not pass through an internal critique of the Saussurean notion of the sign. The archaeological analysis developed in the early works of Foucault aims to analyse the play of discontinuities in the history of discourses (Foucault, 1991: 61). The discourses in question are formed on the basis of a particular episteme, which provides a basic view of the world that unifies intellectual production during a given age (for example, the Renaissance, the Classical Age, or Modernity) (Foucault, 1985 [1969]: 191; Laclau, 1993a: 434). The smallest units of analysis are the statements of a certain discourse. Foucault is not interested in either the truth of statements or their meaning, but rather in the rules of formation that determine the objects, concepts, operations and options of a particular discourse (Dreyfus and Rabinow, 1986 [1982]: 49–50). Analysis of the rules of formation is an analysis of the conditions of existence for discursive events. As such, archaeological analysis involves accounting for the set of rules that define the limits and forms of what can be said, talked about, remembered, re-activated and appropriated (Foucault, 1991: 59–60).

According to Foucault (1985: 157), the rules of formation of, say, a medical discourse must be articulated with its non-discursive conditions. For instance, the establishment of a new medical discourse at the end of the eighteenth century is contemporaneous with a number of political events, economic phenomena, and institutional changes that are not discursive. However, the relation between the discursive and the non-discursive is neither one of determination nor one of expression. Changes in non-discursive conditions do not first change the consciousness of the scientists and then finally their discourse; nor are they first reflected in new concepts, notions and themes, which are subsequently integrated into medical discourse. Rather, non-discursive events transform the mode of existence of medical discourse: its conditions of emergence, insertion and functioning (Foucault, 1985: 162–5, 1991: 66–7). On the other hand, medical discourse is not a passive object subject to transformative pressures from various external forces. Discourse retains a certain autonomy and specificity, which 'nevertheless do not give it the status of pure ideality and total historical independence' (Foucault, 1985: 164–5).

Foucault's insistence upon the distinction between discursive and non-discursive is at odds with the discourse theory of Laclau and Mouffe. However, the shift in his later writings from an archaeological to a genealogical approach brings Foucault's theory of discourse close to that of Laclau and Mouffe,[2] who also to an increasing extent emphasize the role of power in the production of unsutured discursive identities (Laclau, 1993a: 436). While archaeology aims to produce a disinterested and detached description of the rules governing the formation of discourse, genealogy is a method of diagnosing discursive practices from within them (Dreyfus and Rabinow, 1986: 102–3). The genealogist immerses him- or herself in the myriad of power struggles that shape historical forms of discourse (Foucault, 1986b [1971]). 'The task of the genealogist is to destroy the primacy of origins, of final truths. He seeks to destroy the doctrines of development and progress. Having destroyed ideal significations and original truths, he looks to the play of wills. Subjection, domination and combat are found everywhere he looks' (Dreyfus and Rabinow, 1986: 108–9). Laclau and Mouffe clearly share with Foucault the emphasis on subjectivation, power and politics. Indeed, the theoretical affinities between the later works of Foucault and the discourse theory of Laclau and Mouffe are on many scores so significant that the analytics can be viewed as two of a kind (see Dyrberg, 1997).

The Relation between Discourse and the Discursive

Discourse is defined as a relational ensemble of signifying sequences; but if the relational and differential logic prevailed without any limitation or rupture, there would be no room for politics. All identities would be fixed as necessary moments of one and the same discourse, and conflict would only be played out between different intra-discursive variations. However, in the absence of a fixed centre, complete totalization, and thus closure, becomes impossible. Hence, there will always be something that escapes the seemingly infinite processes of signification within discourse. The multiplicity of mutu-ally substituting centres only brings about a precarious order and only manages to produce a partial fixation of meaning. The *partial fixation* of meaning produces an irreducible *surplus of meaning* which escapes the differential logic of discourse. The field of irreducible surplus is termed *the discursive* (or the field of discursivity) in order to indicate that what is not fixed as a differential identity within a concrete discourse is not extra- or non-discursive, but is discursively constructed within a terrain of unfixity. The discursive provides, at once, the condition of possibility and impossibility of a partial fixation of meaning. On the one hand, it provides the differential trace struc-ture that every fixation of meaning must necessarily presuppose. On the other hand, it is never completely absorbed by discourse and thus continues to constitute a field of undecidability which constantly over-flows and subverts the attempt to fix a stable set of differential positions within a particular discourse (Laclau and Mouffe, 1985: 111). In this way, the field of discursivity is precisely what makes possible the articulation of a multiplicity of competing discourses.

The discursive is not an object among other objects (as, of course, are concrete discourses), but rather a 'theoretical horizon for the constitution of the being of every object' (Laclau and Mouffe, 1987: 86). Therefore to ask about the conditions of possibility of the dis-cursive would be meaningless. Indeed, it would be 'equivalent to asking a materialist for the conditions of possibility of matter, or a theist for the conditions of possibility of God' (1987: 86). Nevertheless, concrete discourses constructed within a particular discursive horizon certainly have particular conditions of possibility. These conditions are themselves discursive (Laclau, 1990a: 220).

An example will help to clarify these rather abstract points about the distinction between discourse and the discursive. Let us consider the notion of welfare. In the history of the advanced capitalist societies the term 'welfare' has acquired a host of different meanings according to different traditions and perspectives. Mercantilist theories originally saw welfare as intrinsically linked to the question of the ever-increasing wealth of the nation, achieved through the work of an expanding population. Later, liberalist theories and neo-classical economics came to see welfare as a question of the maximization of private utility within a market economy, eventually through economic state interventions aimed at compensating market failures. Neither of these economic definitions of welfare have dominated the political discourse of the modern welfare state in the post-war era. Welfare has instead been defined in terms of the fulfilment of basic social needs through social insurance or social assistance. However, from the point of view of the predominant discourse of the modern welfare state – the emergence of which was conditional upon the extension of the liberal notion of universal rights to include social rights and the discursive construction of the state as a resource for the weaker and poorer parts of the population – rather than the other way around (Therborn, 1989: 65–72) – the remnants of the long forgotten discourse of mercantilism together with the discourse of neo-classical economics constitute the discursive background for its constitution. And, as we have seen, especially during the recent decades of economic crisis, the discursive background tends to strike back. Thus, growing concern on the part of the central decision-makers for the competitiveness of the national economy in the face of globalization, new technologies, etc. has called into question the old format of the modern welfare state. The growing concern for the structural competitiveness of the national economy have distant roots in the discourse of mercantilism, but is also greatly influenced by the economic ideas of Schumpeter and more recent theories known as 'institutional economics'. In several western European countries the 'neo-mercantilist' critique of the modern welfare state seems to pave the way for what Jessop (1992) has described as a transition from a Keynesian Welfare State to a Schumpeterian Workfare Regime (Jessop, 1992). The structural competitiveness of the national economy must be increased, it is argued, by a combination of economic state interventions on the supply side of the economy and the subordination of social policy to the concern for improved structural competitiveness and greater labour market flexibility. For further discussion, see chapter 12.

The lesson of this illustrative example is that the distinction between discourse and the discursive should be made in terms of differing degrees of fixity/unfixity. That is, while the unfixed elements of a dis-integrated discourse clearly belong to the field of discursivity, the partially fixed moments within concrete discourse do not. The example shows, in addition, that a partial fixation of meaning rests upon precise conditions of possibility, and that its disruption might result from the reactivation of that which the initial fixation necessarily excluded.

Avoiding Some Common Misunderstandings

There are four common misunderstandings regarding the nature of discourse. The *first* is that the construction of every object as an object of discourse involves dispensing with the realist claim concerning the existence of a world external to thought. We have already stressed the compatibility between realist and constructivist assumptions, but because this misunderstanding stubbornly persists it should be repeated that the 'discursive character of an object does not, by any means, imply putting its existence into question' (Laclau and Mouffe, 1987: 82). For example, a stone can be discursively constructed as a projectile or as an object of aesthetic contemplation, but it is still the same physical object. To make this point perfectly clear I shall quote a passage from Derrida's *Limited Inc* (1988a [1977]). Here Derrida talks about his own concept of text, but the argument applies equally well to the concept of discourse. Derrida recalls that,

what I call 'text' implies all the structures called 'real', 'economic', 'historical', socio-institutional, in short: all possible referents. Another way of recalling once again that 'there is nothing outside text'. That does not mean that all referents are suspended, denied, or enclosed in a book, as people have claimed, or have been naive enough to believe and to have accused me of believing. But it does mean that every referent, all reality, has the structure of a differential trace, and that one cannot refer to this 'real' except in an interpretive experience. The latter neither yields meaning nor assumes it except in a movement of differential referring. That's all. (Derrida, 1988a: 148)

The *second* misunderstanding is that the concept of discourse merely designates a linguistic region within a wider social realm. Whereas this might provide an accurate description of the concept of discourse found in the early works of Foucault, it certainly misses the nature of the concept in the works of Laclau and Mouffe. As already mentioned, Laclau and Mouffe (1985: 107–8) reject the distinction between the discursive and the non-discursive, and insist on the interweaving of the semantic aspects of language with the pragmatic aspects of actions, movements and objects. As the reductionist conception of discourse as a linguistic region within the social is widespread and refuses to die, it should be stressed, once again, that discourse is co-extensive with the social and cannot be reduced to either its semantic or its pragmatic aspects. All actions have meaning, and to produce and disseminate meaning is to act.

The *third* misunderstanding is that the relations and identities within concrete discourses are completely arbitrary. This misunderstanding might have been nurtured by Saussure's idea about the arbitrary nature of the sign. According to Saussure (1981: 69), the linguistic sign is arbitrary since there is no natural bond between the signifier and the signified. The proof is that the same signified might attach to different signifiers in different times and places: 'the signified "ox" has as its signifier *b-ö-f* on one side of the border and *o-k-s (Ochs)* on the other' (1981: 68). However, the problem with the examples given by Saussure is that he was *de facto* always thinking about the representation of a real object, in spite of his emphasis that the signified is a concept rather than a thing. In other words, Saussure was thinking about the unmotivated character of the bond that unites the sign to the thing signified (Benveniste, 1971 [1966]: 45–7). As for the relation of the sound-image to the concept, this is by no means arbitrary. The signifieds of language correspond neither to objective essences nor to subjective intentions that have motivations outside language. 'Constituted at the same time as the language, contemporaneous with the attribution made to them of a phonic signifier, they have no unity except for this common signifier, and they dissolve as soon as one seeks to separate them' (Ducrot and Todorov, 1981: 132–3). One might suspect that assertion of the non-arbitrary relation between signifier and signified would compromise the notion of value, since Saussure (1981: 113) claimed that the relative character of value depends on the assertion of the arbitrary nature of the sign. Yet, according to Benveniste, Saussure's claim is wrong: 'to say that the values are "relative" means that they are relative *to each other*' (Benveniste, 1971: 48). Benveniste takes this as proof of their necessity. We might consequently conclude that the relations and identities within a concrete discourse are strictly necessary: not because they are governed by an underlying rationality, but because they are part of a whole which stands in a relation of reciprocal conditioning with its parts (1971: 48). However, the kind of necessity derived from the reciprocal conditioning of part and whole has a local, incomplete and precarious character (Laclau and Mouffe, 1985: 106).

The *fourth* misunderstanding is that discourse comprises nothing but chaotic flux. This might have arisen from Derrida's assertion that in the absence of a transcendental signifier the play of meaning extends infinitely. However, faced with the accusation of speaking of a 'complete freeplay', Derrida assures us that 'there can be no "completeness" where freeplay is concerned' (Derrida, 1988a: 115). Freeplay could be seen as another word for undecidability, although as already mentioned above, undecidability, which penetrates every concrete discourse, involves a *determinate* oscillation between pragmatically determined possibilities. Thus, far from referring to a state of indeterminacy and chaotic flux, the concept of undecidability, and thus freeplay, refers to a determinate openness. It refers to the structurality of the structure, to the field of discursivity which makes possible the formation of metaphysical hierarchies of minor structures in terms of concrete discourses (Derrida, 1978: 155).

The Discursive Operations within Concrete Discourses

In order to analyse concrete discourses we must know what to look for. In his early works Foucault (1985) suggests that we describe enunciative regularities, and the hierarchies between them, as well as their different modalities and points of enunciation. The more formal types of discourse analysis urge us to apply quantitative and qualitative techniques in 'the study of linguistic forms and the regularities in their distribution' as well as 'the general principles of interpretation by which people normally make sense of what they hear and read' (Brown and Yule, 1983: x). Habermas, for his part, wants us to evaluate communicative actions in the light of 'argumentative procedures for directly or indirectly redeeming claims to propositional truth, normative rightness, subjective truthfulness and aesthetic harmony' (Habermas, 1985: 314). What are the focal points of the discourse theory of Laclau and Mouffe? In their focus on the construction of identity, they recurrently refer to *three crucial factors* in the analysis of concrete discourses: the relations of difference and equivalence, the workings of different kinds of overdetermination, and the unifying effect of nodal points. Let us consider each in turn.

The distinction between *relations of difference* and *relations of equivalence* is of considerable theoretical importance. It has been argued above that the unlimited rule of the logic of difference is prevented by the absence of a fixed centre, which renders complete totalization, and thus closure, impossible. The partial fixation of meaning within discourse produces an irreducible surplus of meaning which escapes the differential logic of the discourse in question. However, the expansion of the logic of difference is not only prevented by its lack of a deep foundation in a fixed centre capable of revealing the full essence of all social identities. It is also prevented by the presence of an alternative logic of equivalence which collapses the differential character of social identity by means of expanding a signifying chain of equivalence. Saussure distinguished between syntagmatic and associative relations. The linear combination of linguistic units into sentences establishes a syntagmatic relationship between the linguistic units, while the substitution of one word in the sentence for another word with the same meaning or function establishes an associative, or paradigmatic, relationship. Hence, the following string of words, 'I am thirsty and want to drink a glass of milk', is an example of a syntagmatic combination of words, while the substitution of 'bottle', 'cup', 'jug', etc. for the word 'glass' is an example of a paradigmatic relationship between different words that share a certain sameness in as much as they can contain milk. Now, 'if difference exists only in the diachronic succession of the syntagmatic pole, equivalence exists at the paradigmatic pole' (Laclau, 1988: 256). There is no simple identity between the equivalential identities since they are only the same in one aspect while being different in others (Laclau and Mouffe, 1985: 128). The relation between difference and equivalence is, in other words, undecidable. The discursive identities are inscribed both in signifying chains that stress their differential value, and in signifying chains that emphasize their equivalence. The tension between the differential and equivalential aspects of discursive identities is unresolvable, but political struggles may succeed in emphasizing one of the two aspects. Emphasis on the equivalential aspect by the expansion of chains of equivalence will tend to simplify the social and political space by delimiting the play of difference. The collapse of difference into equivalence will tend to involve a loss of meaning since meaning is intrinsically linked to the differential character of identity. As we shall see in chapter 6, this means that the expansion of chains of equivalence is always related to the construction of a constitutive outside.

An example of a political discourse in which the logic of equivalence played a decisive role is the Jacobin discourse during the French Revolution (1985: 155). The analysis of Furet (1978) shows how the logic of equivalence divided society into two camps. All identities belonged either to the equivalential chain of the 'people' or to that of the *'ancien regime'*. It is interesting to compare the case of the Jacobin imaginary with the development of the Chartist movement in Britain. The Chartist movement was founded in 1835 as an organized protest against the large corn monopolies. As Stedman Jones (1983) has shown, its radical imaginary was greatly influenced by the French Revolution. However, the attempt to invoke a dichotomization of the social and political space failed. The integration of the demands of the middle class, the lack of confrontation with the state, and the failure of the attempt to organize a general strike all contributed to the dissolution of the radical imaginary and the proliferation of difference. The Chartist movement finally recognized the need to advance a plurality of demands within the political system.

The workings of different kinds of *overdetermination* are related to the distinction between relations of difference and equivalence. The concept of overdetermination comes from psychoanalysis, or rather, more precisely, from Freud's famous work on *The Interpretation of Dreams* (Freud, 1986 [1900]). Overdetermination occurs at the symbolic level and takes the form of either condensation or displacement (1986: 383–419). Condensation involves the fusion of a variety of significations and meanings into a single unity. The standard example in the field of politics is the Russian Revolution, which, according to Althusser, condensed a variety of struggles and demands into a single ruptural unity. Displacement involves the transferral of the signification or meaning of one particular moment to another moment. An example would be the construction of the traditional rural culture of the migrant labourers in the shanty towns around the big cities in Latin America as symbols of their resistance to and struggle against the poor living conditions they endure. Condensation occurs when a particular moment receives and concentrates other meanings; displacement takes place when a relation of contiguity is constructed. In Lacanian psychoanalytic theory, condensation therefore becomes equivalent to metaphor, while displacement becomes equivalent to metonymy. An important connection to the distinction between difference and equivalence can now be made. In relations of difference we have neither metaphor nor metonymy. However, the equivalential disruption of relations of difference tends to produce metonymical relations of contiguity, and when the paradigmatic sameness of contiguous elements is fully realized we see the construction of metaphors.

According to Laclau and Mouffe (1985: 112), every discourse is constituted as an attempt to dominate the field of discursivity by expanding signifying chains which partially fix the meaning of the floating signifier. The privileged discursive points that partially fix meaning within signifying chains are called *nodal points* or, in Lacan, *points de capiton* (literally: quilting points). The nodal point creates and sustains the identity of a certain discourse by constructing a knot of definite meanings. According to Žižek, 'this does not imply that it is simply the "richest" word, the word in which is condensed all the richness of meaning of the field it "quilts": the *point de capiton* is rather the word which, *as a word*, on the level of the signifier itself, unifies a given field, constitutes its identity' (Žižek, 1989: 95). It is an empty signifier, a pure signifier without the signified (1989: 97). As such, nodal points like 'God', 'Nation', 'Party' or 'Class' are not characterized by a supreme density of meaning, but rather by a certain emptying of their contents, which facilitates their structural role of

unifying a discursive terrain. What happens is this: a variety of signifiers are floating within the field of discursivity as their traditional
meaning has been lost; suddenly some master signifier intervenes and
retroactively constitutes their identity by fixing the floating signifiers
within a paradigmatic chain of equivalence. In other words:

when we quilt the floating signifiers through 'Communism', for example, 'class
struggle' confers a precise and fixed signification to all other elements: to democracy (so-called 'real democracy' as opposed to 'bourgeois formal democracy' as a
legal form of exploitation); to feminism (the exploitation of women as resulting
from the class-conditioned division of labour); to ecologism (the destruction of
natural resources as a logical consequence of profit-orientated capitalist production); to the peace movement (the principal danger to peace is adventuristic
imperialism), and so on. (1989: 88)

The retroactive constitution of meaning is not an effect of the master-
signifier giving the floating elements their meaning. Rather, the
signification of the floating elements within a paradigmatic chain of
equivalence is a consequence of their reference to a certain symbolic
code (1989: 103). As such, the conception of nodal points reveals the
secret of metaphors: their capacity to unify a certain discourse by
partially fixing the identity of its moments.

The Unity and Limits of Discourse

A final question concerns the unity and limits of concrete discourses.
Foucault (1985: 21–39) has convincingly shown that a discourse can
find no principle of unity in reference to the same object, in a common
style in the production of meaning, in the constancy of its concepts, or
in reference to a common theme. The coherence of a discourse is given
only in the shape of a regularity in dispersion. Laclau and Mouffe
concur that there is no essential principle of coherence and that
discourses are to be conceived as more or less regulated systems of
dispersion. The discursive moments are dispersed, but the ordering
effects of the relations of difference and equivalence, the workings of
different kinds of overdetermination, and the nodal points are factors
that give rise to a certain regularity which can be signified as a
'totality'.

If the unity of discourse is provided in terms of a regularity in dispersion, what remains is the question of how the limits of a discursive
formation are established. Whereas Laclau and Mouffe accounted for
the construction of the regularity in dispersion of concrete discourses

by advancing a theory of hegemony, they have tried to answer the question concerning the construction of the limits of discursive formations by advancing a theory of social antagonism. In chapter 5 we shall take a closer look at the theory of hegemony. The concept of social antagonism will then be examined in chapter 6.

5
Hegemony

One lexical meaning of *hegemony* is 'leadership, authority and influence, especially of one state in a group of states'. Thus, it is common to speak about the hegemony of the USA within the western world in the post-war period. This definition and usage of the concept of hegemony captures the important aspect of leadership, but fails to include the constructivist aspect highlighted by the discourse-theoretical analytics of Laclau and Mouffe. That is to say, the political as well as moral-intellectual leadership of a hegemonic force (state, class, movement, or other) hinges on the construction of a discursive formation that provides a surface of inscription for a wide range of demands, views and attitudes. The construction of a hegemonic discourse is the result of articulation. *Articulation* is defined as a 'practice establishing relations among elements such that their identity is modified as a result of the articulatory practice' (Laclau and Mouffe, 1985: 105). The articulation of discursive elements into contingent moments within a hegemonic discourse takes place in a conflictual terrain of power and resistance, and will therefore always include an element of force and repression. Now, if we put all this together we can define hegemony as the expansion of a discourse, or set of discourses, into a dominant horizon of social orientation and action by means of articulating unfixed elements into partially fixed moments in a context crisscrossed by antagonistic forces.

This definition of hegemony has a general validity for analysing processes of disarticulation and rearticulation that aim to establish and maintain political as well as moral-intellectual leadership. Thus the concept of hegemony refers not only to the privileged position of a nation-state in a group of nation-states, but more generally to construction of a predominant discursive formation. For example,

101

neo-liberalism can be seen as a hegemonic discourse to the extent that it has managed to redefine the terms of the political debate and set a new agenda. Repeated attacks on the centralist and bureaucratic 'nanny state', celebration of the family and individual entrepreneurship, and appraisal of the market as a privileged steering mechanism within both the private and public sectors – all are important moments in the neo-liberalist discourse, the predominance of which has forced oppositional forces to reconsider their conception of the ideal relationship between state, economy and civil society.

Deconstruction and Hegemony

Discourse is a consequence of hegemonic practices of articulation, but it is the play of meaning within discourse and the subversion of discourse by the field of discursivity that provide the condition of possibility of hegemonic articulation. Yet, this is just another way of saying that *hegemony brings us from the undecidable level of non-totalizable openness to a decidable level of discourse.* In support of this assertion, let us reconsider Derrida's notion of an ethico-political decision. According to Derrida (1988a [1977]: 116), the undecidable calls for decisions in the order of ethico-political responsibility. There can be no decision without a trial and a passage by way of undecidability, and such a decision is always an ethico-political one. This dense and abstract argument becomes clearer and more concrete in Derrida's deconstruction of Husserl's phenomenology in *Speech and Phenomena* (Derrida, 1986c [1967]). According to Laclau (1993b: 281), the central question in *Speech and Phenomena* concerns the relation between meaning and knowledge. According to Derrida (1986c: 88–104), there is a formalist moment in Husserl, where he emancipates meaning from knowledge in terms of object intuition. Thus, an expression such as 'The circle is square' has a meaning, since it allows us to say that it refers to an impossible object. Derrida even concludes that if meaning can be separated from knowledge, the essence of meaning is better shown in the absence of such an intuition. However, if Husserl opens up the possibility that we can grasp the meaning of something independently of the intuition of the object, he closes it down by insisting that meaning must always and necessarily await an object intuition. Meaning is subordinated to the telos of knowledge since 'one can well *speak* in saying that "The circle is square"; one speaks *well*, however, in saying that it is not' (1986c: 98). The formalist moment, then, involves only a temporary suspension of the intuitionist moment of true knowledge. However, the fact that there is an oscillation between the formalist and the intuitionist moment means that – from the point of view of meaning – it is undecidable whether meaning will or will not be subordinated to knowledge. This in turn means that if Husserl insists upon subordinating meaning to knowledge, this subordination is consequent upon a contingent intervention in the shape of an ethico-political decision. Such a contingent intervention, which takes place in an undecidable terrain, is conceived by Laclau and Mouffe as a hegemonic intervention (Laclau, 1993b: 282). In fact, Gramsci specifically used the category of hegemony in order to account for the contingent articulation of a plurality of identities into collective wills capable of instituting a certain social order.

Now, 'if deconstruction discovers the role of the decision out of the undecidability of the structure, hegemony, as a theory of the decision taken in an undecidable terrain, requires that the contingent connections existing in that terrain are fully shown by deconstruction' (1993b: 283). Deconstruction points to the fact that metaphysical closure is reached through ethico-political decisions taken in an undecidable terrain; but in order to show that these decisions have the form of hegemonic articulations the constitutive and contingent character of these articulations must be shown by a deconstruction that reveals the undecidability that every decidable inscription must necessarily presuppose. It is at this point that deconstruction and hegemony cross each other. Deconstruction in a certain sense implies a theory of hegemony and the theory of hegemony implies deconstruction. We might even conclude that *deconstruction* and *hegemony* are intrinsically linked in the sense that they constitute the two complementary and reciprocal movements that link decidability with undecidability and vice versa (Laclau, 1993b: 281). Whereas hegemony brings us from undecidability to decidability, deconstruction shows the contingent and constitutive character of decidable hegemonic articulations by revealing the undecidability of the decision.

The Genealogy of the Concept of Hegemony

As Laclau and Mouffe (1985: chs 1 and 2) convincingly demonstrate, the concept of hegemony was introduced into the discourse of Marxism in an attempt to supplement *the economistic logic of necessity* with a *political logic of contingency*. The Marxist conception of 'normal development', grounded in the dialectical development of the forces and relations of production, had run into trouble. An increasing number of exceptions to the putative iron laws of capitalism had to be accounted for in terms of contingent political interventions. The concept of hegemony was introduced to compensate for this perceived deficiency, although, as we shall see, it soon turned out to be a dangerous supplement, which undermined the whole idea that a structural necessity governed the development of capitalist societies.

In western Europe the logic of contingency expanded in response to a theoretical crisis in Marxism that was triggered by important historical events. In his early works Kautsky saw the advent of socialism as guaranteed by the crisis-ridden character of capitalism and by the proletarianization, impoverishment and organization of the masses. Both the crisis of capitalism and simplification of the system of social antagonisms were seen as likely consequences of the unfolding of the inner logic of capitalism, but they also constituted empirically observable facts. These, of course, rested on specific historical conditions of existence. For example, the German proletariat was relatively unified due to the failure of the German bourgeoisie to establish a liberal-democratic state and the failure of the Lassalleans' attempt to integrate the workers into the corporatist institutions of the Bismarckian state. In addition, the great depression of 1873–96 affected the living conditions of all social strata and nurtured the belief in the final collapse of capitalism. However, Kautsky's appeal to reality suffered fatally as the transition to organized capitalism and the economic boom, which lasted until 1914, gave rise to an increasing fragmentation between various social strata and occupational groups and destroyed belief in the imminent collapse of capitalism. The consolidation of capitalism dislocated the simplistic theoretical universe of the early Kautsky and produced a crisis within Marxism.

There were three main responses to this crisis. The first was the establishment of *Marxist orthodoxy*. Kautsky now fully recognized the growing disjuncture between the historical mission of the working class and its actual political practice. The overcoming of this disjuncture required a contingent intervention. In response, Kautsky assigned a new role to theory. Only the scientific insight of Marxist theory into the laws of motion of the economic infrastructure could confirm the transitory character of current tendencies and the future revolutionary reconstitution of the working class (Laclau and Mouffe, 1985: 19). This emphasis on the role of theory in overcoming the disjuncture between the aprioristic knowledge of historical materialism and the current political practices granted intellectuals a privileged role in the struggle for socialism. Intellectuals should help focus on the final socialist object (*das Endziel*) and reinforce the identity of the working class. They also had a crucial role in revealing the essential meaning of history, which is hidden behind a veil of appearances and

contingencies (1985: 20–1). As such, the contingent political mediation of Marxist intellectuals was limited by the fact that this mediation
simply serves as the midwife for the realization of the necessary logics
of capitalism. Notwithstanding this, the minimal space for contingent
political intervention was not reducible to a moment in the chain of
monistically conceived necessity. Marxist orthodoxy thus instigated a
necessity/contingency dualism, which was also to characterize the
open-minded orthodoxy of Labriola and Bauer (1985: 25–9).

The room for contingent political intervention was further expanded by the second response to the crisis of Marxism. Whereas
Kautsky's orthodoxy claimed that the growing fragmentation, characteristic of the new stage of organized capitalism, would finally be
overcome by changes in the infrastructure, Bernstein's *revisionism*
maintained that this was to be achieved through autonomous political
intervention (1985: 30). Hence, contingent political action was no
longer considered to have a secondary midwife function, but to constitute the primary terrain for overcoming fragmentation. Bernstein saw
the social-democratic party as the main source of political unification.
Social Democracy should be a party for all wage earners and all
oppressed, but the political unity it was supposed to bring about would
have a strict class character. This would follow not because the
working class was ontologically or epistemologically privileged, but
rather because of certain historically conditioned 'empirical' advantages (organizational and political capacities) which would be realized
and guided by an underlying ethical impulse. The reductive re-
affirmation of the class character of the political unity of the
underprivileged sectors of the population might seem incomprehensible given the fact that, 'in Bernstein's case, the logical conclusion
would seem to be that political unity can be constituted only through
an overcoming of the class limitations of the different fractions of
workers' (1985: 32). However, as Laclau and Mouffe convincingly
demonstrate, Bernstein was unable to move towards a theory of articulation and hegemony due to his belief that there existed an underlying
ethical impulse in society. His belief in the autonomy of political
intervention was founded on a break with the economic determinism
of Marxist orthodoxy, yet he merely substituted an ethical subjectivism for the mechanist objectivism of historical materialism. That
is, he postulated the existence of an autonomous ethical subject whose
role in the evolutionary process was to assure the ethical progression
of humanity. Clearly, the positing of a transcendental ethical subject
and belief in the idea of an irreversible process of ethical evolution
rule out the development of a theory of hegemonic articulation.
For if the meaning of every political mobilization and achievement

is fixed a priori, there is no room for articulation (1985: 33–5).

Luxemburg, who was Bernstein's arch-enemy, was also unable convincingly to guarantee the class character of the political unity resulting from contingent political interventions. Although she emphasized the important role of the mass strike in the first Russian revolution, she nevertheless recognized that the situation in the West was very different. The dominant trend in the West was the fragmentation of the working class, the isolation of political movements, and the separation between economic and political struggles – factors explained by the more developed nature of liberal democracy in the West *vis-à-vis* Russia (1985: 8–9). In response to the increasing fragmentation in the West, Luxemburg still held to the possibility of a socialist revolution: she believed that the unity of the working class would be recomposed in the course of forthcoming revolutionary struggles. The unity of the working class is a symbolic unity as it results from an overdetermination of each political mobilization by the global struggle against the capitalist system (1985: 10–11). Luxemburg's theory of the uncontrollable spontaneity of overdetermined political mobilizations, culminating in the revolutionary mass strike, clearly broke with the orthodoxy of the Second International. Nevertheless, this theoretical advance was undermined by her insistence upon the necessary class character of the unified political force that emerges as a product of the process of symbolic overdetermination. Such an insistence can only be sustained by reference to the objective laws of capitalist development, i.e. the increasing proletarianization of the middle classes and the peasantry, leading inevitably to a confrontation between bourgeoisie and proletariat. The result of this theoretical regress is a zero-sum game, according to which the logics of necessity and contingency prevent each others' expansion (1985: 11–13).

The third and most radical answer to the crisis of Marxism was provided by Sorel's *revolutionary syndicalism*. Sorel concurs with Bernstein's critique of the rationalism of historical materialism. Indeed, his critique of economism is so radical that he is prevented from repeating Luxemburg's implicit last-minute reliance on the unifying effects of change in the economic base. Put simply, society cannot be conceived in terms of a founding rational substratum to which the process of social unification can be referred. Yet neither can it be conceived in terms of an ethical evolution towards still higher states of humanity. Thus Sorel does not follow Bernstein's attempt to replace mechanistic objectivism with ethical subjectivism (1985: 38). Sorel is therefore compelled from the start to conceive class unity as politically constituted. Sorel's great disillusionment with the socialists for participating in the Dreyfusard coalition government, which led to

a loss of proletarian identity, turned him into a fierce enemy of democratic politics. Consequently, Sorel now, like Luxemburg, pointed to
the unifying effects of the general strike. But for Sorel it does not matter
whether the general strike is achievable or not. Its historical function
is to serve as a myth that provides a point of condensation of working
class unity. The problem is, of course, that the mythically reconstituted
subject is still considered to be a class subject (1985: 40–1). On the
one hand, it must necessarily be so since only violent confrontation
between proletariat and bourgeoisie can regenerate the identity of the
latter and thereby arrest decadence and societal decline. On the other
hand, if historical justification of the actions of the proletariat rests
solely on its opposition to bourgeois decadence, then there is a fundamental split between the actual contents of the proletarian project and
the general function this project fulfils. After all, other classes, projects
or myths could function to arrest decadence and bring about societal
regeneration. In other words, the main problem with Sorel is not that
he insists on the class character of the mythically constructed collective will, since the very logic of his arguments suggests that the relation
between the task and the actor is indeterminate; it lies rather in his
inability to accept that the contingent articulation of task and actor
takes place in and through politics (Laclau, 1994a).

Of the three responses to the crisis of Marxism, Sorel's is the one
that expands the logic of contingency furthest. However, the expansion of the logic of contingency within the prewar discourse of western
European Marxism was linked to a *defensive problem:* how to recon-
stitute the unity of the working class in the face of increasing
fragmentation within the advanced capitalist societies. By contrast,
the *offensive problem* of Russian Marxists like Axelrod, Plekhanov,
Lenin and Trotsky was how to forge a political alliance capable of
bringing about a social revolution in feudal and capitalist societies.
The solution to this problem also involved expanding the logic of
contingency, and this time the contingent logic had a name: hegemony.

The term 'hegemony' first appeared in the writings of Axelrod and
Plekhanov. It described the process whereby the incapacity and failure
of the weak Russian bourgeoisie to carry out the bourgeois revolution
forced the relatively strong working class to intervene decisively to
carry it through. The term 'hegemony' was thus introduced in order
to account for an extraordinary historical situation in which one class
(the proletariat) should carry out the task of another class (the destruction of the feudal order in a bourgeois revolution). Hegemony was first
and foremost a strategic term associated with the dislocation of normal
development. In western Europe dislocation merely invoked a
displacement of the level at which the working class would acquire its

unity – from the economic to the political, ethical or mythical; the historical dislocation in Russia invoked a displacement of the political initiative from one class to another. The relation between the working class and the alien task it had to assume was not one of articulation, since neither the identity of the proletariat nor the character of the bourgeois revolution was altered; it was, rather, one of complete exteriority (Laclau and Mouffe, 1985: 48–9).

The conception of the hegemonic link as external to the hegemonic class also characterized the Leninist tradition (1985: 55). Hegemony is here defined as the *political leadership* of the working class within a broad class alliance. The revolution of 1905 swept away the feudal order and the tsarist regime; the task of the working class now was to lead an alliance of peasants, rural workers and soldiers through to a socialist revolution in Russia. The working class was compelled to give up its ghetto strategy in order to transform itself into the articulator of a multiplicity of demands (1985: 58). However, the hegemonic class alliance did not form a new revolutionary subject as the allied forces retained their preconstituted identities structured around paradigmatic interests. The classes and groups in the hegemonic alliance should 'strike together but march separately' (1985: 55).

It was the dislocation of historical stages that forced the working class to act on a mass basis. In Lenin the concept of hegemony is explicitly linked to what he saw as the uneven and combined development in Russia, where feudalism and emerging capitalism co-existed in a way which weakened the Russian bourgeoisie (as a result the predominance of foreign capital) while strengthening the working class (as a result of the high concentration of capitalist investments). The supplementary logic of hegemony then seems to take its revenge as Trotsky declared uneven and combined development to be the historical condition of our time (1985: 60). The global system of capitalism is perceived as profoundly dislocated, and in this situation hegemony becomes the main political principle for social recomposition.

At this point hegemony was still thought of as an alliance of separate identities held together by the tactical manipulations of leadership within the communist vanguard party. Gramsci, however, replaced this rather authoritarian conception of hegemony with a more democratic notion, embracing *political as well as moral-intellectual leadership* and aiming to articulate a collective will with a national-popular character (1985: 65–7). Hegemony, then, is no longer defined as an alliance of preconstituted identities, but rather as a process of production of a new collective identity. Like Sorel, Gramsci emphasizes the contingent articulation of social forces and political tasks. He even recognizes the importance of ideology, symbols and myths. However, in sharp contrast to Sorel, Gramsci insists that the articulation of collective wills takes place at the level of democratic politics. It is the political struggles within state, economy and civil society that determine the faith of competing hegemonic projects. The fact that Gramsci maintains that the social classes, due to their structural position at the level of the relations of production, have an ontologically privileged role in the struggle for hegemony is regrettable. Nevertheless, as soon as this economistic residue is removed, the contingent logic of hegemonic articulation is able to develop all its theoretical and political potentialities (1985: 69). This last step is taken by Laclau and Mouffe, who define hegemony as an articulatory practice instituting nodal points that partially fix the meaning of the social in an organized system of differences. The discursive system articulated by a hegemonic project is delimited by specific political frontiers resulting from the expansion of chains of equivalence (1985: 134–7).

Hegemony as the General Form of Politics in Mass Societies

The contingent logic of hegemony was seen to expand in response to the crisis in the evolutionary schemes of Marxism, which conceived of history in terms of a necessary succession of stages. In Plekhanov and Lenin the break with the stagist conception of history is delimited to what is perceived as an extraordinary historical situation. However, in Trotsky, where the general law of 'uneven development' seems to explode the somewhat stagist conception of 'combined development' (Laclau, 1990a: 45–50), dislocation becomes a general condition of revolutionary politics within the global system of capitalism. Dislocation is the *sine qua non* for hegemonic articulation. Without dislocation the social totality would be fully sutured and objectivized, and there would thus be no room for hegemonic articulation. Yet, identification of the necessary condition of the contingent logic of hegemony does not explain why hegemony became the general form of politics in modern capitalist societies. Traditional feudal societies were also penetrated by dislocatory forces, and there were certainly political attempts to rearticulate the social in the face of various disruptive events that produced floating signifiers. The political rearticulation of social identity even led to the production of political frontiers, e.g. religious groups not only fought paganism but also struggled over the right interpretation of the words of God. The contingent logic of hegemony can therefore be said to be at work from

109

the very beginning of human history. Thus hegemonic articulation is not exclusively tied to the modern age, as Laclau and Mouffe seem to suggest (Laclau and Mouffe, 1985: 138). Although it should immediately be emphasized that, for example, medieval philosophers were not able to think the concept of hegemony due to the predominance of a highly fundamentalist theological ontology which tended to deny the contingent character of social identity and the presence of floating signifiers. Moreover, there was no room for hegemony in the Gramscian sense of the formation of collective wills through moral and intellectual reform. The capacity to think the contingent articulation of collective wills in and through political struggles is indeed a *distinctively modern phenomenon,* which was conditional not only upon the process of secularization but also upon the entry of the masses into political life. The significance of the latter was recognized by Lenin (1981 [1916]: 117–18), who spoke of the transition to a new bourgeois mass politics, which he labelled 'Lloyd Georgism' after the skilful British Liberal leader Lloyd George. However, whereas Lenin in a reductionist manner conceived mass politics as a part of a bourgeois plot against the proletariat, Gramsci saw it as the very form of politics in advanced industrial societies. The formation of a hegemonic bloc is the ultimate political goal in the new era of mass politics, and just as mass politics cannot be reduced to a bourgeois plot against the proletariat, so hegemony cannot be reduced to a strategy on the part of the proletariat. Instead, hegemony must be conceived as the general form of politics in modern capitalist societies.

The populist aspect of Italian fascism reinforced Gramsci's conviction of the need to address the masses in modern politics. The popular masses had become a key factor in political life as a result of three important developments (Sassoon, 1987: 253). First, the development of the system of organized capitalism spurred the growth of mass political parties, trade unions and pressure groups. Second, the expansion in scope of state intervention, as a consequence of political pressures to include social, educational and health policies, established a direct link between political power and the popular masses. Finally, the expansion of suffrage gave the masses a direct role within the institutional framework of liberal democracy. The historical events that brought about the new era of mass politics also engendered the political forces responsible for the organization of the masses. Thus, the emergence of organized capitalism, state interventionism and liberal democracy heralded the emergence of a new type of intellectual (1987: 253–8). The old model of free-floating intellectual was replaced by a new type, the organic intellectual, whose primary function was to organize the masses rather than to practise the acquired skill of thinking (Gramsci, 1971 [1948–51]: 5–9). Gramsci's conception of intellectuals as 'organizers of the masses of men' differs radically from both Kautsky's and Lenin's conception of intellectuals as conveyors of science who can ally themselves with the proletariat by choosing to become professional revolutionaries. The external relationship between intellectuals and the popular masses, which we find in both Kautsky and Lenin, is in Gramsci replaced by an internal relationship – everybody has the potential to become an intellectual in the Gramscian sense. This opens up a more democratic relationship between intellectuals and the popular masses.

Different Forms of Hegemony

According to Gramsci (1971: 55–9, 106–14, 129–33), it is possible to distinguish between two different forms of hegemony: *transformism* and *expansive hegemony*. Both involve a simultaneous process of revolution–restoration. However, while restoration tends to dominate in the case of transformism, revolution tends to dominate in the case of expansive hegemony. Transformism can thus be seen as a defensive type of politics pursued by the hegemonic force in a situation of political and economic crisis. It involves the gradual but continuous absorption, achieved by methods which vary in their effectiveness, of the active elements produced by allied groups – and even of those which come from antagonistic groups and seem irreconcilably hostile (1971: 59). The preferred method of transformism is co-optation, or, in other words, the expansion of relations of difference. The goal is the formation of a passive consensus which neutralizes antagonistic political forces and disunites the masses (Mouffe, 1979: 182). Transformism is thus a revolution without the people – a passive revolution.

Expansive hegemony can be characterized as an anti-passive revolution in two senses (Sassoon, 1982: 145). Not only is it a strategy which counters the attempt of the bourgeoisie to maintain its leadership by regrouping and recomposing the hegemonic power bloc; it is also an offensive strategy for building an active consensus to mobilize the masses in a revolution involving both ideological and political superstructures and the economic infrastructure. Expansive hegemony involves the formation of a collective will with a national-popular character, which is able to promote the full development of particular demands and lead finally to the resolution of the contradictions they express (Gramsci, 1971: 132–3; Mouffe, 1979: 183).

In Gramsci's view, transformism is the hegemonic strategy of the

111

bourgeoisie in times of political and economic crisis, while expansive hegemony is the strategy of the proletariat. For 'only the working class, whose interests coincide with the limitation of all exploitation, can be capable of successfully bringing about an expansive hegemony' (Mouffe, 1979: 183). Of course, we should not accept the class-reductionist bias in Gramsci's conception of the different forms of hegemony. Not only does it rely on the quite illegitimate assertion that the working class has the historical mission of universal emancipation. It is also problematic on empirical grounds, as there have been numerous examples of both proletarian and bourgeois political forces pursuing both transformist and expansive hegemonic strategies; not to mention many examples of non-class forces involved in exactly the same types of strategies. If we abandon the idea of a neat correlation between, on the one hand, transformism and the bourgeoisie and, on the other hand, expansive hegemony and the proletariat, we still retain an important distinction between the defensive manipulation of consent and the offensive expansion of a hegemonic project. Whereas the Conservative government in Britain headed by Mrs Thatcher provides a clear example of an expansive hegemony, the Clinton administration in the USA seems to represent a transformist, centre-drifting hegemony.

The formation of an expansive hegemony is basically metonymic (Laclau and Mouffe, 1985: 141). A certain contiguity between discursive elements, obtained through a displacement of meaning, is necessary for the expansion of a hegemonic project. Political forces might produce a metonymical sliding by taking on organizational functions within a community that go beyond the traditional practices ascribed to them. Take, for example, the Muslim fundamentalists in Egypt who in 1992 managed to provide the victims of a series of earthquakes in Cairo with first aid, blankets and food. This caused the non-fundamentalist government much grievance, especially as the aid provided by the Muslim fundamentalists was delivered much quicker than that provided by the government. The important thing was not the speed of delivery, however, but rather the fact that the Muslim fundamentalists, by providing that kind of emergency aid, established a relation of contiguity between 'Muslim fundamentalism' and 'social caring'. Indeed, not only did they show themselves to be concerned with social problems and human suffering; they also demonstrated their capacity to run society. However, these actions did not establish a metaphorical sameness between, on the one hand, 'Muslim fundamentalism' and, on the other hand, 'social caring' and 'capacity for governance'. They only gave rise to a metonymical sliding, which provided the conditions of possibility for the articulation of a stronger hegemony based on a metaphorical unity. For metaphor presupposes metonymy, as the discursive articulation of a paradigmatic equivalence requires that the different elements be in a metonymical relation. As such, hegemony based upon metaphor is always the end product of a series of discursive articulations, never the starting point.

The Concept and Function of Ideology

Ideology plays a crucial role in the construction of hegemony. The formation of a strong metaphorical hegemony necessarily involves the creation of an ideological closure. However, in order to specify further the role of ideology for hegemonic discourse, we must first question the traditional Marxist concept of ideology. There are, in fact, two classical approaches to ideology within Marxism, which have often – but not always – been combined. The first conceives ideology as a particular *superstructural level* within the social totality, while the other identifies ideology with *false consciousness* (Laclau, 1990a: 89). The problem with both approaches is that they are grounded in an *essentialist* conception of society and social agency. The essentialist conception of society as a unitary, and fully intelligible, structural totality, which is divided into a base and a superstructure, has been fiercely criticized. Poststructuralists contend that the structural totality 'is always surrounded by an "excess of meaning" which it is unable to master and that, consequently, "society" as a unitary and intelligible object which grounds its own partial processes is an impossibility' (1990a: 90). Likewise the essentialist notion of social agency as a self-identical subject endowed with a set of objective interests, on the basis of which the actual consciousness of the subject can be judged to be false, has come under attack. 'The same excess of meaning, the same precarious character of any structuration that we find in the domain of the social order, is also to be found in the domain of subjectivity' (1990a: 92). Consequently, if when we attempt to determine the real, non-ideological identity of the subject we find nothing but a kaleidoscopic movement of differences, the theoretical basis for the concept of ideology as false consciousness falls apart. The point is made even more strongly in a later article by Laclau on 'The death and resurrection of ideology' (1996a). Quoting Žižek, Laclau argues that the problem with the Marxist notion of ideology is that the extra-ideological reality, which is distorted in ideological representations, is always already ideological. We do not have any access to the real world except through its construction as a discursive form within more or less ideological systems of representation. With the disappearance of an objective world of real essences against which we can measure and finally demask ideological forms of representation, the Marxist notion of ideology no longer has any meaning. However, the death of the Marxist theory of ideology is not a result of the removal of ideological alienation, but rather a result of its own imperialistic success (1996a: 201–3).

The undermining of the essentialist conception of society and social agency as objective essences might lead to the conclusion that the concept of ideology should be abandoned. However, when Laclau insists upon retaining the concept of ideology, it is precisely because both society and social agency are often misrecognized as fully constituted essential unities. The concept of ideology should be retained in the inverted sense of 'the non-recognition of the precarious character of any positivity, of the impossibility of any ultimate suture' (1990a: 92). Any attempt to expand a hegemonic discourse necessarily invokes a totalizing reduction of the infinite play of meaning. And the ideological consists precisely in those discursive forms that seek to construct society and social agency as decidable discursive forms within a totalizing horizon that projects on to a particular discursive form an impossible fullness and transparency. In other words, the ideological is 'the "will" to totality of any totalizing discourse' (1990a: 92). As Laclau remarks, the operation of closure is impossible but at the same time necessary; *impossible* because of the constitutive dislocation which lies in the heart of any structural arrangement, *necessary,* because without that fictitious fixing of meaning there would be no meaning at all' (1996a: 205).

From this it follows that epiphenomenalism and class reductionism must be seen as the ideological support of Marxism. The idea of the self-developing economic substratum and a privileged social class, which together will bring about a full emancipated society, clearly involves ideological totalization. Another example of an ideological form of discourse is the corporatist representation of capitalist society as an 'economic organism', the health of which is ensured by responsible socioeconomic actors who aim to maintain a balance between wages and productivity, employment and inflation, imports and exports, etc. A third example of ideological totalization is found in the belief that the unfettered rule of the market mechanism within both the private and public sectors will finally solve the problems which in western Europe have been identified as 'government failure', 'institutional rigidities', 'Euro-sclerosis', etc.

The conception of ideology in terms of the construction of particular discursive forms within a totalizing horizon with universalist pretensions informs Laclau's argument concerning the role and nature

114

of myth and social imaginary (Laclau, 1990a: 61–5). *Myth* is defined as 'a principle of reading of a given situation' (1990a: 61). The condition for the emergence of myth is structural dislocation and the function of myth is to suture the dislocated space through the constitution of a new space of representation. In other words, the role of myth is essentially hegemonic: 'it involves forming a new objectivity by means of the rearticulation of the dislocated elements' (1990a: 61). The concrete or literal content of myth might include some vision of a promised land or ideal society. However, myth does not merely describe a utopia in the sense of a blueprint for an achieved or achievable society. For Laclau, 'the concrete or literal content of myth represents something different from itself: the very *principle* of a fully achieved literality' (1990a: 63 – emphasis added). In other words, myth is a metaphor for an absent fullness – that is, a fullness which cannot be realized at present.

The metaphoric character of myth permits expression of the very form of fullness itself beyond any concrete or literal content. The indeterminateness of the expression of fullness opens a space for the inverted representation of all possible kinds of structural dislocation. That is to say, myth will tend to provide a surface on which unsatisfied demands are inscribed. If the surface of inscription is hegemonized by what is inscribed on it, then the moment of inscription will be eliminated in favour of the literality of what is inscribed. However, if instead the expression of the very form of fullness continues to dominate, it becomes the unlimited horizon of any social demand. Myth is thereby transformed into a *social imaginary* (1990a: 63–4). A social imaginary is a horizon in the sense that it is not one object among other objects, but rather the condition of possibility for the emergence of any object. In this sense, the Christian millennium, the conception of progress held by the Enlightenment and positivism, and the communist dream of a classless society are all social imaginaries.

The notions of myth and social imaginary conceptualize the ideological forms of discourse that aim to construct society and social agency as positive and fully sutured identities. Social imaginaries provide a horizon for meaning and action that is structured around tendentially empty and essentially ambiguous signifiers (1990a: 65). At a less ambitious level, myth provides a reading principle (embodied in a set of norms, values, presuppositions, etc.) which helps to constitute a new objectivity. In both cases the intervention of an external hegemonic principle results in the construction of a somewhat totalizing and reductive discourse which is striving for a metaphysical closure. From the perspective of meaning, then, the essentializing gesture of ideology involves the non-recognition of the contingent character of any positivity and of the impossibility of any ultimate suture. In other words, ideology involves a forgetting of the undecidability that prevents closure and ensures the limited and precarious character of the decidable forms of social identity. Ideology constructs the real world in terms of a set of fully constituted essences and tends to deny that these essences are contingent results of political decisions taken in an undecidable terrain.

Ideology also involves a certain form of mis- or non-recognition on the part of subjects (Žižek, 1989: 28–33). The point is not that people possess a distorted representation of reality, since in our post-ideological society many people no longer trust ideological truths and no longer take ideological propositions seriously (see Sloterdijk, 1983). The point is, rather, that even when we keep an ironical distance from totalizing ideological representations, we still act according to these representations. That is to say, the illusion is not on the side of *knowledge,* but rather on the side of what people are *doing.* As Žižek puts it:

what they overlook, what they mis-recognize, is not the reality but the illusion which is structuring their reality, their real social activity. They know very well how things really are, but still they are doing it as if they did not know. The illusion is therefore double: it consists in overlooking the illusion which is structuring our real, effective relationship to reality. And this overlooked, unconscious illusion may be called the *ideological fantasy.* (Žižek, 1989: 32–3)

Žižek's standard example of ideological fantasy is commodity fetishism. 'When people use money, they know very well [. . .] that money, in its materiality, is simply an expression of social relations' (1989: 31). They know very well that the fact that money functions as the universal equivalent of all commodities is conditioned by its position in the texture of social relations. However, in what they do, they act as if money, in its material reality, is the immediate embodiment of wealth as such (1989: 31). Many more examples of ideological fantasies come to mind. For example, as conscious consumers we know that advertisements are highly manipulative, but we still use them as primary sources of information and inspiration. We all know that men and women are born equal, but we continue to live in accord with fundamental values of patriarchy. We all know that there is no God, but we still seek comfort in religion. Habermas's theory of communicative action provides a clear example of the role of ideological fantasy at the level of science: even though Habermas admits that the ideal of an unbroken communication will never be realized, the whole theory presupposes that the ideal speech situation has already been realized (Žižek, 1990a: 259).

In ideological fantasy we act as if the totalizing and reductive forms of ideology are true and serious, although we know they are not. This reveals ideological fantasy as 'a means for an ideology to take its own failure into account in advance' (Žižek, 1989: 126). Ideological fantasy compensates for the fact that people, at the level of knowledge, are not convinced by the totalizing and reductive propositions of ideology. The social is structured around a constitutive impossibility and traversed by social antagonisms. The function of ideological fantasy is to mask the void opened by the impossible and antagonistic character of society, which can neither be integrated into the symbolic order nor be represented at the level of the imaginary (1989: 126–7). In other words, ideological fantasy is the safety net of ideology and thus provides the ultimate support of reality.

According to Žižek (1989: 124), there is always a certain *enjoyment* attached to ideological fantasy. We act 'as if', not because it is rational to do so, but because the masking of the failure of ideology marks an eruption of enjoyment in the social field. Not only are we freed from facing up to the impossible and antagonistic character of the social, but the void opened by this fundamental blockage of the social is often – through complex displacements and condensations – embodied in a foreign body (the Jew, the Black, the Communist conspiracy, or the Japanese), which is held responsible for the corruption of the social. This external, corruptive element is undoubtedly an object of fascination, as it is blamed for excessive enjoyment of money, sex, brotherhood, or work – all those things we prize ourselves (Žižek, 1990b: 53–7).

The main consequence of the conceptual couplet of ideology and ideological fantasy is that political critique of ideology must necessarily involve more than simply 'demonstrating how a given ideological field is a result of a montage of heterogeneous "floating signifiers", of their totalization through the intervention of certain "nodal points"' (Žižek, 1989: 125). The critique of ideology as totalizing and essentially reductive will fail to convince the racist, precisely because he or she enjoys being racist. Confronted with the fact that the Jewish neighbour of a racist is in fact a poor, law-abiding fellow worker, the racist might answer that this just proves how good Jews are at deceiving us. The racist might not believe this answer, but it certainly permits him or her to retain the fascinating object of enjoyment: the Jew. It follows, therefore, that in order to undermine the grip of ideology we need to account for how 'ideology implies, manipulates and produces a pre-ideological enjoyment structured in fantasy'

(1989: 125). In other words, we must show the excessive properties attributed to the 'Jew' to be nothing but a response to the constitutive impossibility of the social, which produces in advance the ultimate failure of ideology.

Beyond Subjectivism

Hegemonic articulation is conditional upon the failure of the discourse to constitute a fully sutured space of representation. Notwithstanding this, it hinges upon an attempt to construct an ideological closure. The more or less floating elements that together constitute the ever-present field of discursivity are articulated as moments in a totalizing and essentially reductive discourse. Now, this articulation of discursive elements into partially fixed moments of a concrete discourse requires a certain externality on the part of the hegemonic agent. That is to say, if the structure is undecidable, then the ethico-political decision, which articulates social identity in one way rather than another, must necessarily have an external source (Laclau, 1993b: 283). Yet, does this not produce the image of a rational and wilful subject, which articulates around its project the dispersed elements of a dislocated structure? And does this not replace an *objective closure* of the structure by a *subjective closure* through the intervention of the agent? In other words, is there not a danger that the concept of hegemony smuggles in by the back door an illegitimate subjectivism?

As we have seen above, Gramsci provides a neat response to this danger. He asserts that the identity of the hegemonic agent is constituted at the level of the productive relations while the articulation of collective wills takes place at the level of politics. Gramsci means that 'we can give some free rein to the intriguing game of historical contingency knowing that we have the disciplinary means to bring them back – "in the last instance" – to the stern world of structural constraints' (1993b: 284). The problem with this kind of response is, of course, that it involves a dualist conception of society, one divided into a realm of necessity and a realm of contingency. Such a conception calls for a deconstructive argument that aims to show the undecidable relation between necessity and contingency.

A second, and less essentialist, response to the danger of subjectivism must start with the assertion that the subject is internal to the structure, and discard the idea of a positive differentiation of the constitutive levels of society (i.e. the idea of separate economic, political and ideological regions within the social totality). For the task is to account for the conditions of emergence of an external hegemonic

118

principle within the structure in which the subject is imbedded. This task can be accomplished only by appreciating the full implications of the concept of undecidability. Undecidability prevents the ultimate suturing of the structure. Because of the failure of the structure to constitute itself as a homogeneous space of structural determination, subjectivity can only be formed through acts of identification. 'These acts of identification are thinkable only as a result of the lack within the structure' (1993b: 285). And if in this way the incompleteness of the structure provides the conditions for the emergence of contingent forms of subjectivity, we have a situation where the hegemonic agent is reducible neither to a structural dupe nor to a wilful subject with the character of a *deus ex machina*. In other words, the concept of hegemony does not replace illegitimate objectivism with an equally illegitimate subjectivism.

6
Social Antagonism

Not all articulations are hegemonic articulations. Hegemonic articulation ultimately involves some element of force and repression. It involves the negation of identity in the double sense of the negation of alternative meanings and options and the negation of those people who identify themselves with these meanings and options. The negation of identity tends to give rise to *social antagonism*. The hegemonic force, which is responsible for the negation of individual or collective identity, will tend to construct the excluded identity as one of a series of threatening obstacles to the full realization of chosen meanings and options. If we view the act of exclusion from the perspective of the negated identity, things look a little more complicated as the results from the negation of individual or collective identity can take different forms and have different consequences. In some cases the negation of identity will lead to an open confrontation between the identity negated and the force of negation which is constructed as a part of an opposing conspiracy ('We cannot accept this blunt attack from our enemy!'). In other cases the conflict may be displaced to another field and give rise to seemingly meaningless acts of violence ('I have had a lousy day and I really feel like beating up somebody!'). In other cases the negation of identity will lead to either self-blame or self-denial ('It is our own fault, we are simply not good enough!'), or to a resigned and traumatic incorporation of a lack ('It is really a shame, but I have to live with it as I can do nothing about it!'). The negation of identity may, of course, result in the death of the negated subject(s), and in that case we can hardly speak of a relation of social antagonism, although a political killing will certainly stir up conflict and antagonism.[1] We might therefore conclude that although the negated identity will not always antagonize the force of negation, the negation of identity

120

always gives rise to social antagonism. Thus, what distinguishes hegemonic articulations from other forms of articulation is that whereas the former take place in an antagonistic environment, the latter do not.

The Relation between Politics and Social Antagonism

If hegemony involves antagonism and is a form of politics, it follows that *politics is inextricably linked to social antagonism*. This is implicitly recognized by Schmitt, who claims that 'the specific political distinction to which political actions and motives can be reduced is that between friend and enemy' (Schmitt, 1976 [1927]: 26).[2] According to Schmitt, an enemy is someone who 'must not only be defeated but also utterly destroyed' (1976: 36). From this it follows that there can be no enemies, and thus no politics, within a liberal democracy that clearly does not accept the destruction of oppositional forces. In consequence Schmitt declared war against the unholy alliance between liberalism and democracy. This conclusion is of course totally unacceptable as an alternative, non-liberal democracy will be open to totalitarian developments. Yet Schmitt could have avoided this conclusion if only he had recognized that political antagonists in politics are not necessarily enemies in the strict sense of the term. As Mouffe puts it:

Once we accept the necessity of the political and the impossibility of a world without antagonism, what needs to be envisaged is how it is possible *under those conditions* to create or maintain a pluralistic democratic order. Such an order is based on a distinction between *'enemy'* and *'adversary'*. It requires that, within the context of the political community, the opponent should be considered not as an enemy to be destroyed, but as an adversary whose existence is legitimate and must be tolerated. We will fight against his ideas but we will not question his right to defend them. (Mouffe, 1993a: 4)

The distinction between enemies and adversaries, which permits us to link politics and social antagonism within liberal democracy, is presented in similar terms by Edelman (1988: 67), who boils it down to the question of a distinction between unacceptable and acceptable opponents. Both sorts of opponents negate our identity, but while adversaries follow the rules of the game, enemies do not.

Now, the emphasis on the intrinsic link between politics and social antagonism can be challenged from two angles. *First of all*, it might be argued that politics, defined abstractly as a first order principle for the ordering of the social, should not be tied to social antagonism, but rather to *authority* which is contingent upon conflict/consensus in the sense that it does not necessarily imply the one or the other. However, this argument is vulnerable on four counts. First, it is problematic to distinguish an abstract political principle of social ordering from the concrete modes of this ordering since that tends to reduce politics to an analytical category. Second, authority is not contingent upon conflict/consensus, but tends to invoke the liberalist image of politics as devoid of antagonistic conflicts. Authority involves an undisputed right to act on behalf of the community and a high degree of compliance with this acting. Tacit consent is the rule and conflict the exception. But why is authority needed in the first place? Because of the presence of antagonistic conflicts. Authority is a way of ensuring governance in the face of antagonistic conflict. Third, the attempt to identify politics with authority tends to ground politics in social phenomena which are themselves results of antagonistic struggles. Authority is normally conceived as based either on the weight of tradition (conservatism and communitarianism); on the formal rationality embodied in the legal framework of the state (liberalism); on the morality (Durkheim), truthfulness (Habermas) or charisma (Weber) of those exercising power; or the anticipation of those subjected to the exercise of power that in the normal course of events compliance with regulations and actions will be forthcoming (Easton). Common to all these different conceptions of the source of authority is the idea that something (i.e. tradition, rationality/legality, morality, truthfulness, charisma, or norm-bound anticipations) makes people accept political decisions without protest. However, all these things, which tend to tie politics to a tacit rather than an explicit consensus, are social 'facts' that are constructed in and through political struggles which involve force and repression and thus social antagonism. In other words, politics, defined as authority, hinges on something which is itself a result of the workings of a more fundamental form of politics, defined in terms of hegemonic struggles taking place in a context of social antagonism. Last but not least, there are no sources of authority able to ensure a total consensus that precludes the exclusion of a constitutive outside. Tradition, rationality, morality, etc. are always subject to negotiation; they therefore fail to provide an ultimate ground for everybody to reach agreement, or merely to accept the ruling of others.

The alternative conception of politics in terms of authoritative decisions *also* presents a challenge to our emphasis on the intrinsic link between politics and social antagonism. Thus it might be argued that, by linking politics with social antagonism, Laclau and Mouffe fail to account for '*routine politics*' in the sense of minor policy changes that take place in a highly institutionalized context and do not stir up any antagonistic conflicts. Now, if routine politics refers to a type of politics that has substituted 'the government of things' for 'the government of men', what we have is merely a contradiction in terms: within a totally calculable and programmable institution in which undecidability has become eliminated, there is no politics. However, use of the term 'routine' does not necessarily involve the eradication of undecidability. According to March and Olsen (1989: 21–3), our day-to-day actions are governed by a logic of appropriateness rather than a logic of consequence. Nevertheless, the presence of discursively constructed rules, norms, procedures, etc., which prescribe what is appropriate action, provide no guarantee of the appropriateness of our actions. The rules are often highly ambiguous and inconsistent, and it is often difficult to decide which rule to apply in a given situation. Rule-following is therefore necessarily based upon constitutive interpretations. With regard to the attempt to match rule and situation, this will be based upon legal rather than economic reasoning. 'Rules and situations are related by criteria of similarity and difference and through reasoning by analogy and metaphor' (1989: 25). In sum, undecidability penetrates rule-governed decisions and actions, and that seems to erode the difference between routine politics and the more fundamental forms of politics.

In fact, what might appear as unanimous, routine decisions will often, when submitted to closer inspection, be revealed as the source of all kinds of frustrated desires, unstated criticisms, and endlessly deferred confrontations. If these scattered, micro-level resistances are seldom transformed into major upheavals, this is due to the normalizing aspect of the power strategies that penetrate social and political institutions. The primary objective of these strategies is to efface the traces of the contingent political interventions which constitute the social. What is politically constructed is presented as normal, or natural, and resistance is constructed as deviant, or unnatural. Foucault has brilliantly analysed the subtle logics of self-concealment which political power strategies deploy in order to make political decisions appear as unopposed, routine decisions.

The theoretical argument in favour of routine politics, and the fact that power strategies always attempt to conceal their political character, by no means imply that all routine decisions are at bottom political. The degree of social sedimentation of a certain context of decision-making might be so high that the element of conflict and antagonism tends to evaporate. In that case we should simply speak of social routines rather than routine politics.

123

The Construction of a Constitutive Outside

It is now time to return to the question of how to establish the *limits of a discourse* or discursive formation. We can immediately write off the possibility of appealing to some fundamental ground which would be the source of all the differences within the discursive formation. But could we not then alternatively define the limits of a discursive formation in terms of what are beyond those limits? This is surely the only possible solution, although if what is beyond is merely other differences, then it is impossible to establish if these differences are internal or external to the discursive formation in question. It is therefore necessary to postulate the existence of a beyond that is not simply one more difference, but something that poses a threat to all the differences within the discursive formation. Or, even better, we must assert that a discourse, or a discursive formation, establishes its limits by means of excluding a radical otherness that has no common measure with the differential system from which it is excluded, and that therefore poses a constant threat to that very system (Laclau, 1995a: 151). A radical otherness that, at the same time, constitutes and negates the limits and identity of the discursive formation from which it is excluded is precisely what Laclau (1990a: 17), inspired by Staten (1984: 15–9), calls a *constitutive outside*. And, as 'constitutive outside' is coterminous with 'social antagonism', we can conclude, once again, that social antagonism is, at the same time, the condition of possibility and the condition of impossibility of discursive systems of identity.

The question now is how this constitutive outside, this radical otherness, or this alterity of the Other, is discursively constructed. The constitutive outside introduces a radical negativity that cannot be absorbed by Hegelian dialectics, as it is the conceptual system as such that is negated. This negativity cannot be presented in a direct manner, i.e. as a positive difference. It can only present itself indirectly through chains of equivalence which subvert the differential character of the discursive identities (Laclau and Mouffe, 1985: 128). The differential character of social identities collapses as they become inscribed in chains of equivalence that construct them in terms of a certain 'sameness'. This sameness cannot be given by some underlying essence which is supposed to manifest itself in each of the excluded elements, since that would bring us back to the essentialist position we want to avoid. Therefore, what the excluded elements have in common is solely their negation of the discursive formation in question. That is to say, the chain of equivalence has no positive identity as it annuls all positivity of the excluded elements and thereby gives rise to negativity as such (1985: 128–9). Hence, the constitutive outside of a discourse A, which is discursively constructed by the expansion of a chain of equivalence, is neither B nor non-A, but anti-A. An example will help to illustrate this point. The limit of the discourse of 'western civilization' is established by the exclusion of countries, habits and people that are all somehow considered to be 'barbaric'. However, as the chain of equivalence is expanded to include still more elements, it becomes clear that what all these elements have in common is only the negation of western civilization. Thus, as Africa, India, Asia and South America are caught up in the chain of equivalence, the concept 'barbaric' is gradually emptied to the point where it can only be defined as uncivilized, i.e. as a threat to civilization. Consequently, the discourse of 'western civilization' is established in a confrontation with a constitutive outside which prevents it from being what it is.

Difference and Equivalence

It should be stressed that in social antagonism we do not have a situation in which a negative equivalential pole confronts a positive differential pole, since faced with an external threat a certain sameness of the differential moments will be established (1985: 128). For the sake of illustration, we might envisage the discursive effects of the external threat of Nazism that confronted British society during the Second World War. Faced with the threat of Nazism, the Conservative Party and the Labour Party tended to stress their common commitment to liberal and democratic values. The content of the values shared by the two parties was, of course, emptied to the degree that 'freedom' and 'democracy' became signifiers without a signified; merely symbolizing a communitarian space deprived of its fullness due to the presence of the evil forces of Nazism (Laclau, 1994b).We should remember here that to be equivalent in one respect the Conservatives and Labour had to differ in other ways, otherwise there would exist a simple identity between them. Moreover, we should bear in mind that it is not only the moments articulated within the British political discourse that are either differential or equivalential. The constitutive outside of Nazism, which the British political discourse constructed as equivalent with other evil forces, has a differential character, in so far as it is considered as one of many competing political ideologies. This bears witness to the fact that all social identities are crossing-points between the logic of equivalence and the logic of difference (Laclau, 1995a: 152).

Neither the logic of equivalence nor the logic of difference will dominate completely (Laclau and Mouffe, 1985: 129). They mutually subvert each other. However, the undecidable relation between the two logics can temporarily be fixed in a determinate hierarchy. Which of the two logics gains the upper hand in this hierarchy, and thus manages to assert itself as the predominant logic, depends on the political struggles over hegemony in this area. Two extreme outcomes can be imagined. One possibility is that the equivalential logic has become predominant (1985: 129–30). This was very much the case in the British war-time discourse wherein the space of differentiality was narrowed down by the expansion of the friend–enemy distinction. 'If you are not with us, you are against us' seemed to be the underlying dictum at a time when, despite official espousal of liberal and democratic values, the fear of internal enemies led to serious violations of customary civil rights by way of increased surveillance, censorship, internments and prohibitions. The all-penetrating antagonism between Britain and its constitutive outside did not admit *tertium quid*. This effect of war on political plurality is evidenced by the words of the German Emperor Wilhelm, who during the First World War claimed that he would no longer hear of different political parties, only of Germans.

The other possibility is, of course, that the differential logic has become predominant (1985: 130). To find an example of this we need only consider the development of Britain in the years following the Second World War. The great enemy was defeated and things returned to 'normal'. The post-war discourse of liberal welfare democracy gained ground and gave rise to a true proliferation of legitimate differences. The differential space was thus expanded. Terms like 'the post-war settlement' capture the sense of a stable compromise between different political interests.

Different Types of Social Antagonism

Having thus specified the intrinsic link between politics and antagonism, as well as between chains of equivalence and the construction of a constitutive outside, we shall now briefly consider the two main types of social antagonisms, popular and democratic. As we have seen, the more predominant the logic of equivalence is, the stronger and the more important becomes the particular social antagonism for the structuration of the social. Thus, the infinite expansion of a chain of equivalence tends to establish a clear-cut political frontier which divides the discursive space into two camps: friends and enemies (1985: 131). Examples of social antagonisms that tend to establish a *popular* subject position are numerous. The ancient city-states and

medieval peasant societies were transformed into absolute equivalences when threatened by war and invasion. The forces and
movements behind the bourgeois revolutions in Europe and the anti-
colonial struggles in the Third World have confronted one set of
equivalences (the people) with another set of equivalences (the feudal
parasites and the white imperialists, respectively). The totalitarian
language of equivalence is currently employed by the political leaders
in those countries that are dominated by ethnic and/or nationalist
discourses (the genocide in Bosnia, Chechnya and Rwanda are extreme
and terrifying examples of what this might lead to). In all these cases
the social is dominated by one major social antagonism, to which all
minor antagonisms must necessarily refer. The attempt by socialist and
communist forces to construct the proletariat as equivalent to the
people has failed. Where this attempt was most successful it gave rise
to totalitarian regimes based on severe political repression. In the
advanced capitalist societies its lack of success was due to the failure
of the working class to make the transition from a corporatist class
with rather narrow class interests to a hegemonic class that advanced
a national-popular will.

Popular antagonism involves a simplification of the social space. By
contrast, so-called *democratic* antagonisms make the world increasingly complex. Whereas popular antagonisms divide the entire space
of the social into two opposed camps, democratic antagonisms only
divide minor social spaces. The example *par excellence* is that of the
new social movements, which tend to establish a variety of battlegrounds between polluters and environmentalists, industrialized
agriculture and ecologists, the military-industrial complex and the
peace movements, patriarchal structures and feminists, white people
and blacks, etc.

'Partly because of their very success, democratic struggles tend less
and less to be unified as "popular struggles"' (1985: 133). Popular
mobilizations against a common enemy have not been necessary to
advance the demands of the new social movements. Even relatively
small and loosely organized movements have managed to influence the
political agenda of organized groups. At the same time, different societal trends tend to prevent the rise of popular struggles. First, the
production of frontier effects ceases 'to be grounded upon an evident
and given separation, in a referential framework acquired once and for
all' (1985: 134). Hence, the old separations between people and state,
Left and Right, and East and West seem to have lost their mobilizing
capacity. Second, in most advanced capitalist countries there has been
a tendency towards an increasing sectorization of society into separate
policy arenas. This sectorization, or functional differentiation as

Luhmann (1993) calls it, tends to disconnect and isolate political forces. The result is a polity in which the vertical links between the state and various interest groups and social movements dominate over the horizontal links between the political forces. Last but not least, a tendency towards increasing individualization tends to undercut the possibility of organizing popular struggles. Increasing individualization of working life, leisure, moral questions, political life and the relation to public authorities creates highly unfavourable conditions for collective action.

Social Antagonism and Dislocation

We return finally to discuss the relation between social antagonism and dislocation. In *Hegemony and Socialist Strategy* (1985: 122–7) social antagonism was too readily assumed to be equal to *dislocation*. As such, social antagonism was held responsible for the impossibility of society. As Laclau and Mouffe state, 'antagonisms are not internal but external to the social; or rather they constitute the limits of society, the latter's impossibility of fully constituting itself' (1985: 125). In fact, social antagonism constitutes the limits of every objectivity. It can therefore be depicted as in the figure below.

$$A \leftarrow \text{anti-A}$$

In the original conception of social antagonism it is the external enemy that prevents identity A from becoming fully constituted. However, as Žižek points out in his essay 'Beyond Discourse-Analysis' (1990a), what is negated in social antagonism is always already negated. That is, there is a force of negativity that is prior to social antagonism. According to Žižek, this force is nothing but the Lacanian real, i.e. the traumatic kernel which always resists symbolization. Hence, 'in Lacanian terms we must distinguish antagonism as real from the social reality of the antagonistic fight' (1990a: 253). An attempt at representing this is made in the figure below. The bar through the A signifies the traumatic effect of the real. A-barred is negated by anti-A, and the result is the negation of a negation.

$$\cancel{A} \leftarrow \text{anti-A}$$

Žižek's critical elaboration of the concept of social antagonism helps us achieve a deeper understanding of the view that social antagonism is constitutive of social identity. The point is not that 'we' are

128

nothing but the drive to annihilate the antagonistic force that prevents us from achieving our full identity. Rather, the antagonistic force is held responsible for the blockage of our full identity, and this permits the externalization of our constitutive lack as subjects to the negating Other, which thus becomes the positive embodiment of our self-blockage (1990a: 253). As a result our political actions will tend to be guided by the illusion that the annihilation of the antagonistic force will permit us to become the fully constituted 'we' that we have always sought to be. For example, 'the feminist struggle against patriarchal, male chauvinist oppression is necessarily filled out by the illusion that afterwards, when patriarchal oppression is abolished, women will finally achieve their full identity with themselves, realize their potentials, etc.' (1990a: 251). The working of the ideological illusion that structures our identity and guides our political struggles for emancipation is illustrated in the figure below. A-barred becomes the illusory 'A' as a result of the annihilation of the negating Other.

$\cancel{A} \leftarrow$ anti-A

'A' $\rightarrow$ ~~anti-A~~

Laclau (1990a: xvi) has welcomed Žižek's constructive criticism of the concept of social antagonism presented in *Hegemony and Socialist Strategy*. He claims in response that *social antagonism* should no longer be held responsible for the impossibility of society, but rather be seen as *a discursive response to the dislocation of the social order.* Hence, in *New Reflections on the Revolution of Our Time* social antagonism is defined in terms of the presence of a constitutive outside which, at the same time, constitutes and denies the identity of the inside (Laclau, 1990a: 17). Social antagonism plays an important role in the construction of the spatiality of mythical spaces and social imaginaries. As we know, myths and social imaginaries aim to reconcile the social in the face of structural dislocation, which according to Laclau involves 'the *disruption* of the structure by forces operating *outside* it' (1990a: 50). Mythical spaces and social imaginaries provide a homogeneous space of representation because all forces of negativity have become displaced to an outside that is both constitutive and subversive of the unity of the inside. The various myths and social imaginaries function as surfaces of inscription of social demands and aspirations so long as they are not put into question by external events. 'For longer or shorter periods they have a certain elasticity beyond which we witness their inexorable decline' (1990a: 67). Their final breakdown appears when the spatial forms of representation and the discursive structure they support are confronted with a set of un-domesticable events. The presence of events, which can neither be symbolized by the discursive formation nor inscribed at the level of the imaginary, will undermine the social order, precisely because its ability to sustain order is jeopardized.

Let us try to unpack this dense argument by considering the development of the modern welfare state. The Great Depression in the early 1930s dislocated the discourse of organized capitalism. Institutionalization of the class compromise and intensified regulation of the circuit of capital had produced high economic growth rates and fostered a growing belief in the mutual gains of labour and capital. However, a wave of bankruptcies, mass unemployment and poverty spread from America to most of the western world. Foreign trade crumbled and the roaring twenties came to a close. In the wake of this structural dislocation, and greatly encouraged by the successful experience with state planning during the Second World War, as well as by the new sense of community generated during the war, the modern welfare state emerged as the suturing myth of a society that does not exist. The modern welfare state provided a space of representation for social and economic demands as legitimate differences and displaced all social antagonisms to its constitutive outside. The modern welfare state is a social imaginary with the form of a one-nation project. It is held together only by its exclusion of both left and right extremism, which is seen as a threat to its universalist and rationalist pretensions. At the level of institutions the modern welfare state combined Keynesian demand management with the construction of a comprehensive system of social welfare provisions, which to a wide extent were financed and delivered by the state. The idea was to prevent the social problems associated with mass unemployment by regulating the level of public demand, while at the same time ensuring that these problems were treated and basic needs met. The institutional set-up of the modern welfare state, together with the Fordist combination of mass production and mass consumption, produced an unprecedented level of welfare, prosperity and social harmony. However, in the early 1970s the concurrence of economic stagnation and high inflation shattered the belief in a crisis-free capitalism and gave rise to major societal conflicts. Economic decline and the rise of mass unemployment also revealed some of the more adventurous welfare states to be so generous that they could hardly afford to have clients. In fact, in most countries the persistence of low economic growth rates put into question the institutional matrix of the modern welfare state. We shall return to discuss what might emerge from this profound dislocation of the modern welfare state in chapter 12. In the meantime we shall rejoin the question of the relation between antagonism and dislocation.

As we have seen, Laclau and Mouffe seem to move from consideration of social antagonism as dislocation *per se* to consideration of social antagonism as a discursive response to dislocation. A severe dislocation will not automatically be responded to by the construction of social antagonism – that is, by detecting a cause of the dislocation that can serve as an enemy. Many other possible answers exist: that the dislocation is the result of the wrath of God for our sins; that it is attributed to unforeseen impersonal causes which we can do nothing about; or – even – that it is not answered discursively at all, and instead produces anomie and the disintegration of social identity.

Emphasis on the *stabilizing function* of social antagonism should not allow us to forget that social antagonism is also a *source of dislocation*. At a general level, we might say that 'every identity is dislocated in so far as it depends on an outside which both denies that identity and provides the condition of possibility at the same time' (1990a: 39). Social antagonism is undoubtedly a double-edged sword, as it constitutes and sustains social identity by positing a threat to that very identity. Indeed, in concrete analyses, we often find examples of antagonistic forces which cease to have a stabilizing function and become instead a major source of dislocation. For instance, in South Africa the exclusion of a subversive blackness certainly helped to unify and sustain the identity of both Afrikaners and the English as a white people. However, it did so only by means of introducing a dangerous supplement, which ultimately took its revenge. This pattern is found in many Third World countries. The western discourse constructs the colonized people as a part of an equivalential chain designating a certain 'Oriental', 'African' or 'Hispanic' identity. These identities 'will, at the moment of anti-colonial rebellion, inevitably turn upside down the hierarchy of Western values' (1990a: 32).

131

Part III

Problems and Possible
Solutions

Introduction

We have accounted for the development of the discourse-theoretical analytics of Laclau and Mouffe (Part I) and examined the key concepts of discourse, hegemony and social antagonism (Part II). It is now time to put the theoretical arguments of Laclau, Mouffe and Žižek to work. This will be done by showing that discourse analysis offers some interesting new ways of accounting for the conceptual dyads of structure/agency, power/authority, and universal/particular. In all three cases the problem takes the form of the old dilemma: which comes first, the chicken or the egg? Are social structures the outcome of the actions of an autonomous agency, or is agency always conditioned by facilitating and/or constraining structures? Is power grounded in authority definable as the undisputed right to act, or is all authority ultimately the product of power? Finally, is the particular an embodiment of universal principles, or is the content of the universal nothing but a universalization of the particular? Of course the solution to the problem of 'either/or' is somehow to insist on 'both'. This must, of course, be done without invoking a self-contradiction. In order to be able to argue for both without antinomy, one needs to problematize the underlying assumptions that makes the two alternatives contradictory and to inscribe them within some new undecidable logic that will make room for both in such a way that neither neutralizes the opposition nor sublates it into a higher order synthesis. The kind of performative we are looking for is deconstruction, or, as Derrida would prefer to call it; an argument in a deconstructive style.

The three conceptual couplets that are dealt with in the following chapters have been chosen carefully. All are of central importance for social, cultural and political theory. *Chapter 7* is devoted to a discussion of the structure/agency couplet. The point of departure is

Marxism and the problems it has with reconciling structure- and agency-based explanations. The chapter reviews the attempts of Althusser, Cohen, Elster and Giddens to avoid structural determinism without giving in to voluntarism. The problem with these attempts, however, is their objectivistic conception of structure and agency. The solution proposed by discourse theory starts from the notion of structural dislocation and then goes on to show how the essentially split subject attempts to acquire a stable identity through acts of identification. The chapter concludes with a discussion of the content and limits of hegemonic strategies for societal recomposition.

Chapter 8 aims to develop a non-foundational conception of power as constitutive of any social objectivity, be it structure or agency. The postmodern conception of power as strategy is substituted for the modern conception of power as causation. The relation between power and empowerment is then considered, before the conceptual couplet between power/authority is scrutinized. The crux of the argument here is to show that the relation between power and authority is more important than each of its parts.

Part III finally undertakes to examine the conceptual doublet of universal/particular. The notion of universality is defended against multiculturalist and postmodernist critiques. To this end, it is argued that the authorization of power and resistance always involves a transgression of particularity into universality. This transgression involves two steps: the universalization of demands, sentiments and aspirations through the expansion of chains of equivalence and the embodiment of the universal by a particular hegemonic agency that is split between its universal function and its own particular identity. The concept of representation plays a decisive role when social demands are inscribed within social imaginaries that promise to heal the rift in the social and to provide the dislocated subjects with a fully achieved identity. The act of representation, it is argued, is an essentially impure one as it always involves the transformation of that which it represents.

7

Structure and Agency

Let us begin by clarifying exactly what is meant by the two terms 'structure' and 'agency'. *Agency* in this context refers simply to an intentionally acting subject. No assumptions are made about the subject's degree of control over its actions. Neither are there any assumptions about the rationality of the acting subject. What we have is simply someone who acts in a certain way because he or she wants to achieve or avoid something. It is not important whether the intention is conscious or unconscious. What matters is only that the subject's actions have a direction, i.e. they are not random. It is more difficult to define what is meant by structure. We are concerned here with the traditional concept of structure as a closed and centred totality. But the concept, which could be defined as a fixed system of differences, must in this context be carefully distinguished from the concept of system. We shall thus define a social system in terms of the reproduced patterns of interaction between individual and collective actors. Against this background we can define a *structure* as the complex and relatively enduring relationships that define the basic properties of the system and permit its continued reproduction. While social systems are defined in terms of the interaction between different types of social agency, structures are characterized by the absence of social agency.[1] This explains why agency is to be opposed to social structures rather than to social systems.

That the contraposition between structure and agency is highly relevant to social, cultural and political theory is indisputable. Most social, cultural and political phenomena are explainable both in terms of their structural determinants and in terms of the social actions that brought them about. Many academic disputes arise from fundamental disagreements about the relative importance of structure and agency in explaining social, cultural or political phenomena. For example, is the development of the modern welfare state to be understood as a function of structural determinants such as industrialization, modernization and the capital accumulation, or as an outcome of working-class struggles? Is French Impressionism to be seen as a reflection of societal transformations invoking the rise of the French bourgeoisie, who did not possess enough knowledge about history and religion to be able to decipher classical painting, or as the self-expression of a group of French painters revolting against the orthodoxy of the Royal Academy of Arts? Is the hegemony of liberal democracy explainable in terms of its beneficial effects on economic growth, or is it a consequence of popular-democratic struggles? Such questions have been subject to much discussion over the years. Many have attempted to resolve these seemingly circular debates by claiming that both structure and agency matter. However, such attempts merely to dissolve the opposition between structure- and agency-based explanations are futile, as they fail to sort out the theoretical dilemma posed by the dualistic solution to the structure/agency problem. Faced thus with the persistent tension between structure- and agency-based explanations we should instead commit ourselves to a full investigation of the theoretical problem, the different theoretical attempts to resolve it, and the underlying assumptions that prevent its solution. Only by radically questioning the latter can we hope to make some fruitful theoretical advances.

Structure and Agency in Marx

There are many ways to begin considering the tension between structure and agency. The tension is constitutive of the tradition of modern sociology and is, for example, reflected in the opposing views of Durkheim and Weber. Yet, the tension was already fully exposed in the writings of Marx, in which examples of structure- and agency-based explanations are found side by side. Marx is often portrayed as a hard-headed structuralist who denies the efficacy of social agency. That is a caricature, however, since there are numerous references to both the decisive impact of the economic structure and the role of class struggle. A classical example of Marx's emphasis on the logic of structural determination is to be found in his famous 'Preface to a critique of political economy' (1987c [1859]), where he claims that 'it is not the consciousness of men which determines their being, but, on the contrary, their social being that determines their consciousness' (1987c: 389). By 'social being' Marx understands the dialectical relationship between the productive forces and the relations of production. Hence, social agency is structurally determined by the material transformation of the economic conditions of production. The example *par excellence* of the decisive role of the political logic of class struggle is to be found in 'The Communist Manifesto', where it is claimed that 'the history of all hitherto existing societies is the history of class struggle' (1987b [1948]: 222). Let us here disregard the class-reductionist bias of this claim and simply note that in Marx there are clear examples of both structure- and agency-based explanations.

The two explanatory logics do not have the same status. We note, for instance, that class struggle is *subordinated* to the contradictions at the level of the economic structure in at least three ways (Laclau, 1990a: 7). First, the objective interests of social classes are determined by their structural location in the sphere of production. Second, social classes become conscious of structurally determined class contradictions and fight these out at the level of the superstructure, which is determined by the economic base. Third, the class contradiction cannot be transcended before the forces of production are fully developed within the present relations of production. A clear hierarchy thus exists between structure- and agency-based logics of explanation.

Now, everything depends upon showing that the two logics are compatible. If they are independent of each other the dialectical unity of history would obviously be placed in doubt (1990a: 7). Since we have identified a hierarchy between the two logics, however, we shall only consider here the question of whether it is possible logically to derive the presence of an *antagonistic* relationship between workers and capitalists from the *contradictions* inherent in the capitalist economy.

Capitalism is characterized by the double separation of the direct producers from the means of production and from surplus value. Surplus value arises from the unpaid work of the workers, who because of their separation from the means of production are forced to sell their labour power to the capitalists. The latter appropriate all the surplus value that has been produced by the workers. This might be seen as the direct cause for the rise of an antagonistic relation between workers and capitalists. The development of such an antagonism presupposes that the workers actually resist the extraction of surplus value from the labour however, there is nothing in the economic category 'seller of labour power' which suggests that such resistance is a logical conclusion (1990a: 9). A possible solution would be to introduce the supplementary hypothesis that man is *homo oeconomicus*. That would apparently permit us to assert that the workers will always seek to maximize their share of the surplus value in an antagonistic zero-sum game with the capitalists. Yet, such a solution has been rejected by a majority of Marxists. For not only does it invoke an ahistorical stipulation regarding the essence of human nature. It also, in a completely illegitimate way, introduces a *deus ex machina* which disrupts the attempt to derive antagonism from the contradiction. Last but not least, the presence of a zero-sum game between profit-maximizing workers and capitalists does not give rise to any antagonism. The players can lose or win without breaking the rules of the game, and thus without denying each other's identity as players (1990a: 10–11).

It is not possible to deduce the class antagonism between workers and capitalists from the contradictions of the capitalist economy. This does not mean, however, that the presence of class struggle has no bearing whatsoever on the economic structure of capitalist societies. The point is merely that the relations of production do not *ipso facto* give rise to political class struggles. That is, class conflict 'is not internal to capitalist relations of production (in which the worker counts merely as a seller of labour power), but takes place between the relations of production and the worker's identity outside of them' (1990a: 9). As such, the workers' identity as 'consumers' is denied when wages fall below a certain level. Their identity as 'house owners' is denied by the capitalist business cycle that accompanies regular lay-offs. Their identity as 'democratic citizens' is denied by the absence of workplace democracy. More examples could be provided, but the conclusion is already clear: political class struggle depends on the confrontation between the capitalist relations of production and something outside them.

It must be considered a serious problem that Marx operates with *two hierarchically ordered* but *theoretically unconnected* logics of explanation. In particular, as long as the political logic of class struggle is reduced to the status of external supplement to the logic of structural determination, it is impossible to combat the problems caused by the unchallenged reign of structural determinism. It is undoubtedly the case that a lot has happened since the days of Marx and Engels; it is therefore incumbent to ask whether or not more recent contributions within the Marxist tradition have succeeded in overcoming the problems of structural determinism without surrendering to voluntarism. We shall therefore take a closer look at conceptions of the relationship between structure and agency in the work of Althusser, Cohen, Elster and Giddens.[2]

The Monism of Althusser and Cohen

Althusser's notion of structural causality provides a *monist* picture of the relation between structure and agency: the structure is everything and social agency nothing. The economic, political and ideological instances, or levels, are articulated into a mode of production. The precise articulation of this complexly structured whole determines which of the instances will be dominant in the present conjuncture. The articulation and the effects of the mode of production, and thus also the displacement of dominance between the levels of the structured whole, is, in the last instance, determined by the economic structure. Althusser struggled to escape the problems of economic determinism. He insisted upon the articulation of different modes of production within the social formation; he emphasized the overdetermination of conflicts within the social formation; and he claimed that the structure only exists in its effects. Yet, he was unwilling to give up the idea that everything, in the last instance, is determined by the economic structure. That is, in Althusser 'there is an abstract universal object, the "economy", which produces concrete effects (determination in the last instance here and now)' (Laclau and Mouffe, 1985: 99). We are thus faced with a relation of simple determination. This determination also includes the social agents, who are reduced to mere bearers of the structure (Althusser, 1979b [1968]: 180).

When it comes to the question of the reproduction of the capitalist economy, Althusser (1971 [1969]) emphasizes the role of ideological hegemony, which the ruling class exercises through its control over the ideological state apparatuses (church, education, mass media, etc.). However, the emphasis on ideological hegemony does not undermine the privileged role granted to the logic of *structural determination*. For not only is the hegemonic ideology reduced to its necessary class belonging, but the ideological state apparatuses are also explained functionally in terms of their beneficial effect on the reproduction of the relations of production within capitalist society.

Many have criticized Althusser for his introduction of functional explanation in his essay on 'Ideology and the ideological state apparatuses' (see Hirst, 1976; Applebaum, 1979; and Gane, 1983). Cohen, in fact, welcomes the shift in Althusser from his opaque epistemological conception of structural causality in *Reading Capital* (1979b) to his employment of functional modes of explanation in the ISAs essay (Cohen, 1978: 280). Yet Cohen distances himself from the sloppy use of functional explanation as found in Althusser, and sets out to defend the historical materialism of Marx on the basis of an improved version of functional explanation.

In his prizewinning book on *Karl Marx's Theory of History: A Defence* (1978), Cohen defines functional explanation as 'a distinctive explanatory procedure, in which the reference to the effects of a phenomenon contributes to explaining it' (1978: 250). However, Cohen insists that in order to establish a functional explanation of A, it is not enough to show that A is functional for some fixed referent. A function-attributing statement is explanatory only in so far as it is shown to be an instance of a general law stating that A occurs whenever A has the propensity to generate the effect B (1978: 259–60). In other words, for the statement that A has some beneficial effect B to qualify as a functional explanation, it must be backed by a *consequence law* (1978: 251–9). According to Cohen, a consequence law is a universal conditional statement whose antecedent is a hypothetical causal statement. As such, the consequence law says that 'if it is true that an event of type A occurring at t1 brings about an event of type B at t2, then an event of type A occurs at t3', or in short: 'IF (if A then B) THEN A)'.

Presented in this way, functional explanations become a subset of causal explanations, distinguished by the peculiar feature that the explanandum (A) is some functional instance and the explanans is a dispositional fact of this explanandum (if A then B) (1978: 250). The indisputable advantage of understanding functional explanations as a special type of causal explanation is that the usual violation of the logical time order – which appears when a future effect is supposed to explain a past event – is avoided (1978: 260).

Marx established a conceptual hierarchy between the productive forces, the relations of production and the superstructure. The relations of production are generally said to correspond with the level of development of the productive forces, and in turn to be the foundation on which the superstructure rises. However, according to Cohen (1978: 280), Marx failed to specify the explanatory connections between the three levels. Nevertheless this problem is solved as soon as it is recognized that the key Marxist explanations are functional ones. In fact, Cohen argues, the use of functional explanation is the only way of rendering Marxism consistent, in that it allows for compatibility between the postulated causal power of the upper levels in the hierarchy in relation to the lower, and the granting of explanatory primacy of the lower in relation to the higher ones (1978: 160, 231).

Equipped with his improved version of functional explanation, Cohen claims to be able to explain why, at some point in history, relations of production of type R obtain. These obtain because of their propensity to have a beneficial effect on the development of the productive forces, since whenever relations of production have such an effect they obtain (1978: 261). Cohen can use the same type of argument to explain the superstructural level of the state. However, the productive forces, being the lowest level of the hierarchy, cannot be explained by their functionality. Thus, while contributing to the structuration of the social totality, the development of the forces of production escapes the process of structuration, and thereby calls for a supplementary explanation. Such an explanation is provided by the so-called development thesis, which says that the productive forces tend to develop throughout history due to the fact that, given their inclement situation, whenever knowledge provides the opportunity of expanding productive power, humans will tend to take it, for not to do so would be irrational (1978: 153). This serves to place the entire explanatory burden on the human embodiment of the Absolute Spirit in the shape of a trans-epochal rationality (Laclau, 1990a: 12).

Now, in the standard case of the continued development of the productive forces, the functional explanation of the relations of production works well. The relations of production obtain precisely because they facilitate the continued development of the productive forces. But how can one explain transitional cases where the relations of production fetter the development of the productive forces? Cohen's answer is the following:

In transitional cases the prevailing relations obtain because they recently *were* suitable to the development of the forces, and the class they empower has managed to maintain control despite their no longer being so: it is because ruling classes have an interest in the maintenance of obsolete relations that their *immediate* replacement by freshly suitable relations is not to be expected. (Cohen, 1988: 10)

If we compare the standard case with the transitional ones where the development of the productive forces is fettered, we see that Cohen in the latter makes an exception to the functional mode of explanation by introducing a different kind of explanation that refers to the political power of the ruling classes. Nevertheless, this does not undermine the privileged role of structural determination as the long-term outcome of class struggles is always determined by the dialectic of forces and relations of production (1988: 14). As Cohen puts it: 'class struggle has primary political significance, but the political dimension of society is not itself primary' (1988: 17); i.e. 'the vicissitudes of class struggle decide just *when* a ruling class is supplanted, once a superior social order is *objectively* possible' (1988: 19 – emphasis added). A more clear-cut and explicit example of the *monistic* privileging of structure over agency is hard to find.

143

The Dualism of Elster

Elster (1985: 29) is highly sceptical of the use of functional explanation within the social sciences as no version of it has yet been able to account for a mechanism to support the explanation of A in terms of its functionality. Thus, the problem of the strong functionalism of Cohen is that it fails to account for the causal mechanism linking the dispositional fact of A with the subsequent emergence of A. The hypothetical propensity of the explanandum to have a beneficial effect on some given referent does not create its own fulfilment. The triggering cause of A must always be produced, since if it is not, it becomes difficult to avoid problems of correlation and pre-emption (Elster, 1982: 455 n. 8, 1983: 115).

Despite his general scepticism, Elster insists on retaining a *weak functionalism* which asserts that institutions, or behavioural patterns, may have consequences that are beneficial for some dominant economic or political structure, even though the benefits are unintended and unacknowledged by the beneficiaries (Elster, 1982: 454). What makes Elster's weak functionalism qualify as functionalist is that it still assumes the presence of a referent against which the functionality of A is measured. On the other hand, what makes it weak is that Elster insists that whenever a functional explanation of A is proposed, a feedback-loop between A and its functional effect must be produced (Elster, 1985: 28, 1986: 203–5).

It is one thing to identify such a feedback-loop, and another to explain how it comes about. In order to do so Elster combines three successive modes of explanation, working at different levels of aggregation (Elster, 1985: 5, 18). First, there is *sub-intentional* causal explanation of desires, beliefs and preferences, which are seen to be determined by socioeconomic constraints, by what constitutes the feasible set of options, and by the interaction of social agents (1985: 19–21). Next, there is *intentional* explanation of individual action in terms of the underlying desires, beliefs and preferences of the social agents, assuming that if the individual actors are rational they will act according to their desires, beliefs and preferences. Finally, there is *supra-intentional* causal explanation of aggregate phenomena in terms of the individual actions that go into them. The central point here is that individual actions result in aggregate outcomes which are either intended or unintended, or a combination of both (1985: 22–4).

The combination of these three modes of explanation helps us to understand the reproduction of the capitalist mode of production. The functional correspondence between the productive forces, the relations of production, and the superstructure, which tend to ensure

144

the reproduction of capitalist social relations, is seen as an intended and/or unintended outcome of individual actions motivated by the actual beliefs, desires and preferences of social agents. Moreover, the status quo is maintained so long as these agents perceive that the costs of transformation exceed the benefits within a reasonable time horizon. Since the touchstone of this argument is the intentional explanation of individual actions, I shall give it closer examination.

By contrast to explanations in terms of functionality, intentional explanation cites the intended rather than the actual consequence of behaviour in order to account for it (1985: 27). A subset of intentional explanations is dealt with by rational choice theory, which considers only rational actions that are performed because they are rational (1985: 8–9). The much-celebrated game theory constitutes a special branch of rational choice theory that stresses the interdependence of decisions (Elster, 1982: 464). This theoretical complex rests on the basic premise 'that structural constraints do not completely determine the actions taken by individuals in a society' (1982: 463–4). With this assertion Elster breaks decisively with the structural Marxism of Althusser. In contrast to Althusser, who reduced social agency to structural dupes, Elster insists that there is always a margin for undetermined individual choice. Intentional explanation starts exactly where structural determination ends. Structure- and agency-based explanations are complementary, and Elster thus moves from a monist to a *dualist* conception of structure and agency.

The Duality of Structure in Giddens

According to Giddens (1982: 534–5), Elster's hypostatization of structure and agency bears witness to his failure to see that structure is not only a constraint upon action but also something which facilitates action. However, the double presence of the structure as both a constraint and a facilitator of action does not imply that social agency is fully determined by the structure. On the contrary, Giddens takes it to be a defining condition of social agency that it could act otherwise. Hence, social agency is capable of intervening in the world and making a difference *vis-à-vis* the structure (Giddens, 1976: 75). In this sense Giddens is clearly an action theorist. Now, in order to understand how structure and agency are *mutually* involved in the production of each other, it is necessary to take a closer look at Giddens' reformulation of the concepts.

Giddens warns us against reducing social systems to their underlying structure (Giddens, 1979: 59–64). Such a reduction would from the outset deprive us of the crucial dimension of social action. *Structure* should thus be defined in terms of the structural properties that are recursively implicated in the reproduction of various praxis-forms within social systems (1979: 64). Structural analysis is thus an investigation of those rules and resources that bind social praxis-forms in time and space. The more the social praxis-forms are stretched across time and space, the more institutionalized they become, and the more deeply layered are the structural properties that contribute to their reproduction (1979: 64–5).

Turning to the concept of *social actors*, Giddens (1979: 55–6) defines their actions as a continuous flow of conduct, which, to the extent that it acquires a certain regularity, takes the form of a social praxis. Social actors have the capacity for *reflexive monitoring* of their conduct (1979: 56). That is, they continuously relate their actions to one another as well as to the world in which these take place. A part of the actors' reflexive monitoring of their conduct is the ability to account for their actions. These actions are for the most part intentional, although they are far from always guided by a clear and well-defined goal. The actors are to a great extent capable of rationalizing and motivating their actions. The reasons for actions can be more or less explicit, and the motives for actions can be more or less conscious. To act for a reason and with a specific motive requires that the social actors possess a minimum degree of knowledge about their structured surroundings (1979: 57). This knowledge is either discursively formulated, or a tacit knowledge that is skilfully applied in the course of actors' conduct. It is precisely the *knowledgeability* of the social actors that, together with their capacity for reflexive monitoring of conduct, makes it possible for them to resist the determining power of the structure. The social actors are capable of evaluating their actions in relation to structural constraints and facilities, and they know how to regulate and adjust their conduct in the light of these. This gives the social actors autonomy as it creates a certain degree of manipulative control over the structural conditions for their actions. Nevertheless, this control is always limited by the unacknowledged conditions and unintended consequences of social action (1979: 57–9).

Giddens' reformulation of the concepts of structure and agency makes it possible to understand the interaction of structure and agency as part of a *structuration process*. Structuration here refers to the way in which a social system and its structural properties are produced and reproduced in and through the interaction of social actors, who apply different generative rules and resources while acting in a context of unacknowledged conditions and unintended consequences (1979: 66). The implicit conception of structure as both medium and outcome of the actions of social agency enables Giddens to describe the relation between structure and agency in terms of neither a monism nor a dualism, but of a duality (1979: 4–5).

The first point to note is that Giddens' solution to the problem of structural determinism is achieved by means of a 'rationalistic' conception of social actors as knowledgeable and reflexively self-monitoring. The idea that social agency could act otherwise suggests that agency is not entirely determined by the structures, which provide an ever present condition for agency. When social actors are capable of resisting structural pressures, it is because in the continuous flow of human conduct there is a kernel of *theoria* in the ancient Greek sense of an insight into the state of affairs, obtained by means of either contemplation or reflexive observation. It is this kernel of *Theoria* that permits social actors to exercise a minimal degree of manipulative control over the structural conditions of action. Thus, social actors are neither structural dupes nor absolute choosers, but strategically thinking actors, who, in spite of their epistemological capacities, are capable of manoeuvring with a certain efficiency within the limits set by the structure of the social system.

Second, Giddens' solution is achieved more by 'definitional fiat than by analytical rigour' (Hay, 1995: 198). On the one hand, he offers an idiosyncratic definition of structure in terms of instantiated rule- and resource-sets. On the other hand, he defines social agency as referring 'not to the intentions people have in doing things but to their capability of doing things' (Giddens, 1984: 9). When these definitions are combined there is of course no dualism between structure and agency. In fact, nobody has ever claimed that a dualism existed between the social actors and the rules and resources that condition their action. What is frequently claimed, though, is that the intentional actions of social agency often clash with structural traits of the system (in terms of complex relations between institutionalized orders, meanings and contexts that are often unacknowledged by social agency) that are beyond the control of a particular set of individual or collective actors, or at least not alterable in the short term.[3] This tension between social agency and what Giddens for some odd reason tends to call the social system (see Outhwaite, 1990: 67) remains unresolved and seems to haunt Giddens as a *dualism* between macro- and micro-practices (Hay, 1995: 198–9).

Beyond Structural Determinism

Althusser, Cohen, Elster and Giddens have all, in different ways, sought to reconstruct Marxist theory, but not one of them has succeeded in solving the problem of structural determinism in a satisfactory way. The monism of Althusser and Cohen merely reiterates the problem; Elster's dualism gives in to voluntarism; and Giddens' attempt to see structure and agency as two sides of the same coin relies on an essentialist conception of the subject as possessing specific epistemological capacities, and on a question-begging redefinition of both structure and agency. What is clear, though, is that Althusser, Cohen, Elster and Giddens *all share a belief in the possibility of structural determination.* They all conceive structure as a fully constituted, objective whole which has a series of calculable effects. Now, it is precisely this analytical premise that is the source of all the problems. That is, as soon as structural determination is accepted as a principle, there exist only two possibilities: either one can, like Althusser and Cohen, attempt to figure out how this structural determination takes place and how social agency can be said to be an effect of the structure, or one can, like Elster and Giddens, construct sophisticated arguments about how social agency either *escapes* (Elster) or *resists* (Giddens) structural determination. A more satisfactory solution to the problem of structural determinism, however, starts by problematizing the whole idea of structural determination. This is not done merely by dispensing with the notion of structure; or, indeed, by substituting the idea of a fully structured whole with the notion of an unstructured chaos of individual actions. What is required is a precise account of what exactly it is that deprives the structure of its determining capacity.

It is not enough to redefine the concept of structure as a discursive structure within which the absence of a fixed centre prevents closure. Undoubtedly, the possibility of a full determination of the identity of the subject, once and for all, is undermined by the extension of the play of meaning within discursive structures; however, one could still argue that discursive structures, despite their playfulness, will be capable of determining the subject in the sense of providing it with a complete and unquestionable guide for how to understand itself, the world and the appropriate forms of social and political action. In other words, the discursive character of the structure does not problematize its effectiveness. According to Laclau, what really undermines the determining capacity of the structure is *dislocation*. Dislocation refers to the emergence of an event, or a set of events, that cannot be represented, symbolized, or in other ways domesticated by the discursive structure – which therefore is disrupted. In contrast to Althusser, who tended to

148

see dislocation as a conjunctural disturbance which did not affect the fundamental aspects of the structure, Laclau conceives dislocation as a permanent phenomenon inasmuch as there is always something that resists symbolization and domestication, and thereby reveals the limit, incapacity and contingency of the discursive structure. It follows that dislocation continuously prevents the full structuration of the structure. Dislocation is the traumatic event of 'chaos' and 'crisis' that ensures the incompleteness of the structure; it is precisely this incompleteness, this lack of objectivity, that deprives the structure of its determining capacity. Dislocation is, in other words, the concept of the impossibility of structural determination. As Laclau (1990a: 41–3) puts it, dislocation is the very form of *temporality, possibility* and *freedom*.

Subject, Identification and Hegemony

With the objectivity of the structure goes also the objectivity of social agency. Put simply, social agency cannot be seen as a structurally determined subject position, which is stamped upon the subject through the process of social determination and ideological inter-pellation, precisely because the incompleteness of the structure prevents structural determination of such objective positions within the structure (1990a: 43–4). Neither can social agency be seen as having an objective essence that the dislocation of the structure liber-ates. The identity of the subject is only given in relation to the structure (1990a: 44).

The subject is internal to the structure, but the structure is dislocated by an event which cannot be domesticated by the structure. The dis-location of the discursive structure prevents the full structuration of the structure and also prevents the subject from being determined by the structure. However, the fact that the subject does not have a struc-turally determined identity does not imply that the subject is characterized by a complete *lack of structural identity,* as the existen-tialists would have it. The subject, rather, has a *failed structural identity* (1990a: 44). The incompleteness of the structural identity constitutes the subject as the locus of a decision about how to estab-lish itself as a concrete subjectivity with a fully achieved identity. The subject is thus partially self-determined in the sense that it constitutes the locus of a decision that is not determined by the structure, which is always already dislocated (1990a: 30).

We have here arrived at the notion of *the subject before its subjectivation.* This subject is characterized by a constitutive lack.[4] In

Lacanian terms we might say that the subject is a bearer of signification which is desperately searching for a signifier that can express its
identity within the symbolic order (Žižek, 1989: 175). However, the
symbolic order is disrupted by the Lacanian Real, which introduces a
radical negativity in the shape of a traumatic event that resists symbolization (1989: 170–1). The result is that the subject cannot find a
signifier which is really its own. One tends to say either too little or
too much. Therefore, the act of symbolic representation fails and
produces a lack. The subject of the signifier is precisely this lack, this
impossibility of fully expressing its identity at the level of the symbolic.
What is crucial to see here is that the subject's failure of representation is its positive condition. In the words of Žižek: 'the subject of the
signifier is a retroactive effect of the failure of its own representation'
(1989: 175).

The subject before its subjectivation is penetrated by a constitutive
lack, and the process of subjectivation (that is, of becoming somebody)
takes the form of an attempt to fill the empty space of the lack through
identification. The split and divided subject may seek to acquire a fully
achieved identity through acts of identification (Laclau, 1990a: 60;
Žižek, 1989: 181). However, these acts of identification – or of decision – take place within an undecidable terrain revealed by the
dislocation of the discursive structure. The subject will, in this situation, aim to identify with one of the emerging hegemonic projects that
seem to offer a 'solution' to the 'crisis' of the structure. The subject is
thus nothing but the distance between the undecidable structure and
the decision of how to heal the rift in the social which has been caused
by dislocation (Laclau, 1990a: 30).

There are many possible *points of identification* for the split and
divided subject. A state functionary in eastern Europe who has lost his
job as a consequence of the collapse of Communism might identify
with the nationalist cause, with the reforms of progressive liberals, or
with forces who want to return to the safe haven of Stalinist rule. A
student who is expelled from the university might seek to restore the
full identity she never had by becoming either a militant who rebels
against the 'system', the perfect mother for her two children, or an
independent artist who cares nothing for formal education. Finally,
millennialist, socialist and popular discourses may offer alternative
ways of reconstituting the identity of peasants who have been expelled
from their land.

A single subject may identify with many different things and may
thus occupy many different 'subject positions'. A *subjectivated individual* is thus a masquerading void. There might be inconsistencies and
irresolvable contradictions between the different identifications of the

subject; however, these aporias might be perfectly acceptable to the subject. After all, everybody is a little schizophrenic. Nevertheless, a minimal consistency or accommodation between different subject positions is brought about by hegemonic strategies which aim to articulate different struggles and identities around a nodal point. Such strategies will tend to have important frontier effects as they will give rise to antagonistic divisions within the social.

Filling the Gap

A dislocated structure does not possess the means of its own future rearticulation (1990a: 50). It cannot determine its own reconstitution, precisely because it is dislocated. The *dislocated structure* is an open and decentred structure, and its crisis can be resolved in many ways. Structural rearticulation will take place within an undecidable terrain and will therefore be an eminently political rearticulation. The gap opened by the dislocation of the structure will be filled by emerging *hegemonic projects* that have the character of myths. The mythical filling of the gap in the dislocated structure also entails the constitution of the identity of the subject (1990a: 50). Social and political agency is constructed as a part of the emerging hegemonic strategies for societal restructuration. Hence, as Laclau contends:

> The question of *who* or *what* transform social relations is not pertinent. It's not a question of 'someone' or 'something' producing an effect of transformation or articulation, as if its identity was somehow previous to this effect. [. . .] It is because the lack is constitutive that the production of an effect constructs the identity of the agent generating it. (Laclau, 1990a: 210–11)

Social and political agency are constructed as a part of the solutions they are advancing, but there are often intense struggles about the content of these solutions and the emerging hegemonic strategies are constantly reformulated as a result of the articulation of a plurality of discourses and identities. There is no master subject capable of governing the formation and advancement of hegemonic strategies. However, there will be different sorts of organic intellectuals, who will aim to establish a certain leadership within the emerging hegemonic projects. This leadership will have a relative, and discursively constructed, capacity to impute meaning to their expectations, experiences and interpretations. The organic intellectuals will often know what they do and why they do it, but they will not know the effects of what they do.

The hegemonic attempt to fill the gap in the dislocated structure by the construction of a myth raises the question of the relation between the function of the myth and its concrete content (Laclau, 1994a: 9–10). The relation between *the filling* and *the filling function* seems to depend upon the size and scope of the dislocation of the structure. When structural dislocation goes deep down to the very bottom of the social, the need for order expands infinitely. As a result the filling function tends to become more important than the filling. This is very much the situation in eastern Europe following the Communist collapse. It seems to be of little importance to the voters whether the politicians they support are fascists, reformed communists or neo-liberals, so long as they promise to restore order and put an end to chaos, misery and despair. By contrast, in the advanced industrial countries, where societal dislocation is not that deep, the filling tends to become more important than the filling function. As a consequence, debates over concrete proposals for solving the socioeconomic crisis are intense. Thus, whereas in the former case the mere *availability* of political projects for social restructuration counts more than their *credibility*, in the latter case credibility becomes extremely important (1990a: 66). Credibility should not, in this connection, be seen as a question of providing rational solutions that would not be too difficult to implement. It is, rather, a question of whether or not a concrete proposal is in accordance with some of the basic principles that organize the life of different social groups and individuals. To be judged as credible a political project must show itself to be consistent with rules, norms and values cherished by the section of the population which is interpellated by the particular project. On the other hand, credibility can also be achieved as a result of a demonstrable willingness to bury what are considered unsustainable and discredited principles. In short, credibility is a question of responding adequately to the 'problems' by means of offering a 'solution' that leads to a simultaneous conservation–dissolution of institutionalized ways of life.[5] This emphasizes the importance of tradition and leads us to the question of the limits to the possible.

Limits to the Possible?

That dislocation is the very form of temporality, possibility and freedom might seem to imply that there are no limits to the possible within a dislocated structure. However, nothing could be more wrong than to turn the assertion that everything is discursively constructed into the proposition that everything can be discursively constructed in

any possible way. On the contrary, in the case of structural dislocation 'there is a temporalization of spaces or a widening of the field of
the possible, but this takes place within a *determinate* situation'
(1990a: 43). In other words, despite the disruptive force of dislocation, there is always *a relative structuration of the social* which might
block the advancement of a certain hegemonic project.

In addition, the form of social and political institutions might influence the fate of political strategies. This has been described by Jessop
as *the strategic selectivity* of institutions.[6] As for the genealogy of the
concept of strategic selectivity, it can be traced back to Althusser's
concept of structural causality, which emphasized the independent
effects of the state within a structure organized in a specific hierarchy,
the variation of which is determined in the last instance by the
economic level (Althusser, 1979b). The structuralist orientation of this
concept was weakened by Poulantzas (1980 [1978]), and by Offe
(1974), who talked instead about the structural selectivity of the state
– defined as the structural qualities of the capitalist state that guarantee the effective elimination of anti-capitalist issues and policies.
Dissatisfied with the structural-functionalist overtones of this conception of structural selectivity, Jessop finally developed it into the
strategic selectivity of the state (and the economy). This refers to
the asymmetrical manner in which the relationship between the institutional forms of state (and economy) and the different political
strategies adopted towards them facilitate and/or constrain the elaboration, realization and redirection of these very strategies (Jessop, 1990:
260–2, 1992: 233, n. 3). What immediately appears as a structural
constraint, in the sense of a highly sedimented institutional blockage, might over time be eliminated or transformed into a conjunctural
facilitation.

Finally, the authoritative and allocative *resources* of social and political actors are also important, and they certainly play a decisive role
in struggles for hegemony. However, it is often extremely difficult to
say which resources count in a specific confrontation as the determination and distribution of the relevant resources tend to be subject
to constant displacements. Even in situations where the determination
and distribution of the relevant resources are relatively stable, it might
be that the ostensibly greater force is not strongest but weakest. In
other words, there is always the possibility of 'a mutation of meaning
not limited to the semantics of discourse or the dictionary but which
produces itself as history' (Derrida, 1988a [1977]: 149).

In sum, structural and institutional conditions, together with
the given distribution of resources, impose important limits on the
possible. Indeed, the most important limit to the possible remains

the opposition from *antagonistic forces* of various kinds. The struggle for hegemony always takes place in a field crisscrossed by antagonistic forces which at once affirm and block each other's identity. However, the struggles between the hegemonic agents are conditional upon sedimented institutional structures that possess a certain strategic selectivity.

8

Power and Authority

There has been much discussion about the relation between power and authority. Some tend to view power as grounded in authority, defined as the legitimate right to act, while others insist that the authorization of power is itself an act of power and imposition. The argument presented in the latter part of this chapter aims to take us beyond both the reduction of power to authority and the reduction of authority to power. The question to be answered is: what does the authorization of power imply? Before answering this question, however, it is necessary to define power, which is an 'essentially contested concept' (Connolly, 1974). We need to understand the precise nature of the power that is authorized. If power is defined narrowly, for example in terms of the repressive power of a sovereign ruler, authority is reduced to a question of the juridical legitimacy on which the exercise of power is founded. A broader definition of power will enable us to reveal the multiple forms of authorization; this will finally help us to establish precisely what the authorization of power implies. To go beyond the concept of sovereign power involves the development of a *nonfoundational concept of power,* one which does not reduce power to an effect of either structure or agency, and does not conflate power with either domination or empowerment. The elaboration of such a concept of power clearly hinges on the discussion of structure and agency in the previous chapter. As the answer to the question of how power is authorized touches on the relation between the universal and the particular, which is examined in the next chapter, the present chapter can be seen as a bridge in the present discussion of the three conceptual doublets.

Power as Causation

Hobbes and Machiavelli can both be seen as precursors of the modern concept of power. Of the two, it is undoubtedly the political writings of Hobbes that have been the more influential. Hobbes' *Leviathan* came more than a century after Machiavelli's *The Prince* and his metaphors of sovereignty and community accorded better with the spirit of modernity than the military metaphors of strategy and organization deployed by Machiavelli (Clegg, 1989: 4). Moreover, writing as he was in the aftermath of the Civil War in England, Hobbes had no problem convincing his readers that the creation of order was urgent. Hobbes saw the sovereign monarch as the solution to the ultimately horrifying chaos associated with the state of nature. The contractual basis of the monarchy was to ensure that each actor identified with the sovereign, whose role is to institute and maintain the social order by means of laws, prohibitions and punishment. Political community is thus conditioned by a sovereign subject exercising power. Power is thus the source of the social. It is conceived in terms of a 'society-effect' (Laclau and Zac, 1994: 17), or, in the words of Hobbes himself, 'Power and Cause are the same thing' (Hobbes, 1839: 72). The conception of power as *causation* refers, first and foremost, to sovereign power, which directly limits those subjective powers whose unrestrained exercise is deemed antithetical to social order. This identification of power with causation can be generalized to social actors as a whole. Hence, the 'Power of *a Man* ' says Hobbes, 'is his present means, to obtain some future apparent Good' (Hobbes, 1986 [1651]: 150).

The model of causality on which Hobbes builds his notion of power was ultimately derived from the new science of mechanics pioneered in the seventeenth century (Ball, 1975: 214; Clegg, 1989: 41). In Hume's elaboration of the early formulation of Galileo, causality can exist between separated but contiguously related entities. Intentional actors were a perfect analogue of such entities, since their desires, wants and preferences were individually embodied. Social individuals thus became the example *par excellence* of ontologically autarchic entities (Ball, 1978: 102). This permits us to conclude that the causal model of power is indeed also an *agency model* of power.

The causal and atomistic concept of power answers the questions of what power is and who has power, rather than the questions of what power does and how its exercise is organized (Clegg, 1989: 31). This leads on to the question of the distribution of power, which was central to the American community power debate in the 1950s. Most of the political scientists who participated in this debate were under the spell of Hobbes' mechanistic conception of power (Ball, 1975). A causal and atomistic conception of power was articulated with the behavioural science approach to politics, to which the 'obscure' notion of intentions was wholly foreign. The result was a reformulation of power in terms of a causal relation between the actual doings of individuals (Clegg, 1989: 41–4).

The limits of the behavioural concept of power as causation are analysed by Lukes in his seminal study *Power: A Radical View* (1974). Lukes critically evaluates what he sees as the three faces of power, and finally advocates a three-dimensional view of power. The first face of power Lukes finds in the works of Dahl, who defines power as the successful attempt of A to get B to do something that B would not otherwise do (Dahl, 1957). This definition is directed against elite theorists such as Hunter (1953) and Mills (1956), who tended to mistake potential power for actual power and thus failed to specify the scope of the power of the would-be ruling elite (Dahl, 1958, 1971). The identification of a power elite requires showing that the preferences of a well-defined group regularly prevail over those of opponents on key issues (1971: 359). Dahl's study of community power in New Haven, which tended to follow these methodological criteria, concluded that there existed a pluralist distribution of power.

Dahl's analysis of the distribution of political power focuses on '*behaviour* in the making of *decisions* on *issues* over which there is an observable conflict of (subjective) *interests*, seen as express policy preferences, revealed by political participation' (Lukes, 1974: 15). The problem with Dahl's analysis is that the explicit focus on overt conflicts over key issues tends to blind him to the less visible forms of power. Of course, power is exercised when A gets B to do something which B would not otherwise do. However, 'power is also exercised when A devotes his energies to creating or reinforcing social and political values and institutional practices that limit the scope of the political process to public consideration of only those issues which are relatively innocuous to A' (Barach and Baratz, 1970: 7). According to Barach and Baratz (1962, 1963), power has two faces: decision-making and nondecision-making. A exercises power over B when A's preferences regularly prevail in decisions on key issues about which there is overt conflict, and when A succeeds in controlling the political agenda through so-called nondecisions so as to prevent potential issues that threaten the interests of A from becoming actual. The reference to nondecisions indicates the limits of the behavioural approach. Nevertheless, Barach and Baratz (1970) insist that their so-called nondecisions, which confine the scope of public political decisions, are themselves decisions. Now, the limit case is, of course, the situation where B does not articulate a formulated issue due to his or her antici-pation of A's reaction. Notwithstanding this, as long as A has deliberately given B reasons to anticipate A's reaction, we remain within the confines of the behavioural approach. We might therefore conclude 'that the two-dimensional view on power involves a *quali-fied critique* of the *behavioral focus* of the first view' and that it 'allows for consideration of the ways in which *decisions* are prevented from being taken on *potential issues* over which there is an observable *conflict* [overt or covert: JT] of (subjective) *interests,* seen as embodied in express policy preferences and sub-political grievances' (Lukes, 1974: 20).

Barach and Baratz go further than Dahl's one-dimensional view on power, but not far enough. They remain too tied to decisions and actual observable conflicts. As a consequence, they fail to account for collective action and systemic effects that are not reducible to indi-vidual decisions or behaviour, and fail to see that power also involves the attempt of A to prevent conflicts by means of influencing, shaping or determining the wants of B (1974: 21–3). In response to his own critical evaluation of Barach and Baratz's two-faced concept of power, Lukes emphasizes the role of manipulated consensus, which he takes to be an effect of either patterns of collective action or institutional-ized inaction. Power not only involves decisions and nondecisions but also no-decisions. It is not only bound to overt or covert conflicts but also to latent conflicts. The suppression of latent conflicts by both action and inaction is power's third face (1974: 24–5). Power is exer-cised when wants are products of a system working against the real interests of B (1974: 34). The latter are not derived from the under-lying structure of society, but are to be determined in a hypothetical counterfactual situation where B is not subject to the effects of the third face of power.

The reference to institutionalized inaction as an integral part of the exercise of power clearly brings Lukes into conflict with the be-havioural approach. Yet his commitment to a Kantian ethics of responsibility prevents him adopting a structuralist position that emphasizes the biased effects of anonymous structures. It should always be possible to hold someone responsible for the exercise of power, and the problem with the structural Marxism of Althusser and Poulantzas is therefore that, 'within a system characterised by struc-tural determination, there would be no place for power' (1974: 52–6). Having drawn a clear line between power and structural determina-tion, Lukes still wants to maintain some notion of structural effects. This he does, first, by asserting that social actors through action and internalized inaction shape the wants and actions of other people, and, second, by insisting that those actors must act within structurally determined limits, but nonetheless retain a certain relative autonomy in the sense that they could always have acted differently. In sum, Lukes can be said to solve the structure–agency problem by privileging agency over structure. As such, Lukes' three-dimensional concept of power remains loyal to the causal and atomistic model of power. The third face of power can ultimately be reduced to the causal effect of relatively autonomous actors on their opponents' state of mind.

Lukes holds that 'the supreme and most insidious exercise of power' is 'to prevent people, to whatever degree, from having grievances by shaping their perceptions, cognitions and preferences in such a way that they accept their role in the existing order of things' (1974: 24). A clear theoretical parallel to Lukes is thus the 'dominant ideology thesis', which has helped disappointed Marxists explain why the working class has not yet revolted against the oppressive system of capitalism. Restating the old Marxist dictum that 'the ruling ideas are always the ideas of the ruling class', writers such as Abercrombie et al. (1980) and Althusser (1971 [1969]) have emphasized the role of ideology in reproducing the beliefs and motivations of the workers. Among those supporting the dominant ideology thesis one often finds an illegitimate reduction of Gramsci's theory of hegemony to the issue of providing an ideological legitimation of capitalism. No matter how the concept of ideology is defined, the core of the argument remains that conflicts are prevented by the workers' ideological misrecognition of their objective interests. Power is thus generally conceived in terms of the causal effect of some social class agency on the wants, beliefs and cognitions of the masses.

Now, the concept of power as causation does not necessarily rely upon celebration of the actions and inactions of social actors. For instance, the causationist alternative to Lukes is a *structural* grounding of power. A structuralist notion of power as causation is to be found in both Parsons and Poulantzas. Parsons does not conceive power in terms of a relationship between social agencies, be they individuals, groups or states. Power is, rather, conceived as a property of social systems. The survival of a social system is conditional upon the fulfilment of four basic functions: goal attainment, patterns maintenance, adaption and integration. These functional prerequisites correspond to different social subsystems. The political subsystem is concerned primarily with the problem of goal-attainment. Collective goal-attainment requires the performance of binding obligations by the units of the system, and power is defined as the generalized capacity to secure such binding obligations when these are legitimized with reference to their bearing on the collective goals, and when in the case of recalcitrance there is a presumption of enforcement by negative sanctions (Parsons, 1986 [1963]: 103). Power is a means of acquiring control over outputs, or as Parsons puts it, 'a *specific* mechanism operating to brings about changes in the action of other units, individual or collective, in the processes of social interaction' (1986: 95). Thus, as in Lukes, power is conceived in terms of a causal effect on social agency. However, the origin of this causal effect is not another social agency, as it is in Lukes, but rather a social subsystem.

Poulantzas also conceives power in systemic terms. Power is defined as '*the capacity of a social class to realize its specific objective interests*' (Poulantzas, 1987 [1968]: 104). However, as Poulantzas explains:

> just as the concept of class points to the effects of the ensemble of the levels of the structure on the supports, so the concept of power specifies the effects of the ensemble of these levels on the relations between social classes in struggle. *It points to the effects of the structure on the relations of conflict between the practices of the various classes 'in struggle'.* (1987: 99)

To make this perfectly clear, Poulantzas concludes that 'power is not located in the levels of structure, but is an effect of the ensemble of these levels, while at the same time characterizing each of the levels of the class struggle' (1987: 99–100).

Some have attempted to ground the Marxist conception of power as a causal effect of a specific structure in a transcendental realist argument, which clearly takes us beyond the behaviouralist approach (Isaac, 1987). Transcendental realists like Benton (1977) and Bhaskar (1978 [1975]) deal with the transcendental question of what the world must be like for science to be possible as a meaningful practice. Epistemologically, they subscribe to the post-positivist view that knowledge is constructed rather than merely given by empirical facts. Indeed, it is not only our knowledge about the world which is constructed, but also the social world of wills, habits, norms and institutions. Knowledge and our immediate life-world are constructed, but that does not mean that they are incorrigible (Clegg, 1989: 119). According to the transcendental realists, what we know, experience and act upon is only the tip of the iceberg. Beneath the surface is a set of deep structures to which our knowledge, experiences and actions must ultimately adjust. The world possesses ontological depth. The structure of social phenomena and the structure of the relation between phenomena possess causal powers, which under certain conditions combine contingently to produce a series of actual effects. In the light of this, 'power would thus be the freedom to act in such a

160

way as to realize the inherent *dispositions* of either the structure of a thing or its place in a structure of relations' (1989: 121). A has power to get B to do something that B would not otherwise have done, in the appropriate conditions, in virtue of its intrinsic nature or constitution. This can easily be translated into the Marxist vocabulary of Poulantzas: the capitalist class has the power to sustain capitalist rule due to its position in the capitalist mode of production.

A variety of contingencies are involved in the production of the effects of the structural powers: the standing conditions are contingent; the causal powers combine in a contingent way; and, last but not least, in the social world intransitive causal effects are mediated by the transitive appearances of wills, habits, norms and institutions. Yet ultimately none of these contingencies puts into question the necessity of the causal mechanisms embodied in the deep structure of society. We are thus left with the postulation of a metaphysical hierarchy between an unconditional structural necessity and the accidents it suffers. The deep structure of society thus remains impenetrable to contingency.

Power as Strategy

Lukes is absolutely right: power should not be assimilated to structural determination. The reason is not because power should instead be tied to a responsible agency, as Lukes would have it, but rather because *dislocation of the structure is the condition of possibility of both power and contingency*. It is easy to see why this is so. Dislocation reveals the undecidability of the social – an undecidability that calls for an ethico-political decision, which necessarily involves the exclusion of a constitutive outside. The act of exclusion is an act of power. Power constitutes social identity in an act of exclusion, and the continued repression of what is excluded is the condition of possibility not only of the existence but also of the essence of the social identity in question (Laclau, 1990a: 32). The constitutive outside is the condition of possibility of the identity constructed through the act of power. As the constitutive outside is present within the inside as its always real possibility, the constructed identity is revealed as a purely contingent identity (Mouffe, 1996a: 247). We can, therefore, conclude that all social relations are power relations and that contingency penetrates the very heart of the social (1990a: 31; Mouffe, 1994a: 320). These crucial insights do not, as one might think, deprive the social of its objectivity. For, as Laclau remarks, 'objectivity – the being of objects – is nothing but the sedimented form of power, in other words a power whose traces have been erased' (Laclau, 1990a: 60).

The identification of power with the constitution of social identity by means of the exclusion of a constitutive outside undermines the conception of power as an external relation of causation between preconstituted entities – a conception which underlies both the behaviouralist and realist approaches.[1] Power cannot be viewed as a causal effect of either structure or agency since these are constructed in and through power (Mouffe, 1994a: 320, 1996a: 247). This explains why we cannot be content with substituting Lukes' agency-based concept of power for the structure-based concept of power in Poulantzas. Neither structure nor agency is a preconstituted identity providing a pre-political source for the exercise of power. Both are constructed in and through political power struggles, and since they are thus internal to political power, the causal model of power with its emphasis on the external relation between cause and effect must be abandoned.

Laclau and Mouffe's conception of power as constitutive of social identity squares well with Foucault's Machiavellian conception of power, which emphasizes the role of strategy and organization. According to Foucault (1990 [1976]: 93), power is neither an effect of institutions or structures nor a certain strength that we are endowed with. Power must be defined nominalistically 'as the name one attributes to a complex strategical situation in a society' (1990: 93). This complex strategical situation provides a relatively institutionalized terrain of crisscrossing power strategies, which conditions the ways in which the various strategies transform, strengthen and subvert each other (Dyrberg, 1997).

Foucault addresses the crucial questions of what power is doing and how it is organized. The traditional answers are that power essentially involves the repression of wills and desires and that it is organized in terms of a network of censorship, prohibitions and taboos which together constitute the Law (Foucault, 1990: 81–5). This is the repressive, juridical notion of power, which fails to account for 'everything that makes for its productivity, its strategic resourcefulness, its positivity' (1990: 86). Foucault's alternative concept stresses the productive aspects of power. Power often involves the proliferation of discourse and the constitution, multiplication and transformation of identity. As such, power is intimately related to knowledge. 'We are subjected to the production of truth through power and we cannot exercise power except through the production of knowledge' (Foucault, 1986c [1976]: 93). However, power is not a wholly positive force as the constitution of identity and the production of knowledge are always conditional upon acts of exclusion. As for the organization of power, Foucault emphasizes the role of local institutions, apparatuses and other '*dispositifs*'. These institutions and apparatuses host two overlapping power technologies: *normalizing regulations,* which contribute to the self-correction of the soul in the face of discursively constructed truths through confessional practices, evaluative judgements and medical pathologizations; and *disciplinary techniques,* which aim to extend social control to the body through institutional regulations, surveillance and punishment (Dreyfus and Rabinow, 1986 [1982]: 143–83).

Foucault's power analytics can be summarized by the following propositions: (1) power is everywhere, not because it embraces everything but because it comes from everywhere; (2) power cannot be acquired, seized or shared – it is not something that can be possessed; (3) power comes from below, but the multiplicity of local forces form the basis for wide-ranging effects of cleavage that run through the social body as a whole; (4) power is intentional, but non-subjective – power strategies are guided by a series of aims and objectives, but they cannot be mastered by an individual subject; and (5) resistance is not in a position of exteriority in relation to power, but always works within and against it (Foucault, 1990: 93–6). This last proposition has given rise to heated discussion about the possibility of emancipation. I shall not attempt to summarize this discussion here, but only note that in a Foucauldian perspective emancipation can not be the emancipation from power (Laclau, 1992a, 1993b). Quite simply, 'if emancipation eliminates power through a contingent act of struggle, it must itself be power' (1993b: 293). However, this assertion does not lead to the nihilistic conclusion that emancipation is impossible. For 'if all emancipation must constitute itself as power, there will be a plurality of powers, and, as a result, a plurality of contingent and partial emancipations' (1993b: 293–4). Emancipation in this sense cannot be thought in terms of a transgression into a land of freedom in which the essential human nature is fully liberated. It should rather be seen as involving pragmatic forms of experimentation that seek to undermine and/or transform the prevailing power relations so as to make them more acceptable and less oppressive (May, 1994: 112–19).

Power: Domination or Empowerment?

There has been much debate within the social sciences as to whether power essentially involves domination or empowerment. Some argue that power is always power over somebody, i.e. the bending of wills, while others claim that power should merely be seen as the power to do certain things, i.e. the ability to draw on various rules and resources in the course of action. Foucault aims to escape the choice between 'power over' and 'power to' by claiming that power is neither an empowerment, potentiality or capacity, nor a relation of domination (Foucault, 1986d [1982]: 217–19). Power is thus neither the ability to use, consume or destroy things, nor simply a relationship between partners, individual or collective. For Foucault, power is first and foremost the way in which certain actions modify other actions by means of shaping the identities of the acting subjectivities. However, that does not mean that power is clearly separated from empowerment and domination. As we shall see, both empowerment and domination are central elements in any exercise of power.

Let us start by considering more closely the relation between power and *domination*. Foucault clearly views power as an exercise-concept. However, the exercise of power is not reducible to the power of a fully constituted A over a fully constituted B. As we have seen, power is conceived in terms of a network of discursive strategies which simultaneously produce the identity of A and B. Power thus accounts for how human beings are made subjects. It is important to realize that the word subject has two meanings: 'subject to someone else by control and dependence, and tied to his own identity by a conscience or self-knowledge' (1986: 212). As such, power involves both subjectivation and subjection. Identities are constructed, and as a part of this construction they are placed in specific relations of control and dependence. Take, for example, the relations between doctors and patients, men and women, teachers and students, etc. Each of these identities is constructed in and through a more or less institutionalized network of power strategies that define specific relations of dominance – of doctors over patients, men over women, teachers over students, etc. When, for example, doctors are said to be exercising power over their patients, this basically means that the doctors have become vehicles for the power strategies shaping the relationship between doctors and patients. However, doctors' active and self-conscious exercise of power over patients presupposes that the identity of doctors *vis-à-vis* patients is constructed as if it was already there in the first place. That is, doctors' exercise of power over patients presupposes the retroactive construction of their identity as doctors in and through the unmasterable network of power strategies. In other words, doctors are not the original source of the power they exercise over patients.

Relations of dominance are an immanent effect of power, but what about *empowerment*? What is the relation between power and empowerment? Transcendental realists define power in terms of capacities and outcomes. For example, according to Benton (1981:

173–82), A's successful exercise of power, measured in terms of A's achievement of a specific objective, depends upon A's control and mobilization of his capabilities and resources. However, against this conception of power as a certain empowerment it can be argued that capabilities and resources are defined, structured, distributed and mobilized in a specific discursive context that is shaped and reshaped by crisscrossing power strategies. As such, the forms of empowerment on which the exercise of power depends are themselves circumscribed by discursive power strategies. That is to say, power and empowerment tend to 'overlap one another, support one another reciprocally, and use each other mutually as the means to an end' (Foucault, 1986: 218). We can therefore conclude that both domination and empowerment are intrinsic features of a more generalized notion of power as strategy.

The Authorization of Power

In the terms established by the impact of the French Revolution upon traditional society, power and authority were represented as mutually exclusive phenomena (Nisbet, 1966: 111–12). Thus conservatives and radicals alike saw the rational, centralized and popular-democratic force of political power as expanding at the expense of the traditional, decentralized and paternalistic forms of social authority embodied in the family, the guild, the church and the state. The conservatives demurred at this development while the radicals praised it as yet another step toward the liberation of man from oppressive authorities.

Later, when the problem of how to re-establish and maintain social order resurfaced, modern sociologists aimed to establish a positive link between power and authority. Indeed, the history of sociology reveals a persistent effort to ground political power in some kind of social authority. The starting point of this effort was the proposition that power requires authorization, if it is not to rely entirely on positive and/or negative sanctions. But how should we define authority? The Hobbesian notion of authority is that of legitimate power. Authority involves a right to exercise power (Hobbes, 1986: 218). However, this juridical notion of authority must be discarded as it builds on the notion of sovereign power, which we have criticized above. We shall, therefore, define *authority* as an exercise of power that is accepted by those who are subjected by it, at least to the extent that they 'voluntarily choose' not to put up any resistance against what is implied by the exercise of power.[2] From this definition it follows that power is not derivative of authority, as Parsons would have it. Power may, or may not, be authoritative. If it is not authorized, power will have to rely upon 'naked force'.

However, authority should not only be distinguished from coercion through positive and negative sanctions, but also from persuasion through argument (Arendt, 1954: 93). According to Arendt, persuasion takes place between equals and this explains why authority, which is a form of power, cannot be equated with persuasion. Even if we assume that persuasion always involves power, authority should be clearly distinguished from persuasion. Hence, while persuasion may involve the exercise of authoritative power, the latter does rely on persuasion. Authority is not a particular form of power that makes people agree with, or even like, the content and/or outcome of the exercise of power. Rather, authority is where people voluntarily accept a content and/or outcome of an exercise of power, which they do not agree with and which they do not like. This acceptance may flow from a number of sources which alone or together produce the feeling that the exercise of power must or ought to be obeyed (Easton, 1971 [1953]: 132).

Let us briefly consider some of *the main sources of authority*. If somebody submits to a certain exercise of power because it appears to be in accordance with the rules prevalent in society, we might speak of a *de jure* authority. According to Weber (1978 [1921–22]: 212–41), the source of *de jure* authority is either tradition or bureaucratic rationality/legality. An exercise of power might be accepted because it is judged to be in accordance with traditional norms and values or because it is in accordance with the formal rationality and laws on which modern bureaucracies are based. However, it might be that people submit to a certain exercise of power because they consider the judgements or claims of those exercising power as rightful authorities. In that case we might speak of a *de facto* authority. We may variously think that those exercising power are moral (Durkheim), truthful (Habermas) or charismatic (Weber). It is difficult to distinguish *de facto* authority from *de jure* authority, as the former seems to rest on the latter (Gissurarson, 1993: 38). Morality, truthfulness and charisma might disrupt both tradition and rationality/legality, but in the final analysis all three features presuppose the prevailing rules of society. As Winch (1967) remarks, Jesus did not come to break the law, but to fulfil it. Thus even the actions of charismatic persons depend upon some pre-established rules.

We finally come to the sources of what we might call pragmatic authority. In this case the exercise of power is accepted not because it is considered to be lawful, and not because it is advanced by a rightful agency, but rather because people anticipate that in the normal course of events obedience will be forthcoming (Easton). For example, people might refrain from protesting either because they believe that such protest is too demanding, too risky or too inefficient, or because they think that the unlawful and unrightful exercise of power will in fact serve to produce solutions that work for society as a whole. In this last case, voluntary acceptance of a certain exercise of power clearly rests upon a norm-governed anticipation of the effects of protest and obedience, respectively. As the norms informing the anticipated reaction will be dictated either by tradition or by the rationality and legality of modern bureaucracy, this third form of authority owes a great deal to the first form, *de jure* authority.

The emphasis on voluntary acceptance tends to establish a hierarchy between the good authority and the bad power. However, it has been argued by political realists like Pareto and Mosca that such a hierarchy cannot be sustained. Authority does not come into existence through shared beliefs or conventions, but through power and imposition (Gissurarson, 1993: 39). In fact, all the various sources of authority are ultimately political and are constructed by power strategies in a complex strategic situation. We have already, in chapter 6, emphasized the political character of the various sources of authority. This insight now confronts us with an urgent problem. For if the source of authority is established through power, how do we then prevent authority from becoming indistinguishable from power? The answer is that we can do so only by invoking a split between the universal form and the particular content of authority. That is to say, the authorization of power should be seen as involving reference to a universal and thus neutral ground beyond power, which contributes to rendering a particular exercise of power acceptable. What inhabits this ground, its content, should nevertheless, despite any appearance to the contrary, be conceived as a particular product of political power strategies. What makes the sources of authority capable of functioning as the privileged reference points for the authorization of power is the fact that they are always 'posed as presupposed' (Žižek, 1991: 201–3, 214–19). History is written backwards. The sources of authority, which are constructed in and through political power struggles, are posed as if they were always already there in the first place. This ideological concealment of the contingent and particularistic character of the source of authority is what Spivak has called a *strategic essentialism* – a term which captures well the strategic necessity of essentializing that which cannot be essentialized.

9

The Universal and the Particular

The neo-Aristotelian moral philosopher MacIntyre (1984) claims that there is no mediation between Aristotle and Nietzsche: either we retain the notion of a common good, or we give up all reference to universal values. There are no Kantian, utilitarian or existentialist stations on the road between universalism and particularism. MacIntyre's bold statement concerning the fundamental gulf between the universal and the particular is widely accepted, even by people who draw the opposite conclusion to MacIntyre by insisting upon the primacy of the particular over the universal. The discourse theory of Laclau and Mouffe also accepts the idea that there is a chasm between the universal and the particular, but it challenges the idea that a radical choice must be made between universalization of the particular and particularization of the universal. The fundamental claim of discourse theory is that by rethinking the notions of the universal and the particular we can account for their mutual conditioning. As a consequence, the *metaphysical hierarchies* privileging either a pure universality or a pure particularism are revealed as political and ideological attempts to arrest the *undecidable game* between the universal and the particular.

The Primacy of the Universal over the Particular

A deconstructive reading of the relation between the universal and the particular might start by showing how the primacy of the universal over the particular was established in classical ancient philosophy, within Christian thought, and within the discourse of modernity (Laclau, 1992b).

168

Classical ancient philosophy maintains that there is a strict dividing line between the universal and the particular and that the pole of the universal is fully graspable by reason. No mediation is possible as the universal and the particular are mutually exclusive poles. Either the particular becomes universal by transforming itself into a transparent medium for the actualization of the universal, which is seen as the source of all possible meaning; or it negates the universal by asserting its own particularism, which because of its irrationality can have no entity of its own and thus can only exist as a corruption of being (1992b: 84–5).

Christian thought sees the universal as the eschatological succession ordered by God. As such, the universal is completely inaccessible to human reason. The eschatological succession only shows itself to finite human beings through revelations. It follows that the dividing line between the universal and the particular can no longer be thought in terms of a distinction between reason and its other. The dividing line is, rather, drawn between two temporal series of events: (1) a contingent series, which is the result of the choice and interaction of the finite human being; and (2) an eschatological series, which is governed by God's Master Plan. Now, since each of the universal, God-given moments in the eschatological series must necessarily realize itself in a finite world of contingent particulars with which it has no common measure, the relation between the two temporal series must be opaque and radically incomprehensible. This incomprehensible relation is established through incarnation: the universal is incarnated in the particular. Hence, mediation is possible, but God is the only mediator (1992b: 85).

With the emergence of the discourse of *modernity* the divine foundation of all existing reality was replaced by a rational foundation, which was not external but internal to the totality it was supposed to ground. The rational ground has a logic of its own, which, unlike the designs of God, is fully transparent to human reason. The universal principle of rationality transcends all particular human beings, but as the former is fully comprehensible by the latter, human beings can identify themselves with the universal principle of rationality and start transforming society and nature in its image. This gives way to a complete subsumption of the particular under universal rationality. In Descartes there is still a duality between the universal principle of rationality and the real world. But the Enlightenment saw in rationality a universal principle for reorganizing social and political life. Feudalism, religion and patrimonial administration finally had to give way to market economy, science and bureaucratic administration. The highest point in modernity's advance of this rationalistic hegemony was when the gap between the universal principle of rationality and the irrationality of the particular forms of reality was entirely closed. This task was accomplished by Hegel and Marx, who both asserted that 'the real is rational'. An interesting consequence of this identity between the real and the rational is that it cancels the distinction between universality and particularity, so that incarnation is no longer needed. Hence, in Marx, the liberation of the proletariat and that of humankind become indistinguishable.

The chasm between the universal and the particular has been dealt with in different ways. In classical ancient philosophy there is a strict separation of the universal and the particular, and no mediation is possible. There is also a strict separation between the universal and the particular within Christian thought, although here mediation in the form of incarnation is made possible by divine intervention. Finally, the need for incarnation is removed in the discourse of modernity as the particular is completely universalized. A common feature of all three accounts is the metaphysical hierarchy privileging universality over particularity. The latter is either seen as a corruption of being, a passive object for the incarnation of universal events, or something that is entirely absorbed by the universal principle of rationality.

Towards a Radical Particularism?

The metaphysical privileging of the universal over the particular has recently been challenged by certain *multiculturalist* and *postmodernist* currents (Laclau, 1995a). Some of the advocates of multiculturalism tend to attack universal values, which they perceive as an ethnocentric preserve of western imperialism. Certain postmodern theorists fuel the fire by criticizing the very idea of universal values for being a totalitarian remnant of the foundationalist ontology of the Enlightenment. In the most radical formulations, multiculturalist and postmodernist writers have advocated what we might call a pure particularism, i.e. a monadic particularism that does away with any reference to universal values. Nevertheless, it should be noted that multiculturalist values are not always accompanied by the appraisal of a pure particularism, and that many postmodern theorists seem to sustain 'a notion of "weak" identity which is incompatible with the strong cultural attachments required by a "politics of authenticity"' (1995a: 147). Bearing in mind this important caveat, we can begin to examine the multiculturalist and postmodernist arguments in favour of a pure particularism that makes no appeal to universality.

Idealizing descriptions of societies with a high degree of cultural diversity have for a long time used the metaphor of the 'melting pot'. The different cultural groups should not only live peacefully side by side, but also aspire to blend with each other and thus to become a part of a larger community. In the case of California the melting pot metaphor no longer seems to offer an adequate description of the multicultural society. The metaphor of the 'fruit bowl' seems to capture better the lack of integration and community that is the daily experience of most people in Los Angeles. And this metaphor is not only considered an adequate description of the large multiracial cities in the West. A growing number of multiculturalist intellectuals seem to conceive the harnessing of separate cultural identities as a normative good. Segregation and cultural autonomy have become celebrated values for a new generation of politically correct activists. The University of California was at the beginning of the 1990s the centre of militant actions carried out by a group of students demanding the establishment of a Centre for Asian Studies. Carrying stylized images of Vietcong soldiers and banners proclaiming that 'Material hunger is nothing compared to intellectual hunger', a large group of Asian upper-middle-class students struggled not only for more research into their own cultural roots and background but also for Asian studies to be undertaken by Asian professors and for the right of students to submit essays written in their mother tongue. Clearly the reinforcement of segregation and cultural autonomy is the underlying goal of such political struggles fought in the name of authenticity.

Assertion of the value of one's own particular cultural identity might be a necessary stepping stone in the struggle for a more equitable society. Nevertheless, the recent celebration of separate and differential cultural identities endowed with a radical autonomy is both theoretically and politically self-defeating. It is *theoretically self-defeating* because the constitution of a separate, differential identity must necessarily include relations to the other identities within the system of differences as a part of its own identity. These relations will clearly have to be regulated by rules and norms that transcend the singularity of any particular identity. Thus, a pure particularism is not theoretically sustainable (1995a: 147).

Assessment of the *political impact* of the celebration of a pure particularism must take into account two situations. The *first* is where a particular cultural identity withdraws from the level of public debate and policy-making and becomes preoccupied with the purity of its particular identity. Politically, such a withdrawal will contribute to the maintenance of the status quo in the power relations between the various groups in society. In other words, we will have a situation not entirely different from the vision of 'separate developments' within separate 'homelands' that was part of the official doctrine of apartheid in South Africa (Laclau, 1992b: 88). Few will count that as an example of a progressive politics of liberation. The *other situation* is where a particular cultural identity seeks to manifest itself politically in terms of its own particularity. The problem here is that an attempt by a cultural minority to assert itself politically in the public realm entirely on its own premises will eventually lead to political marginalization, and thus to erosion of the identity that was to be asserted. Hence, a particular identity, for example an ethnic group of immigrants, will not be able to represent itself, let alone advance its particular interests, without making some reference to the universal right to proper housing, education, etc. Even the struggle to gain respect for the integrity of the group has to be waged in terms of everybody's right to the same. However, if the reference to universal values is the condition of possibility for the advancement of the interests of a particular group, it is at the same time the condition of impossibility for the maintenance of its particularity. That is, the inscription of the interests of a particular group within a communitarian space of universal values will inevitably contribute to the hybridization of the particularistic identity of the group (Laclau, 1995a: 148–9). Whether the particularity of the identity will be entirely lost, or only slightly modified, as a result of its insertion into a communitarian space that has been ideologically and culturally moulded by the dominant groups is an open question to be decided in and through political struggles for hegemony (1995a: 149).

We shall now move on from the multiculturalist arguments in favour of a pure particularism and instead consider those *postmodern* arguments that seem to lead to the rejection of the idea of universal values as ethnocentric and ultimately totalitarian. The basic argument is this: since all values are contextual, and all contexts are incommensurable due to the absence of a common ontological ground, we must defend cultural pluralism. This argument is quite plausible and we certainly have no reason to argue otherwise (1995a: 151). However, it is problematic simply to conclude that the presence of a multiplicity of incommensurable contexts and identities renders the reference to universal values obsolete. Again we seem faced with two different situations. Both are premised on the assumption that the absence of universal values, norms and rules will lead to some kind of Hobbesian state of nature, within which the incommensurable identities will gradually destroy each other in antagonistic clashes. Against this background, the *first situation* is one in which the mutual destruction of the plurality of separate identities is prevented by the construction of a stable system of differences. However, this

Hobbesian solution will lead us straight back to the theoretical arguments against the multiculturalist appraisal of a system of a pure particularism, which has been shown to be a contradiction in terms because every system of differences rests upon universal norms and rules. The *second situation,* in contrast, is one where the mutual destruction of the plurality of separate identities engaged in antagonistic clashes is prevented by some pre-established harmony of purely differential identities, which are related in and through their separations and exclusions, but which do not form part of a system of differences in the sense of an internally differentiated totality. However, here we need to account for the total ground that constitutes the differences as differences (Laclau, 1992b: 88, 1995a: 157). Indeed, 'the pre-established harmony of monads is as essential a ground as the Spinozean totality' (1995a: 157). In other words, even assertion of the presence of some purely differential identities ultimately requires a reference to some kind of universalism. The conclusion is that even the fiercest multiculturalist and/or postmodern attack on the notion of universal values seems to presuppose what it excludes.

The Universal as an Empty Place

It is not enough simply to reject the multiculturalist and postmodern arguments in favour of a pure particularism as politically dangerous and theoretically flawed. In order to face up to the challenge presented by the retreat and return of the universal, we must show how the relation between particularity and universality can be rethought in a way that *prevents* reduction of the particular to the universal (as in the case of classical ancient philosophy, Christian thought and the discourse of modernity) as well as reduction of the universal to the particular (as in the case of multiculturalism and some versions of postmodern theory).

Laclau's attempt at such a rethinking starts from the proposition that all systems – whether they have the form of an internally differentiated totality or a relational totality of separate identities – must establish some more or less stable limits. Without boundaries there can be no system. The limits of a system are constitutive of its systemic character. But then, how are the limits of a system established? We can immediately write off any reference to an underlying positive essence. Yet, can we alternatively establish the limits of a system in terms of its differential relation with identities outside the system? The answer is: not if we accept that all identity is differential, since in that case it would be impossible to see which differential identities were internal or external to the system. According to Laclau (1994b: 168–9, 1995a: 151), we are left with only one possibility: to establish the limits of a system in terms of the exclusion of a radical and threatening otherness, which does not present itself as yet another difference, but rather involves the expansion of a chain of equivalence. In other words, construction of the limits of a system involves the construction of a social antagonism.

This latter is an important point since it permits us to rethink the relation between particularity and universality. The argument is that whenever a system is constructed through the exclusion of a radical and threatening otherness, a universalistic chain of equivalence will be established between the particular identities that are a part of the system. An example will serve to illustrate the point. Since the case of the construction of a relational totality of separate and differential identities seems to be the most challenging, the example we shall look at is the formation of a national resistance movement that brings together a large variety of separate demands, struggles and groupings. A far from unfamiliar situation in many Third World countries is the presence of a totalitarian regime that rests upon a combination of military power and lucrative alliances with foreign investors. Now, in the absence of a transformist strategy of co-optation and marginal reforms, such a regime will tend to accumulate a large number of unsatisfied social demands. These demands are certainly particular ones, as they are advanced by many different groups. If the government continuously denies the demands of a variety of different groups, these groups will share the common experience of a threat to their particular identities. They will also share the feeling that something is equally present in all the demands, namely that they are in opposition to the regime. They will finally start to share the ambition to construct a new social order in which their particular identities can be fully developed. Hence, trade unions, ethnic groups, women's organizations, political minorities, poor urban dwellers, etc. will tend to become united, not by an overarching ideology that reduces their particular identities to differential positions within a unified whole, but by the construction of a chain of equivalence that expresses a common feeling of a lack of fullness. As the chain of equivalence expresses a sameness that transcends the particular identities (without undermining their particularity), and as it often becomes extended into a horizon for the inscription of social demands, it certainly possesses a dimension of universality (1995a: 153).

The universal emerges out of the particular as an irreducible dimension of the chain of equivalence expanded as a result of the negation of the particular identities. As such, the dimension of universality reached through equivalence does not take the form of an unconditional a priori principle. Neither does it take the form of a regulative idea in the sense of an empirically unreachable telos that consistently guides our actions. The kind of universality we are discussing here cannot exist prior to, and independently of, the system of equivalences from which it proceeds (1995a: 154). This is a universality that only exists as a dimension of the chain of equivalence that links the particular identities. This universality has its roots in the experience of a common destiny, and it might even invoke the idea of a common cause: a popular struggle against the oppressor and the realization of a fully fledged community of fully achieved identities. However, as the chain of equivalence is expanded to include all the various demands, struggles and groupings, it becomes clear that it does not possess a positive content of its own. The dimension of universality is 'just an empty place unifying a set of equivalential demands' (1995a: 155). Thus, far from being something positive, the universal is the very principle of positivity, a pure Being in which all the particular beings are mirrored.

The universal is an *empty place* whose content is partially fixed in and through political struggles between the particular groups caught up in the chain of equivalence (1995a: 158). The various groups will aim to hegemonize the empty place of the universal. The particular identity that succeeds in filling the empty space of the universal has established a hegemony. Such a hegemony does not take the form merely of a precarious agreement between different political forces that 'strike together, but march separately'. Neither does it take the form of an imposition upon other political groups of a pre-given organizational principle provided by a political vanguard. Rather, hegemony involves the construction of a collective will, in the Gramscian sense of a political project that is shaped in and through the political struggles for hegemony (Laclau, 1994b: 175–6). Not all groups are equally capable of becoming hegemonic. The unevenness of the structural positions in society prevents this: not by determining once and for all which among the various political forces is capable of becoming hegemonic, but rather by constraining and facilitating the formulation and realization of the political strategies of those forces (1994b: 174–5).

This last twist in the story concerning the relation between the universal and the particular permits us to conclude that there seems to be a circular relation between the two: *the universal emerges out of the negation of the particular identities, but its content is fixed in and through political struggles for hegemony, in which particular demands are universalized and others are marginalized.* There is much more to

175

say about the hegemonic incarnation of the universal by a particular social agent. Yet, before we can advance further in the understanding of this process, and its consequences for the social agent who assumes the function of representing the universal, we must address the question of how the empty universal is signified within the social.

Universalism and Empty Signifiers

As we have seen, the dimension of universality reached through equivalence does not possess a positive content of its own, but rather constitutes the very principle of positivity. It invokes reference to a communitarian space that is only present in its absence. That is to say, it refers to a community that is lost because it is denied by the antagonist force which is the constitutive outside of the system.

How, then, can the empty place of the universal be signified? Since what we are trying to signify is not a positive, differential identity, but rather an empty universality produced by the expansion of a chain of equivalence, it is clear that 'no production of *one more* difference can do the trick' (1994b: 170). Indeed, as 'all the means of representation are differential in nature, it is only if the differential nature of the signifying units [the signs: JT] is subverted, only if the signifiers empty themselves of their attachment to particular signifieds and assume the role of representing the pure being of the system – or, rather the system as pure Being – that such a signification is possible' (1994b: 170–1). In other words, the dimension of universality can only be signified by what Laclau calls an *empty signifier*. We recall that an empty signifier is neither a signifier attached to different signifieds in different contexts (an equivocal signifier) nor a signifier simultaneously attached to different signifieds which overdetermine or underdetermine its meaning (a floating signifier) (1994b: 167). Rather, an empty signifier is a signifier that is not attached to any signified due to the incessant sliding of the signifieds under the signifier. Empty signifiers – 'the people', 'order', 'unity', 'liberation', 'revolution', etc. – have been employed, on various occasions, to signify the absence of a community of fully achieved identities. Why one signifier rather than another assumes the function of signifying the absent communitarian fullness is determined in and through political struggles for hegemony.

This brings us back to the question of how a particular political force manages to *hegemonize* the empty place of the universal. Clearly a particular political force cannot simply fill the empty place of the universal by asserting its unmediated particularity and advancing its own particular interests. As Gramsci says, a class or group is

176

hegemonic only 'when it is not closed in a narrow corporatist perspective but represents itself as realising the broader aims either of emancipating, or ensuring order, for wider masses of the population' (1994b: 175). In other words, for a class or group to become hegemonic it must be able to present its particularity as the incarnation of that empty signifier which refers to the absent communitarian fullness (1994b: 176). For instance, if the call is for order and unity, it must show that its political project will bring about order and provide unity. If the call is for emancipation and revolution in the name of the people, it must show that it holds the key to that. That is to say, for a social group or class to become hegemonic, it must be able to speak in the name of the impossible object of society, and in order to do so it must turn the particular content of its demands into an embodiment of the signifier of an empty universality. Put another way, shifting the point of enunciation implies a transformation of the content of the enunciation. This is the core of all hegemonic operations.

The Constitutive Split of the Hegemonic Agent

The successful attempt by a social group to present its particular project and demands as an embodiment of the empty signifier that signifies the empty universal has important consequences. It might help the particular political force to become hegemonic, but the hegemonic victory would be achieved only at the expense of a loss of identity, the direct result of the universalization of the particular content of the project and demands of the hegemonic agent. As such, the hegemonic agent seems to be *constitutively split* between the particularity of its particular project and demands and the universal function of the latter, which requires the transformation of this very particularity into a surface of inscription through which all political struggles will be expressed (1994b: 177).

An example of this is the transformation of the social-democratic parties in Scandinavia from ghetto parties to popular-democratic parties. At the beginning of the twentieth century social-democratic ideology was somewhat sectarian in its celebration of the so-called ghetto party model, which aimed at narrowly pursuing the class interests of the workers while immunizing them from bourgeois influence. The means by which it proposed to achieve the realization of these interests was the formation of mutual aid societies and insurance funds within the trade unions. However, when in the 1930s the social-democratic parties became the decisive hegemonic force, this was facilitated by a gradual shift in social-democratic ideology in the direction of a popular-democratic imaginary. That is, although the social-democratic parties in their practical politics continued to think first and foremost of the interests of the working class, they started to interpellate the people as a whole in the name of redistributive justice. The result was the formation of a still more universalistic welfare state that provided social welfare to all citizens as of right. It must be said that the universalization of the particular project and demands of the social-democratic parties was not without serious political costs. The emptying of the original content of signifiers such as 'class struggle' and 'liberation' was conceived by some as treason and embourgeoise-ment. The result was a deepening of the political division within the workers' movement. Not only were the social-democratic parties in-ternally divided between the centrist party leadership and the often more militant party members and trade-union activists. They also faced a serious political competition from the communist parties and the New Left. What is interesting is that this political division within the workers' movement is constitutive for a hegemonic force. As it is irreducible, all we can do is to think of different ways to institution-alize an open dialogue between the pragmatic party leaders and militant activists.

The universal is an empty place and the hegemonic forces that aim to fill that place are 'constitutively split between the concrete politics that they advocate and the ability of those politics to fill the empty place' (Laclau, 1995a: 159). According to Laclau (1995a: 160–4), this constitutive split has been widely recognized within western political philosophy, which has dealt with the split between the universal and the particular in and through the construction of different images of the ruler – Plato's philosopher-king, Hobbes' sovereign, Hegel's hereditary monarch and Gramsci's hegemonic class.

No tension exists between the universal and the particular in *Plato* as the particular is fully absorbed by the universal. The universal is not an empty place to be filled from outside, but rather the fullness of Being which expresses itself in particular beings. However, only one par-ticular form realizes universal fullness. Only one form of social arrangement and political organization is compatible with what community is in the last instance. As ruling is a matter of knowledge rather than of prudence, only those with knowledge of the only par-ticular form of polity to realize the essence of community should be allowed to rule. Only philosophers possess such a knowledge: there-fore the ruler should be a philosopher-king (1995a: 160–1).

Hobbes is the antipode of Plato. For where in Plato the universal is the only place of fullness, in Hobbes it is an absolutely empty space. Faced with the threat of radical disorder in the state of nature, the universal need for order is more important than the actual order which fulfils that need. Indifference as to the content of the actual social order gives way to an exclusive concentration on the ordering function of the latter (1995a: 161). This is precisely what legitimizes the sovereign, the mortal God who has *ex hypothesis* the function of ensuring order. No other force can guarantee order since power in the state of nature is equally distributed among the members of society, thus preventing the generation of effects of domination that could lead to the construction of partial and competing orders around different power centres (Laclau, 1994a: 9–10). Politics is not eliminated once but twice: first in the state of nature, where everybody has an equal share of power, and then in the commonwealth, where Leviathan fills the empty place of the universal once and for always (1994b: 177). In sum, there is both difference and similarity between Hobbes and Plato. They disagree with regard to the nature of the universal and its relation to the particular. For Plato the universal is the fullness of being that fully absorbs the particular, while for Hobbes the universal is an empty place that is ultimately reduced to the particular order imposed by Leviathan (1994b: 177–8). However, they agree 'not to allow the particular any dynamics of its own *vis-à-vis* the full/empty place of the universal' (Laclau, 1995a: 161). In Plato the particular actualizes a universality that transcends it, while in Hobbes the particular order imposed by Leviathan becomes the unchallengeable Law of the community. It is this failure to account for the transient forms of the particular filling of the universal which in both cases prevents the development of a theory of hegemony.

In *Hegel* the particularism associated with each stage of social organization is sublated by still higher forms of rationality within a universal system of dialectical reasoning. Having reached its highest state, through the successive sublation of its particularistic content, this dialectical system needs to signify itself as a totality. This signification is obtained through a constitutional monarch whose physical body is exactly the reverse of the spiritual totality it represents. The constitutional monarch must be a hereditary one. If he was elected, reasons for his election would be required; this would imply that the full development of society had not been achieved independently of the monarch, who implicitly would be admitted a greater role than the one of ceremonial representation (1995a: 161–2).

Hegel appears to go beyond Hobbes as he allows the particular a certain dynamics. However, this dynamics is governed by a transcendental rationality, the telos of which is the moment of total closure reached in and through the achievement of absolute knowledge. Thus, we are not, after all, talking here of a dynamics which is independent of a universality transcending it. Nevertheless, there is a striking difference between Hegel and Hobbes (1995a: 1962–3). Whereas Hobbes assumes the presence of a radical disorder, Hegel's image of social crisis is less radical. In Hegel social crises are partial and take place against a relatively structured background. This important difference between Hobbes and Hegel has consequences for their conception of the social order and the role of the ruler within that order. Hobbes emphasizes the moment of construction and ascribes to the sovereign the decisive role of providing a particular social order that satisfies the universal need for simply any order. Hegel on his part views society and state as much more self-structured. Social crises are overcome by sublation, and social order is the telos of the dialectical unfolding of world history, and therefore not something that needs to be constructed. Consequently, the hereditary monarch is not supposed to contribute anything at all to the social order. His function is, as already stated, purely ceremonial.

We finally arrive at *Gramsci* and his notion of the hegemonic class. A class becomes hegemonic to the extent that it succeeds in presenting its particular project and demands as the embodiment of an empty universality, one that symbolizes an absent communitarian space and is signified by empty signifiers. There is nothing that a priori determines the particular content of this empty universality. The actual filling of the empty place of the universal is a consequence of political struggles for hegemony. Now, if we compare Gramsci with Hobbes and Hegel, the unique position held by the hegemonic class between the Hegelian monarch and Hobbes' Leviathan is revealed. Gramsci leans towards Hobbes inasmuch as both emphasize the moment of constitution and the active and independent contribution of the ruler. Nevertheless, when it comes to the conception of society in the light of the distinction between order and disorder, Gramsci leans towards Hegel as his notion of social crisis invokes the idea of a partial dislocation that always leaves some areas of the social fabric relatively intact. The conclusion is clear: the hegemonic operation is a constitutive political act that is made possible by dislocation, but that must always take into account and aim to hegemonize the sedimented social relations. Thus, in the words of Laclau, 'the succession of hegemonic regimes can be seen as a series of "partial covenants" – partial because, as society is more structured than in Hobbes, people have more conditions to enter into the political covenant; but partial also because, as the result of that, they also have more reason to substitute the sovereign' (1995a: 163).

180

The Limits of Hegemony

The concept of hegemonic regimes as partial covenants touches on the question of the *limits* of the attempt to hegemonize the empty place of the universal. The question may be phrased in the following way: is it possible for a particular content to suture fully the empty place of the universal? Is it possible for the content of the universal to be constructed in such a way so as to eliminate all opposition and rule out further discussion? Writers like Habermas and Rawls will tend to answer yes. Both underline the constructed character of the universal and think that under certain circumstances the process of negotiation will lead to a true universality. In the case of Rawls it is a hypothetical contract between reasoned individuals under the veil of ignorance that does the trick. With Habermas it a dialogue based on a communicative rationality. Neither Rawls nor Habermas aims to answer the question regarding the limits of hegemony. The filling of the empty place of the universal is not seen by them to be the result of a hegemonic operation, but rather as arising from the result of the working of either a subjective or intersubjective rationality, which completely eliminates the dimension of politics in the sense of antagonistic articulations.

It is clearly not enough to reject the conclusions of Rawls and Habermas on the basis of a critique of their ontology. For it might be that another argument, more in line with the ontology of discourse theory, could do the trick of attaching the empty signifiers of the universal to a transcendental signified. In order to rule out this possibility it must be shown why particular embodiments of the universal always fail to deliver the goods. To this end Laclau points to the 'paradox implicit in the formulation of universal principles, which is that all of them have to present themselves as valid without exception, while, even in its own terms, this universality can be easily questioned and never be actually maintained' (1995a: 155). The case of universal rights illustrates the paradoxical nature of the attempt to fill the empty place of the universal. Universal rights are formulated as limitless principles. They express a universality that transcends the particularity of the context of their emergence, and it is precisely this claim to universal validity that makes possible a chain of equivalential effects: different people in different situations can claim to have the same right to privacy, to speak, to determine their own affairs, etc. There might be numerable contexts in which such universal rights are perfectly valid. However, as the universal rights are applied in still more contexts, problems will eventually arise as the particularity of new contexts will not allow the application of universal rights formulated in another and entirely different context. As Laclau puts it, universal rights are 'sooner or later entangled in their own contextual particularism and are incapable of fulfilling their universal function' (1995a: 156). Laclau's example is the right to national self-determination, which is formulated as a limitless principle and which works well in a great number of cases, but nevertheless tends to produce tensions and ambiguities when applied in a situation where genocidal practices are taking place within a particular nation-state.[1]

Laclau's argument concerning the limits of the attempt to hegemonize the empty place of the universal are paralleled by Žižek. Žižek (1991: 121–2) not only shows how the passage into universality is secured by a rhetorical shift from a judgement of reflection where empirical entities are predicated ('All men have the right to . . .') to a judgement of necessity that invokes the self-determination of the Notion as such ('Man has the right to . . .'). He also shows how, when 'confronted with the multitude of particular crimes, the Universal law reveals itself as the absolute, universal crime' (1991: 42). When faced with so many particular crimes, which it is its task to constrain, law is doubled into its opposite. This occurs not because the concretely applied law must necessarily resort to physical violence, capital punishment, etc., but rather because it can only legitimize itself by referring to the incomprehensible and essentially violent assertion that 'law is law'. In sum, 'the first law ("law is . . .") is the universal law in so far as it is abstractly opposed to crime, whereas the second law (". . . is law") reveals the concealed truth of the first: the obscene violence, the absolute, universalized crime as its hidden reverse' (1991: 34). According to Žižek, the conclusion to be derived from this argument is that:

the Particular is always deficient and/or in excess with regard to its Universal: in excess, since it eludes the Universal; since the Universal – in so far as it is 'abstract' – cannot encompass it; deficient, since – and this is the reverse of the same predicament – there is never enough of the Particular to 'fill out' the universal frame. (Žižek, 1991: 43–4)

Thus, the encounter between the universal and the particular is always missed. This has important theoretical consequences, since, according to Žižek, 'the subject exists only within this "failed encounter" between the Universal and the Particular – it is ultimately nothing but a name for their constitutive discord' (1991: 46). If, on the contrary, the universal fully absorbs the particular, or the particular fills out the universal in a way that leaves no remainder, it is because we are located within an objective structure, which does not permit the emergence of a subject. Laclau reaches the same conclusion, as he sees the constitutive split between ordering and order as implying that the subject, in the sense of the subject of lack and identification, can never be superseded by a fully fledged identity. However, the constitutive split between ordering and order is not only the condition of emergence for the subject; it is also the very condition of politics. Indeed, the management of the incompleteness of society, which derives from the constitutive split between the universal and the particular, is the very essence of politics (Laclau and Zac, 1994: 37).

The Role of Constitutive Representations

Representation plays an important role in relation to the constitutive split between the particular and the universal. Representation can thus be viewed as the process through which unachieved particular identities are inscribed within a universal context, be it an emancipatory project, the institutions of liberal democracy, or some other discursive horizon with universal pretensions. The link between the unachieved particular identities and the hegemonic agent, which at the same time provides the particular filler and undertakes the filling function, is established in and through representation. *Hegemony* thus revolves around relations of *representation*. It is vital to understand that these relations of representation are constitutive of what they represent, and therefore will always result in the hybridization of the particular identities represented by the hegemonic agent. We have briefly touched upon this issue above, but let us now elaborate the argument in order to reveal its political consequences.

Representation can initially be defined by the *fictio iuris* that somebody is present in a place in which he or she is not present in the first place (Laclau, 1993b: 289–90). That is, representation describes the process whereby some representative presents the interests, wants or opinions formulated in point A of society in another point B of society, where these interests, wants and opinions are not already present. It follows that even the case where the represented and the representative are the same person should be seen as a process of representation in so far as the interests presented in point B cannot be deduced from the interest initially formulated in point A. In other words, one can undoubtedly be said to represent oneself in court when one is called to present or defend one's interests (Laclau, 1993c: 229).

According to the traditional modernist view, perfect representation involves a transparent transmission of the preconstituted will of the represented by a neutral representative. However, the conditions of a perfect representation are obtained neither on the part of the represented nor on that of the representative. And, as Laclau (1993b: 290) remarks, this is not a result of what is empirically (un)attainable but rather a result of the very logic inherent in the process of representation. The problem with regard to the represented is that if he or she needs to be represented it is because his or her basic identity is established in a place A, which is different from the place B where important decisions affecting this basic identity are to be taken. The absence of a full presence at the decisive level of political decision-making can be seen as a flaw in the identity of the represented. The represented does not have a fully fledged identity, and representation can thus be seen as providing the supplement necessary for achieving a fully constituted identity. The function of the representative is to inscribe the interests of the represented in a complex reality different from the one in which these interests were originally formulated. As the process of inscription must necessarily take into account a whole series of rules, values, norms and other interests, which are present at, say, the level of national politics as opposed to a local or regional level, it will always require negotiation and rearticulation of the original interests. Thus, in order to present and defend the interests of the represented, the representative will have to reconstruct and transform the interests and identity that he or she represents. The supplementary act of representation will therefore ultimately lead to the hybridization of the identity of the represented (1993b: 290–1).

We must give up the idea of a perfect representation, which, as we have seen, is denied by a logical impossibility. Yet, that does not mean that there are no relations of representation. Representation plays an important role in the construction and expansion of universalizing hegemonic projects, but representation is an essentially impure phenomenon. Recognition of the constitutive impurity of representation carries important political consequences as it urges us to think twice before accusing political representatives of having become 'sell outs' who ignore, distort or betray the interests they represent. Actual instances of ignorance, distortion and betrayal may occur and should be fiercely criticized, but what the bold and sweeping criticisms of political representatives overlook is the fact that the act of representation must necessarily negotiate and rearticulate the interests of the represented (1993b: 291, 1993c: 229–30). According to Laclau, this means that:

184

the problem of democratic control is not one of making the relation of representation transparent, so that it fully expresses the will of the represented, because that will was not there in the first place. Rather it consists in making the represented participate as much as possible in the formation of a new will, to ensure as much as possible their complicity in all the impurities and unevenness that the process of representation presupposes. (Laclau, 1993c: 230)

Now, the constructed character of what is represented can also be viewed from the perspective of the hegemonic agent who claims to represent the absent communitarian space of unachieved social identities. In democratic societies the hegemonic agent will tend to authorize its dominant position in the network of power by referring to its embodiment of the will of the people. The hegemonic agent will aim to present itself as the true and only incarnation of popular sovereignty. However, the existence of a plethora of unachieved particular identities reveals the representation of these in terms of a popular will as a constitutive representation. The will of the people must be constructed out of the manifold interests of the particular groups that are interpellated in the name of the people. It is a matter of fact that the constitutive role of political representatives is currently becoming more visible as the particular social agents increasingly become 'multiple selves' (Laclau, 1993b: 291). In the postmodern world of today people are becoming less and less able to refer to a single or primary ground on which their basic identity depends. The proliferation and circulation of points of identification tend to produce loosely integrated and highly unstable identities. In this situation the process of representation can no longer be seen as merely a supplement to relatively well-defined identities, but rather becomes a primary terrain for the construction of such identities. The risk is, of course, that the loosely integrated and highly unstable identities are represented, and thus rearticulated, by political forces celebrating a harnessing of separate and differential identities only loosely connected within a 'thin' community. Such a scenario carries the danger that a dual structure will develop, consisting of a private sphere of law-protected segregation and a public sphere governed by a quasi-omnipotent technocracy. This would be a scenario leading us back to a new Middle Age. The alternative is not necessarily the development of a 'thick' community, as proposed by communitarian theorists like MacIntyre. Another scenario would be to take difference, particularity and the lack of well-defined identities as the starting point, and then attempt to inscribe this plurality in equivalential logics by emphasizing common vocabularies, experiences and hopes. This could open the way to a relative universalization of values that could be the basis for a popular

185

hegemony (1993b: 164). Once the empty place of universality is constructed through the expansion of chains of equivalence, competition between political representatives, who seek at once to provide the particular filler and to symbolize the filling function, becomes a crucial condition for the reinvigoration of liberal democracy.

Part IV

Discourse Theory at Work

Introduction

The emphasis so far has been on the *theoretical* aspects of discourse theory. Part I considered the intellectual development of Laclau and Mouffe and aimed to account for the decisive influence of Žižek on their work. Part II examined the theoretical concepts of discourse, hegemony and social antagonism. Part III demonstrated the theoretical contribution of discourse theory to an understanding of the relation between structure and agency, power and authority and universal and particular. There is a tendency among those broadly unsympathetic to theories committed to gauging what the consequences of post-modernity are for the social sciences to write off poststructuralist, post-Marxist and psychoanalytical theories of discourse as mere theoretical sophistry, with no relevance to the analysis of concrete social, cultural and political phenomena. It is therefore important to show that discourse theory provides a novel and productive frame-work for analysing phenomena, events and developments of great importance to people in their daily lives. To this end Part IV seeks to put discourse theory to work within three important areas of research: nationalism and racism, mass media, and the modern welfare state.

These subject areas, which are normally the domain of social, cultural and political theory, respectively, will be dealt with in an identical manner. A general framework for understanding the different phenomena will first be established, and then some concrete discourse-theoretical studies presented. The modest attempt to establish a general framework of analysis will draw on theories which are not directly informed by the discourse theory of Laclau and Mouffe. However, the various theories will be reinterpreted from a discourse-theoretical perspective. The aim is to show that the new theories of discourse advanced by Laclau, Mouffe and Žižek provide an abstract, 'metatheoretical' basis for the various theories dealing with nationalism and racism, mass media and the modern welfare state. The empirical illustrations draw on concrete studies which all have a certain theoretical affinity with the discourse theory of Laclau and Mouffe. In order to highlight this affinity the concrete studies are redescribed using the vocabulary of Laclau and Mouffe. The aim of this exercise is to indicate the relevance of discourse theory for the study of *concrete* social, cultural and political phenomena.

Chapter 10 emphasizes the relation between the democratic revolution, the question of the nation, and the discourse of nationalism and racism. The theoretical reflections are followed by a brief summary of recent studies of nationalist revival in eastern Europe and the Arab countries, and of racism in South Africa and Britain.

Chapter 11 deals with the modern mass media culture. It reviews key arguments in the discourse-theoretical study of mass media, and shows why it is necessary to go beyond the traditional mass communication model. It briefly assesses the discursive effects of electronically wrapped language, before concluding with a discussion of the emancipatory effects of modern mass media culture.

Chapter 12 sets out to answer the fundamental issue of how to define and explain the modern welfare state. There follows a brief summary of some discourse-theoretical studies of the genesis and expansion of the modern welfare state. The chapter concludes with a discussion of the present crisis of the modern welfare state and the strategies for renewal.

The aim in combining theoretical reflection and concrete studies is to show the value of taking a discourse-theoretical approach to social, cultural and political analysis.

10
The Politics of Nationalism and Racism

Introduction

The categories '*nation*' and '*race*' are essential components of the discourse of modernity. The nation, conceived as a community that is both limited and sovereign, has become the predominant way of imagining the cultural and political community of modern societies (Anderson, 1983); the classification of human beings according to their race has been central to the modern sciences, in which man is conceived as both the subject and object of knowledge (anthropology is a good example). However, the ideological correlatives of 'nationalism' and 'racism' are held by both liberal and Marxist thinkers to be antithetic to the discourse of modernity. Modernity, with its emphasis on enlightened reasoning and the universal right to human equality, was supposed to wipe out the irrational and excessive ideological phenomena of nationalism and racism. Nevertheless, nationalist and racist discourses continue to play an important role in providing the myths and social imaginaries that organize and guide social and political action. Rather than viewing this as an exceptional development, an unfortunate anomaly, or an unenlightened residue, this chapter argues that nationalism and racism are not only intrinsically linked but are also integral features of modern democracy.

Democracy, Nation and Nationalism

Nations and nationalism are traditionally seen either as a functional response to the structures of modern societies or as a primordial, and thus natural, form of human belonging (Smith, 1995). Marxist and liberal theorists conceive nationalism as the ideological cement of the nation-state, which in turn is seen as providing the best political shell for the capitalist market economy (Hobsbawm, 1990), fulfilling the cultural needs of modern growth-oriented societies (Gellner, 1983), or masking the class conflicts and factions of modern societies (Sklair, 1991). Reversing the causal relation between structure and super-structure, other theorists (Armstrong, 1992; Fishman, 1980; Greenfeld, 1992) tend to view nations and nationalism as basic forms of human association and sentiment, which determine the contents of modernity (Smith, 1995: 53). Unconvinced by these functionalist and essentialist conceptions of nation and nationalism, we shall here alter-natively view *nationalism as a certain articulation of the empty signifier of the nation, which itself becomes a nodal point in the political discourse of modern democracy and generally functions as a way of symbolizing an absent communitarian fullness.*

This conception of nationalism takes Lefort's study of the Democratic Revolution as its point of departure.[1] In a language that is not foreign to Lacanian psychoanalysis, Lefort claims that society can only be unified in relation to a symbolic power outside society. The constitutive power is a symbolic power rather than an actual power of prisons and armed men, i.e. a state apparatus (Lefort, 1986: 279). The relation between society and this symbolic power is an imag-inary one, as the symbolic power that provides the unification of society is itself imagined by the individuals in the society, which the symbolic power retroactively constitutes (Ifversen, 1989: 33).

In the *ancien regime* the Prince occupied the locus of symbolic power (Lefort, 1988: 16–17). Under the monarchy, then, power was embodied in the person of the Prince. In order to maintain his legiti-macy, the Prince had to mediate between mortals and gods. If he associated himself with one of the two poles he would either reveal the gulf between his particular body and the universality he was supposed to incarnate, or become a despot who ruled only in his own name. Now, with the secularization of society and the breakdown of the absolute monarchies, the role of the Prince in the configuration of society is rendered obsolete. The Democratic Revolution invokes 'the dissolution of the markers of certainty' and undermines the possibility of embodying symbolic power in a particular body (Lefort, 1988: 16–19). As a result the locus of power becomes an empty place. The locus of power cannot be occupied. No individual or group can be consubstantial with it. No government can appropriate power, as its exercise is subject to procedures of periodical redistribution and controlled contest (1988: 17). In the national elections atomized individuals choose a government that promises to unify society. This 'leads to the emergence of a purely social society in which the people, the nation and the state take on the status of universal entities, and in which any individual or group can be accorded the same status' (1988: 18).

The symbolic power is not only empty but also invisible. What is visible are only the various attempts to exercise power in the name of society. Paradoxically, the attempt to represent the unity of society always tends to reveal conflicts and antagonisms. It follows that, in order temporarily to occupy the empty space of symbolic power, an expansive hegemony must be established. This will require the authorization of power by referring it back to the empty signifiers of 'the nation' and 'the people', which are the nodal points in the political discourse of modernity.[2] In short, the 'I speak' must be transformed into 'the nation/the people speaks' (Ifversen, 1989: 38). That is to say, in order to become hegemonic one must be able to speak in the name of the nation and the name of the people. However, it is not enough to refer abstractly to what is good for 'the nation' and/or 'the people'. To exercise hegemonic power one needs to hegemonize the empty signifiers of 'the nation' and 'the people' by giving them a particular content.

Against this background, nationalism can be defined as a myth that provides the empty signifiers of 'the nation' and 'the people' with a particular, substantial embodiment. Thus, nationalism tends to construct the *nation-as-this* and the *people-as-one*. As such, nationalist myth aims to guide social and political action in the name of a particular *ethnos* (being French) and a certain imagined national space (France as the locus of Frenchness).

The homogenization and substantialization of the national space will take the form of a number of predicative statements defining what the nation is. However, no matter how many essential predicates of the nation are listed, there is something missing. The true essence of the nation escapes predication. Hence, in the final instance the homogenization and substantialization of the nation can only be obtained in and through the discursive construction of 'enemies of the nation', which are simultaneously outside and inside the nation (as Orwell's science-fiction novel *Nineteen Eighty-Four* shows, reference to 'the traitor' and 'the enemy within' is indispensable for the unification of the nation). Enemies of the nation may be constructed through the expansion of a chain of equivalence that invokes the idea of a conspiracy against the nation in question. Consider, for instance, Germany's conception of the allied vanquishers in the First World War, who subsequently humiliated Germany in the Treaty of

Versailles. A more recent example would be Huntington's (1996) ideas about the 'clash of civilizations': after the collapse of the communist enemy, the western democratic states are threatened by the fundamentalist alliance between China, North Korea and the Islamic countries. However, enemies of the nation may also be constructed as legitimate adversaries. This is the case, for example, when other nations are considered to be a competitive threat within the global market economy. Thus, eastern Europe, Japan, the Asian Tigers and the USA are in different ways perceived as causes of the weak economic position of Europe, metaphorically described as 'Euro-sclerosis'. Whether an antagonistic or adversarial relation is predominant in the construction of national identity is an empirical question.

According to Žižek (1990b), enemies of the nation are generally accused of 'excessive enjoyment'. Hence, the nation 'exists only as long as its specific enjoyment continues to be materialized in certain social practices, and transmitted in national myths that structure these practices' (1990b: 53). As such, the nationalist myth is always concerned with the possession of the national Thing. The enemies of the nation want to steal our enjoyment and/or gain access to some secret, perverse enjoyment. By imputing to the Other the theft of enjoyment, we conceal the fact that we never had what was allegedly stolen from us (1990b: 54). Moreover, by fantasizing about, or even hating, the special enjoyment of the Other, we reveal our own enjoyment, or the hatred of our own enjoyment (1990b: 57). It gives us satisfaction to think about the inaccessible enjoyment of the Other, and by denouncing the Other's excessive enjoyment it becomes possible for us to externalize our own excess of enjoyment, which prevents us from being fully ourselves. Hence, the Americans hate the Japanese for their workaholism and ridicule their inability to relax and enjoy life. Why? Because the Americans hate their own obsessive relation towards work.

The homogenization and substantialization of the empty signifier of the nation, which is a defining feature of nationalist discourse, undoubtedly invokes a totalitarian closure, a violent reduction of difference to sameness. However, nationalism should not be discarded as a totalitarian aberration, since if the place of power was really empty, 'then those who exercise it are perceived as mere ordinary individuals, as forming a faction at the service of private interests and, by the same token, legitimacy collapses throughout society' (Lefort, 1986: 279). In other words, nationalism is not a totalitarian exception to the rules of democracy, since a certain amount of strategic essentialism is needed in order for power to be authorized. In fact, the substantial filling of the empty signifier of the nation is not only a necessary feature of democratic societies but also totally ineradicable. Nationalism represents the repressed other of democratic universalization, which is necessitated by liberal democracy, but which, nevertheless, threatens the very logic of the latter and prevents its ultimate closure. Hence, the democratic insistence on the formal and empty notions of 'the nation' and 'the people' can never be fully realized as there is always a particular, substantial content of 'the nation' and 'the people' that resists universalization (Sumic and Riha, 1994: 153–4).

The necessary and ineradicable substance of the nation may vary in size and function. Thus we might distinguish between, on the one hand, a *'thin'* and *'good'* nationalism that is based on right and constructs nations in terms of formal political communities (*Gesellschaft*) and, on the other hand, a *'thick'* and *'bad'* nationalism that is based on might and destroys nations – either from the inside (separatism) or from the outside (imperialism) – in the name of the superior virtues of an organic community (*Gemeinschaft*) (Balibar, 1991a: 47). Where the first type of nationalism ends and the other type begins is hard to say. Even if we accept that good and bad nationalism can only be defined relationally as polar extremes on a continuum from thin to thick nationalism, the interpretation of a particular nationalism as either good or bad still depends upon the vantage point taken. The actors within a nationalist movement might describe its actions as a struggle for independence founded on the right of the people to self-determination, while external spectators describe the same actions as an instance of separatism or imperialism (Sumic and Riha, 1994: 149). The fact is that there is no final truth since, rather than being either good or bad, the particular nationalisms are unclear, fragmented and highly ambiguous (1994: 151).

Whether good or bad, nationalism provides a surface of inscription of social demands, hopes and aspirations. Nationalism and the social antagonisms to which it gives rise can thus be seen as a discursive response to dislocation. Dislocations emanating from internal or external events that question, destabilize or dismantle the current regime foster an acute need for a hegemonic project able to rearticulate the floating signifiers within a new discursive order that promises the full realization of the dislocated identities within a unified communal space. The role of the hegemonic project of nationalism is thus to provide the empty signifier of the nation, which symbolizes an absent fullness, with a precise substantive content that people can identify with. With the transformation of the mythical space of nationalist discourse into a social imaginary there seems to be no limit to the demands, hopes and aspirations that can be inscribed on the ideological surface. This was very much the situation in the regional states in Russia following the collapse of Communism. Everything good was supposed to follow from the gaining of national independence. From the perspective of the nationalist movements the worst that could happen was for the regional states actually to gain national independence, since that would eventually reveal the limitations of the nationalist social imaginary. The painful recognition of such limitations is today forcing some of the independent states to re-establish some form of confederal unity with Russia.

Nationalist Revival in Eastern Europe and the Arab Countries

Drawing upon the analytical framework presented above we shall now briefly consider two discourse-theoretical studies of nationalism. Both are concerned with the current revival of nationalism. The first study focuses on *the surge of nationalism in eastern Europe,* while the other examines *the expansion of the discourse of Arab nationalism and its relation with the discourse of Islam.*

Political commentators in the West have been fascinated by the reinvention of democracy in the post-Communist countries in eastern Europe (Sumic and Riha, 1994: 147–8; Žižek, 1990b: 50). What engaged the western gaze was not the prospect of eastern Europe inheriting our model of liberal democracy, which is in fact showing increasing signs of decay and crisis. The real object of fascination was the naive gaze with which the historical actors in eastern Europe stared back at our western democracy. For their fascinated gaze carried the promise of a new beginning, to be obtained through the rediscovery of democracy in its pure and undistorted form. However, the fascinated gaze of western spectators faded as the idyllic picture of the prospects following the collapse of Communism was replaced by the reality of resurgent nationalism.

In Yugoslavia, as in the rest of the post-Communist states, the nationalist movements were strong. In the eyes of western spectators, EU officials and left-wing intellectuals alike, there seemed to be nothing but bad separatist nationalism (Sumic and Riha, 1994: 151). Slovenes, Serbs and Croats were all considered to be national chauvinists. This reductionist ideological fantasy on the part of western commentators has proved problematic, since the rejection of all demands for national autonomy as separatism, and the failure to recognize the sedimented, socioeconomic and political interests of the historical actors in ex-Yugoslavia, contributed to the development and hardening of the different national identities. The western spectator thus became a historical actor. The West can thus be said to be co-responsible for the failure to realize the possibility of creating a confederate state – a possibility that, in Sumic and Riha's (1994: 150) opinion, still existed in the early 1990s.

In the light of the swift recognition given by the EU to the national independence of first Slovenia and then Croatia, accusations that the West was dismissive of all demands for national autonomy is unsustainable. However, Sumic and Riha's description of the western obsession with the Balkan disease of excessive nationalism seems to be quite precise. What is particularly interesting is their point about the discursive function of this ideological fantasy: that it made it possible for the West to avoid confrontation with the 'really existing' nationalisms, which, as we have seen, constitute the repressed Other of modern democracy, the substantial leftover of the process of democratic universalization (1994: 153). This point brings us back to Žižek's claim that the hatred of the Other's enjoyment is the hatred of our own excess of enjoyment. The West scorns the excessive nationalism in the former Yugoslavia because the West hates to be reminded of the ineradicable substance of nationalism which is necessitated by, but also threatens, liberal democracy.

The West has aimed to avoid dealing with the 'really existing' nationalisms in Yugoslavia. Yet how do we explain the re-emergence of this nationalism? Let us start with the more general question of how to explain the current eruption of nationalism throughout eastern Europe. Žižek (1990b: 58) provides a strong argument against the standard explanation of eastern European nationalism as a reaction to the alleged Communist suppression of nationalist sentiments. Marx claimed that the workers have no fatherland, but the Communist regimes in eastern Europe produced a 'compulsive attachment to the national cause' (1990b: 58). Hence, what we get, once the Communist regimes are overthrown, is simply nationalism stripped of its Communist clothing (1990b: 59). In Žižek's alternative interpretation, the re-emergence of nationalism in eastern Europe is a response to societal dislocation. The collapse of the Communist regimes created a systemic vacuum, which was to be filled by the creation of a capitalist market economy. In this situation national chauvinism constituted 'a kind of "shock-absorber" against the sudden exposure to capitalist openness and imbalance' (1990b: 60). The capitalist market economy embodied the promise of freedom, wealth and prosperity, but the demand was for the establishment of a social body that would restrain capitalism's destructive potentials (1990b: 61). The democratic opposition had fought the Communist regimes in the name of 'civil society', conceived in terms of an organic national community (i.e. a *Gemeinschaft* rather than a *Gesellschaft*). Communism was depicted as the primary source of the destruction of civil society. When the struggle against Communism was won, it was unthinkable that the excess of Communism should be replaced with the excess of capitalism. Hence the desire for a capitalism-cum-*Gemeinschaft*, i.e. a capitalist market economy restrained by the corporate force of the national community.

At a more concrete level of analysis, discourse theory can help us to understand the events that led to the declaration of an independent Slovenian nation-state.[3] The condition of possibility for Slovenia to struggle for independence from the Yugoslavian federation was the shift in the Slovenian discourse on Slovenia and Yugoslavia from a logic of difference to a logic of equivalence. The Yugoslavian federal model was dominated by a logic of difference. There was a common political identity at the federal level, but a relational totality of cultural, religious, social and economic differences at the republican level. However, during the 1980s the Yugoslavian model was increasingly attacked by social and political forces in Slovenia. The new social movements saw the Communist regime as the main obstacle to the establishment of a plural democracy based on a democratic civil society and a *Rechtsstaat* (Mastnak, 1991). And the influential circle around the literary journal *Nova Revija* drew attention to 'the general retardation and decline of the Slovenian nation', caused by 'the ideologically rigid, economically ineffectual and politically illegitimate communist regime' as well as by the 'antagonistic map of the former Yugoslavia, which, almost since its inception in 1918, could be held together as a state only by a dictatorship' (Grafenauer, 1991: 1–2). Articulation of the demand for democracy with the national cause was a consequence of the rallying of the non-establishment groups, the new social movements and the *Nova Revija* circle around the Human Rights Committee. This process of unification, which was largely an effect of the allegedly unjust trial in 1988 of a number of progressive Slovenian journalists, resulted in a further nationalization of Slovenian politics, as the new social movements now began to view national independence as a necessary precondition for the development of a plural democracy. According to Mastnak (1989: 46–7), the nationalization of Slovenian politics was further spurred on by the Serbian press, which one-sidedly constructed the Slovenian opposition as nationalist separatism. The result was a breakdown of the differential totality at the republican level as an equivalential chain between plural democracy and Slovenian independence was constructed in direct confrontation with the Communist, Yugoslavian enemy, which was to an increasing extent identified with Serbia. A nationalist discourse was expanded, and when the reformists within the Slovenian Communist Party took over and began to address the national question, finally walking out of the extraordinary congress of the League of Communists in Yugoslavia in 1990, the movement towards national independence had reached the point of no return. In the years following the declaration of national independence in June 1991 the two chains of equivalence were further expanded as Slovenia was increasingly constructed as a part of Europe, while Serbia and indeed Croatia, were described as elements of the Balkan disorder. In the words of the Slovenian Minister of Foreign Affairs, Mr Thaler:

European public opinion perceives us through many stereotypes still linked to the past. They think the Balkan slaughterhouse starts here. In some ways we're to be blamed for such views, but we are ready to demonstrate the opposite. Slovenia is not Croatia. (Quoted from Manzin, 1994–95: 29)

Although nuances exist in the Slovenian representation of Croatia, the construction of an antagonistic relation between Europe and the Balkans, and its subsequent articulation with the chains of equivalence linking democracy with Slovenia and communism with Yugoslavia, have clearly helped to sustain the newly won independence of the Slovenian nation-state.

Whereas, in the extreme cases of Yugoslavia and Czechoslovakia the nationalist movements in the post-Communist eastern European countries led to the break-up of relatively well-established nation-states, Arab nationalism has led to the harnessing of the post-colonial nation-states and tended to inscribe these within a pan-Arabic Islamic community.

The politics of Arab nationalism is analysed by Al-Azmeh in his insightful book on *Islams and Modernities* (1993). According to Al-Azmeh (1993: 19), the general view of Orientalist literature is that the universalist historical forces of nationalism, democracy and socialism have failed to make headway against the plethora of pre-constituted, particular identities. The Arab countries are taken to consist of a multitude of religious, sectarian and ethnic groups, which as a whole are insensitive to the unifying force of the modern metanarratives. At best the latter are 'subjected to an almost immediate degeneration: nationalism to sheer religious xenophobia, democracy to corruption and manipulation, socialism to extortion and travesty' (1993: 19). In marked contrast to this Orientalist view, Al-Azmeh claims that the discourse of Islam has not been insulated from the modern discourse of nationalism and that the nation has functioned as a nodal point in recent Islamism.

Al-Azmeh draws our attention to the fact that modern political Islamism has a distinctive nationalist orientation. It aims to establish a political order that is defined in terms of a collection of singular acts and entities unified by their common reference to the empty signifier of Islam (1993: 24–6). The discourse of political Islamism can be seen as a hegemonic response to the dislocatory forces of social pulverization that hit large sections of the populations in the big cities in the Arab countries (1993: 32). It affirms its Islamic identity against 'its corruptions by otherness, such as non-Islamic people and religions, schisms, heresies and a manifold of enemies' (1993: 27). A highly voluntaristic notion of action leads to direct, unmediated and often terroristic actions, which contribute to the homogenization of the surface of society and help to maintain Islam as an empty signifier by introducing a pure violence that does not seek to realize any particular aims but is rather directed against the system of domination as such (1993: 30–1; cf. Laclau, 1994a). This discourse of modern political Islamism, which is a product of the last two and a half decades, has increasingly associated itself with Arab nationalist ideology. Indeed, it owes its current strength to the attempt to rearticulate and carry forward the Arab nationalist project that was defeated in the Arab–Israeli war in 1967 (Al-Azmeh, 1993: 28).

In order fully to understand the nature of the articulation between Arab nationalism and Islamism we have to go back to the notion of authenticity, which refers to a *sui generis* originality that ascribes a noble descent and privileged status for certain humans (1993: 41). When predicated on historical collectivities, be they Arab, Muslim or other, the notion of authenticity generates a discourse of revivalism. In the case of Arab and Islamic revivalism, history is divided into alternating periods of decadence and health. The present corruption of Arab and Muslim authenticity prescribes a return to the pristine beginnings described in the teachings of the Koran and the example of the prophet Muhammad (1993: 42). Revivalism was initially Islamist, but it received its most thorough grounding in the secular discourse of Arab nationalism (1993: 42–3). However, contemporary Islam has taken on board most of the organismic and vitalist elements in Arab nationalism, which conceived the nation as an organic body infused with a vital force that permeates its individual organs. In so doing, it has resurrected the romanticism of Afghani (1839–97), who saw religion rather than ethnicity as the bond of nations, and thus has paved the way for a pan-Arabic Islamism (1993: 43–4, 54).

According to Al-Azmeh (1993: 60–1), Islamism and Arab nationalism do not relate as pre-existing *sui generis* identities. They are instead articulated by a hegemonic practice that establishes a relation between them such that their identity is modified as a result of that practice. As such, the articulation of Islamism and Arab nationalism invokes the Arabization of the former and the sacralization of the latter (1993: 61). Emphasis on the articulation of the religious discourse of Islamism and the secular discourse of Arab nationalism serves to demonstrate that the link between the two discourses is established neither in terms of a common essence, an accidental concordance, nor as the parasitic use of one by the other (1993: 62). In short, there is no intrinsic relation between the two discourses, but rather a relation of contiguity (metonymic or paradigmatic) (1993: 67–8). Nevertheless, a sort of hierarchy between the two discourses can be identified, as Arab nationalist ideology regards 'Islam as but one moment of Arab glory, albeit an important one' (1993: 43). Thus, in the vocabulary of Laclau and Mouffe, Arab nationalism has the status of a limitless social imaginary, while Islam has that of a somewhat limited myth. However, the hierarchical relation between Islamism and Arab nationalism does not imply the absorption, or consummation, of the former by the latter. The hierarchy between the two discourses is not one of integration, but rather one of mutual support. The association of the elitist discourse of Arab nationalism with the populist discourse of Islam helps to expand the social basis and civic orientation of Arab nationalism. Conversely, the association of the civic discourse of Islamism with the political discourse of Arab nationalism tends to increase the political role of Islam (1993: 67).

At the level of rhetoric, the occasional power of mutual convertibility has been ensured by the word *umma*, which means both nation and Islamic community. Nationalism and religious guidance are the means to restore the moment of primitive innocence defined by the *umma* (1993: 70). However, the association between Islam and Arab nationalism is not secured by a single equivocal word alone; it is also a result of the discursive construction of a common enemy, the West. The discursive operation that sanctions this construction involves a double displacement, according to which the crusades are conceived as an early manifestation of colonialism, and imperialism is conceived in terms of a cultural invasion (1993: 70–2). This displacement assures the nationalist and the Islamic reformer alike that my enemy is your enemy and your enemy is mine.

Nationalism and Racism

Leaving the analysis of nationalist discourse behind us, we shall move on to consider the transition from nationalism to racism. The term 'nation' is an empty signifier symbolizing an absent fullness, i.e. a cultural and political community that is imagined precisely because it is not fully realized. The aim of a nationalistic movement is to hegemonize the content of the empty signifier of 'the nation' by attaching it to a transcendental signified able once and for all to arrest the play of meaning. As such, nationalistic movements will tend to define the nation in terms of *patria*. *Patria* involves a transcendental reference to a necessary relation between blood and soil: 'France for the French!' We are here in the area of what Derrida calls *ontopology*, which can be defined as an 'axiomatics linking indissociably the ontological value of present-being [on] to its situation, to the stable and presentable determination of a locality, the topos of territory, native soil, city, body in general' (Derrida, 1994: 82). The onto-pological essentialization of the relation between being and place is a constitutive feature of nationalism. It hinges, however, on the essentialization of a being in terms of a definition of a privileged, distinctive and unified *ethnos* that inhabits the national territory. The auto-referential interpellation of a superior race with a privileged link to the national soil is conditional upon a hetero-referential inter-pellation of other inferior races, which are either inside or outside the nation. The auto-referential and the hetero-referential interpellations of individuals as belonging to a certain race (defined either in bio-logical or cultural terms) together constitute the defining gesture of racism, which should not be confused with other phenomena of 'xeno-phobia' or 'intolerance' seen in the past (Balibar, 1991a: 49, 1991b: 6). Racism is a historical phenomenon that emerges within the discourse of nationalism. That is to say, racism has nothing to do with the exist-ence of objective biological or cultural races and should not be seen as an invariant trait of human nature. Rather, racism is a discursive construction that develops within the field of nationalism (Balibar, 1991a: 37–8).

Nationalism is the determining condition of the production of racism, and although racism is not always equally manifest in all nationalisms, it is nonetheless a necessary element in their constitution (1991a: 48). Racism thus contributes to the constitution of nationalist discourse as it produces the fictive *ethnos* which interpellates concrete individuals as members of a nation. This reveals the relation between nationalism and racism as one of mutual conditioning. Nationalist and racist discourses are intrinsically linked, but the relation between nationalism and racism is not a matter of perversion, formal similarity or causation (mechanical or spiritual). Racism is '*a supplement of nationalism*, or more precisely *a supplement internal to nationalism*, always in excess of it, but always indispensable to its constitution and yet always insufficient to achieve its project' (1991a: 54).

Racism produces the fictive *ethnos* around which nationalist discourse is organized. The fictive *ethnos* is produced by nationalist movements by means of excluding a constitutive outside that is constructed through the rearticulation of differential moments as parts of a chain of equivalence. This chain of equivalence may construct different ethnic groups as belonging to an undifferentiated mass of people who are conceived as inferior due to their biological race. However, racism may also operate within a system of differences by means of associating certain separate ethnic identities with certain essential cultural traits that are strictly incompatible with the norms and values of the predominant *ethnos*. Both biological and cultural racism involve the stigmatization of otherness. This latter inscribes itself in social practices of elimination, violence, intolerance, humiliation, discrimination etc., as well as in fantasmatic representations that invoke the need to purify the social body, to preserve its identity, to protect it from all forms of mixing, interbreeding and invasion, etc. (Balibar, 1991b: 17–8). The fantasmatic representations of racism might be spontaneously developed as a part of racist practices, but they might also be the result of the carefully developed theoretical doctrines that organize these. The strength of such doctrines is that they provide the 'interpretative keys not only to what individuals are *experiencing* but also to what they *are* in the social world' (1991b: 19). In other words, the strength of racist doctrines lies in their mythical function of providing a reading principle that allows people to make sense of a divided and chaotic world and to assess their own role in its re-organization. A myth refers to an absent fullness, but if this universal reference to an absent fullness continues to dominate over the particular content of the hegemonic attempts to fill the empty place of the universal, the myth is transformed into a social imaginary that provides the ultimate horizon of meaning and action. In that case the reading principle provided by racism is no longer merely one among many possible reading principles, but the only true reading principle, able to reveal the secret of the social order and the enemies that have conspired to deprive it of its fullness.

Racism in South Africa and Britain

There is no single racism, but many racisms. We shall here look at two different forms of racism: first, *the discourse of state racism typified by the South African apartheid system,* which was initially rooted in a biological conception of a hierarchy between superior and inferior races; and second, *the racist discourse within the British nation-state*, which, like the later apartheid discourse, has tended to underline the insurmountability of cultural differences rather than the biological superiority of certain groups or peoples in relation to others (1991b: 21). Despite the differences between these two different forms of racism, the studies of Norval and Smith reveal a common feature of the racist discourses in South Africa and Britain, both of which seem to be organized around a complex game between 'the inside' and 'the outside'. Exactly how this game is played out we shall see by considering first Norval's *Deconstructing Apartheid Discourse* (1996), and then Smith's *New Right Discourse on Race and Sexuality* (1994a), books that demonstrate well the fruitfulness of the discourse theory of Laclau and Mouffe.

The aim of Norval's study is to account for the emergence, operation and crisis of the South African apartheid discourse (Norval, 1996: 2). Apartheid is initially defined as a hegemonic discourse that constructs its political frontiers on the basis of race and ethnicity. The apartheid discourse emerged in response to a series of dislocations in the 1930s and 1940s. Industrialization, proletarization and urbanization spurred the growth of white and black trade unions, but also generated crucial problems arising from the poor conditions of the white workers and the mixing of races, which led to interbreeding and loss of moral values (1996: 114, 18–24). What was at stake, it was argued, was no less than the identity of the white race. Association of race and nation made it possible to perceive the threat to the white race as a source of denationalization. The immediate solution to 'the poor whites problem' and 'the native question' was segregationism, which was intended to bring the workers, women and the youth back to the national fold. However, the advocates of segregationism failed on two counts. First, their control over the native Africans was so liberal that the National Party was able to argue that segregation did not solve the problems (1996: 28–35). Second, their attempt to establish a unity between the Afrikaans-speaking and English-speaking whites ignored the grievances of the large Afrikaans-speaking underclass and its mobilization along ethnic lines; this made it possible for the National Party to argue that a unity between equals was out of the question (1996: 35–9). As a result the National Party was able to advance a hegemonic apartheid discourse that was not so much based on an antagonism between whites and blacks as on an antagonism between Afrikaners and non-Afrikaners. Thus the racism of the apartheid discourse was not simply of a biological kind, as the native Africans were only one among the many groups to be excluded from the domain of acceptability (1996: 44). To the excluded natives were added the Coloureds, the Indians and the Jews, as well as the communist and English-imperialist dangers, and it was through this exteriorization of a series of 'others' that Afrikanerdom gained its identity (1996: 54).

Norval's account of the operation of the apartheid discourse takes issue with the traditional idea of a sharp distinction between a period of negative, race-based apartheid (1948–53) and a period of positive, ethnicity-based apartheid (1958–61) (1996: 104–5). The problem with this reading of the historical development is that it ignores the fact that the apartheid discourse was already, at the beginning of the 1950s, marked by an ambiguous conception of apartheid as based either on race or on ethnicity. Thus, the goal of apartheid was to protect the white population while encouraging the development of separate ethnic groups (1996: 117–18). In Norval's reading there was no clear break between apartheid as 'white supremacy' and apartheid as 'separate development', but rather a gradual transformation of the apartheid myth into a social imaginary (1996: 9). The apartheid myth revolved around the impossible object of the *volkseie*, which defined the authentic core of Afrikanerdom: 'what is ours and ours alone'. The apartheid myth offered a reading principle for the dislocations experienced by the white Afrikaner population, and as such the early apartheid discourse had a limited and particularistic character. However, the metaphorization of the literal content of the myth was achieved by 'the movement in which the *volkseie* increasingly came to be regarded as a *universal* ordering principle' (1996: 143). That is, the Afrikaner nationalist movement saw it as its duty to extend the conception of *volkseie* to other groupings. Thus, *volk* (people) no longer referred exclusively to the white Afrikaners and the English-speaking whites. Every ethnic group constituted a *volk*, and the Zulu, Sotho, Venda and Xohsa 'national units' also had the right to affirm their differential position within the national community. This paved the way for the establishment of self-governing 'Bantu-homelands' (1996: 171). The formation of a multi-racial state involved the creation of a complex hierarchy wherein the rights and degree of freedom of each *volk* depended on the stage of its development (1996: 149). Accordingly, 'while the discourse privileged the production of "ethnic difference", it, nevertheless, in one and the same moment, excluded all Africans, as a whole, from the polity' (1996: 171). Hence, while the logic of difference had come to the fore it had not eliminated the logic of exclusion. Blacks could not vote and were subjected to all kinds of discriminating regulations, although not always overtly racist ones.

The period from 1970 to 1985 was characterized by the simultaneous operation of repression and reform (1996: 177). We shall here focus on the transformist strategies of co-optation. Segregationism had developed under the Verwoerd regime into the celebration of separate developments, and the Vorster government subsequently opted for a multi-nationalist state. (1996: 186). However, the status of the Coloureds and the Indians as an appendix to the white community made it impossible to establish a separate nationhood for these groups (1996: 189). In a situation where the black resistance movement was becoming stronger, and the South African neighbour states were decolonialized, a solution to this difficulty was badly needed. The solution could be none other than the introduction of a limited form of power-sharing whereby the Coloureds and Indians were co-opted into the white political community (1996: 197–9). The Conservative Party split from the National Party in protest against these transformist strategies. The rest of the National Party was confused about the acceptability of sharing political power with the Coloureds and Indians. Nevertheless, the tri-cameral parliament was finally created in 1984 (1996: 206–16). The political co-optation of the Coloureds and Indians was paralleled by the economic co-optation of the urban blacks, who were to be integrated into the discourse of free enterprise. However, when, contrary to expectations, the formation of black trade unions led to an intensification of the political struggles, and when the Coloureds and Indians formed a political alliance with the blacks and the progressive white democrats, the failure of the transformist strategies became evident (1996: 218, 231). The transformist strategies had undermined the logic of exclusion, and the formation in 1983 of the United Democratic Front, which mobilized people on a non-racial basis, undercut the logic of difference. In this situation nothing could prevent the conjunctural crisis from developing into an organic crisis. A nation-wide state of emergency was declared in 1986. However, as we know, the mounting resistance, not only from the black organizations, the mass democratic movements and the white anti-apartheid organizations, but also from the international community, finally caused the South African apartheid regime to fall.

According to Norval, 'apartheid discourse was premised upon the construction of closed, organic identities, still evident today, in varying degrees, in the discourse of the far right, Inkatha and the new NP [National Party: JT]' (1996: 302). The post-apartheid regime is founded upon the rejection of apartheid, and thus on the rejection of the identitary logic that celebrates the closure of essential identity. Nevertheless, the non-racist discourse will need to establish some kind of closure, although it is important that it continues to emphasize the non-substantiality of 'the people' and 'the nation' in order to be able to deal with the political enemies of the post-apartheid regime in terms of adversaries.[4] Only in that way can the democratic future of South Africa be ensured.

Whereas the South African apartheid system entered into crisis during the 1970s and 1980s, the racist discourse in Britain was strengthened in the same period in response to the social, political and economic crisis. Smith has scrutinized the racism and homophobia of Thatcherism and the New Right in a recent study that, *inter alia*, deals extensively with Enoch Powell's contribution to the formation of an anti-black-immigration movement (Smith, 1994a). Her basic contention is that the standard accounts of Thatcherism have focused almost exclusively on the economic policies, and generally treated racism as if it were only a minor issue within the New Right discourse (1994a: 1–5). Her point is not that racism was the essence of Thatcherism and the New Right discourse, but rather that it constituted a central strategic element in the attempt to articulate a new hegemonic project. Political scientists like Kavanagh (1987) and Gamble (1988), for their part, recognize the importance of the racist element, but tend to reduce it to a single issue (the question of immigration control) and thus fail to see that racism constitutes a nodal point in the discourse of the New Right. That is to say, not only is racism an important aspect of many different policies (urban, educational, etc.); it also plays an important role in the symbolization of the lost communal space of the nation, which is under continuous threat from the post-colonialist enemy within.[5] Thus, according to Smith, 'the relation between the white defenders of the true British nation and the anti-British black "invader" became a nodal point: racial antagonism operated as the key which made the disintegration of the nation – and the inevitability of national recovery – intelligible' (Smith, 1994a: 8).

The racist myth of the New Right was unleashed by the Conservative MP Enoch Powell in a series of speeches at the end of the 1960s. Powellism provided a popular alternative to the consensus approach of both the Conservative Party and the Labour Party, and thus laid the groundwork for legitimation of the authoritarian populism of the Thatcherite project (1994a: 6). Powell's anti-black-immigrants movement problematized the business-as-usual approach to crisis, and thus paved the way for a new hegemonic project. In his 'Rivers of blood' speech in 1968 Powell spoke in the name of the people against the political consensus of the two dominant parties (1994a: 154–62). Powell cited a letter from an old white lady trapped in her home in the midst of racial invasion. According to Powell, it was bad enough that the system of control governing the borders of the white British 'Home' could not withstand the pressure from the post-colonial, black intruders, but things got even worse as the old lady was finally called a racist by a young female government official who represented the pro-tolerance approach of the official system in general and the Labour Party in particular.

Powellism not only contributed to the dismantling of the post-war political settlement; it also promised a revitalization of the white British nation in the face of the black threat. People became supporters of this hegemonic project not because the racist claims were considered to be true and consistent, but rather because the racist myth offered a principle of order and intelligibility in a situation of profound dislocation (1994a: 38–9). In Smith's words, the hegemonic project of today's New Right represents an example of 'hegemony-as-normalization' as opposed to a 'hegemony-of-domination' (1994a: 40).

Smith analyses a series of discursive operations within the racist myth of Thatcherism and the New Right. I shall here briefly summarize her analysis of the 'logic of supplementarity' and the 'proliferation of differences'. The first analysis relates to the racist discourse of Powell (1994a: 70–84). Powell portrays the black immigrant as, at once, a foreign invader and an insidious enemy within. The black immigrants live in unintegrated enclaves which are merely detachments of communities in the West Indies, India or Pakistan, while at the same time they are said to have penetrated deep into educational curricula and local government policies. This paradoxical doubleness can be understood in terms of Derrida's notion of supplementarity. Essentialist and metaphysical discourse tends to make a distinction between the privileged, self-identical essence and its harmless, non-constitutive supplement, which can be added or subtracted without affecting the essential identity. However, a deconstructive reading of the essentialist and metaphysical discourse tends to reveal the subversive character of this external supplement, which positions itself as a necessary completion of the inside, and in this manner shows that the inside has always remained incomplete on its own (1994a: 74). Now, the speeches of Powell seem to be structured in accordance with this logic of supplementarity. The black immigrants are depicted as a pure addition, members of foreign population groups that can be repatriated back to their home countries without damage being caused to the white British nation. Yet the blacks are also portrayed as a dangerous supplement, as an enemy within which must be countered by a white British solidarity and a patriotic commitment to rebuilding the nation (1994a: 75).

Moving from the Powellite discourse of the 1970s to the Conservative discourse of Thatcher in the later 1980s it is interesting to see

208

that, while the former was strictly exclusionary, the latter tends to establish a complex game between inclusion and exclusion. That is, 'the new racism defines the blackness which it wants to exclude not as that which is not-white and therefore inferior, but as that which is inherently anti-British' (1994a: 95). The blacks should not be excluded because of their skin colour. They should be excluded only in so far as their behaviour, values and norms constitute a threat to the British nation. This cultural racism opens into a disciplinary differentiation of blacknesses, which takes the form of a counterpositioning of assimilatory blacks who are included in the British nation to non-assimilatory blacks who are to be excluded. This counter-positioning is embodied in discursive practices, where the prohibition of racial discrimination goes hand in hand with strict immigration controls (1994a: 99). The inherent differentiation of otherness carries important political consequences, as resistance to the new racism cannot be waged simply in the name of the subaltern black population. Resistance will have to establish a chain of equivalence with other excluded minorities as a first step in challenging the existing hegemony and forging a new one.

11
The Politics of Mass Media

It is a truism that mass media have a decisive political, social and cultural importance. Mass media have lost and won wars (Vietnam and the Gulf), removed and elected political leaders (Nixon and Berlusconi), and generally contributed to the manufacturing of consent. Mass media are also engaged in the production of the fabric of everyday life as they organize our leisure time, shape our social behaviour and provide the material out of which our very identities are constructed in terms of class, race, nationality, sexuality, and distinctions between 'us' and 'them'. Last but not least, mass media produce, store and reinvoke the symbols, myths and values that constitute what we consider to be our 'common culture' (Kellner, 1995: 1). The globalization of mass media tends to detach the symbols, myths and values that constitute the backbone of ethnic cultures from their social and/or territorial 'origin' and boundedness. This would appear to counteract the strong tendency towards a world-wide homogenization of popular culture, as the result of this process is a kind of globalized heterogeneity.

Mass media comprise television, radio, film, music, print media, and computers that privilege either sound or sight, or any mix of the two. Mass media culture is an *industrial culture*, and the predominant regime of accumulation is that of capitalist mass production (Fordism), although new forms of flexible specialization (post-Fordism) are gaining ground. Mass media culture is also a *high-tech culture* that exploits the technological innovations in the field of computers and audio-visual equipment. Above all, however, mass media culture is a *site* where battles over identity, distribution and societal control are fought out (1995: 35). Mass media help to establish and maintain the hegemony of specific political groups by producing and promulgating social myths and imaginaries, but they also provide the means and material for resistance and counter-hegemonic struggles. In sum, mass media culture tends to provide a new articulation of capitalism, media and technology within what some call an 'information society'. However, the information society is not an established fact, but a terrain that is sustained and divided by social antagonisms and constantly reshaped by hegemonic struggles.

The study of mass media, and of their political, social and cultural effects, was previously an integral part of *sociological communications studies*. Today the study of mass media is most often a part of what is commonly known as *cultural studies*. Kellner (1995: 27–8, 43–9, 94–101, 112–17) portrays cultural studies as inherently transdisciplinary work that is informed by postmodern and post-structuralist metatheories, and that is supposed to be critical, multiculturalist and multiperspectival. Cultural studies utilize the concept of articulation in order to define how cultural artifacts are overdetermined by political ideologies, and by social and political identities in terms of class, race, nationality and gender, and how these ideologies and identities are related in and through their cultural representations (1995: 25). In order to avoid conceiving the relation between cultural artifacts and the social and political phenomena that overflow them in terms of the inscription of a plurality of pre-constituted contents on a neutral surface of cultural forms, we might benefit from Laclau and Mouffe's definition of articulation, which emphasizes the mutual modification of the elements articulated. Articulation is here defined as a practice that establishes a mutually constitutive relationship between social, political and cultural elements (Laclau and Mouffe, 1985: 105).

The works of the *Frankfurt School* critical theorists might inspire some engaged in cultural studies to maintain a critical focus on the ideological effects of the products of the culture industries, and to further develop qualitative methods of analysis. However, we must reject the Frankfurt School's distinction between an ideological low culture and a potentially emancipatory high culture, together with its class reductionism and pessimistic view regarding the possibility of political upheavals and societal change (Laclau, 1990a: 51–2). In the light of these criticisms of the Frankfurt School the importance of *British cultural studies* can be clearly envisaged. Not only did the scholars attached to the Birmingham Centre for Contemporary Cultural Studies reject the notion of mass culture for being elitist and contemptuous of the masses; they also invoked Gramsci to produce critical studies of the cultural mediation of social antagonisms. The emphasis on the antagonistic relation between political groups and

211

social classes is important as it highlights the fact that we are not merely dealing with the effect of mass media culture on a plurality of differential identities. We are interested first and foremost in the asymmetrical effects of mass media on the social and political forces constituted in and through the expansion of chains of equivalence (Kellner, 1995: 31–2). In other words, we are primarily concerned with relations of power and resistance and how they are shaped in and through mass media. The emphasis on power and resistance might in turn help us to bridge the gap between the text-centred analysis of the cultural studies approach and the sociological focus on the production, distribution and consumption of mass media texts that is found within traditional communication studies (1995: 30, 41–3). For the forms of power and resistance engendered by mass media are the outcome of what takes place both inside and outside the mass media message. Power and resistance are both conditional on the articulation of meaningful sequences and the dissemination of these within society.

In the remaining part of this chapter I shall review some of the key arguments to be found in the *discourse-theoretical studies of mass media,* as advanced by writers such as Fairclough (1995), van Dijk (1985), Derrida (1988a) and Poster (1990). In the course of the presentation I shall demonstrate the relevance of Laclau and Mouffe's concepts of discourse, hegemony and social antagonism. I first seek to establish the exact nature of the object of analysis, and then critically assess the basic model of communication advanced by traditional communications studies. I proceed to investigate the effect of electronically wrapped language on the conception of the self, before concluding with a brief discussion of the undecidability of the so-called information society with regard to its totalitarian and/or emancipatory effects.

Mass Media and Discourse

I shall start by defining the object of analysis of the discourse-theoretical studies carried out in the field of cultural studies. There appear to be three different ways of relating mass media with the notion of discourse. One possibility for pairing 'mass media' and 'discourse' would involve focusing on the political and/or theoretical *discourse about mass media* and their overall function in society. How do various actors perceive the role of mass media in relation to the production and reproduction of the social order? Although this is undoubtedly an important research question, the macro-sociological focus on the discourse concerning the societal role of mass media is far too narrow and by no means exhausts the potential of the discourse-theoretical approach.

A second possibility for linking up mass media with discourse is to focus on the *discourse of mass media*. What are the form and content of the discourse produced by various kinds of mass media? This important question, which pays specific attention to the mass media message, has been answered by various sorts of content analysis; these aim to provide an objective, replicable and quantitative description of mass media texts (see Holsti, 1969; and Krippendorff, 1980). Content analysis here includes socio-linguistic analyses of the socially conditioned use of language, ethno-methodological analyses of the formulations employed by interviewers, semiotic analysis of ideological codes, and critical linguistic analysis of the ideological content of vocabulary choices (Fairclough, 1995). The limitation of these forms of analysis is, besides their narrow focus on the mass media message, that they fail to see that mass media texts are not only socially shaped but also socially constitutive. In other words, such analysis fails to assess the effects of mass media texts on the relations of power and resistance.

The third possibility is to focus on *mass media as discourse*. This is the approach of the Birmingham school (Hall, 1980: 128–38), Fairclough (1995: 16, 57–68) and van Dijk (1985: 5), who maintain that the study of mass media should include micro-, meso- and macro-levels of analysis. At the *micro-level,* mass media studies are concerned with the analysis of the syntax, semantics, lexical style and rhetorical devices of the text as well as its presentation and organization. The notion of text is here broadly defined as the various forms of spoken, written or audio-visual signs that are articulated in the signifying chains of the different units of production, i.e. television programmes, newspaper advertisements, pop songs, etc. At the *meso-level* the focus is on the institutional forms of production, distribution and consumption of mass media messages. Analysis of the intertextuality of the text plays a key role at this level of analysis as the 'rules' of production, distribution and consumption might give rise to a particular blend of different textual genres. Finally, at the *macro-level* the analysis concentrates on the political regulations of mass media and the economic forms of ownership and control.

What is important is that the analysis at all three levels is concerned with discursive terrains, i.e. socio-political terrains composed of discursively constructed meanings, rules, norms, procedures, values, knowledge forms, etc. That is to say, the signifying chains articulated in the text are shaped by the rules of formation, which are defined by the hegemonic forms of discourse. The institutional forms of production, distribution and consumption are guided by professional norms, formal and informal rules of broadcasting, and discursively constructed household routines. Finally, the politics and economics of mass media are framed by pre-constituted assumptions, political ideologies, institutionalized economic rationalities, etc. Together these discourses add up to produce a discursive formation of mass media, which is not passively expressing or reflecting underlying phenomena in culture and society, but actively produces, reproduces and transforms such phenomena (van Dijk, 1985: 5). Needless to say, such a broad definition of discourse, which cuts across any distinction between mental and material, linguistic and non-linguistic, and semantic and pragmatic, is supported by Laclau and Mouffe's definition of discourse as a relational 'totality' of signifying sequences, in and through which the identity of subjects, objects and social actions are shaped and reshaped.

One of Laclau's central assertions is that 'the constitution of a social identity is an act of power and that identity as such *is* power' (Laclau, 1990a: 33). This assertion is reflected in the works of Hall et al., Fairclough and van Dijk, who all emphasize importance of analysing the relations of power and resistance (re-)produced within the discursive formation of mass media. It is this concern with the relations of power and resistance that takes us from the *archaeological* study of the form and content of mass media messages, which is found in the bulk of content analysis, to the *genealogical* study of the hegemonic mass media configurations, which is undertaken by different sorts of discourse theorists.

The *Birmingham school* broke with the assumption that the mass media message was a transparent medium for the dissemination of pre-constituted meanings (Connell and Mills, 1985: 35). Meanings are, rather, constructed by socially determined practices of signification inherent to mass media (Hall, 1977: 27-9). This insight was linked to the study of ideology through the assertion that mass media were important ideological state apparatuses. However, although the Birmingham school did a valuable job in analysing the discursive construction of popular ideologies, it nevertheless failed to provide a systematic discourse analysis (van Dijk, 1985: 3-4). Another problem, arguably, was its tendency to focus on the way groups with pre-constituted identities resist or conform to ideological pressures, rather than on the way cultural experiences constitute the identity of different groups (Poster, 1990: 16).

Fairclough and van Dijk both confront and resolve the first problem, the absence of a systematic analysis of discourse. *Fairclough* (1995: 57-62) analyses three aspects of what he defines as discursive communicative events: (1) the mass media text itself; (2) the discourse practice, including the institutional forms of production and consumption that produce a particular kind of intertextuality; and (3) the socio-cultural practices organizing the field of mass media as a whole. These three aspects largely correspond to the micro-, meso- and macro-levels of analysis discussed above. Fairclough's primary focus is on what he calls the orders of discourse (1995: 55–7). These provide the discursive background for the construction and chaining of communicative events produced by mass media. The analysis of orders of discourse focuses on the configurations of discourses and genres that inform the production of communicative events. Discourses here refer to power–knowledge complexes, i.e. different forms of scientific, professional and lay knowledge. Genres refer to the use of language – including styles, modes and voices – that corresponds to some particular social practice (1995: 56). Fairclough uses the term 'discourse types' to describe the relatively unitary and stable configurations of discourses and genres within the order of discourse, and he sees Gramsci's concept of hegemony as a helpful tool for understanding how specific discourse types are constructed out of the multiplicity of cultural forms pervading the field of mass media (1995: 66–7). The hegemonic discourse type in many mass media, and especially within broadcasting, tends to privilege entertainment over information and to shift the emphasis from a formal public language to a private conversational language. According to Fairclough (1995: 12–13), the ideological function of this particular discourse type is to divert attention away from public political issues and to naturalize the terms in which reality is presented.

Whereas Fairclough has been concerned with analysing the discursive context for the construction of communicative events in, for example, the field of news production, van Dijk (1985) provides the tools for a systematic analysis of the organization of news in the daily press. His focus is on what he calls 'schematic superstructures' and how these organize 'thematic macrostructures' (1995: 69). The thematic macrostructure of a news discourse is defined as the overall organization of the global 'topics' that a news item is about, e.g. an IRA bombing is seen as an act of 'terrorism'. This thematic macrostructure is structured by a certain schematic superstructure, which is defined by the ensemble of norms, rules and categories that determine the possible orderings and the hierarchical organization of the textual units in news discourse, e.g. terrorism is related to important questions about 'social order' and 'national security'. The news schema is shaped by the social and professional routines of reporters and news editors, but it serves as the cognitive map for the processing of news discourse by both the news producers and the news consumers (1995: 70).

The organization of the themes of the news discourse by a pre-established, conventional news schema is likely to produce specific ideological effects, for example by downplaying the socioeconomic background of social riots, etc. Thus, it seems that the discourse-theoretical studies of mass media all link up with the notion of ideology. Ideology is often seen as involving distortion or falsehood. Fairclough (1995: 14–15) recognizes the problems associated with this conception of ideology, and offers an alternative definition: the textual presence of pre-constituted presuppositions in the service of power. He recognizes, first, that the ideological naturalization of meaning in and through the positing of taken-for-granted assumptions helps to reproduce the relations of power, and second, that ideological naturalizations are independent of judgements of truth and falsity. However, Fairclough's conception of ideology lacks a precise understanding of the process of naturalization. Ideology cannot be reduced to a question of an appeal to sedimented meanings, and it is not something that is present in some texts and not in others, and that in the last instance can be reduced to a mechanism of power. In other words, ideology is not an empirical phenomenon, but an ontological dimension.

As indicated in chapter 5, Laclau offers a way of understanding the ontological dimension of ideology. If discourse is co-extensive with the social, it is not possible to criticize ideology from an extra-discursive point of truth, reality, etc. However, according to Laclau (1996a: 200–9), this does not mean that ideological critique is impossible, but rather that we cannot criticize ideology as such since all critique of ideology is intra-ideological. This assertion of the omnipresence of ideology might lead to the abandoning of the notions of distortion and false consciousness, and to a conception of society as an objective field of incommensurable ideological discourses. Yet, it might lead instead to the reconceptualizing of ideology as a constitutive distortion. The latter option, which is the one chosen by Laclau, conceives ideology not as the distortion of reality but as a construction of reality through distortion. The kind of distortion we are discussing is not the distortion of a pre-constituted identity, but rather a discursive operation that constructs a constitutive closure of social and political identities. Distortion involves concealment of the dislocation and undecidability of what ultimately presents itself as a closed identity. The act of concealment projects onto that identity the closure it lacks. Ideology can thus be seen as the positing of meanings as presupposed, i.e. as unitary, decidable and natural (as, for example, when neo-liberal politicians claim that human beings are self-interested, rational individuals, or when communitarian thinkers claim that human beings are guided by the common good). By the same token, we might conclude that deconstruction will have a destabilizing effect on ideology as it seeks to undermine and unravel all kinds of metaphysical closure. Deconstruction thus represents an important weapon in the political effort to resist the ideological effects of mass media texts.

Beyond the Traditional Mass Communication Model

The question concerning the construction of subjectivity through the discursive forms of mass media will be dealt with from two different angles: first, through a critique of the traditional model of mass communication, and second, through an assessment of the impact of electronically wrapped language on the conception of the self and its relation to the world.

Whereas the Birmingham school analysed communication processes in terms of a complex structure articulating interrelated but distinctive moments of production, distribution, consumption and reproduction (Hall, 1980), the traditional sociological *communication model* pictures the communication process in terms of a linear relation where an intentional *sender* (S) encodes a *message* (M) that is transmitted through a certain channel and finally reaches the *receiver* (R), who decodes the message and acts upon it (Mcquail, 1975: 14–18). The basic S–M–R model is sometimes further elaborated by the introduction of a feedback loop from receiver to sender, a description of the environment in which the communication process takes place, and an account of the relative closure, or openness, of the relation of communication (1975: 21–7). According to Mcquail (1975: 31), it is not possible to rely on a single model of communication, due to empirical variations in the social situation in which communication occurs (1975: 31). However, the bottom line is that within this sociological perspective communication is conceived as merely a question of message exchange.

The basic model of message exchange can be adapted to cover the special case of *mass* communication. What is particular about mass communication is its collective character, the reliance on advanced and expensive technical means of communication, the distantiation of senders and receivers in time and space, and the lack of truly interactive communication (Fairclough, 1995: 36–42; Mcquail, 1975: 163–7). Its most significant feature, however, is the importance of the mass media organizations, and the people who work in them. These people seem to occupy an intermediary position between the senders and the receivers as they handle and shape mass media messages (Mcquail, 1975: 168–72). Journalists, film producers, publishers, editors, and the like are crucial (co-) producers of mass media texts. They are the 'real communicators', as opposed to the 'would-be communicators' outside the mass media organizations. In this connection, one might also draw attention to the army of professional PR workers, who are employed by governments, political parties, interest organizations, etc., and whose work it is to establish and cultivate the link between the real and the would-be communicators. This layer of PR workers plays an increasingly important role as agenda setters and opinion leaders.

In the last instance, mass communication, like all other forms of communication, is about the channelling of streams of information and messages in time and space (1975: 19). It is therefore no surprise that the free flow of information and messages is often depicted as the essential telos of the process of mass communication. Nevertheless, accidental obstacles that produce *noise* and *distortion* frequently occur, and there exist numerous *limitations* on senders' and receivers' access to mass media. The would-be communicators are often manipulated by the real communicators, who generally act as gate-keepers, and the mass audience often misinterprets the mass media message and tends to suffer from overload.

The linear model of message sending has stimulated analyses of communication as an *influence process*. Mcquail (1975: 138–43) defines influence as an interest-driven communication between a sender and a receiver which may have a predictable effect on the latter in terms of securing his or her compliance with, or internalization of, the content of the message. The agency concept of power traces the source of power and influence to the properties of the sender, who may be capable of rewarding and/or punishing the receiver, of providing a normatively regulated submission, of establishing trust and credence, or of providing a point of identification (1975: 145–7). There are many sources of influence through communication, although according to Mcquail (1975: 193) the influence gained through the mass media is limited due to the voluntary character of reception and the relative lack of attention.

The claim I wish to make is that the adoption of a discourse-theoretical perspective destabilizes the traditional model of communication and undermines the sociological account of the telos and influence of mass media. In support of this claim I make three contentions. First, the essence of communication is not the exchange of messages. Second, the message does not possess a pure, intentional content, but is discursively constructed in and through the hegemonic (mass) media configuration. Third, not only the message but also the would-be communicator, the real communicator and the audience are discursively constructed in and through forms of power that are not reducible to the interest-driven and relatively predictable effects of the communicative actions of the sender. I shall be brief in my effort to sustain these contentions, restricting my argument to a few remarks that merely indicate the lines along which further research may be conducted.

First, according to Derrida (1988a), communication is neither generally nor essentially involved with the communication of meaning between senders and receivers. Indeed, as Derrida remarks, 'one characteristic of the semantic field of the word *communication* is that it designates nonsemantic movements as well' (1988a: 1). We might, however, choose to focus on the communication of meaning through writing, in the broad Derridean sense of the term. The point here is that for written communication to retain its function as writing it must remain readable despite the radical absence of both sender and receiver (1988a: 7–8). Hence, the essence of written communication is not to be found in the actual exchange of a message, but rather in its iter-ability, i.e. in the possibility of repeating the signifying sequence in, through and even in view of its alteration (1988a: 53). In other words, communication does not acquire its identity from the transmission of intent from the sender to the receiver, but rather from the iterability of the mark in the absence of any empirically determined subject.

Second, according to Derrida (1988a: 9), the written sign carries with it a force that breaks with the context of its inscription: 'by virtue of its essential iterability, a written syntagma can always be detached from the chain in which it is inserted or given without causing it to lose all possibility of functioning' (1988a: 9). In other words, the written message cannot be entirely enclosed in any context or chain of signification. One may, therefore, 'come to recognize other possi-bilities in it by inscribing or *grafting* it onto other chains' (1988a: 9). Everything thus depends on the discursive construction of the message, i.e. on its articulation within the (un)decidable contexts that make up the hegemonic mass media configuration. There is no pure, original meaning, but only possible discursively constructed meanings.

Third, it is not the case that the content of the message is dis-cursively constructed by various types of actors whose identity is given outside and independently of the discursive chains of signification. According to Laclau and Mouffe (1987: 82–4), there is nothing outside discourse. Both the meaning of the message and the identity of the media actors are discursively constructed. That is to say, not only the message but also the would-be communicator, the real communicator and the audience are constructed in and through discursive strategies of power and resistance.

Beginning with the *message,* the crucial question is: what can be said, how, and when? The hegemonic discourse establishes a truth regime that defines what can be considered as true and false and a value regime that provides criteria for judging what is good and what is bad. The normalizing practices of the discourse will seek to natu-ralize repression, justify hierarchies, and objectivize constructed meanings so that their political 'origin' is forgotten. The question of how things are said is very much a question of the choice of what Fairclough calls genre and discourse, but it also depends upon the rules of the game, which define what van Dijk sees as the cognitive schema of organization and presentation. Finally, the question of when certain things can be said in a particular way must be answered in terms of an analysis of the discursive construction of the agenda, in and through hegemonic struggles.

With regard to *would-be and real communicators*, it should be emphasized that, in so far as this relation involves the representation of the views, ideas and interests of the would-be communicator (for example, a politician) by the real communicator (for example, a political journalist), this representation is an essentially impure one. This is so not because journalists have made a living out of distorting political statements in the eternal hunt for cover stories, but rather because the act of representation partially constructs the necessarily incomplete views, ideas and interests by inscribing them into news contexts framed by discursively constructed rules, norms and values. Laclau's argument concerning the impurity of representations does not entail that we should stop comparing representations in terms of their particularity, completeness and interestedness. We constantly evaluate and make judgements about the relative (un-)truthfulness of repre-sentation, and although these evaluative judgements are always made from particular positions and points of view, they can still be compared in terms of how 'public-spirited' or 'self-interested' they are (Fairclough, 1995: 47).

More generally, the relevant question concerning the discursive construction of would-be and real communicators is: who permits whom to talk from which position? We have a host of real communi-cators who might be constructed as servants of the public, as professionals with professional standards and norms, or as career-driven employees in private business firms. The real communicators might permit the would-be communicators – politicians, interest organizations, business firms, professionals or citizens – to speak as legitimate political combatants, public entertainers, objective experts, or vox pop. Social antagonisms play a major role in the staging of a multiplicity of voices. Who is constructed as inside and who as outside the community? Who are our friends and who are our enemies?

Finally, the key question concerning the *receivers* of mass media messages is: who is interpellated and how? Is the mass audience empowered or disempowered by mass media communication? Are the receivers constructed as a passive, receptive audience or as active, co-producers of the world? In addition, how are different social groups targeted and portrayed? Which points of identification are on offer, and which are denied? These questions are all crucial to a mapping of the discursive construction of today's mass audience.

The Discursive Effect of Electronically Wrapped Language

Poster's (1990) analysis of the impact of electronically wrapped language on the conception of the self invokes the notion of *mode of information*. The justification for this notion, which seeks to conceptualize discontinuous historical configurations, is drawn from the fact that the rise of new technology intended to streamline, simplify or enhance the communicative conduct of familiar routines may prove to be a dislocatory event that paves the way for new patterns of communication (1990: 5). One such new pattern might be conceptualized as a mode of information that structures symbolic exchange. Three different modes of information can be identified in the course of history: (1) face to face, orally mediated exchange; (2) written exchanges mediated by print; and (3) electronically mediated exchange (1990: 6). These modes of information, it should be emphasized, are not sequential, but rather different overdetermined structures in which former modes of information are inscribed within a new logic. They do not constitute a set of transcendental categories, but are the result of an attempt to write what Foucault called the history of the present. Last but not least, they are not a consequence of the progressive realization of some telos of history, but rather discursive totalizations of communicative practices, which have different historical conditions of existence (1990: 6–7).

To make the point quite clear, the analysis of modes of information is more concerned with the discursive aspects of information exchange – which Poster denotes *the wrapping of language* – than with the efficiency of communication (1990: 8). Thus, Poster's main thesis is that the shift from oral and print-wrapped language to electronically wrapped language reconfigures the subject and its relation to the world (1990: 11). The electronic mode of information with its endless

221

production of simulacra undermines the representational function of language. As a consequence the identity of the subject starts to float and society increasingly becomes the practice of positioning subjects to receive and interpret self-referential messages (1990: 8–15). Speech constitutes the subject as an organic member of a community. Print media constitute the receiving subject as a rational and autonomous ego who instrumentally interprets, logically connects and critically scrutinizes linear symbols. Finally, electronically mediated communication – which is contextless, monologic and self-referential – invites the recipient to reconstruct his or her self in conversation with different discourses. The subject thus becomes engaged in a practice of self-constitution, which increasingly takes the form of a practice of reading that emphasizes multivocality (1990: 65). In the postmodern world of electronic communication we therefore gradually become nomadic and multiple selves. This certainly poses a major political challenge to the political strategies of hegemonic articulation. The crucial question becomes how to construct a hegemonic project that can unify the scattered and multiple selves into a collective will without stifling the play of meaning in which the postmodern subjects are enmeshed.

The Information Society: Salvation or Damnation?

I shall conclude this chapter by addressing the crucial question of the emancipatory effects of our present *information society*. The modern discourse of Enlightenment conceives free and undistorted communication as having a tremendous emancipatory effect which must be safeguarded through public anti-monopoly regulations, the achievement of a critical media literacy, and the advancement of a certain discourse ethics. In the light of this, the anarchic character of computer networks and the growing attention paid to critical media analysis in schools, public debates and higher education are welcomed. Unconstrained access to the means of mass communication and the de-masking of distorted forms of communication are thought likely to remove the blindfold of the oppressed and allow them to speak the truth. As such, transparency and revolution are considered as two sides of the same coin within the discourse of modernity.

However, if there is no such thing as free and undistorted communication due to the fact that media messages are discursively constructed in and through power–knowledge complexes, we have to pose a different question. The point is not whether the demands for free and undistorted communication are realized and the freeing of essential human aspirations from repressive forms of power carried through.

222

What we need to ask is: what scope is there for pursuing political strategies of resistance, dissent and pragmatic experimentation in the field of mass media in order to change the state of affairs so it accords more with the values we cherish? What potential is there for mobilizing subjugated knowledges, for playing out different values against each other, and for advancing new political projects?

In past decades the answer to these questions was highly pessimistic. Hence, the theories of media manipulation that flourished in the 1960s and the early 1970s portrayed mass media as an all-powerful force of social control that was capable of imposing a monolithic dominant ideology on the population (Kellner, 1995: 3). It certainly remains possible that mass media might impede the advancement of crucial political values such as democracy, freedom and equality by promoting nationalism, racism and sexism, and by naturalizing the 'ways things are', i.e. by justifying totalitarian tendencies, 'unfreedom' and inequality. However, audiences today may well be able to resist the effects of the dominant media configuration and create their own readings and appropriations. The content of the messages disseminated by the hegemonic media configuration is only partially fixed. There is always a surplus of meaning and a multiplicity of voices, which destabilize the dominant meanings and provide material for the articulation of new meanings and alternative political projects. In addition, organic intellectuals in many countries have gained access to relatively inexpensive electronic means of reproduction and mass communication. Finally, computer-mediated communication might possess a democratic potential, although the realization of this potential hinges on the advancement of interactive forms of communication and the political empowerment of disempowered populations (Hacker, 1996).

Against this overly optimistic view, it should be noted that the fusion of capitalism, media and technology tends to produce an increasing concentration of money, control and technological facilities in the hands of multinational media corporations. This negative development should, of course, be resisted on all fronts, not least by the development of alternative forms of mass media networking. On the other hand, it might also be the case that the more the large media corporations exploit their capacities to capture our hearts and minds, the more the mass media messages they produce and circulate will take the form of noise, in the sense of empty messages that we neither trust nor pay attention to. Likewise, against the unrestrained computer-age optimism, it should be noted that the new forms of computer-mediated communication tend to produce an ambiguous effect, providing not only increasing autonomy and diversity of choice but also new forms of surveillance and control (Kellner, 1995: 16). Nevertheless, we might be comforted by the fact that it has so far proved difficult to control the World Wide Web of computers. On the other hand, the uncensored flow of information of the World Wide Web seems to facilitate the circulation of all kinds of discriminating and abusive texts. As such, we can conclude that there remains a certain undecidability about the totalitarian and emancipatory effects generated by the advent of the information society.

12

The Politics of the Modern Welfare State

Discourse theory has in general paid little attention to the study of the historical forms of state and economy, the stable institutions in modern capitalist societies, and the question of societal reproduction. The focus has instead been the study of ideological formations in civil society, the construction of the identity of new political subjectivities, and the disruptive effects of societal dislocation. However, I have elsewhere attempted to compensate for the benign neglect on the part of Laclau and Mouffe by aiming to direct discourse theory to the study of the reproductive aspects of the institutional ensembles of state and economy (see Torfing, 1991, 1998). In this chapter I shall further pursue this endeavour by analysing the politics of the modern welfare state.

How Do We Define the Modern Welfare State?

In an attempt to define the term *'welfare state'*, we might say that health, housing, education, social assistance, full employment, etc. constitute an equivalential chain that establishes the meaning of the welfare state. The chain of equivalence appears to enrich our understanding of what the welfare state is; yet what is actually achieved is the opposite, since 'the more the chain expands, the more differential features of each of the links will have to be dropped in order to keep alive what the equivalential chain attempts to express' (Laclau, 1996a: 208). The notion of the welfare state is an empty signifier that functions as a *nodal point* in the sense that it retroactively constitutes that which it signifies. Thus, discursive formations of political strategies, institutional forms and power networks have been unified under the

225

popular banner of the welfare state. Within society at large the discursive formation of the welfare state has generally contributed to filling the gap opened up by the recognition that capitalist market economy lacks capacity to reproduce itself (Katznelson, 1988: 519–25). The welfare state has been a response to societal dislocation, and it has generally helped to secure the reproduction of capitalism by modifying the market forces. The welfare state has thus functioned as a subversive supplement to the rule of the capitalist market.

Historically the welfare state concept has been construed in a number of ways. In *Germany* Bismarck used the concept of *Wohlfahrtsstaat* in the 1880s to denote the social reforms intended to create a national system of social insurance. In order to curb the threat of a socialist revolution during the great depression of 1873–96, the Iron Chancellor appropriated the thoughts of Wagner and Schmoller and introduced a compulsory insurance system (Girvetz, 1968: 515). The idea was to pre-empt popular initiative by introducing social reforms from above (transformism). The strongly paternalistic overtones of these reforms made later generations prefer the notion of *Socialstaat* as the name for the continental welfare system.

More than half a century after the Bismarckian reforms in Germany, the welfare state concept was reinvigorated as part of the post-war reconstruction discourse in *Britain*. The famous Beveridge Report of 1942 proposed the establishment of a comprehensive welfare system able to provide social security for everyone from the cradle to the grave. The goal of the modern welfare state was the abolition of want, and the means was 'first and foremost, a plan of insurance – of giving in return for contributions benefits up to a subsistence level, as of right and without means test' (Beveridge, 1942: 7).

If, as such, the concept of the modern welfare state in Britain was seen as an integral part of a comprehensive policy of social progress with universal pretensions, the social-democratic parties in the *Scandinavian countries* contributed significantly to its ideologization. The Social Democratic Party in Denmark was left in an ideological vacuum following the obvious failure of its post-war programme of wide-ranging nationalizations and central state planning of the economy. A host of young academically educated politicians consequently set out to establish a pragmatic political platform for their struggle to build a new society different from both capitalism and communism. In the creation of a universalistic and solidaristic welfare state they found the means to remedy the defects of capitalist market society. While in Denmark the social-democratic congresses of the 1950s and 1960s clung to the idiom of democratic socialism, the loosely defined idea of the modern welfare state gradually became accepted as the unifying goal of the practical politics of the Social Democratic Party. Within society at large, there was a growing distrust in the ideological doctrines of socialism and economic liberalism; in this situation 'welfare politics' appeared as a more neutral and pragmatic, but no less ideological, slogan (see Poulsen, 1960).

The *classical studies* of the modern welfare state carried out by Marshall (1965) and Titmuss (1974) provide stimulating insights and widely accepted typologies. Marshall (1965: 71–2) describes the history of the modern welfare state in terms of a development from civil rights to individual freedom, via political rights to participate in the exercise of political power, and finally to social rights to live as a civilized being according to the welfare standards prevailing in society. Titmuss (1974) offers a similar typology. Whereas Marshall seeks to distinguish the modern welfare state from its prehistory, Titmuss aims to distinguish between different welfare state models, which he defines as residual, performative and universal-institutional (1974: 30–32). While the first two models are associated with private market institutions (private and corporative insurance schemes, respectively), the latter is associated with public government institutions (social insurance, social assistance and public social services). However, neither the attempt to distinguish the welfare state from its prehistory nor the effort to distinguish between different welfare state models helps us establish a general definition of the welfare state. The welfare state cannot be reduced to the presence of social rights, and is not exhausted by the reference to its different historical forms.

In our search for an analytical definition of the welfare state in terms of its forms and functions, we might start off by assuming that, generally speaking, the welfare state is concerned with the provision of political, economic and social conditions for the extended reproduction of the population. Judged against this background, it is highly problematic that the welfare state is often conceived *narrowly* either in terms of a high level of public social expenditure, as in many liberal theories, or in terms of a combination of state-run welfare programmes and state governing of the economy, as in most Marxist theories. The general limitation of such conceptions is that they say little about the economic and social aspects of the modern welfare state, as they tend to focus almost exclusively on the role of the state in the narrow sense of the term.

I shall therefore, alternatively, conceive the welfare state in somewhat *broader* terms: as the articulation of historical forms of state, economy and civil society in a historical bloc, which is capable of generating a high level of wealth, welfare and social harmony. Following from this conception, I shall define the modern welfare state, which was established in the leading capitalist countries in the post-war era, in terms of its articulation of a socially responsible state, an organized capitalist market economy, and a civil society of private associations and households that to an increasing degree are organized around consumption.

The intrasocietal relationships that define the matrix of the modern welfare state can be described in terms of the institutional forms of societal governance advocated by Keynes, Ford and Beveridge. As for the state–economy relation, economic liberalism was at the beginning of the century challenged by ambitious plans for the creation of large-plan economic systems and the nationalization of major industries and banks. However, in most countries these plans were discarded in favour of *Keynesian-type* economic state interventions (Mishra, 1984: 17). The Keynesian orthodoxy accelerated economic growth by means of counter-cyclical demand-management (Keynes, 1971 [1933], 1977 [1936]), which contributed to the moderation of economic fluctuations, thus permitting private business firms to anticipate market stability on the basis of which investments could be committed.

Now, if Keynesian demand-management was the accelerator and brake of economic growth, the *Fordist compromise* – which after the Second World War organized the relation between economy and civil society in most western countries – was the engine. The much-less-than-roaring 1920s gave way in the 1930s to an economic recession that owed its existence to the fact that capitalist mass production was not matched by an adequate level of mass consumption. However, in the post-war period, imitation of the USA led to the spread of the Fordist compromise, according to which the workers' acceptance of the introduction of new means of mass production was paid for by real wage rises, which in turn enabled the workers to purchase the standardized consumer goods they themselves produced at the semi-automatic assembly lines (Ford, 1926).

Finally, the relation between the state and civil society generally took the form of a *Beveridgean welfare system,* which generalized the Fordist norms of mass consumption by expanding a comprehensive social welfare system based on state-funded insurance schemes, social-assistance programmes, and public health care (Beveridge, 1942). Thus, in most western European countries political struggles and social compromise spurred the development from private charity associations driven by altruism, via private insurance schemes appealing to human self-interest, to public welfare systems based upon social solidarity (Einhorn and Logue, 1989: 131–3, 140–3).

The concrete institutions of the modern welfare state, and the power networks they embody, are pervaded by the belief that the social sciences can provide the overall guidelines for the piecemeal social engineering of society (Mishra, 1984: 12–16). Politicians and professionals share the basic conviction that the social sciences can help society to manage its affairs rationally rather than leaving them to chance and drift. Hence, prediction, planning and control have been the main tenets of the central decision-makers in both the public and private sectors. The concrete mode of organization of administrative and economic institutions was informed, first, by the discourses of Weberian bureaucracy (hierarchical control) and Taylorism (scientific management) and, later, by the discourse of Human Relations (manipulation of informal norms and habits). Common to these discourses was the attempt to increase efficiency, maximize control, and unify complex and fragmented institutions. However, complexity and fragmentation were inevitable consequences of the growing size of public and private institutions, which was motivated by economists' appraisal of the economies of scale. Indeed, the large Fordist factories were constructed as the exemplary model for the design of both public and private organizations.

The large bureaucratic organizations that constitute the backbone of the modern welfare state target both the macro-body of the population and the micro-bodies of the individuals with their power strategies. Both are seen as important resources for the generation of wealth. Individual bodies are disciplined by anonymous forms of regulation such as bureaucratic rules and machine-paced labour processes, as well as by panoptic forms of surveillance in factories, schools and welfare institutions. The creation of docile bodies is also, and to an increasing extent, achieved through practices of normalization, i.e. through the internalization of standards of appropriate behaviour by means of formal education, social learning and role-constitutive mass media messages.

The discursive formation of the modern welfare state has been held together by a social imaginary. This tends to invoke the image of a society that does not exist: a fully integrated society based upon freedom, equality and solidarity; a society in which everybody by way of their social citizenship is inscribed within a social community that protects them from the hazards of the market, from the disruptive effects of class struggle, and from most of the perils of life. Citizenship is clearly an equivalential logic referring to peoples' status as members of a fully constituted community that grants everyone some basic economic, political and social rights. Whether you are rich or poor, young or old, black or white, you possess the same fundamental rights. The egalitarian logic of citizenship tends to cancel out the differential character of social identities by constructing a certain sameness in terms of membership of a fully constituted community. However, this process of equalization gives way to a process of stratification. The recipients of social benefits and the users of social welfare services, as well as economic actors in the corporate policy networks and employees in the Fordist factories and the public sector, become divided, differentiated and classified according to type, skills, competence, function, etc. The undecidable play of equalization and stratification tends to undermine the potential for popular struggle and resistance, and thus helps to sustain the vision of society as a corporate body. In the Scandinavian countries society is generally represented as an organic unity of particular identities. No antagonisms exist between particular identities as everyone is constructed as a partner in the gradual development of society towards still higher states of humanity. However, social antagonisms are not entirely eliminated by the one-nation project of the modern welfare state; rather, they are displaced to a constitutive outside. The constitutive threat to the modern welfare state takes a variety of forms: political movements on the extreme Right or the extreme Left that reject the universalist and rationalist pretensions of the welfare state; competitive pressures from the other capitalist economies upon the national growth model; a pre-modern lack of social understanding, which is represented as the dark past of the Enlightened welfare state; allegedly 'postmodern' tendencies towards individualization and fragmentation, which supposedly undermine solidarity; etc.

How Do We Explain the Development of the Modern Welfare State?

The first generations of welfare state theorists were not only guilty of conceiving the welfare state narrowly in terms of either a high level of public social expenditure (liberal theories), or a combination of state-run welfare programmes and state governing of the economy (Marxist theories). They also ran into serious *methodological problems,* for they tended to explain the historical development of the modern welfare state as a function of either structure or agency. This tendency is found in both liberal and Marxist theories. For instance, some liberal theorists emphasize the impact of developmental determinants such as industrialization, economic growth and modernization (Wilensky, 1975; Flora and Alber, 1982), while others emphasize the role of public choice and the institutional barriers in deciding rationally on the size of public social expenditures (Downs, 1957, 1960; Kristensen, 1987). Marxist theorists tend to reproduce

230

this structure–agency dualism by accounting for the development of the modern welfare state in terms of either a response to the structural imperatives of the capitalist economy (O'Connor, 1973; Fine and Harris, 1979), or the outcome of political pressures by the working class (Gough, 1979; Korpi, 1983). Notwithstanding their *one-sidedness*, the problem with structure-based and agency-based explanations of the historical development of the welfare state is that they tend to suffer from all the methodological problems associated with functionalist, rationalist and instrumentalist modes of explanation.

The problem at the ontological level is that both structure-based and agency-based explanations of the welfare state have an *objectivist bias*, inasmuch as they tend to see either structure or agency as a fully constituted starting point for the analysis of the modern welfare state. Under the spell of the metaphysics of presence – constitutive for the entire field of the social sciences in the modern age – liberal and Marxist theories cling to the idea that social and political analysis should have an objective starting point. That is, there is an implicit assumption that only by stripping the analytical starting point, in terms of structure or agency, of anything contingent is it possible to gain true scientific knowledge. The bottom line is that this objectivist bias tends to invoke systematic marginalization of the role of politics in terms of hegemonic struggles over the construction of political and social identities. Thus, whereas functional explanations of the welfare state in terms of developmental determinants or structural imperatives tend to reduce politics to a supplementary logic, rationalistic and instrumentalist explanations of the welfare state in terms of either public choice or working-class mobilization tend to delimit the impact of politics by grounding political action in pregiven rationalities or pregiven class interests.

To counter the one-sidedness, methodological problems and object-ivist bias of the traditional explanations, I propose that the development of the modern welfare state be explained in terms of *the interplay of open-ended political strategies and ambiguous structures and institutions*. An explanation along these lines can be developed from the latest works of Esping-Andersen, who aims to transform the original class-mobilization thesis into a class-coalition thesis. The class-mobilization thesis can be criticized on three points: (1) for failing to account for the formation of the proletariat into a class; (2) for failing to recognize that the 'workers have sometimes found their interests best served by distinctively unsolidaristic measures, and conversely, solidaristic welfare policies have in certain circumstances been pursued by the middle classes and the parties at the centre and right' (Baldwin, 1996: 37); and (3) for failing to account for institutional conditions in the realization of political strategies for social welfare. Esping-Andersen responds to the first criticism in his book *Politics Against Market* (1985: 30–1), where he explicitly addresses the question of proletarian class formation. The other two criticisms are met by the advancement of his class-coalition thesis in *The Three Worlds of Welfare Capitalism* (1990). The basic idea is that the welfare state should be explained in terms of the forging of political alliances between workers and small farmers or between workers and public employees (1990: 18). The realization of the political strategies of such hegemonic alliances is said to be conditioned by the historical legacy of various welfare state regimes (1990: 29). Although one might object that the emphasis on class-based agency is still too reductionist and that the account of structural and institutional conditions is too vague, this is certainly a promising starting point for a hegemony approach to the study of the modern welfare state.

As part of his thesis, Esping-Andersen also redefines the object of analysis. He does not set out to explain either the level of public social expenditures or the ideal of the universalist, comprehensive and redistributive welfare state in the Scandinavian countries. He instead envisions three distinctive welfare state regimes: liberal, conservative and social-democratic. These exhibit different decommodification and stratification effects, as the social right to welfare is tied to need, contributions and citizenship, respectively. However, the difficulty of fitting the actual welfare state regimes into Esping-Andersen's typology (see Castles and Mitchell, 1990; van Kersbergen, 1991; Leibfried, 1993; Jones, 1993) suggests that we should seek instead to account for the family resemblances between the different welfare states on the basis of a description of their defining characteristics (Baldwin, 1996: 40–3). Nevertheless, this still leaves us with a narrow conception of the welfare state with regard to its social policy dimension. To overcome this last problem we only have to follow the line taken by Esping-Andersen in his latest writings, where he is concerned with the Fordist system of production and the function of private households as settings for leisure and mass consumption (see Esping-Andersen, 1993).

The Genesis and Expansion of the Modern Welfare State

In order to shed light on the genesis and expansion of the modern welfare state I shall briefly discuss two important works: Dean's study of the transition from workfare to welfare, in his book *The Constitution of Poverty* (1991), and Donzelot's study of the articulation of Beveridgeanism, Fordism and Keynesianism, in his book *L'invention du social* (1994 [1984]). Both studies takes a discourse-theoretical approach to the study of the conflictual emergence of the modern welfare state.

Dean (1991: 7) claims that the governance of poverty in Britain during the eighteenth and nineteenth centuries was marked by a decisive break with the mercantilistic workfare discourse in favour of a liberal welfare discourse. This fundamental transformation in the discourse of poverty has two aspects: 'one concerning ways of theorising, knowing, and classifying; the other, forms of treatment, relief, discipline, deterrence, and administration' (1991: 9). The inter-linking of these aspects serves to constitute poverty in a definite historical form.

The mercantilistic workfare discourse dominated British social policy from the middle of the seventeenth century to the beginning of the nineteenth century. The aim of the poor laws during this period was to provide work for those willing to work, to punish those who were not, and to provide bread to those unable to work (1991: 25). Those among the poor who were unwilling to work and those who were willing, but either out of work or corrupted by the taint of sloth, constituted the idle poor. The key question of the workfare discourse was: how will the idle poor be set to work? The answer was: through forced labour in workhouses. The workhouse emerged as the ideal institutional solution to the more fundamental problem of linking the large numbers of the idle poor to the wealth and strength of the nation (1991: 35–42). According to mercantilist thought, the number of poor equalled the wealth of the nation, in the broad sense of the term, provided that the idle poor were forced to labour. Thus, the popula-tion, conceived in terms of a 'stock of labour', was seen as an invaluable resource of the state. The mobilization of this resource was the primary aim of the governance of poverty within the highly paternalistic workfare discourse.

According to Dean (1991: 75–86), the publication in 1798 of Malthus' *Essay on the Principle of Population as it Affects the Future Improvement of Society* was the event that, more than any other, contributed to the dislocation of the mercantilistic workfare discourse. The population could no longer be celebrated as a resource of wealth-creation, as there was held to be an omnipresent tendency for the population to outgrow the means of subsistence, which invariably led to vice and misery. Malthus' theory of overpopulation also under-mined the principles guiding the poor laws, as these tended to increase the population without increasing the supply of food. In other words, the poor laws tended to create the poor they were set up to maintain

233

(1991: 81). However, if the poor laws only made things worse, then how were the problems of overpopulation and poverty to be solved? Through the private exercise of moral restraint, calculative behaviour and worldly asceticism, was the response of Malthus. Hence, the Malthusian state is not a paternalistic one. This does not mean that it is not a patriarchal one. 'The Malthusian prescription for the poor is about allowing those laws of nature to operate which bind the poor man to the yoke of wage-labour and the poor woman to the yoke of conjugal dependence' (1991: 85).

Malthus' critique of the poor laws did not lead to the abolition of the poor laws but rather to their redirection. The 1834 Poor Law Amendment Act emphasized self-reliance, encouraged reproductive prudence and the foresight of saving, and abolished relief to able-bodied males and their dependants (1991: 97). The new poor laws, with their emphasis on self and familial responsibility, were heavily influenced by Malthusianism. However, the impact of Malthus' essay went far beyond the scope of the new poor laws: it constituted and structured the new liberal welfare discourse, of which it was itself an instance.

An important political point emerges from Dean's study of the transition from workfare to welfare. Today many political commentators reject the new workfare discourse as a neo-liberal invention. However, as we have seen, the liberal welfare discourse was constituted through a major break with the workfare discourse. As such, workfare is not essentially liberal, or neo-liberal. If anything, the 'original' workfare discourse was conservative. Nevertheless, today workfare is open to many different political articulations, and the neo-liberal appropriation of workfare is only one such possible articulation. In Scandinavia a neo-statist, social-democratic workfare strategy is currently gaining ground.

Whereas Dean focuses on the British debate on pauperism only towards the end of his study, *Donzelot* (1984) takes the French debate on pauperism and social economy as the point of departure for his study of the genealogy of the welfare state during the Third French Republic (1870–1940). There are important differences between the two approaches; however, the shared interest of Dean and Donzelot in the discursive construction of practical solutions to social problems establishes a point of continuity between their studies.

According to Donzelot (1984: 395),[1] the proclamation of rights gave rise to conflicting interpretations of the role of the state. Some wanted the state to live up to its new political responsibility and abolish capitalist relations of production, which were perceived to undermine the requirement for justice. Others feared that such a step would eventually undermine respect for the freedom of the individual. The proposed solution to this conflict inherent to the Republic's political foundation was the advancement of a discourse of solidarity, social rights and state intervention. The answer lay in an attempt to promote justice, not by reorganizing society but rather by mitigating the effects of poverty and reducing the effects of oppression (1984: 396–7). Hence, the state reassumed responsibility for society, but its interventions were to act on the forms of the social bond rather than on the structure of society (1984: 405). The discursive condition of possibility for the advancement of the discourse of solidarity, rights and intervention was the basic conviction that social problems should be solved by improving the social milieu rather than by declaiming moral and political maxims (1984: 398). This conviction was a very long way from the moral economy of Smith and Ricardo.

At the practical level, solidarity was realized through the application of the insurance technique. It was thanks to this technique that the New School succeeded in ensuring that the discourse of solidarity prevailed over rival schools of thought (1984: 399). Social insurance was proclaimed as superior to the liberal reliance on legal compensation and savings. It was extremely difficult for the poor to save, and legal compensation for injury, sickness or death was seldom obtained, and if it was it could bankrupt the company (1984: 399–400, 402). Social insurance was also superior to that provided by the English mutual societies, advocated by the traditionalists, as it made for a more equal protection across all social categories and could not be used to finance strikes (1984: 402). Finally, the social insurance model clearly dissociated itself from the socialist dream of a social revolution: 'the principle of a pre-existing debt provides it with the means for dealing with social problems as eventualities calling for compensation rather than as a fruit of original injustices calling for the global reconstruction of society' (1984: 403). In sum, social insurance was able, through its emphasis on the socialization of risk, to present itself as an alternative to liberal individualism without giving in to socialist collectivism.

Social insurance could help to mitigate the effects of poverty, but would it also help to reduce the effects of oppression? Despite the unequal terms of exchange offered by the labour contract, the employers were highly dissatisfied. They felt they were the victims of the free labour contract, threatened by the unstable and elusive character of the workers. To compensate for this threat the bosses were granted three further means of paternalistic control. Industrial tribunals, workers' pass books, and, above all, the system of factory regulation were the state's concession to the employers' complaints (1984: 406–8). The particular powers given to the bosses were justified by the reference to the singular character of each enterprise, which made general laws and regulations impossible. However, 'with social right, the boss is called upon to apply rules not of his own making but whose authority stems from the solidarity of the whole of society and the necessary generality of sanitary norms, and which *can only have the effect of reducing the arbitrariness of power*' (1984: 409 – emphasis added). In other words, the discourse of solidarity, social rights and state intervention undermined the paternalistic system of industrial control that had served as a means of increasing the relative surplus value appropriated by the capitalists.

The advancement of the discourse of Fordism and Taylorism provided the solution to the breakdown of the paternalistic system of control. It could be shown that the attempt to increase the production of relative surplus value would be better realized by the rationalization of production (time-and-motion studies and vertical integration of an increasingly divided labour process by the use of machine-paced assembly lines), which would generate large and increasing productivity gains (1984: 411). The workers were persuaded to support the introduction of Fordism on the grounds that their means of consumption were augmented by indexing real wages to rising productivity rates. The outcome was the articulation of the Fordist system with the discourse of social rights – later epitomized by the Beveridge report.

Fordism gives rise to intense fights over the minimum time in which a job can be done. If the norm is set low, it will increase profits. If it is set high, it will enhance the workers' protection. In the first instance economic rationality predominates, and in the second instance social rationality. From the point of view of social rationality (social protection), economic rationality (profit maximization) constitutes an irrational threat (1984: 412–13). Therefore, by inscribing their struggles within the prevailing social rationality, trade unions can forge an important alliance with the state in favour of social protection. Such an alliance cannot be reduced to a purely instrumental arrangement as it is conditional upon the universalization of the particular demands of the working class. It thus eventually leads to transformation of the contents of working-class solidarity from a class solidarity based on everyone within the group to a generalized solidarity based on everybody who shares the same social predicament (Schmidt, 1995).

The Fordist normalization of production did not eliminate the class struggle but merely displaced it to the level of wage negotiations, where the norms of production were agreed. The conflict between labour and capital was inscribed within the two antagonistic logics of social rationality and economic rationality, and the state was caught in the crossfire between the trade unions and the large companies, both of which claimed to incarnate modern rationality (Donzelot, 1984: 415). Labour and capital both wanted the state to take sides in the conflict, and this made it difficult for the state to preserve its republican neutrality. Against this background it is easy to understand why the state enthusiastically embraced the Keynesian doctrine. The discourse of Keynesianism articulated the economic and the social rather than allowing one to prevail over the other. This articulation was a direct consequence of the economic policy of demand-management. The economic and the social are conjoined in a circular mechanism. As Donzelot says:

the theory [Keynesianism: JT] makes the social the means of 'reinflating' the economic when the latter is at risk of being affected by weak demand [. . .] through the artificial but effective injection into society on an increased capacity to buy and employ. Equally, the economic, thus maintained in a constant state of good functioning, is the means for sustaining the pursuit of a social politics which provides safeguards for the workers that keep them in a state of availability for work, rather than leaving them to the possibility of sinking below a threshold of poverty which makes them unfit to work when economic activity picks up again. (1984: 421)

The economic and social are articulated in and through the economic interventions of the state. The state is thus assigned the ultimate responsibility for the progressive development of society.

The Present Crisis and Strategies for Renewal

In the post-war period the articulation between Keynesianism, Fordism and Beveridgeanism was in western Europe reinforced by a series of hegemonic compromises and, sustained by the development of a social imaginary that constituted the welfare state, became the surface of inscription of all social demands. The state had the overall responsibility for promoting the social and mitigating the effects of poverty and oppression, and it had no problem living up to this responsibility. In many western countries the virtuous circle of Keynesianism, Fordism and Beveridgeanism produced an un-precedentedly high level of wealth, welfare and social harmony. High economic growth rates, full employment and rising living standards were maintained by the tandem of Fordism and Keynesianism, and social problems were countered by a Beveridgean welfare system, which in the Scandinavian countries developed social insurance into an all-public, comprehensive and very generous system of welfare provision.

The modern welfare state ran into severe problems at the beginning of the 1970s. New types of socioeconomic problems and political protest contested the habitus of the modern welfare state, and revealed a symptomatic lack of fast and flexible responses. Various counter-measures were launched, but a hard kernel of undomesticable issues remained, and societal dislocation was thus unavoidable. What could not be domesticated was first and foremost the effects of the collapse of the Fordist mode of development, which resulted in a stagflation crisis. This crisis, triggered by decreasing productivity growth rates due to technical limitations and industrial micro-conflictuality, put both countercyclical economic state interventions and tax-financed welfare provisions under pressure. Rising unemployment and fiscal problems were the inevitable result (Mishra, 1984: 19).

In most countries the mass basis of the modern welfare state seemed to remain intact. People continued to support the overall goals of the welfare state, despite the fact that in some respects it failed to deliver the goods. The modern welfare state had, nevertheless, become the target of popular struggles waged by a proliferation of new social movements that opposed the concomitant increasing commodification and bureaucratization of social life (Mouffe, 1988a: 91–5). As the demands of the new social movements could not readily be domesti-cated by the discourse of the modern welfare state, the decisive challenge to the political forces within the establishment was to retain the main goals of the modern welfare state while changing its insti-tutional forms and articulations.

The 1970s and the 1980s passed without any offensive attempts to reshape the intrasocietal relationships of the modern welfare state. Keynesian rescue attempts were followed by the monetarist disaster and neo-liberal attempts to roll back the state. However, none of these efforts was based on a vision of a new socioeconomic settlement. This situation changed during the 1990s with the emergence of political strategies (neo-liberal, neo-corporatist and neo-statist) aiming to effect a transition from the *Keynesian Welfare State* (KWS) to a *Schumpeterian Workfare Regime* (SWR) (Jessop, 1993, 1994a, 1994b).[2] With regard to the general mode of economic state inter-vention, the KWS aimed to maintain full employment within a relatively closed economy through demand-side interventions, while the SWS aims to promote permanent innovation and structural competitiveness within a relatively open economy through inter-ventions on the supply side. As for the form of the social welfare regime, the KWS tried to regulate collective bargaining within limits

238

consistent with full employment levels of growth; to generalize norms of mass consumption beyond those employed in Fordist sectors so that all national citizens might share the fruits of economic growth (and thereby contribute to effective domestic demand); and to promote forms of collective consumption favourable to the Fordist mode of growth. By contrast, the SWR tends to subordinate social policy to the requirements of labour market flexibility, especially where it concerns the working population, and otherwise puts downward pressure on public social spending.

In earlier work (Jessop, 1993, 1994a, 1994b) the structural economic pressures prompting the shift from the KWS to the SWR were seen as comprising: (1) growing internationalization and globalization; (2) the rise of new technologies; and (3) the paradigm shift from Fordism to post-Fordism. However, in order to avoid legitimate accusations of economism future research should seek to establish the relative and combined effect of both economic and political factors. Thus, in addition to elaborating the economic analysis of the transition from the KWS to the SWR as associated with the crisis of Fordism and the search for new modes of societal regulation that would stabilize an emergent system of post-Fordism within a globalized world economy, we must introduce and develop an account of the political logics behind this transformation. An important argument in this regard relates to the fact that politicians tend to disclaim responsibility for full employment and state provided welfare. There is an important discourse on 'state/government failures' which is informed by right-wing arguments about the failure of mixed economy and left-wing arguments about the failure of the welfare state to prevent social problems and enhance social and economic equality. This discourse links up with another discourse on the 'crisis of legitimation' which draws on neo-liberal arguments about the inefficiency of bureaucratic rule and leftist arguments about the disempowering effects of bureaucratic institutions. Finally, the discourse on the 'fiscal crisis of the state' – due to the budget squeeze, the increasing interest burden on public debt and the ageing of the European populations – further contributes to the undermining of the KWS. In this situation the SWR is welcomed by the politicians because it legitimizes an austerity, recommodification and retrenchment response to the crisis of the KWS. The SWR justifies a response based upon macro-economic discipline, recommodification and privatization since the SWR is merely aiming at creating a framework for the free-enterprise of business and individuals/families. The assessment of the relative importance of political and economic logics for the transition from the KWS to the SWR is an important task for

239

the future. However, in the following discussion we shall focus mainly upon the economic logics.

Now, the problem of the earlier work on the transition from the KWS to the SWR is not only that it is economistic. Another problem is a direct product of the way the basic research question was initially formulated. Hence, by asking the question of 'which type of state will provide the best political shell for the post-Fordist mode of development in the face of growing internationalization and globalization' we were inclined to produce a functionalist argument which saw the transition from the KWS to the SWR as a functional response to structural imperatives. However, the problems associated with functionalist arguments can be avoided if the thought experiment carried out at a high level of abstraction is modified and re-specified at lower levels of abstraction in order to account for the politics which shape and reshape the structural couplings between the economic, political and social institutions and practices. Hence, at the level of concrete analysis we must shift the focus from economic and political pressures to the constitutive role of changes in political discourses in the course of societal restructuration. Economic and political problems are manifested in an interdiscursive field in which competing social forces seek to interpret them in terms of failures and crises understood from their own distinctive perspectives. Events which cannot be domesticated by the traditional discourses on the welfare state will tend to dislocate the socioeconomic framework of meaning (consider the devastating impact of stagflation on the Keynesian orthodoxy). The dislocation of the hegemonic discourses produces a growing number of floating signifiers and intensifies the political struggles between social forces who seek to redefine the subjects, objects and sites of regulation; to propose alternative societal paradigms; and to enter negotiations over the terms of a new compromise. The hegemonic struggles at the level of political discourse will lead to the formulation of a more or less adequate response to what is perceived to be the major sources of crisis and dislocation (i.e. to the structural pressures which are constructed as objective causes of necessary economic and political changes).

The discursive responses to crisis and dislocation will invoke changing visions of the good life. In this case we can already see how 'full employment' is being replaced by 'the enterprising society', and how 'solidarity and equality' are replaced by 'independence and opportunity'. In future research it is important to establish why different narratives have proved to have more or less appeal and mobilizing capacity. This will involve examining the resonance of these accounts with the everyday experiences of different actors, their link to wider institutional and public (meta)narratives, and their capacity to give discursive expression to underlying structural contradictions and strategic dilemmas in the economic and political systems.

The emphasis on discourse and politics helps us to combat the functionalist bias found in the earlier work on the transition from the KWS to the SWR. The actual shifts in the mode of regulation are guided by discursive changes which are brought about by social forces engaged in hegemonic struggles over the authoritative response to societal dislocation. People act upon discursive constructions of the 'real world' rather than upon the hard facts themselves. Or, rather, they act upon what is constructed as facts in and through discourse. Moreover, our actions are not governed by a logic of consequence but rather by a logic of appropriateness which is imbedded in discursive frameworks of meaning and knowledge as well as in sedimented forms of rules, norms and procedures. However, it should be clearly emphasized that the fact that we act upon discursive constructions by no means implies that the content of the actual policies affecting business firms and the unemployed is dictated by the official discourse behind the various policy changes. The official discourse will be challenged and transformed by other, and competing, discursive strategies all the way down from the first stipulations of motives and intentions to the processes of policy-making and policy implementation. Therefore, one should not be surprised if the content of the implemented policies are not in strict accordance with the content of the official discourse stating the motives and intentions behind the new mode of regulation.

Part V

Political Perspectives

Introduction

The new theories of discourse not only provide stimulating theoretical arguments and fruitful empirical analyses. They also carry important *political implications*. Although the new theories do not in themselves support any particular politics, the Marxist ambition to change the world is taken very seriously by Laclau, Mouffe and Žižek. In the words of Rosenau (1992: 14–17), they are *affirmative* as opposed to *sceptical* postmodernists. Rather than offering a pessimistic, negative and gloomy assessment of the possibility of a social revolution in our time, they tend to believe that postmodernity makes thinkable a whole range of new political projects.

Underlying their relatively optimistic assessment of the possibility of a democratic postmodern politics is the underlying view that postmodernity is a crisis of the self-foundation of modernity and not a crisis of its political project. Both Habermas and Lyotard tend to assimilate the political project of modernity into its epistemological and ontological underpinning (Mouffe, 1989: 31–3). While Lyotard thinks that we have to give up both the political project and its theoretical underpinning, Habermas aims to rework the latter in order to rescue the modern project of emancipation. In contrast to both Habermas and Lyotard, Rorty claims that we can abandon the theoretical underpinning of modernity and keep the political project. However, whereas Rorty identifies the political project with liberalism, which he understands as capitalism-*cum*-democracy (Mouffe, 1996b: 4–6), the aim of Laclau and Mouffe is not only to disentangle political liberalism from the rationalism of Enlightenment but also to free it from its association with capitalism and its correlate of economic liberalism (Mouffe, 1987: 105–6, 1992a: 2–3). The first stage of this endeavour is achieved through the elaboration of a concept of democratic citizenship that goes beyond liberalism and its communitarian critics. The second is realized through the advancement of the concept of radical plural democracy. 'Democratic citizenship' and 'radical plural democracy' are considered by Laclau and Mouffe as nodal points in a social imaginary that should replace the Jacobin imaginary of the Left. Thus their aim is to breathe new life into the Left by furnishing a new hegemonic project that articulates liberal and communitarian values with traditional socialist goals.

The advancement of a radical plural democracy is considered in *chapter 13*, while the concept of democratic citizenship is discussed in *chapter 14*. As the advocacy of a specific political project is informed by a particular ethics, it is necessary to confront the question of the possibility of a postmodern ethics. This is done in *chapter 15*, which closes this final section on the political perspectives of the new theories of discourse.

13

Towards a Radical Plural Democracy

Introduction

According to Mouffe, 'the objective of the Left should be the extension and deepening of the democratic revolution initiated two hundred years ago' (Mouffe, 1992a: 1). The Left must learn from the tragic experience of totalitarianism and should seek to advance a *radical plural democracy*. Liberal democracy should not be rejected as a sham, but should rather be radicalized through an immanent critique of its limitations. The progressive potential in extending and deepening liberal democracy is great for it is clearly not possible to find a more radical principle for organizing society than that all human beings are free and equal.

In order fully to comprehend the meaning and implications of a radical plural democracy we should first seek to understand the conditions of possibility of democracy and the contingent articulation of the liberal and democratic aspects of liberal democracy. The re-articulation of liberal democracy in terms of a plural democracy will then permit us to consider the call for a radical plural democracy. We shall finally deal with the question of the form of democratic institutions and the present challenge to our plural democracy.

Modern Democracy

Modernity is characterized by a *Democratic Revolution* that renders power an empty place. No individual or group can occupy the locus of power that provides the imaginary unification of society. In democratic societies sovereignty truly lies with the people. The point is, however, that *the people* does not exist as a homogenous unity capable of governing itself (Žižek, 1989: 147). The people is an empty signifier, and the political parties in democratic societies are all aware of the gap between the universality of the people and their own particularity. Recognition of the constitutive nature of this gap is the condition of possibility of modern democracy (Laclau, 1994b: 178). No party can embody the will of the people and all attempts to do so must necessarily be viewed as temporary, 'as a kind of surrogate, a substitute for the real-impossible sovereign' (Žižek, 1989: 147). In totalitarian societies the people exists in the shape of the Party, which claims to realize its objective interests. The Party embodies the will of the people, leaving no residue. Hence, 'the People always support the Party because any member of the People who opposes Party rule automatically excludes himself from the People' (1989: 147).

Democratic politics are conditional upon recognition of the *indeterminate* character of the universal and the rejection of all attempts to fix its final meaning (Mouffe, 1994a: 323). Different political forces will nevertheless constantly aim to hegemonize the content of the universal. The attempt to hegemonize the universal will necessarily involve the production of empty signifiers other than that of 'the people'. The imprecision of the key signifiers of political language helps them to function as a surface of inscription for any kind of social demand. The proliferation of indeterminate signifiers like 'welfare', 'order' and 'progress' makes it possible for a large number of political forces to participate in the more or less sedimented forms of democratic politics. Almost everybody will feel that they can identify themselves with the broad and abstract headline on the political agenda. In consequence, democratic opposition, negotiation and compromise will thrive. The conclusion is thus that, not only is indeterminacy the precondition for democracy, but 'the more the political imaginary is organized around empty signifiers, the more democratic that society will be' (Laclau, 1993c: 231). However, total indeterminacy and total toleration would also mean total disintegration of the social fabric. Thus 'the sliding of the political signified under the democratic signifiers has to be arrested at some point' (1993c: 232). For instance, intolerance with regard to anti-democratic Nazi propaganda is actually the condition of possibility for democratic tolerance of other political forces (Laclau, 1996b: 51). It follows that all democratic societies must necessarily be partly based on *force* and *exclusion*. As Mouffe puts it, 'a political form of government requires a specific ordering of values which precludes a total pluralism' (Mouffe, 1994a: 324). However, if this is true, then no political regime can be entirely democratic. It turns out, therefore, that the condition of possibility of modern democracy is also its condition of impossibility.

Liberal Democracy

The contingent articulation of the *liberal* and *democratic* aspects of what we have come to know as liberal democracy was progressively established throughout the period of the nineteenth and the beginning of the twentieth centuries. Liberalism never constituted a unified and consistent doctrine. It has, rather, been an amalgam of different doctrines, including the *Recht Staat*, the defence of individual freedom and basic rights, the recognition of pluralism, representative government, the separation of powers, the limitation of the role of the state, rationalistic individualism, and capitalist market economy. Democracy, for its part, emerged as a discourse of popular sovereignty, universal suffrage and equality. The two terms were for a long while opposed to each other as democracy was identified with mob rule and carried a mainly pejorative meaning (Laclau, 1993c: 222). The articulation of liberalism and democracy in and through intense political struggles took the form of a democratization of the liberal state, in which process democracy was also liberalized. Hence, not only was democracy reduced to the competition between different political elites for the votes of the masses (Macpherson, 1972 [1965]: 5–11); it was also restricted to the public sphere, which was strictly opposed to the private sphere of capitalist economy and patriarchal gender relations (Bowles and Gintis, 1986: 66–7). However, the masses used their political voice to demand state-run welfare programmes (Beveridgeanism) and state governing of the economy (Keynesianism). The growing scope of economic state interventions has, together with extension of the democratic rights to equality to include the sex/gender system, clearly undermined the attempt to establish a rigid boundary between the public and private spheres. However, as we shall see, most liberal theorists continue to argue ideologically as if a rigid boundary existed.

The contingent articulation of liberalism and democracy has by no means produced a harmonious unity. There exists a persistent *conflict* between the traditional liberal appraisal of *pluralism, individualism* and *freedom* and the democratic principles of *unity, community* and *equality*. Both arch-liberalists such as Hayek and Nozick and fierce anti-liberalists such as Schmitt recognize the conflict between liberalism and democracy. Whereas the former are ready to abandon those forms of democracy which constrain the unfolding of the principles of liberalism, Schmitt is ready to give up liberalism in favour of what he defines as democracy. We shall return to the question of the political consequences of Schmitt's 'democratic' anti-liberalism when we have established the precise content of the conflict between liberalism and democracy.

First, as indicated in the previous section, there exists a profound conflict between the liberal appraisal of *pluralism* and the need for a basic social and political *unity* of democratic society. The principle of pluralism cannot reign unchallenged, as a (minimal) consensus concerning the values informing a mode of societal coexistence is required. The obvious problem with this is, of course, that a consensus based upon a comprehensive moral ideal would seriously harm the principle of pluralism as it would privilege, in an arbitrary manner, a particular controversial conception of the good (Mouffe, 1994a: 315). Political liberalists like Rawls (1971, 1993) and Larmore (1987) are not only opposed to such a perfectionist assertion of a common substantial good. They are also dissatisfied with the idea of a Hobbesian *modus vivendi* in terms of a consensus on a set of institutional procedures based on self-interest. They alternatively set out to provide a rationalistic grounding for a moral consensus (Mouffe, 1994a: 317). They want to solve the conflict between pluralism and the need for socio-political unity by showing that people, who privately have different and conflicting conceptions of the ideal of the good life, will agree on a set of common values informing the way we construct our public, political institutions. This 'overlapping consensus' (Rawls, 1993) not only differs from a consensus in terms of a *modus vivendi* but also from a constitutive consensus, where there is agreement about the basic principles for regulating political conflict while disagreement about their interpretation (Mouffe, 1996a: 251). Rawls' overlapping consensus goes deeper than the constitutional consensus as it seeks to fix the content of the principles of the liberal constitution once and for all. People who disagree with the precise content of the liberal principles organizing society should be forced to agree through coercion. This also includes those who merely disagree with the interpretation of the principles of Justice as Fairness around which well-ordered societies will tend to establish an overlapping consensus. Hence, in Rawls' liberal utopia 'legitimate dissent would have been eliminated from the public sphere' (1996a: 252). Rawls tends to downplay the size of this problem since the conception of Justice as Fairness must be able to gain support from all 'reasonable' citizens, despite their doctrinal differences in other respects. In the recent works of Rawls (1993), those disagreeing with the overlapping consensus tend to be written off as 'unreasonable'. However, Rawls'

(1993: 55) definition of reasonable citizens clearly demonstrates that the distinction between 'reasonable' and 'unreasonable' is really a distinction between those accepting and opposing the political principles of liberal democracy (Mouffe, 1996a: 249). Thus, we can conclude that the overlapping consensus is not a moral consensus between people with different private beliefs, but rather a political consensus that relies on a particular conception of the good. Consequently, the attempt to furnish a solution to the conflict between liberal pluralism and democratic unity by means of advancing the idea of a moral consensus based on Reason has failed.

Second, there is a clash between the moral and ontological *individualism* of liberalism and the *communitarianism* implicit in democratic thought. Take, for example, the notion of popular sovereignty, which refers to the existence of a collective will that is more than the sum of individual wills and whose realization will often be in conflict with some of these individual wills. The implicit conflict between liberal individualism and democratic communitarianism is not removed by the fact that a homogeneous community does not exist. It is certainly true that all attempts to construct a 'we' necessarily involve the exclusion of a 'them', and that therefore no fully inclusive political community can exist. However, it is precisely the politics of collective will formation, hinging upon the construction of antagonistic relations between 'friends' and 'enemies', that liberal individualism is unable to understand. Liberalism sees the individual as the starting point and destination of social action, and politics is consequently defined as the selfish pursuit of private interest (Mouffe, 1990: 60–1). Liberalism is essentially a theory of atomistic individualism, and is thus radically incompatible with the communitarian aspect of democracy.

Third, there is direct conflict between the liberal principle of *freedom* and the democratic principle of *equality*. The liberal concept of liberty emphasizes the negative freedom of individuals from the tyranny of political authorities and institutions. Individuals should be free to do what they want providing they are responsible for their actions and allow other people the same degree of liberty. In accordance with the ideology of possessive individualism (Macpherson, 1962), the inviolable integrity of the individual is stretched to include not only its actions and opinions but also its natural possessions in terms of its body, capabilities, property and relentless drive to appropriate material as well as immaterial resources. Hence, the individual is only free if these possessions are protected from interference by public authorities and institutions. Such a negative freedom is not necessarily in conflict with the demand for equality, at least not if equality is defined either as the equal right to freedom, or as the equal right to take part in the political decision-making process. A minimal and non-interfering state is undoubtedly enough to guarantee such a formal equality. However, the problem is that the combination of possessive individualism and negative freedom tends to generate an immense socioeconomic inequality, which tends to hollow out the formal equality. Historically this has resulted in increasing democratic demands for real equality in the sense of equality of opportunity. This has in turn led to the formation of a solidaristic welfare state, the socioeconomic interventions of which are often in conflict with the liberal concern for the negative freedom of the individual.

It might be possible to find ways of *mediating* the persistent conflicts between pluralism and unity, individualism and communitarianism, and freedom and equality. For example, Walzer's concept of complex equality might help to balance the demands for equality with the demand for liberty. According to Walzer (1983), different social goods should be (re-)distributed in accordance with different principles of justice that reflect the character and social meanings of the goods in question. That is to say, the principles of justice should be pluralistic in form; we do not need excessive state intervention to enforce a total equality in all possible respects. However, none of the possible forms of mediation will manage to *reconcile* the immanent conflicts of liberal democracy. Liberal democracy is based on an irreconcilable tension between liberal principles of pluralism, individualism and freedom and the democratic concern for unity, community and equality. In the last instance we are talking about a fundamental tension between a liberal logic of difference and a democratic logic of equivalence. According to Mouffe (1990: 65–6, 1991a: 14–15, 1994b: 111–12), it is the un-decidable game between these two logics that keeps liberal democracy alive and secures the primacy of politics.

Democracy as Agonistic Pluralism

'Pluralism, understood as the principle that individuals should have the possibility to organize their lives as they wish, to choose their own ends, and to realize them as they think best, is the great contribution of liberalism to modern society' (Mouffe, 1990: 58). Any democratic project must therefore find a way to come to terms with *pluralism*. According to Mouffe, this will necessarily lead us 'to discard the dangerous dream of a perfect consensus, of a harmonious collective will, and to accept the permanence of conflicts and antagonisms' (1990: 58–9). The relation between pluralism, democracy and social antagonism can be further elucidated by considering the democratic anti-liberalism of Schmitt and the political liberalism of Rawls.

According to Mouffe, we can learn from *Schmitt* why democracy must necessarily be plural and why pluralism is intrinsically linked to social antagonism. Schmitt (1985 [1923]: 26) defines democracy in terms of an identity of rulers and ruled; he admits that this definition makes it possible to view authoritarian regimes like Communism and Fascism as democratic in so far as they achieve the identity of governing and governed (1985: 16). The political implications of this definition of democracy are clearly unacceptable. The lesson to learn is thus:

that the logic of democracy alone does not guarantee the defence of individual freedom and a respect for individual rights. It is only through its articulation with political liberalism that the logic of popular sovereignty can avoid becoming tyrannical; then one cannot speak of the people as if it was one homogeneous and unified entity with a single general will. (Mouffe, 1990: 60)

Democracy should be plural. In this respect Mouffe is in complete agreement with the liberal tradition. However, the problem is that liberalism fails to grasp the intrinsic link between pluralism and social antagonism. Here Schmitt's criticism of liberal theory can help us. According to Schmitt (1985: 35), liberal pluralism is characterized by endless conflicts between different opinions (it is these conflicts that prevent the identity between rulers and ruled). However, 'every religious, moral, economic, ethical or other antithesis transforms into a political one if it is sufficiently strong to group human beings effectively according to friend and enemy' (Schmitt, 1976 [1927]: 37). In other words, pluralism entails politics and social antagonism, as disagreement between different concepts of the good will divide people into friends and enemies (Mouffe, 1996b: 8–9). If liberalism fails to see this, it is because its individualist conception of politics as the rational pursuit of private interests 'annihilates the political as a domain of conquering power and repression' (Schmitt, 1976: 71). It is therefore necessary to abandon the ontological individualism of the liberal tradition in order to grasp the collective character of the political struggles that pluralism facilitates.

Mouffe considers *Rawls* a paradigmatic example of the failure of political liberalism to deal with the antagonistic forms of politics within plural democracy. Rawls (1971) originally presented his principle of Justice as Fairness as the consequence of a 'free agreement' of rational individuals who, in a hypothetical 'original' position, are free, equal and ignorant of their future position in society (Mouffe, 1994a:

320–1). Rational individuals will under these circumstances realize that it is to their mutual advantage that liberty, income and wealth should be equally distributed, since that will permit everybody to pursue their different conceptions of the good. Rawls (1993) has recently emphasized the historicity of his principles of justice and explicitly distanced himself from rational choice theory. We shall return to discuss the implications of this move for his conception of citizenship in the next chapter. Here we shall only consider the fact that the very idea of an overlapping consensus between rational, self-interested individuals tends to preclude the existence of social antagonism at the level of politics. As earlier mentioned, Rawls seems to apply a somewhat totalitarian argument: either people within the political community take part in the rational consensus about the way political institutions in society should be organized, or they are unreasonable and excluded from the political community. This argument tends to remove social antagonism from the political community, not by eliminating social antagonism but by displacing it to the relation between the political community and its constitutive outside (the unreasonable). The reason for the evacuation of conflict and antagonism from the political community is to be found in the fact that 'politics is not affected by the existence of pluralism, which Rawls understands only as the multiplicity of the conceptions of the good that people exercise in the private sphere, perfectly separated from the public sphere where consensus based on self-interest reigns' (Mouffe, 1987: 115). In Rawls there is no room for a political pluralism between different hegemonic forces that are fighting over the 'correct' interpretation of the empty signifiers of freedom and equality. Social antagonism exists either in the private sphere or between the political community and its constitutive outside. Thus Rawls' deliberative democracy is a perfect liberal utopia in which disputes over the principles of justice are eliminated once and for all by a political consensus obtained by reasonable, self-interested individuals on the basis of public deliberation.

The liberal idea of a deliberative democracy based on political consensus is challenged by the recent surge of political conflicts. At the threshold of the twenty-first century we are witnessing a world-wide proliferation of social antagonisms of great political significance. The forces that overthrew the Communist regimes in Russia and eastern Europe have become divided by ethnic, regional and religious antagonisms, and the loss of the West's enemy seems to have paved the way for the eruption of the same kind of antagonisms in the western democracies (Mouffe, 1994b: 105–7). In the Middle East fundamentalist movements are gaining ground, and in the Third World there are signs that the end of the cold war has fuelled antagonistic conflicts at the political level of the state. Now, some might try to construe the proliferation of political conflicts and antagonisms as a temporary interruption of the march towards a liberal democracy freed from antagonism. However, if we are to face up to this huge challenge the belief in a consensus without conflicts and exclusions must be abandoned. 'The prime task of democratic politics is not to eliminate passions, nor to relegate them to the private sphere in order to render rational consensus possible, but to mobilize these passions, and give them a democratic outlet' (1994b: 109). Thus, rather than seeking to dissolve political conflicts and antagonisms within the framework of a consensual, deliberative democracy, we should aim to find ways of making social antagonisms compatible with pluralist democracy. The trick is to turn *antagonism* into *agonism*. This would be done by securing a political consensus on basic democratic values and procedures while allowing dissent over the interpretation of the precise meaning of these values and procedures and their implications for our political choice between different ways of organizing society. Within such an agonistic democracy enemies would not be destroyed, but rather turned into adversaries whose politics we might disagree with, but whose existence would be legitimate and should be tolerated (Mouffe, 1993a: 4, 1995: 501–2, 1996c: 8–9). As mentioned above, the limit for the agonistic inclusion of enemies as legitimate adversaries is, of course, those who apply anti-democratic means in their attack on the basic democratic values and procedures.

Post-structuralist insights might help to sustain an *agonistic democracy* that is capable of transforming enemies into adversaries. Clearly it is unhelpful to demand of an ethnic-nationalist movement that it sticks to the democratic rules of the game and commits itself to basic democratic values. However, the nomadization and hybridization of identity might contribute to the dissolution of antagonistic frontiers (Mouffe, 1994b: 110–11). Nomadization refers to the attempt to undercut the allegiance of a specific identity to a certain place or a certain property, and thereby to show that all identities are constructed in and through hegemonic power struggles. This will tend to denaturalize social and political identities and make them more negotiable. Hybridization refers to the attempt to make people realize that their identity is multiple in the sense of constituting an overdetermined ensemble of identifications. For example, as soon as people see that they are not only 'Serbs' but also 'women', 'poor', 'Europeans', etc., their loyalties, and therefore their passions, will be divided.

255

The Call For a Radical Plural Democracy

The addition of the term '*radical*' to what we have described above as '*plural democracy*' can produce two different meanings. It might indicate that democracy should be radically pluralist in the sense that the plurality of different identities is not grounded in any transcendent or underlying positive ground. A radical plural democracy will in this interpretation involve 'the struggle for a maximum autonomization of spheres [of struggle: JT] on the basis of the generalization of the equivalential-egalitarian logic' (Laclau and Mouffe, 1985: 167). The other possible meaning of radical plural democracy is that plural democracy, and the struggles for freedom and equality it engenders, should be deepened and extended to all areas of society (Mouffe, 1989: 39, 1990: 57). In this interpretation radical plural democracy entails the pluralization of democracy and the displacement of the Democratic Revolution to more and more fields of the social.

Whereas liberal democracy aimed to draw a rigid line of demarcation between the public sphere of democratic politics and the private sphere of economic liberalism, the struggle for a radical plural democracy seeks to displace the quest for freedom and equality to the economic sphere, thereby undermining the traditional private–public divide. Such a displacement makes it possible to envisage the intrinsic link between the struggle for *radical plural democracy* and the struggle for *socialism*. As Laclau and Mouffe contend, 'every project for radical democracy implies a socialist dimension, as it is necessary to put an end to capitalist relations of production, which are at the root of numerous relations of subordination; but socialism is *one* of the components of radical democracy, not vice versa' (Laclau and Mouffe, 1985: 178). The struggle for a radical plural democracy will involve the socialization of production, but this 'cannot mean only workers' self-management, as what is at stake is true participation by all subjects in decisions about what is to be produced, how it is to be produced, and the forms in which the product is to be distributed' (1985: 178).

It should be noted that Laclau and Mouffe's understanding of radical plural democracy differs from many other forms of radical or participatory democracy inasmuch as it does not involve a rejection of the liberal democratic regime. 'The aim is not to create a completely different kind of society, but to use the symbolic resources of the liberal democratic tradition to struggle against relations of subordination not only in the economy but also those linked to gender, race, or sexual orientation, for example' (Mouffe, 1990: 57–8).

This brings us to a crucial aspect of radical plural democracy, which has to do with its capacity to engender political struggles and unify them into a new hegemonic project for the Left. The argument starts from the observation that hierarchical relations of subordination provide the necessary but not sufficient condition for the rise of political struggles against oppression. Relations of subordination are only transformed into sites of democratic antagonism when they are confronted with the liberal democratic quest for freedom and equality (Mouffe, 1988a: 94–5). Thus the proliferation of new social movements in the 1970s and 1980s was a result of the negation of the liberal-democratic ideology by new forms of subordination produced by the increasing commodification, bureaucratization and homogenization of social life (Laclau and Mouffe, 1985: 159–65). The extension of the Democratic Revolution to still new areas of society provides sufficient condition for the creation of democratic antagonism, but it does not predetermine how these democratic antagonisms are to be articulated. Democratic antagonisms do not necessarily lead to democratic struggles as they can be articulated with different kinds of discourse, even with anti-democratic right-wing discourses demanding 'less state and more market'. However, the project of radical plural democracy offers a way of turning democratic antagonisms into democratic struggles directed towards a wide-ranging democratization of social life (Mouffe, 1988a: 96). Unification of the different kinds of democratic struggles against sexism, racism, and new forms of subordination under the banner of radical plural democracy is the primary task of the Left. However, 'these struggles do not spontaneously converge, and in order to establish democratic equivalences, a new "common sense" is necessary, which would transform the identity of different groups so that the demands of each group could be articulated with those of others according to the principle of democratic equivalence' (Mouffe, 1989: 42). The task, then, is not to establish an alliance between dominant and subordinate agencies, but rather to produce a new collective will that makes sure that the interests of one group are not pursued at the expense of the interests of other groups.

The struggle for a radical plural democracy provides the Left with a new hegemonic project potentially capable of engendering and unifying a broad range of progressive political struggles. However, radical plural democracy provides neither an actually realizable blueprint nor in principle an achievable utopia that we should seek to realize as far as possible. The reason for this is to be found in the fact that plural democracy can be conceived as radical in at least two senses. The first has to do with the gradual displacement of the democratic imaginary to all spheres of society. The second concerns the basic tension between the liberal and democratic aspects of plural democracy, and the fact that the condition of possibility of a further democratization of society is also the condition of impossibility. From the latter it follows that radical plural democracy will always be an incomplete and conflictual project. The attempt to establish a fully democratic society in which people 'will be perfectly free because they are entirely equal, and where they will all be perfectly equal because they are entirely free' would necessarily involve the creation of a totally transparent society in which all tensions and all forms of repression are themselves repressed. That would bring forth a totalitarian nightmare. The paradox is that the concept of radical plural democracy 'is precisely not "radical" in the sense of pure, true democracy; its radical character implies, on the contrary, that we can save democracy only by taking into account its own radical impossibility' (Žižek, 1989: 6). It is the very impossibility of a fully achieved democracy that prevents radical plural democracy from constituting a distant, but perfectly realizable, *telos*. We might, therefore, conclude that radical plural democracy, rather, takes the form of a promise: the promise of a democracy to come in the Derridean sense of the term (Mouffe, 1994b: 111–12).

The Search For Appropriate Democratic Institutions

Whereas Schmitt scorns parliamentarism and conceives a true democracy as being based on a *substantial* homogeneity, Kelsen presents the *procedural* rules associated with parliamentarism as the necessary instruments for arriving at political decisions within a democracy (Mouffe, 1991a: 10–11). This seems to confront us with the dilemma as to whether we should advance a substantial definition of liberal democracy, and accept the implicit dangers implied by such a definition, or we should opt for a strictly procedural definition of liberal democracy, and run the risk of impoverishing the very concept of democracy (1991a: 11). However, the concept of democracy as *agonistic pluralism* helps us avoid this dilemma (1991a: 12). As such, it might be argued that because democratic procedures are not sufficient for creating the political unity of democratic societies a more substantial homogeneity is required. However, as the political principles of freedom and equality give rise to multiple interpretations, and are far too abstract to constitute any precise guide for political decision-making, we need to establish a number of procedures for arriving at political decisions within the undecidable terrain of liberty and equality. These procedures must, of course, be in strict accordance with the constitutive principles of liberal democracy. But given the undecidability and indeterminacy of these principles there is plenty of room for disagreement over the precise form of the procedural forms of liberal democracy, and this is exactly what spurs the search for *appropriate democratic institutions*.

The discussion of the strengths and weaknesses of different kinds of democratic institutions is scarcely developed in the works of Mouffe. Her interest lies primarily in the field of political philosophy. Nevertheless, she has some interesting comments on the works of Macpherson, Bobbio and Hirst. All three share the ambition of articulating liberal democracy with socialism. However, when it comes to the form of democratic institutions Macpherson seems to be much more critical of the institutions of liberal democracy than, for example, Bobbio (Mouffe, 1993c: 102–5). Hence, whereas Bobbio (1987) wants to adapt the institutions of liberal democracy to make way for more equality and a greater democratic accountability, Macpherson (1973 [1964], 1977) recommends the replacement of the liberal form of representative democracy (parliamentarism) with a direct participatory democracy organized in terms of a socialist council democracy. Bobbio claims that the process of democratization should not be conceived as a transition from representative to direct democracy, and he thinks that representative democracy is the best response to the three enemies of democracy in terms of the complexification, bureaucratization and massification of society. Representative democracy should not only be maintained and adapted to these challenges; it should also be extended to all spheres of society (Mouffe, 1993c: 92–4).

Now, while Mouffe thinks Bobbio is right to stress the importance of representative democracy and the need to abandon the illusions of direct democracy, she thinks that Bobbio somehow overstates the case for representative democracy and fails to confront the fundamental problems of parliamentarism (Mouffe, 1993c: 96). Bobbio recognizes the fact that parliamentarism is being undermined by the invisible power of neo-corporatist interest politics and that the actual circumstances have turned parliamentary discussions into a 'empty and trivial formality', as Schmitt (1985: 50) succinctly puts it. However, Bobbio leaves it there and does not offer any suggestions as to how liberal democracy can be renewed in the light of the shortcomings of representative democracy.

It is here that Hirst's thoughts about the development of an *associational democracy* become relevant (Hirst, 1988, 1994). According to Mouffe, 'Hirst sees associational socialism as representing the only challenge to corporate capitalism that respects the principles of liberal

259

democracy' (Mouffe, 1993c: 98). The central idea of associational socialism is that economic units should be cooperatively owned and democratically managed. Associational socialism 'encourages the organization of social life in small unities and challenges hierarchy and administrative centralization' (1993c: 98–9). This means that also the public bodies providing education, health, welfare and community services can be democratized according to the general principles of decentralized, democratic governance. As such, Hirst's vision of an associational democracy provides us with an important model for how to democratize *both* the private and the public sector. If we want more democracy, we must make room for a multiplicity of democratically managed associations and communities. An associational democracy needs a state. The pluralist state should not be seen as merely one association among others, as it is involved in different forms of meta-governance. Hence, according to Hirst, we must insist upon the need for a reflexive pluralist state whose legal task is to ensure equity between associations, police their conduct and protect the rights of both individuals and associations (1993c: 99).

A crucial condition for the establishment of an associational socialist democracy is that we relinquish the individualist conception of the individual as an unencumbered self which exists prior to and independently of social communities. The recognition of individuals as encumbered, multiple selves leads to a new understanding of the idea of social rights. Rights are not to be seen as a property of the individual herself. Hence, 'it is through her inscription in specific social relations, rather than as an individual outside society, that a social agent is granted rights' (1993c: 97). Neither the individual nor the community possesses universal rights; the individual has rights in and through his or her constitutive membership of a community. It is in this sense that, for example, social rights must be understood as collective rather than individual rights.

The Present Challenge to Plural Democracy

The growth of private interest government constitutes a major challenge to representational democracy, but the advancement of an associational socialist democracy provides us with an effective counter-measure. However, as Hirst indicates, associational democracy should be advanced only in order to renew the traditional forms of liberal democracy. Representative democracy should not be abandoned, but should rather be supplemented by new forms of democratic institutions. And as a matter of fact, the political parties will have an important role to play within an agonistic democracy in giving expression to cross-cutting forms of social division and political conflict. The problem here is that if the political parties *fail to do their job* a whole range of ethnic, religious, and nationalist movements are likely to take over with the possible result that the democratic creed of society is jeopardized (Mouffe, 1993a: 5).

In the light of this the celebration of the 'end of ideology', the 'demise of the Left' and even the 'end of politics' constitutes another challenge to plural democracy (Mouffe, 1993a, 1993d, 1995). In western Europe consensus at the centre has created a *political vacuum* that has facilitated the growth of the extreme Right. People feel that they can no longer tell the difference between the political parties, who all claim to inhabit the political centre. This is a frustrating experience in the light of the many unresolved problems of unemployment, environmental destruction, and deteriorating standards of public service, and it is this frustration which feeds the political parties at the extreme Right, which are not exactly strong supporters of liberal democracy. What we need in this critical situation is a new confrontational politics. We need political forces with new political vocabularies which can construct new political frontiers in their attempt to deal effectively with the political and social problems of today. 'A healthy democratic process calls for a vibrant clash of political positions and an open conflict of interests. If such is missing, it can too easily be replaced by a confrontation between non-negotiable moral values and essentialist identities' (Mouffe, 1993a: 6). In aiming to tackle this challenge an agonistic democracy seems to constitute a much better starting point than a deliberative democracy in the Habermasian and Rawlsian sense of the term. For whereas a deliberative democracy aims to establish a consensus through free and unconstrained public discussion, agonistic democracy seeks to make room for a confrontation between adversaries who agree on the liberal-democratic rules of the game while disagreeing not only about substantial, political and moral issues but also about the precise interpretation of the rules of the game (Mouffe, 1995: 502).

14
Beyond Libertarianism and Communitarianism

Introduction

The Left needs to rally around the idea of a *democratic citizenship* (Mouffe, 1992a: 3–4). First, because the demand for the extension of rights, based on an egalitarian notion of citizenship, would help the Left to recover the radical impetus behind the popular struggles that once brought down the *ancien régime*. Second, because the idea of democratic citizenship would help the Left defeat neo-liberalism by reinvoking notions of community, civic virtue and active participation, which have been buried by the surge of moral individualism and the advent of the hyper-market society. Third, and most importantly, the Left should embrace the idea of democratic citizenship because, as we shall see, it provides a vital means in the struggle for a radical plural democracy. Whereas the first two reasons follow directly from the liberal and communitarian notions of democratic citizenship, the latter is conditional upon reformulation of the notion of democratic citizenship, which seeks to go beyond both liberalism and communitarianism. The present chapter aims to provide such a reformulation. It examines the weaknesses of liberalism and communitarianism, discusses the possibility of a synthesis between the two philosophical traditions, and reworks their notions of democratic citizenship, before aiming to elaborate a concept of radical democratic citizenship. The chapter concludes with a brief discussion of the idea of a gendered citizenship. However, before entering into discussion about liberalism and communitarianism, it is necessary to provide a sketch of the genealogy of the liberal notion of democratic citizenship.

The Genealogy of the Liberal Notion of Democratic Citizenship

Today most people agree that democratic citizenship has to do with the rights and obligations the individual obtains through his or her membership of a political community. The *liberal* notion of democratic citizenship tends to privilege *rights* over *obligations*. In a nutshell, the citizen is conceived as an individual bearer of universal rights. However, even the liberal notion of citizenship hinges on a reference to community. Hence, the universal rights of the individual are to be defended collectively by society at large. Citizen rights are thus granted in and through an instrumental political community, i.e. a political community the *raison d'être* of which is to protect the universal rights of the individual. Thus the liberal notion of democratic citizenship invokes a reference to both the individual and the community, and takes the rights of the individual to be dependent on the community. This is interesting as it is precisely what makes it possible for the liberal notion of democratic citizenship to mediate the tension between individualism and communitarian collectivism. The individual is not constituted by the community, yet he or she can only be a free and autonomous individual due to the presence of an instrumental community that can protect, and extend, his or her rights.

The liberal notion of democratic citizenship not only privileges rights over obligations but also conceives the citizen as *passive* rather than *active*. The transformation of the Ancient Greek conception of the citizen as an active participant in the government of society (in Greek: *polités*) to a passive bearer of universal rights (in French: *citoyen*) might be explained as a consequence of the expansion of the Roman Empire, which conferred on an increasing number of people in the conquered territories the status of citizen (in Latin: *cives*), thereby making it impossible for everybody to be actively engaged in affairs of state (Walzer, 1989: 214–15).

The size of the Roman Empire may have impeded active political participation, and the political obligation of the conquered subjects may have been rather small. Nevertheless, the transformation of the active citizen with political obligation into a *passive bearer of rights* was first and foremost the consequence of two important discursive developments (Balibar, 1994: 8–12). The *first* took place in the transition between Ancient Greece and medieval Europe, or, say, between Aristotle and St Augustine. Aristotle placed man as a citizen in a public sphere of reciprocity and equality with his fellow men; at the same time, he placed beside and indeed below him various types of dependent and imperfect beings – the woman, the child (the pupil) and the slave (the servant or the labourer) (1994: 9). The relation between

263

the man-citizen and the inferior beings, who are excluded from the civic space, involves the man always talking and the inferior always listening. This is in stark contrast to the relation between fellow citizens, who alternately talk and listen (1994: 10). The whole discourse of citizenship changed with the breakdown of the Ancient structure and the advent of Christianity and secular absolutism. According to St Augustine, everybody is equal in the face of God and the Sovereign, and it is this equality of the people in their subjection to the will of God and the will of the Sovereign that constitutes them as citizens. People face a transcendental law that is present, not as an external authority founded in some natural inequality (as, for example, between men and women), but as an inner voice that everybody is bound to obey (1994: 10). In short, the first event takes us from the Greek man-citizen, whose autonomy and equality hinge on the subjection of other people, to the Christian man, whose citizenship is conditional upon his own subjection to both a divine and a secular sovereignty.

The *second* event is produced by the declaration of human rights in the French Revolution in 1789. The Christian man obtained his citizenship in and through his subjection to the law. Through their subjection the Christian citizens obtained an equal protection from the sovereign. The French Revolution and the declaration of human rights abolished the double subjection of the people to God and the absolute monarch. Man was no longer called before the law by his inner voice, but instead constituted as a responsible law maker and the possessor of a number of universal rights. According to Balibar, this second transition from a citizenship based on equal subjection and equal protection to a citizenship based on equal rights means that 'citizenship is not one among other attributes of subjectivity; on the contrary: it *is* subjectivity, *that form* of subjectivity that would no longer be identical with subjection for anyone' (1994: 12). Thus, we end up with liberal democratic citizenship, which is not fully achieved by many people (as it is difficult to avoid subjection), but which, nevertheless, constitutes the subject as a free subjectivity.

The Problems of Liberalism and Communitarianism

In the *liberal perspective* the citizen is, first and foremost, an individual bearer of universal rights. These rights are protected by the law, which is enforced by the state. The constitutional rights of the individual are dependent on the collective defence of these rights by the community. However, while the individual is dependent on the community, the latter is not taken to be dependent upon the individual. Hence, liberal thought is not concerned with the active participation of citizens in the development of civic virtues and common norms and values. Liberalism reduces democratic citizenship to a question of the legal status of the individual, and views social cooperation only as a means of enhancing our productive capacities and increasing each person's individual prosperity (Mouffe, 1988b: 29). The absence of a common, political obligation fosters a gradual weakening and impoverishment of the political community, which in turn may result in a failure to secure the rights of the citizens and uphold the liberal democratic regime. Thus the problem with the liberal notion of democratic citizenship, which affirms that there is no common good and that each individual should be able to define and seek to realize his or her own conception of the good, is that it runs the risk of *sacrificing the citizen to the individual* (Mouffe, 1992b: 29).

Communitarian critics like Taylor (1985), MacIntyre (1984) and Sandel (1982) have rightly emphasized the growing phenomenon of *anomie*, which seems to accompany the hegemonic forms of liberal individualism (Mouffe, 1992b: 29). However, whereas it is certainly true that we need to counter the atomistic individualism of the liberal tradition by emphasizing the citizen's active participation in the development and defence of common norms and values, we must reject the communitarian attempt to revive republican ideas of a substantive community based on a comprehensive conception of the common good. The problem is not so much that the republican communities in Ancient Greece and medieval Europe were highly undemocratic – for example, excluding women from participating in the formulation and administration of the common good. Such undemocratic exclusion belonged to the pre-modern age and is not likely to be reproduced in the consolidated western democracy of today. The problem is rather that the idea of a substantive community based on a comprehensive conception of the common good creates a *Gemeinschaft* type of community that is clearly pre-modern and incompatible with the pluralism which today is a constitutive component of modern democracy. The problem is, therefore, the opposite of that of liberalism, as the communitarian critics of liberal thought tend to *sacrifice the individual to the citizen* (Mouffe, 1992b: 29).

The crucial question is how to conceptualize democratic citizenship in a way that does not sacrifice the citizen to the individual or vice versa (1992b: 29–30). According to Mouffe, an attempt to answer this question must necessarily begin by seeking to develop a conception of political community that is compatible with the pluralism of modern democracy. That is, we should aim to envisage 'a form of communality

265

that respects diversity and makes room for different forms of individuality' (1992b: 30).

Yet, is it really possible to create a synthesis of *liberal individualism* and *republican communitarianism*? Is the liberal celebration of the negative freedom of individuals not radically incompatible with the existence of a political community that is more than merely a minimal protective shell of individual rights? According to Mouffe (1988b: 30, 1988c: 203–5), Berlin (1975 [1969]) believes that such a radical incompatibility exists, while Skinner (1991) thinks that it is perfectly possible to reconcile negative freedom with an active participation in the development of common norms and values. Skinner finds in the classical republicanism of Machiavelli an argument that reconciles virtuous public service with negative freedom. According to Machiavelli, free states are those that avoid external servitude and are able to govern themselves according to their own will (1991: 194–5). Free states, which constitutionally must have the form of a *res publica*, are the primary condition for ensuring the negative freedom of the citizens (1991: 195). However, self-governing republics can only be kept in being if their citizens cultivate civic virtue through active participation in government and in the development of common norms and values (1991: 197). It follows that, to ensure our own liberty and avoid the servitude that renders its exercise impossible we must commit ourselves to pursue the common good (Mouffe, 1988b: 30). In other words, common, political obligation is perfectly compatible with individual liberty in the negative sense of the absence of any element of constraint and, thus, of freedom to pursue one's own chosen ends.

Reworking Liberalism and Communitarianism

The attempt to create a synthesis of liberal pluralism and the communitarian emphasis on the constitutive character of the political community requires a substantial reworking of both the liberal and the communitarian traditions. The synthesis we are aiming to construct must 'go beyond the conceptions of citizenship of both the liberal and the civic republican traditions while building on their respective strengths' (Mouffe, 1991b: 70). In other words, we must in relation to the liberal tradition show how individual rights can be defended within a politically constructed political community. In relation to the communitarian tradition we must show how the political community can be redefined in terms of 'what we can call, following Wittgenstein, a "grammar of conduct" that coincides with the allegiance to the

266

constitutive ethico-political principles of modern democracy' (Mouffe, 1992b: 30).

Let us begin with the *liberal tradition*, which shall here be represented by its most distinguished and sophisticated scholar, Rawls. The works of Rawls challenge the views of hard-line libertarians such as Hayek and Nozick; nevertheless his concept of democratic citizenship does not go beyond liberal individualism. Rawls rejects the idea of natural rights, while being unable to accept that it is only as citizens within a community that we have rights (Mouffe, 1987: 119). Alternatively Rawls aims to provide a rationalistic foundation for democratic citizenship. Citizenship is defined as the legally ensured capacity of each person to form, revise and rationally pursue his or her conception of the good. That is, citizens are individuals who use their civil, political and social rights to pursue their own interests within constraints imposed by the exigency to respect the rights of others (Mouffe, 1992a: 6). Democratic citizenship is defined in terms of liberal democratic rights, and in Rawls' initial formulation these rights are guaranteed by a rational agreement between free and equal individuals who, at the moment of the agreement, are ignorant of everything that could be prejudicial to their impartiality (Rawls, 1971). Because the rights of the democratic citizens are rooted in this Archimedean point of rational agreement, the right is claimed to have priority over any conception of the common good.

This position has been fiercely attacked by Rawls' communitarian critics. According to Mouffe (1988c: 199), Sandel is perfectly correct in claiming that Rawls does not succeed in justifying the priority of the right over the good in a convincing manner. The priority of the right over the good cannot be justified independently of a particular political community, since it is 'only through our participation in a community which defines the good that we can have a sense of the right and a conception of justice' (1988c: 199). However, the inadequacy of Rawls' attempt to justify the priority of the right over the good does not prove the superiority of a communitarian politics of the common good over a liberal politics of defending rights. So, rather than abandoning the conception of justice as the primary virtue of society, we should recognize that the assertion of the right over the good is only possible within a particular political community, or regime, which is defined by the common political good it puts to work, i.e. the principles of freedom and equality for all. Hence, Rawls is right to defend pluralism and individual rights, but wrong to believe that this defence requires the rejection of any notion of a common good (Mouffe, 1987: 110–11). What we need to do is make a clear distinction between the common political good, which justifies the priority of rights, and the common moral good, which is claimed to be secondary to pluralism and the defence of rights (Mouffe, 1988c: 199). The common political good is defined by a collective will at the level of regime, whereas the common moral good is defined by a multiplicity of singular wills.

In his later works, Rawls (1985, 1987, 1993) tends to move in this direction as he recognizes the historicity of both individuals and the principles of justice; he also tends to grant priority to reasonable actions of context-bound deliberation over rational, self-interested choices. However, according to Mouffe (1987: 112–16), Rawls does not go far enough in his conception of justice as political. According to Rawls (1985: 6), the undisputed principles of justice are informed by certain fundamental intuitive ideas that are latent in the public political culture of a democratic society. However, these intuitive ideas are in the last instance derived from individual moral capacities and not from the presence of a certain political regime (Mouffe, 1987: 113). Rawls not only fails to provide an adequate understanding of the political in the sense of *politeia*; he also fails to account for the role of politics in the form of hegemony and social antagonism. Rawls accepts that the formulation of the principles of justice must start from the basic values of freedom and equality, but he tends to think that these values are self-evident and uncontroversial. This is far from being the case: freedom and equality are sedimented values, which in the last instance are the result of a political decision taken in an undecidable terrain; they therefore invariably involve the exclusion of the alternative values of both the adversaries, who are tolerated, and the enemies, who are not (Mouffe, 1993e: 143–4).

In sum, the reworking of the liberal notion of democratic citizenship entails an emphatic insistence on the role of a particular hegemonic form of political community for sustaining the rights of individuals. It is because the political community is founded on a particular political common good that democratic citizens have the rights they have. If citizens want to enjoy these rights in the future they must actively engage in the communal activities and political struggles that re-enact the common political good.

Turning now to the discussion of the *communitarian notion* of democratic citizenship, we shall start by recalling the critique of the implications of liberal individualism. The problem is that the liberal notion of democratic citizenship only allows for an instrumental community. According to the communitarians, such a 'thin' conception of community will invariably lead to an impoverishment of the notion of citizenship. In their view the 'thin', instrumental conception of community should be replaced with a 'thick' community that constitutes individuals as active members of an organic community organized around a substantive conception of the common good (Mouffe, 1991b: 71). As we have seen above, the problem with such a 'thick' conception of the political community is that its pre-modern ideal of an all-embracing substantive unity is incompatible with liberal pluralism. Nevertheless, the totalitarian implications of the communitarian conception of community can be removed without giving up the emphasis on the constitutive character of the community. This can be achieved by insisting that 'what makes us fellow citizens in a liberal democratic regime is not a substantive idea of the good but a set of political principles specific to such a tradition: the principles of freedom and equality for all' (1991b: 75). Such principles constitute what, borrowing from Wittgenstein, we can call a grammar of conduct, and it is the individuals' recognition of the ethico-political principles embodied in this grammar of conduct that constitutes them as citizens with both rights and obligations.

According to Mouffe (1991b: 75–6), the conceptualization of the political community in terms of a certain grammar of conduct re-establishes the lost connection between ethics and politics. The liberal tradition stripped politics of its ethical components as it relegated normative concerns to the private sphere of morals and religion, and as the instrumental community of mutual interests did not foster any principles for the ethical guidance of civic activities. The moral vacuum of liberal politics tends to undermine the social cohesion of democratic societies. However, the attempt to reconnect politics and ethics should not seek to revive the pre-modern fusion of politics and morals. That is, we should not aim to subordinate politics to the moral values specified by the common good, but rather emphasize the role of the grammar of conduct, whose ethical-political principles cannot be derived from any comprehensive moral. Thus the solution to the problem of how to re-establish the lost connection between ethics and politics seems to hinge upon the distinction between a common moral good and a common ethical-political good.

The notion of a political grammar of conduct is provided by the conservative philosopher Oakeshott, who in *On Human Conduct* (1975) draws a distinction between human associations conceived in terms of *universitas* and those conceived in terms of *societas*. *Universitas* refers to engagement in an enterprise defined by a common purpose or interest. By contrast, *societas* refers to a formal engagement in terms of the ethico-political rules that specify the conditions to be subscribed to in choosing performances. Individuals becomes citizens within a certain *societas* (or *res publica*) not by subscribing to a common goal but rather by recognizing the authority of a certain 'practice of civility' which specifies the grammar of conduct of the political community (Mouffe, 1991b: 76).

Oakeshott's conception of *societas* as a constitutive community of ethico-political principles goes beyond both the liberal conception of an instrumental community defined by the rule of law and the communitarian conception of a substantive community defined by the common good. Two problems remain to be solved, however. The first concerns the fact that the conservative content of Oakeshott's *res publica* is incompatible with the advancement of a radical plural democracy. This problem can be solved simply by redefining the content of the *res publica*. Henceforth, the ethico-political principles with which people should identify in order to become citizens within a *societas* are those of freedom and equality for all and everywhere. People might be engaged in different purposive enterprises and hold different conceptions of the good, but what binds them together as citizens within the *res publica* should be their submission to a radical interpretation of the principles of freedom and equality. In this interpretation citizenship is neither one identity among others, as in liberalism, nor the dominant overriding identity, as in communitarianism. Rather, citizenship is a social imaginary that affects all the different subject positions of social and political agents (1991b: 79).

The second problem is more fundamental, having to do with Oakeshott's flawed conception of politics (1991b: 78). For Oakeshott politics is something that takes place within the shared language of civility, which defines the 'we' of the *res publica*. Oakeshott has no conception of politics as hegemonic struggles over the constitution of the political community, involving the construction of a 'we' and the positing of a 'they', whether in the form of an adversary or an enemy. Consequently, he cannot account for the above attempt to redefine the content of the *res publica* through hegemonic struggles.

By introducing politics and antagonism into Oakeshott's argument, and by changing the content of the ethico-political principles of the *res publica*, we arrive at a conception of democratic citizenship according to which citizenship is a matter of adhering to the ethico-political principles defined by a politically constructed political community. Thus the reworking of the liberal and communitarian positions tends to lead to exactly the same result: community is constitutive of citizenship. However, the community in question is neither an instrumental nor a substantive community, but a social imaginary that defines a political common good, shaped in and through exclusionary hegemonic struggles. In other words, political community should not be conceived as an empirical referent, i.e. as a group of people unified by the presence of a mechanical or organic solidarity; instead it should be understood as a discursive surface of inscription that permits the construction of a 'we' by advancing a particular conceptualization of the empty signifier of the 'common good' (Mouffe, 1992b: 30).

Towards the Notion of a Radical Democratic Citizenship

The deconstructive reworking of the liberal and communitarian notion of democratic citizenship suggests that we envisage democratic citizenship 'as a form of political identity that is created through identification with the political principles of modern pluralist democracy, i.e. the assertion of liberty and equality for all' (1992b: 30). In this view, democratic citizens are neither mere bearers of universal rights nor servants of a state governed by a substantive conception of the common good. Rather, democratic citizenship is a 'common political identity of persons who might be engaged in many different communities and who have differing conceptions of the good, but who accept submission to certain authoritative rules of conduct' (1992b: 30–1). The democratic citizens take an active part in the interpretation and constant re-enactment of the rules of conduct and the correlative ethico-political principles, which, rather than prescribing a substantive consensus, function as a kind of vanishing point around which plural democracy is organized.

Democratic citizenship can thus be viewed as a communitarian discourse that urges us to treat everybody as free and equal. The constitutive principles of freedom and equality for all can be interpreted in many different ways. In recent decades, neo-conservative and neo-liberal forces have criticized what they see as an excess of democracy and an excess of equality, respectively. A host of distinguished intellectuals have suggested that plural democracy should be narrowed in scope, and that liberal values such as individualism and free market economy should take precedence over democratic values such as political and socioeconomic equality (Laclau and Mouffe, 1985: 171–5; Mouffe, 1988c: 193). In the context of this anti-democratic offensive, which has taken the form of a frontal attack on the welfare state, Rawls' principles of justice are commendable. However, while Rawls' interpretation of democratic citizenship is certainly progressive, it has a limited political role, being too individualistic and failing to take into account the demands of the new social movements and the various forms of anti-state resistance (Mouffe, 1987: 117–18). As an alternative to both the anti-democratic offensive and Rawls' defence of the present form of

271

liberal democracy, a radical democratic interpretation of democratic citizenship aims to extend the principles of plural democracy to all spheres of society. A *radical democratic citizenship* will thus involve the creation of a collective form of identification that constructs a 'we' through the expansion of a chain of equivalence between workers, women, gays, blacks and others who struggle against illegitimate forms of subordination (Mouffe, 1992b: 31). It will also involve the articulation of a new egalitarian ideal that is sensitive to present political struggles. Such an egalitarianism might be founded upon Walzer's notion of complex equality or upon a de-construction of the state–market dichotomy (Laclau, 1990a: xii-xv; Mouffe, 1987: 118).

A radical democratic citizenship would challenge illegitimate sub-ordination in all social spheres, for it is a fact that no sphere is immune from the principles of freedom and equality (Mouffe, 1992b: 32). However, this does not mean that the private is eradicated because it is invaded by public concerns for freedom and equality. 'The distinc-tion between private and public can be maintained as a distinction between individual and citizen' (1992b: 32). Our wants, choices and decisions are private because they are our own individual responsi-bility, but our performances are public because they must subscribe to the conditions and principles specified by our democratic citizenship. 'The identities qua individual and qua citizen are preserved, and none is sacrificed to the other; they coexist in a permanent tension that can never be reconciled' (1992b: 32).

A Gendered Citizenship?

A final question is whether we should aim to develop a *gendered concept* of *citizenship*. Pateman (1988, 1989) rightly affirms that citizenship has traditionally been conceived as a formal status obtained by men, within a public space, based on the negation of women's participation. Confronted with this public world of citizenship, women face what Pateman calls Wollstonecraft's dilemma: either they obtain the status of citizens by aiming to become like men, or they insist on their particular identity as women and continue to be excluded from citizenship. Pateman's solution to this dilemma, according to which one cannot be both a woman and a citizen, is the elaboration of a gendered notion of citizenship. She asserts that women should obtain citizenship qua their identity as women in exactly the same way as men obtain citizenship qua their identity as men. Whereas men become citizens in and through their willingness to serve and die for their country, women should become citizens in and through their capacity to create life, to be mothers.

Pateman's attempt to attach political significance to women's so-called specific tasks breaks down the rigid distinction between the public and the private, which has served as a means to keep women in a subordinate position. However, Pateman's deconstruction of the public–private divide is founded on an essentialist conception of men as men and women as women (Mouffe, 1993f: 82). Pateman never deconstructs the opposition between men and women, and thus fails to realize the implications of conceiving the masculine/feminine distinction as discursively constructed in and through hegemonic struggles. Once we accept that the precarious unity of our multiple selves is not determined by some essential sexual identity, it becomes clear that 'the limitations of the modern conception of citizenship should be remedied, not by making sexual difference politically relevant to its definition, but by constructing a new conception of citizenship where sexual difference would become effectively irrelevant' (1993f: 82). Mouffe agrees with Pateman's critique of the liberal, male-dominated conception of citizenship, but maintains that a gendered notion of democratic citizenship is not the answer to the problems of liberalism and patriarchalism. The exclusivity of the liberal (and republican) concept of citizenship should, rather, be combated by conceiving citizenship as something we can all obtain by identifying with the ethico-political principles of modern democracy. The subordination of women, which is often based on a certain construction of the masculine/feminine distinction, should be fought by expanding the quest for freedom and equality to all spheres of society. In other words, a radical democratic citizenship is Mouffe's alternative to a gendered notion of democratic citizenship. It should be noted that the project of a radical plural democracy does not do away with the distinction between the public and the private, but aims to reformulate it. We all live in a state of permanent tension between our private identity as different individuals and our public identity as equivalential citizens (Mouffe, 1991b: 81). It is only when our acts and values have direct consequences for our common social hopes and living conditions that we can be held responsible as radical democratic citizens.

15

The Contours of a Postmodern Ethics?

Introduction

Having recommended a particular form of democracy and society, as well as a certain type of citizenship, we must now confront the pressing question of how such political recommendations can be morally and ethically justified within the ambit of the postmodern theorizing of Laclau, Mouffe and Žižek. The more general question is whether a postmodern ethics is possible. Many will claim that a postmodern ethics is a *contradiction in terms*, since moral and ethical claims must necessarily have a solid foundation and postmodern theorizing is inherently anti-foundationalist. Some will even draw the conclusion that without foundations discourse theory is unable to advance any ethical claims at all. To this end, it has been suggested that the difference between the discourse theory of Laclau and Mouffe and the joyous nihilism often attributed to deconstructivist politics is not explained (Howard, 1989: 95–6). Likewise, discourse theory has been blamed for sliding into a 'bottomless relativist gloom' and for leaving us in a 'normative vacuum' (Geras, 1987: 67, 77). Although it is tempting merely to shrug one's shoulders in the face of such mistaken and unqualified criticisms, this chapter seeks to answer these and similar criticisms by sketching the contours of a postmodern ethics.

Modern and Postmodern Ethics

To this end we might start by recalling how Laclau and Mouffe define postmodernity. *Postmodernity* involves challenging the foundational status of the modern metanarratives rather than undermining the

274

validity of their political and ethical values (Laclau, 1989: 63; Mouffe, 1989: 34). Thus postmodernity does not imply any rejection of the emancipatory project of modernity. Rather, it urges us to take an anti-foundationalist approach to ethics that denies the existence of an ethics beyond discourse. We can continue to celebrate ethical values such as tolerance, freedom, equality, fairness and decency, and we can continue to struggle for the eradication of human suffering. Nevertheless, we should abandon any attempt to ground our ethical values in an extra-discursive essence that brings our common deliberations over good and evil, right and wrong, to a premature close.

According to Bauman (1993), the question of foundations plays a decisive role in understanding the difference between modern and postmodern ethics. *Modern ethics* was conceived of as man-made rather than God-given. Rather than being a 'natural trait' of free individuals, ethical behaviour was something to be designed and injected into human conduct (1993: 6). People should learn, and be forced to obey, a comprehensive and unitary code of ethics guided by reason. They should discipline themselves through the exercise of 'better judgement', and be convinced that 'doing wrong does not pay'. That is to say, reason should do what belief could no longer do. Reason thus provided modern ethics with a new foundation, and this foundation secured the universality of modern ethics as all human beings were considered to possess, or to be capable of acquiring, that reason which informed moral rules (1993: 68). The constitutive outside of an ethics founded on reason was feelings and affection. The emotional impulse could not be ascribed any moral significance.[1]

Modernity was animated by a belief in the possibility of a non-aporetic ethical code rooted in reason and universal validity for all human beings. Disbelief in such a possibility is what marks the emergence of postmodernity (1993: 10). Postmodernity, for its part, affirms that ethics is incurably aporetic, as few choices are unambiguously good; that ethics cannot be grounded in reason or any other extra-discursive essence, as the very attempt to subordinate ethical demands to something preceding it is detrimental to ethical judgement; and finally that ethical codes are not completely universalizable, as what is believed to be moral in one place and time is certain to be frowned upon in another, and as ethical codes are always the result of political struggles that can only pretend to promote a universal ethics (1993: 10–14).

Postmodernity is not devoid of ethics, but recognizes the absence of ethical foundations. Postmodernity is modernity without illusions. It aims to provide new anti-foundational answers to old (and new) ethical questions. The critique of essentialism implies that ethical judgement cannot be made a priori, not even in the sense of establishing a minimal content for a categorical imperative. However, this does not logically imply that a *postmodern ethics* cannot be based upon less than a priori dictated judgements (Laclau, 1997: 17). However, such general assurances of the ethical commitment of the postmodern condition fail to convince hard-line modernists, who insist that the absence of unshakable foundations inevitably leads to immorality and weakening of the social bond of society, and claim that the emphasis placed on the discursivity of meanings and values leads to the relativist assertion that 'everything goes'.

This commonplace view has been rejected by Rorty (1989). Countering the prediction that the loss of foundations will lead to immorality and social dissolution, Rorty argues that similar predictions regarding the consequences following from the secularization of western societies have not come true. As religious faith declined, people remained moral, and the social glue was preserved. A concern for our grandchildren replaced our belief in heavenly rewards after death, and society was held together by new common vocabularies (1989: 85–6).

Rorty counters the charge of *relativism* by rendering it a non-problem. The world is out there, but truth is not (1989: 4–5). Truth cannot be out there – cannot exist independently of the human mind – because descriptions of the world cannot exist in that way, cannot be out there. Only descriptions of the world can be true or false, and such descriptions are made within discourses, or vocabularies, that are always underdetermined by the world. 'The world can, once we have programmed ourselves with a language, cause us to hold beliefs. But it cannot propose a language for us to speak' (1989: 6). If this view is accepted, relativism ceases to be a problem. For there will be no extra-discursive moral truth to accept or challenge. There will be no attempt to scrutinize competing values within competing vocabularies to see which ones are morally privileged. In short, 'there will be no way to rise above the language, culture, institutions, and practices one has adopted and view all these as on a par with all the others' (1989: 50). We will always approach the question of what is true and false, good and evil, right and wrong, within the discursive framework we find ourselves in. We can establish what to us seems true, right and good, but the possibility of a transcendental grounding of our beliefs is forever ruled out.

Moral judgement is intra-discursive, and the clash of different discursive morals will either create an antagonism or produce a new discourse in which moral claims from the different discourses are articulated. However, as Žižek points out, there is a limit to the idea that moral truth is relative to the discursive context in which it is established. For within this discursive context a contingent detail will always emerge to reveal a repressed trauma and shatter our self-delusions (Žižek, 1991: 196). Thus, although truth is context-dependent, in the sense that there is no truth in general but only the truth of some situation, 'there is nonetheless in every plural field a particular point which articulates its truth and as such cannot be *relativized*' (1991: 196). When suddenly, forced by a minor incident, we realize that our moral conduct produces a hitherto unacknowledged effect that undermines all that we believe in, we are confronted with a truth that is not 'determined' by the discursive context of moral judgement. In other words, dislocation, and the eruption of the Real, will tend to produce a hard kernel of non-relativizable truth. The truth effect of dislocation will subsequently be accounted for within new discursive truth regimes.

In sum, postmodern ethics recognizes its own *discursivity*. All attempts to ground ethics in an extra-discursive instance beyond play are doomed to failure, and can at best be described as hegemonic attempts partially to fix the discursive context of ethical judgement. Now, as discourse is always penetrated and destabilized by the field of discursivity, the discursive context of ethical judgement opens up an inherently undecidable terrain in which antagonisms over ethical questions will prevail and a final reconciliation never be achieved. We might advance a good and plausible argument for our ethical stance, but we will never arrive at a moment of absolute truth. This does not cause us to slide into a relativist gloom as we will always be capable of justifying our ethical stance from within a certain discourse. Although there always exists room for manoeuvre, the discourse in question leads us to prefer this to that and never allows us to think that what we prefer is on a par with what people within other discursive contexts prefer. We never arrive at a situation where we believe A to be just as true as non-A or anti-A.

Towards an Ethics of Deconstruction?

According to Laclau (1997), *antifoundationalism* does not lead to immorality or to a relativist gloom. On the contrary the postmodern 'experience of the radical contingency of any particular content claiming to be valid is the very condition of that ethical overinvestment that makes possible a higher moral consciousness' (1997: 17). Hence, it is only when we experience the absolute as an utterly empty place that we can project into contingent courses of action a moral depth that they, left to themselves, lack. In other words, it is because we know that God is dead and Reason cannot take his place that we are forced to assume the immense responsibility of inventing and safeguarding the ethical 'ground' of our actions.

The postmodern disbelief in the possibility of providing a firm foundation for ethical claims constitutes a considerable challenge for the postmodern intellectuals who, like Laclau, think that anti-foundationalism opens up a land of opportunity for humankind. It also represents a considerable challenge to all those who recognize, intuitively, that the bedrock foundations of the modern meta-narrative have eroded, but who are afraid of the consequences. Anti-foundationalism is strictly incompatible with the idea of a universal ethics grounded in some outer-worldly or inner-worldly essence. In the light of the widespread view that the strength of an ethical claim derives from its transcendental universality, it is quite understandable that many people feel uncomfortable with the prospect of living in a postmodern world. The uncertainty arising from the disappearance of unshakable ethical foundations is indirectly nurtured by those postmodern intellectuals who, like Foucault, recommend an aestheticization of ethics, whereby each subject must constantly re-invent himself by constructing his own mode of enjoyment and self-mastery. This proposed celebration of unadulterated individualism is undoubtedly an unacceptable alternative for traditional considerations about what is good and what is right, and as such has provided an easy target for the hard-line modernists' ill-informed attacks on postmodern philosophy for being ethically irresponsible.

Many people in the post-industrial West respond ideologically to the uncertainty of the postmodern condition by continuing to live *as if* absolute ethical foundations could still be provided. However, most people seem to respond to the postmodern challenge by putting to one side the big ethical questions of what is good and evil and focusing instead on *conventional morals* – the formal codes and the informal rules that ought to guide our conduct as parents, professionals, scientists, experts, politicians, etc. Although this latter response seems plausible inasmuch as it tries to retain an ethics in the face of the loss of foundations by retreating to a consensual morality of context-bound prescriptions and demands, it is nevertheless a wholly inadequate and, indeed, rather unfortunate response to the post-modern challenge. The problem with the ethical epidemic, which has turned philosophers and theologists into experts on ethics, is that it builds on the assumption that the ethical, defined as the *good* to be pursued by human beings, can be reduced to moral codes and rules that prescribe the *right* conduct in a particular situation. For example, in the discussion concerning the professional ethics of doctors, it is suggested that doctors should not lie to their patients. Yet, such a moral rule is a poor substitute for the ethical claim that personal autonomy should be respected and the patient should have the right to take important decisions, including whether to let the doctor take them on his or her behalf. In the face of such an ethical claim, the moral rule 'doctors should not lie to their patients' crumbles and becomes insignificant. This shows that there is, after all, an ethical conception of the good to pursue, which can never be exhausted by what we have agreed it is morally right to do in a given situation.

However, the problem is not solved merely by highlighting the importance of claims about the ethically good. The ethical conception of the good can always be deconstructed and redescribed in a way that makes the good look bad. Faced with this problem many have drawn the conclusion that a postmodern, deconstructive ethics is a contradiction in terms, as deconstruction deconstructs any ethical foundation. In stark contrast to this defeatist conclusion, Critchley (1992: 2) claims that there is an *ethical moment in deconstruction,* which is perhaps even the goal towards which Derrida's work is directed. The kind of ethics seemingly present in the deconstructive double-reading of texts (recall Derrida's extended meaning of 'texts', which is close to Laclau and Mouffe's concept of discourse) is an ethical experience in the Levinasian sense of the term. The ethics discussed by the phenomenological and Judaist philosopher Levinas is not reducible to the socio-political order of ethics and morals that organizes and improves human life (1992: 4). That is, Levinasian ethics can be reduced neither to a branch of philosophy nor to the predominant set of moral conventions, but is best described as an ethics of ethics, an ultra-ethics (1992: 18). Thus we are not talking about an ethics in the traditional sense of the term, but rather an ethical experience that cannot be exhausted by ethical and moral claims.

The ethical experience refers to the relation of a singular I to the alterity of an Other, who is not lost in the crowd as 'one of many' (1992: 17). The ethical experience of the Other is constituted through my way of relating to the face of the other, defined as 'the way in which the other presents himself, exceeding the idea of the other in me' (Levinas, 1969: 50). What makes my relation to the Other ethical is my *non-reciprocal* and *unconditional* acceptance of the obligation to *respond* to the Other's demand. The Other demands me, and thereby calls me to justice, to justify myself in terms of my responsiveness. However, the Other's demand on me is a non-humiliating demand, as the Other can also demand me to demand her. That is, the ethical relation to the face of the Other does not invoke the destitution of the self through a submissive self-sacrifice. The important thing is that here I am for the Other. 'It is precisely in this privilege accorded to the irreducible particularity of my obligations to the singular Other, prior to procedures of universalization and legislation, [. . .] that the word "ethics" is able to exceed its traditional determination' (Critchley, 1992: 18).[2]

But where is the moment of Levinasian ultra-ethics to be found in the deconstructive double-reading? *Deconstruction* aims to show, first, how a text is dependent on the presuppositions of what Derrida names the metaphysics of presence, or logocentrism, and second, how the same text radically questions the metaphysics it presupposes and thus points towards a thinking that is not logocentric (1992: 20–1). Deconstruction reveals the texts's attachment and subversion of the metaphysical tradition, but does not claim to be able to transgress metaphysics. Derrida refers to this double refusal of the limits of metaphysics and the possibility of transgression in terms of a closure. 'Closure is the hinge that articulates the double movement between logocentrism, or metaphysics, and its other' (1992: 21), and Levinasian ultra-ethics signifies the articulation of this hinge. In other words, deconstruction involves an ethical openness towards the alterity of the Other, conceived as the constitutive outside that cannot be domesticated and therefore remains *un*thought precisely because it is un*thought* (1992: 29). Deconstruction thus acts ethically against any attempt to instigate a metaphysical closure of self-identity by denying the demanding (non-)presence of the wholly Other.[3]

From Ultra-Ethics to Ethical Bricolage?

It should be noted that Critchley is not claiming 'that the relation between deconstruction and ethics is one of inference or derivation' (1992: 2). Levinasian ultra-ethics is identified, rather, as a particular moment in the deconstructive double-reading. The ethics of deconstruction consists in its performative openness towards the alterity of the Other, which we can neither comprehend nor domesticate. As for the status of this ethics of deconstruction, it should be made clear that it belongs to the realm of undecidable infrastructures. Critchley (1996: 34–5) aims to show this by recalling the fact that Derrida tends to equate the Levinasian ethics of 'the relation to the Other' with his own concepts of 'justice' and 'democracy to come'.

Derrida (1992: 14–15) defines *justice,* as distinguished from the law, as an 'experience' of the undecidable, and thus as something which cannot itself be deconstructed. By contrast, law is something that must necessarily be deconstructible for politics and political progress to be possible. Justice can never be exhausted by or instantiated in finite laws since justice 'always addresses itself to singularity, the singularity of the other' (1992: 20). It is thus easy to see the equivalence between Derrida's concept of justice and the Levinasian ethics of 'the relation to the Other'. Both involve a singular relation to a heterogeneous otherness. The same goes for Derrida's notion of *democracy to come,* which 'does not involve any teleological assertion – not even the limited one of a regulative idea – but simply the continual commitment to keep open the relation to the other, an opening that is always *"à venir"'* (to come) (Laclau, 1995b: 91).

As Laclau (1995b: 90–1) notes, Derrida (1994) remains committed to ethical values of emancipation such as the elimination of exploitation and discrimination, the assertion of human rights, the consolidation of civil and political freedom, etc. This immediately poses the question of how to account for the relation between the undecidable, ethico-political infrastructures of Levinasian ultra-ethics, justice and democracy to come, and the particular ethical values and moral conventions that organize and improve our human existence. It is tempting to think that the latter can somehow be derived from the former. However, as Laclau (1995b: 93; 1996b: 52–3) rightly points out, this is a dangerous path to take as it presupposes the idea of foundation merely by substituting an abyssal *Ab-grund* for a solid *Grund,* and undermines the explicit indifference of deconstruction, undecidability and discourse theory to particular political, ethical and moral projects. On this score Critchley is in complete agreement with Laclau. He assures us that his 'claim is not that *an* ethics can be derived from deconstruction, like an effect from a cause, a superstructure from an infrastructure, or a second critique from a first critique' (Critchley, 1992: 2).

Now, if the particular contents of our ethical and moral claims cannot be derived from the undecidable, ethico-political infrastructures, does that not leave us in an ethical and moral vacuum? The answer is no, for as Laclau says:

We live as *bricoleurs* in a plural world, having to take decisions within incomplete systems of rules (incompletion here means undecidability), and some of these rules are ethical ones. It is because of this constitutive incompletion that decisions have to be taken, but because we are faced with incompletion and not with total dispossession, the problem of *total* ethical grounding – either through the opening to the otherness of the other, or through any similar metaphysical principle – never arises. (Laclau, 1995b: 94)

It is arguably unfair to label the Levinasian ethics of deconstruction metaphysical, but Laclau is certainly right to emphasize the importance of ethical *bricolage*, i.e. of our pragmatic acceptance and application of ethical and moral claims that we come across in the meeting place of tradition and our daily actions.

We return now to our initial question: how should we account for the relation between the undecidable, ethico-political infrastructures and our ethical bricolage? One way of conceiving this relation would be to see Levinasian ultra-ethics as both the condition of possibility and the condition of impossibility of ethical *bricolage*. This squares well with Laclau's claim that the empty signifier of the universal is something without which concrete emancipations cannot take place, but also something that can never be fully exhausted or embodied in particular emancipatory projects (Laclau, 1992a: 132–4). The argument would be as follows. The deconstruction of ethical and moral foundations forces us to be ethical *bricoleurs* who take up and articulate the context-bound, ethical and moral claims that we come across and think will serve as reasonable and appropriate guides for our belief and actions. Our decision to apply a certain ethical or moral standard is not and should not be governed by any metaphysical principle (Laclau, 1996b: 53), and Levinasian ultra-ethics does not constitute a hard and fast rule limiting our choice of ethical and moral standards. Rather, it calls on us to recognize our infinite responsibility towards the Other, which we cannot comprehend or domesticate (Critchley, 1996: 35). Faced with this infinite responsibility, which cannot be generalized into a rule and cannot be given a particular content, we finally recognize that our ethical *bricolage* is endlessly deconstructible. In other words, in light of our infinite responsibility towards the wholly Other, we will realize that what we take to be good and right is never good and right enough. We are thus forced to live with the anxiety that even when we really try to do what we think is good and right, we are not living up to our infinite responsibility. This anxiety is what keeps the discursive field of ethical and moral revision and negotiation open.

Before further discussing the practice of ethical *bricolage*, I should like to make one last remark concerning the parallel between Levinasian ultra-ethics, conceived as experience of the undecidable and what Žižek (1991: 271–3) denotes the Lacanian ethics of the Real. According to Lacan, the drive is inherently ethical. Why? Because drive 'is not "blind animal thriving", but the ethical compulsion which compels us to mark repeatedly the memory of a lost Cause' (1991: 272). That is, drive is precisely the compulsion to encircle again and again the site of all lost causes, of all shattered and perverted dreams and hopes. These should be remembered neither out of nostalgic longing for something that was essentially good and only contingently corrupted (Communism), nor as a concrete warning against the repetition of some traumatic event (Nazism), but rather because the marking of all lost Causes marks the general impossibility of all totalizing ethics and morals. Therefore, by transforming ourselves into a monument of past catastrophes, by preserving the traces of the traumas of both Nazism and Communism, we contribute to the destabilization of all ethical and moral Causes. In other words, through our experience, in our memory of the traumas of the past we keep open the empty place of the universal and thereby clear the ground for ethical *bricolage*.

Postmodern Ethics and its Conversational Support

According to Laclau (1992a), the modern discourses of *emancipation* have been historically constituted through the articulation of two incompatible lines of thought. The *first* is based on the idea of an absolute chasm between the emancipatory moment and the oppressive system that is rejected.[4] The *second* invokes the idea that emancipation takes place at the level of the ground of the social; that it affects all levels of society; that it brings about a complete transparency by eliminating the distorting relations of power; and that it is guided by an immanent rationality, which in the moment of full emancipation becomes one with the real. Whereas the first line of thought emphasizes a dichotomous discontinuity, the second emphasizes the continuous unfolding of a social objectivity.

Now, the problem is that we cannot simply renounce either line of thought as both are necessary to produce the discourse of emancipation (1992a: 125–7). Instead of abandoning the conception of emancipation as a self-contradictory impossibility, we should recognize that the logically incompatible logics that are constitutive of the concept of emancipation are both linked to the *destiny of the universal* (1992a: 132–4). This will enable a productive interplay between the two logics, both of which are modified by their interplay. The basic premise of the argument is that emancipation, to be a true act of radical re-foundation (the first line of thought about emancipation), cannot be the work of any particularistic social agency. In order to become hegemonic, an emancipatory movement whose identity is constituted by the social antagonism it constructs must necessarily invoke some notion of ground, totality, transparency and rationality (the second line of thought about emancipation). However, the meaning of these terms is deformed by the fact that they are not dimensions of an un-limited, and fully achieved, universality. As such, they are rather particular, and thus limited, embodiments of the empty universality to which the emancipatory movement must necessarily refer (1992a: 134–7). As the attempt to fill the empty universality is the *sine qua non* of the radical chasm invoked by the act of emancipation, the logic of radical discontinuity is deformed in exactly the same manner as the logic of continuity. From the implicit assertion that the emancipatory dichotomy can neither be absolute nor be totally eradicated it follows that there is no act of completely revolutionary foundation and no final reconciliation of society.

Derrida makes the same intellectual move as Laclau. He seeks to abandon the eschatological notion of emancipation without giving up the notion of emancipation as such. This is achieved by moving from the eschatological notion of emancipation to the emancipatory promise of a justice that is distinguished from any law and a democracy that is always yet to come (Derrida, 1994: 59). Such an emancipatory promise, which promises to be kept, to produce events, new effective forms of action, organization, etc., must be liberated from any form of metaphysical determination. The metaphysical determination of the content of the promise by God, by the iron laws of the mode of production, or the ethical progress of humankind will tend to undermine the radical effects of the promise as the promise of that which is never there but always to come. That is to say, true emancipation must necessarily be premised on a messianic affirmation that is clearly distinguished from any concrete messianic movement and any messianism (1994: 89).

It is the empty universality of the promise – of justice, of the democracy to come, and of our infinite responsibility – that makes possible and destabilizes our ethical *bricolage*. Our ethical bricolage is governed by the Aristotelian notion of *phronesis*, which is basically an ethical knowledge or reasoning, as distinct from 'rational', scientific knowledge known as *episteme*. According to Mouffe, phronesis is 'dependent on the ethos, the cultural and historical conditions current in the community, and implies a renunciation of all pretence to universality' (Mouffe, 1989: 36). Phronetic reasoning thus respects the postmodern weakening of the foundations of modernity. However, 'even if we cannot decide algorithmically about many things, this does not mean that we are confined to total nihilism, since we can reason about the *verisimilitude* of the available alternatives' (Laclau and Mouffe, 1987: 102). Moreover, when compared with epistemic reasoning, phronetic reasoning seems to entail some favourable political consequences. For as Laclau and Mouffe convincingly argue:

284

An argument founded on the apodicticity of the conclusion is an argument which admits neither discussion nor any plurality of viewpoints; on the other hand, an argument which tries to found itself on the verisimilitude of its conclusions is essentially pluralist, because it needs to make reference to other arguments and, since the process is essentially open, these can be contested and refuted. The logic of verisimilitude is, in this sense, essentially *public and democratic*. (Laclau and Mouffe, 1987: 102)

Our ethical *bricolage*, which has nothing but a *conversational support*, is indeed highly precarious and calls for active participation and constant re-enactment. Sustainment of one's preferred conception of the good and the right requires recognition of the primacy of politics. However, this does not mean that everybody must be politically active all the time and within all spheres of society, as the process of sedimentation will tend to establish a tradition of cherished values and norms that are neither usually nor generally contested.

Another important question concerning our ethical *bricolage* is the question of ethico-political responsibility. According to Laclau:

The role of deconstruction is, from this perspective, to *reactivate* the moment of decision that underlies any *sedimented* set of social relations. The political and ethical significance of this first movement is that by enlarging the area of structural undecidability it enlarges also the area of responsibility – that is, of the decision. (In Derridean terms: the requirements of justice become more complex and multifaceted *vis-à-vis* the law.) (Laclau, 1995b: 93)

The intrinsic link between *deconstruction* and *responsibility* is also stressed by Žižek. According to Žižek (1991: 189), we are called to responsibility by our very condition of being *subjects* in the Lacanian sense of the term. The dislocation of the symbolic order, the sudden eruption of the real, constitutes an impossible moment of openness which is also the moment of subjectivity. In this moment of subjectivity, '"subject" is the name for that unfathomable X called upon, suddenly made accountable, thrown into a position of responsibility, into the urgency of decision in such a moment of undecidability' (1991: 189). In other words, the subject becomes ethically and politically responsible in the course of taking a decision, because the decision is called for by the dislocation of the structure, which reveals its undecidability and implies the absence of a voice of structural necessity speaking through the subject. The subject is forced to invent new solutions and make unheard-of moves in a situation in which there are no solid foundations to build upon. However, the absence of such foundations does not make the subject an absolute chooser with no grounds to choose. The dislocation of the structure creates a situation in which the subject simultaneously is faced with a mere possibility and forced to choose. As such, the subject enjoys a freedom that is at once liberating and enslaving. The structure is dislocated and the subject is free to choose, but as the dislocation of the structure penetrates the subject, who tends to suffer from the loss of his or her identity, the subject is forced to shoulder the burden of decision in order to create a minimum of social order and identity in accordance with the ethical and moral principles that are still intact and accepted as valid.

As ethical *bricoleurs* we are responsible for arriving at ethical decisions in an undecidable terrain in which we are forced to posit our own presuppositions, to invent our own grounds, and to establish our own foundations (strategic essentialism). Yet, it is important to recognize, not only the contingency but also the essential impurity of these grounds. The discourse of political correctness, which is sweeping the university campuses in the USA, fails to do this. Political correctness is nurtured by a strong belief in the possibility of constructing a non-discriminating and thus emancipating language. We should not, of course, make use of discriminatory expressions, but the idea of a political correct 'new-speak' purified of all kinds of chauvinist language might, unintendedly, have totalitarian effects. However, most importantly the idea of an absolute purity is utterly problematic. As Laclau in a different context notes:

> The totalitarian dreams of an absolute purity – with its counterpart of an impurity without appeal – have a deplorable and negative result. It leads one to think that what is this side of the frontier of exclusion is uncontaminated fullness, purity, presence. But this is far from being the case. Radical contextualization of meaning, when it is coupled with the recognition of the unstable character of all context, means that there is no meaning that contains in itself the guarantee against its own corruption. (Laclau, 1990b: 95)

Hence, even the most cherished values such as democracy, equality and anti-chauvinism are capable of being corrupted and of producing adverse effects.

The Liberal Ironist as Postmodern Hero?

How, then, do we conceive of the subject of ethical decisions? Who is the postmodern hero capable of facing a world of radical contingency while insisting on acting in a way that can be justified ethically?

According to Rorty (1989: 73–4), the postmodern hero is a *liberal ironist*, i.e. someone who believes that cruelty is the worst thing we do and who realizes the contingency and fragility of his or her final vocabulary. Rorty himself claims to be a liberal ironist; he thinks that the problem with Foucault is that he attempts to be an ironist without being a liberal, and that the problem with Habermas is that he aims to be a liberal without being an ironist (1989: 65–9). According to Rorty, we should recognize liberal democracy as a net contributor to the reduction of cruelty, but we should not aim to ground liberal democracy in a universalistic theory of undistorted communicative action which claims that we can have access to some transcendental truth. The celebration of liberal ironism might give the impression that liberalism and ironism are intrinsically linked. However, as we have already seen, Rorty draws a rigid line between the private realm of ironist thinking and the public realm of liberal hope (1993: 83). Ironism should be limited to the realm of private self-development since the practising, in public, of the endless ironic re-descriptions of the world and other people's selves is definitely cruel (1989: 89).

Now, the question is whether it is possible to be, at the same time, a *private ironist* and a *public liberal*. Or, as Rorty (1989: 88–95) puts it, is ironism compatible with a sense of human solidarity, or are ironists naturally anti-liberal? In answering this question Rorty compares the liberal ironist with the liberal metaphysician. The difference between the two, says Rorty, is that whereas the metaphysician seeks an answer to the question 'Why should I avoid humiliating others?', the ironist merely wants to know the answer to the question 'What humiliates?'. Whereas the metaphysician wants our wish to be good to be backed by an argument that refers to some shared ground in terms of God, rationality or the essence of Man, the ironist considers that it is enough to be able to perceive humiliation as a common danger and to know how the actual suffering of human beings can be reduced. In other words, what distinguishes the metaphysician from the ironist is that the former wants philosophy to provide answers to questions like 'Why not be cruel?' and 'Why be kind?', while the latter knows that this is precisely what philosophy cannot provide.

Thus, what Rorty is saying is that we should forget about the universal foundations of our ethics since such foundations cannot be provided. However, according to Laclau (1991: 97), this is an unnecessarily defensive answer to the question regarding the compatibility of ironism and liberalism. For 'without a universalism of sorts – the idea of *human* rights, for instance – a truly democratic society is impossible' (1991: 97). However, as Laclau says:

in order to assert this it is not at all necessary to muddle through the Enlightenment's rationalism or Habermas' "domination-free communication." It is enough to recognize that democracy needs universalism while asserting, at the same time, that universalism is one of the vocabularies, one of the language games, which was constructed at some point by social agents and which has become a more and more central part of our values and our culture. It is a *contingent* historical product. (Laclau, 1991: 97)

This argument can be refined by invoking Laclau's distinction between the universal as an empty signifier signifying the absence of a fully achieved community and the particular filling of that empty space of the universal. Thus, human rights and democracy are contingent historical discourses that have been advanced by particular political forces. However, these discourses owe their status as social imaginaries to the fact that they have managed to hegemonize an empty universality which is there to be filled, but which can never be completely filled by any particular content. What the political actors contingently construct, therefore, is not the vocabulary of universalism, but rather the particular filling of the empty signifier of a universalism that will always be there as a vanishing mediator of political struggles.

It is important to appreciate the political advantages that flow from the historicist recasting of universalism. The first is that recognition of the historicity of Being, of the fact that human beings are the exclusive authors of their world, will have a liberating effect on humankind. For, if people realize that 'the world that they inhabit is only the result of the contingent discourse and vocabularies that constitute it, they will tolerate fate with less patience' (1991: 97). In short, people who realize that the world is a political construction will generally be inclined to change and improve things not to their liking.

The second advantage is 'that the perception of the contingent character of universalist values will make us all more conscious of the dangers that threaten them and of their possible extinction' (1991: 97). If we believe that what is ethically good and morally right is guaranteed by God, rationality or the essence of Man, we might be less inclined to participate actively in the preservation of those ethical and moral values than if we realized that only our responsible defence of what is good and right will ensure the persistence of our ethical and moral standards.

We have finally arrived at the point where 'philosophy comes to an end and the realm of politics begins' (1991: 98). There is nothing beyond discourse, and what is constructed as discourse is *politically* constructed on the basis of a radical undecidability that reaches the very ground itself. The postmodern hero operating in this ethical realm of deconstruction and hegemonic politics should not be portrayed as an ironist, as this term invokes the image of a playful and uncommitted intellectual who is merely interested in the enhancement of self-enjoyment. Rather, the postmodern hero should be portrayed as a *strong poet* in the Nietzschean sense of one who both acknowledges and appropriates contingency, who both affirms the contingency of the world and knows how to take political advantage of that contingency by imagining and seeking to realize a host of new political projects that aim to make the world better and more agreeable. The strong poet is 'a new type who has still not been entirely created by our culture, but one whose creation is absolutely necessary if our time is going to live up to its most radical and exhilarating possibilities' (1991: 98).

Conclusion: The Tasks Ahead

This book has aimed to provide a comprehensive and accessible account of the new theories of discourse developed by Laclau, Mouffe and Žižek. To this end it has discussed the theoretical development in the works of Laclau and Mouffe and emphasized Žižek's positive influence on this development. The main concepts and arguments of the new theories of discourse were assessed in Part II, and the applicability of the theories to theoretical and empirical studies was explored in Part III and Part IV. In the concluding part of the book the political perspectives opened up by the theories have been discussed in relation to democracy, citizenship and ethics.

It is impossible to derive a general theoretical and/or political conclusion from the arguments advanced by the new theories of discourse. However, a few concluding remarks on the *strengths* and *weaknesses* of their discourse are called for. Laclau and Mouffe radicalize the undogmatic and highly innovative Marxism of Gramsci as a stepping stone to the advancement of a new type of postmodern theorizing that is of great relevance to social, cultural and political studies. The postmodern theory of discourse focuses on the question of the construction of identity. Social and political identities are disrupted by societal dislocation, rearticulated in and through hegemonic struggles, harnessed through the construction of social antagonisms, and 'naturalized' by their claim to universality. The concepts and arguments of Laclau and Mouffe's discourse theory are geared towards a study of the discursive construction of meaning, but the construction of meaning is not confined to a particular ideological region within society. Discourse is taken as coextensive with society. However, the general impression is that most discourse-theoretical studies focus on ideological configurations within civil society, the formation of new social and political subjectivities, and the disruptive moments of crisis and dislocation where pre-established identities are undermined and new identities are forged. Thus it is the study of ethnic, national and subcultural identities that is in the forefront. This is in itself fine, but tends to carry with it a benign neglect of the study of state–economy relations, the institutional underpinning of relatively enduring social and political identities, and the stable reproduction of capitalist societies. Questions relating to the reproduction of state, economy, classes and society were central to Gramscian and neo-Gramscian analysis, but today they are overlooked and forgotten areas of research. A great challenge lies in re-approaching these key questions from the vantage point of a postmodern theory of discourse. I have myself made a modest contribution to this particular field (Torfing, 1991, 1998), and would encourage further attempts to direct discourse theory to the study of the institutions of the advanced capitalist societies. As indicated above, several recently developed theories have a theoretical affinity with discourse theory. In the field of economics and political theory we might mention here the French regulation theories, certain neo-Marxist state theories, and branches of the new institutionalism. In the field of sociology many theories of mass media, urban spaces, consumerism and the so-called risk society come close to the discourse-theoretical approach, and the area of cultural studies is pervaded by poststructuralist studies of identity construction (feminism, racism, nationalism, etc.).

This leads me to issue two final caveats. The first concerns the application of discourse theory in *empirical studies*. Although the concepts and arguments of the new theories of discourse are developed in specific analytical contexts, they are pitched at a highly abstract level. That is to say, because discourse theory has a metatheoretical character, it is often difficult to apply it in an unmediated way in concrete empirical studies. Discourse theory provides us with a basic understanding of the key aspects of discursive world formation, but has no ambition of furnishing a detailed and fully operationalized framework for the study of all kinds of social, cultural and political relations. I would thus warn against attempts to apply discourse theory directly and instrumentally in empirical studies. For instance, if one was interested in the impact of the emerging European Union on the social policies in a particular country, it would be necessary to study the traditional theories in that field in order to select the most promising ones for a closer scrutiny. Discourse theory could be drawn upon in such a study in order to reveal the weaknesses of the theories in question and to develop a new theory consistent with the anti-essentialist and anti-foundationalist assumptions of discourse theory. The proof of the pudding would then be to show how well the new theory was capable of hegemonizing the empirical findings in the pragmatic sense of making sense of them and integrating them within a coherent narrative.

The second caveat concerns the quest for a *methodology* able to utilize discourse theory in the concrete study of the construction of identity. Such a recipe does not exist and should not be developed. For, whereas there is a great need to develop our critical reflections on how to apply discourse theory in concrete studies, we should not aim to solve the methodological question once and for all. Discourse theorists must remain methodological bricoleurs and refrain from developing an all-purpose technique for discourse analysis. The methodology to be applied will vary from study to study, and the development of a totalizing master methodology would serve only to repress new and alternative forms of analysis.

There are good reasons to be optimistic about the further development of discourse theory, not only with regard to the theoretical argument but also with an eye to a much needed widening of the analytical focus and the development of critical reflections on methodology. An increasing number of students of social, cultural and political phenomena find that discourse theory provides insights that help to overcome old theoretical problems and to respond to the political challenges of today in a novel and fruitful way. With interest in discourse theory increasing within many different disciplines, new research agendas are likely to emerge. It is my modest hope that this book will help stimulate interest in, and further development of, the new theories of discourse.

Notes

Chapter 1 A Gramsci-Inspired Critique of Structural Marxism

1 The merits of Laclau and Mouffe's critique of structural Marxism should be judged elsewhere. Here I am merely interested in summarizing Laclau and Mouffe's critical reading of Althusser, Balibar and Poulantzas rather than judging their validity.

Chapter 2 The Advancement of a Neo-Gramscian Theory of Discourse

1 The word 'hegemonic' in the term 'hegemonic practices' means hegemonic in intent rather than hegemonic in effect (= hegemony). Hence, the term 'hegemonic practices' refers to attempts to dis- and re-articulate social elements in and through antagonistic struggles in order to become hegemonic. Whether such attempts succeed in constructing a hegemony is not important in this regard.

2 The emphasis on the historicity and discursivity of 'class' and 'class strug- gles' (or any other concept) by no means implies a rejection of the use of such concepts. The discourse theory of Laclau and Mouffe is not advocating a kind of new-speak, according to which certain essentialist concepts should be abandoned. Discourse theory merely wants us to pay attention to the historical and discursive conditions of possibility of certain concepts, so as to avoid treating them as essentialist categories with an unlimited validity.

Chapter 3 Towards a New Type of Postmodern Theorizing

1 Some define 'politics' in terms of the institutionalization of the competition between political parties within the confines of state and parliament, while

293

reserving the notion of 'the political' for the truly constitutive decisions that shape the institutions of politics. As Laclau and Mouffe are ambiguous on this score I have felt free to call the constitutive dimension of the social 'politics', and to denote the institutional level of the state 'the political'.

2 Such quasi-logical argumentation is defined by Perelman and Olbrechts (1969 [1958]) as 'rhetoric'. However, because of the pejorative connotations of 'rhetoric' in terms of manipulation through the display of oral skills, I prefer to use the notion of quasi-logical argumentation.

Chapter 4 Discourse

1 Defining discursive systems in terms of pure forms does not mean that distinctions in terms of substance are cancelled out of existence, but only that such distinctions are seen as discursively constructed.

2 The shift from the archaeological to the genealogical approach is by no means a ruptural break. The archaeological approach continues to constitute an important analytical aspect of the new genealogical approach.

Chapter 6 Social Antagonism

1 In fact, we can hardly speak of a relation of negation either, since this ultimate form of negation tends to eliminate itself by eliminating its object of negation.

2 Schmitt's use of the terms 'the political' and 'politics' differs from the usage introduced in chapter 3. Schmitt calls constitutive political actions and motives 'the political' and uses 'politics' to denote the parliamentary struggles between the political parties, which take place at the level of the state.

Chapter 7 Structure and Agency

1 That social agency is absent from the definition of structure does not prevent it being conceived as internal to the structure. Although social agency is not a part of the structure, it can be internal to the structure in the sense that it can only be conceived of in relation to the structure of the social system.

2 Giddens does not consider himself a Marxist, but he clearly places himself within the intellectual terrain provided by Marxist theory, as he claims to be engaged in a critical appraisal of Marxism, which he thinks provides crucial elements to a general theory of human *Praxis* (Giddens, 1981: 1–2).

3 The claim that structures cannot be reduced to instantiated rule- and resource-sets does not force us into the arms of the transcendental realists, who view structures as 'real causal mechanisms' that operate in accordance with the concept of 'natural necessity'. Structures are not natural givens, but discursive constructs that have become so sedimented that they may selectively block the realization of the political strategies of a particular set of social agents.

4 The lack is constitutive precisely because the subject *is* this lack in the sense that the subject only exists in the attempt to overcome the lack. To avoid misunderstandings it should be stressed that the 'constitutive lack' does not provide a new essentialistic ground. The lack cannot be seen as providing a new ground precisely because nothing determinate can follow from the lack. It is possible to deduce some rational actions from the knowledge of the wants, preferences, or interests of a social agent, but nothing can be derived from a lack, which is exactly the absence of a positive essence.

5 For the first use of the concept of conservation-dissolution effects see Poulantzas (1978 [1974]: 109–55).

6 Jessop subscribes to a transcendental realist ontology that is not immediately compatible with the constructivist ontology of discourse-theoretical analytics. Nevertheless, Jessop shares many of the theoretical ambitions of Laclau and Mouffe – for example, in terms of anti-reductionism and anti-determinism. Moreover, it is possible that the incompatible ontologies might be reconciled – as attempted, for example, by Torfing (1998).

Chapter 8 Power and Authority

1 While the behaviouralists build on Hume's episodic notion of causality, according to which cause and effect, like billiard balls, are separated and only contiguously related, the transcendental realists insist that in order for a cause to produce an effect there must be a generative causal mechanism which relates cause and effect and produces the latter. As such, the realists can be said to conceive causality in terms of internal relations. However, they still insist on the possibility of separating the structurally imbedded cause from its actual effects. It is this kind of external relation that is referred to here.

2 The slippery expression that maintains people 'voluntarily choose' not to put up resistance refers to an acceptance of what is implied by the exercise of power, which is result neither of brainwashing nor terror.

Chapter 9 The Universal and the Particular

1 A similar emphasis on the structural necessity of exceptions to the law is found in Derrida (1992).

Chapter 10 The Politics of Nationalism and Racism

1 The argument presented here draws heavily on Ifversen's (1989) discussion of Lefort's understanding of the French Revolution.

2 According to Anderson (1983: 41–9), the condition of possibility for the spread of the discourse of the nation, which eventually led to the unification of cultural and political borders within separate nation-states, was the interplay between capitalism, the new print technologies and the fatal diversity of human languages, which together produced the sense of a common destiny of a people that was held together by particular solidarities.

3 I here draw extensively on a paper by Hansen (1995), who explicitly discusses the contribution of the discourse theory of Laclau and Mouffe to an understanding of the construction of Slovenian identity.

4 The distinction between 'enemies' and 'adversaries' is fully developed in chapter 13.

5 Smith goes on to show that the demonization of homosexuality was framed not only in terms of the AIDS-panic discourse but also in terms of a racist conception of the dangerous black immigrant. We shall here deal only with the basic function of the racist aspect of the New Right discourse. Readers interested in the Thatcher government's treatment of homosexuality should consult chapter 5 in Smith (1994a).

Chapter 12 The Politics of the Modern Welfare State

1 What follows is a brief summary of the third chapter of *L'invention du social*, which is the only chapter that has been translated into English (Donzelot, 1984).

2 Such policies are implemented in a situation where we are seeing a transition from a nationally-focused government system to a more de-centred and multi-tiered system of socio-economic governance. Within the emerging governance structures the state may retain the overall responsibility for the central state functions, but the responsibility for actually carrying out these functions is to an increasing extent shared with different non-state actors within self-organized policy networks. The SWR is accordingly more appropriately termed regime rather than state.

Chapter 15 The Contours of a Postmodern Ethics?

1 The modern ethics of obligation, which replaced the pre-modern ethics of virtue, assumed that the free individual was essentially bad. By contrast, humanist and Marxist intellectuals have claimed that Man is only contingently evil. Hence, he is only evil because he has not yet become fully emancipated. However, this kind of emancipatory ethics is no less essentialistic and rationalistic than the liberal ethics of moral obligation. Man is potentially good and the actualization of this potential is the outcome of the unfolding of the necessary laws of history: either in terms of an ethical *Entwicklung* or in terms of the dialectical development of the forces and relations of production, which will finally set Man free.

2 I tend to bracket Levinas' metaphysical conception of ethics as a 'first philosophy', and thus also his attempt to establish a metaphysical opposition between ethics and ontology. Derrida has sought to deconstruct the metaphysical ideas of Levinas. Levinas himself tends to move away from them in his later writings (see Critchley, 1992: 13–16).

3 Although he does not establish a link between deconstruction and Levinasian ultra-ethics, Bauman (1993: 47–61) conceives the idea of a moral responsibility interpellating the singular self to be for the Other as a postmodern ethics that resists codification and universalization.

4 This idea presupposes the pre-existence of the identity to be emancipated *vis-à-vis* the act of emancipation since without such a pre-existence the idea of something being liberated from the radical otherness of the oppressor is undermined.

Glossary

This glossary provides brief definitions of the terms, concepts and neologisms that it is important to understand in order to follow the arguments of Laclau, Mouffe and Žižek. The glossary can be used both in relation to this book and when reading the original works of Laclau, Mouffe and Žižek.

Absolute historicism
In Gramsci absolute historicism refers to the idea that unity of a social formation cannot be reduced to a moment in the progressive unfolding of an abstract, trans-historical logic, but is a result of political struggles taking place within a particular historical terrain. Althusser criticized Gramsci's absolute historicism because it undermined the structural Marxists' assertion of 'the determination in the last instance by the economy'.

Articulation
Articulation is a practice that establishes a relation among elements such that their identity is modified as a result of the articulatory practice. When an ethnic identity is articulated with a class identity both identities are modified by the established relation. Articulations that take place in a context of antagonistic struggles and conflicts are defined as hegemonic articulations.

Authority
Authority is a result of the authorization of power. Power is authorized through an appeal to a universalized particularism, which functions as a justifying 'foundation' for the exercise of power. Hence, politicians justify their policy in terms of what is 'good for society', what is 'rational to do', or in 'accordance with the national tradition'.

Classism
The belief in the privileged role of the working class *vis-à-vis* other forms of social and political agency.

Class reductionism
The claim that every legal, cultural, political or ideological element has a necessary class belonging. Involves the assertion that non-class identities are really class identities in disguise.

Collective will
Collective will is a result of the fusion of singular wills into an organized, collective identity which is capable of intervening in the process of creating a new kind of society.

Condensation
Condensation is one of two forms of overdetermination. It involves the fusion of a variety of identities and meanings into a single unity; e.g. a revolutionary situation may condense different ethnic, nationalist, and socialist struggles.

Connotation
Connotation is when a sign functions as a signifier for another signified; e.g. when the British flag, which is in itself a sign, is taken to signify 'imperial greatness'.

Constitutive outside
The constitutive outside is a discursive exteriority that cannot be related to the moments within the discourse in question through relations of simple difference, as it has the form of a radical alterity, which threatens and disrupts the discursive system of differences. The constitutive outside is an outside which blocks the identity of the inside, but it is nonetheless a prerequisite for the construction of the identity of the inside. The constitutive limits of a discourse are constructed in relation to the threatening outside. For example, the neo-liberal discourse assumes that the old, bureaucratic forms of social democratic welfare statism is the real threat to market-led economic regeneration.

Contingency
A social identity is contingent in so far as its conditions of possibility are also its conditions of finitude. During the cold war the West constituted its identity in relation to the Communist regimes in eastern Europe and the Soviet Union. What the former US president Ronald Reagan saw as the 'evil empire' in the East at once confirmed and threatened the contingent identity of the West.

Decentring of structure
Decentring involves not only the rejection of the idea of a fixed centre that structures the structure but itself escapes the process of structuration. It also involves the construction of a variety of centres that partially fix the identities within an open-ended structure.

Decentring of subject
The rejection of the idea of a privileged, transcendental subject (e.g. God, Class or Humanity) in favour of an analysis of different subject positions within a discursive structure.

Deconstruction
Derrida uses the notion of deconstruction as a name for the destabilization of essential identities which derives from the fact that the effort to determine the essence of something always fails because there exist ambiguities and undecidables that resist ultimate fixation.

Democratic antagonisms
Democratic antagonisms tend to divide minor social spaces into antagonistic battlegrounds. The struggles erected by the new social movements are good examples of democratic antagonisms.

Denotation
Denotation is the kind of meaning which is established when a signifier is conjoined with a signified within a sign. Barthes argues that denotative meaning is a result of the naturalization of connotations.

Difference (logic of . . .)
A way of relating discursive moments in and through their mutual differences. The logic of difference constructs a relational 'totality'. The differential relations between the discursive moments are constitutive of their very identity.

Discourse
Discourse is a relational totality of signifying sequences that together constitute a more or less coherent framework for what can be said and done. The notion of discourse cuts across the distinction between thought and reality, and includes both semantic and pragmatic aspects. It does not merely designate a linguistic region within the social, but is rather co-extensive with the social.

The discursive (the field of discursivity)
The partial fixation of meaning within discourse produces an irreducible surplus of meaning. The field of irreducible surplus is termed the discursive (or the field of discursivity).

Discursive formation
A discursive formation is a result of the articulation of a variety of discourses into a relatively unified whole. Liberal democracy is a discursive formation as it consists of a variety of different discourses which have been articulated in and through hegemonic practices.

Dislocation
A destabilization of a discourse that results from the emergence of events which cannot be domesticated, symbolized or integrated within the discourse in question. For example, the concurrence of inflation and unemployment in the early 1970s dislocated the Keynesian orthodoxy which basically claimed that 'stagflation' would never occur. Likewise, the process of globalization tends to dislocate the idea of the nation-state as the privileged terrain for economic activity.

Displacement
One of the two forms of overdetermination. Displacement involves the transferral of the meaning of one particular discursive moment to another discursive moment.

The economic
Refers to capitalist commodity production, which is based on the commodification of labour power.

Empiricist epistemology
The idea that the subject can only gain valid knowledge about the object through sense data that have been collected through observation.

Empty signifier
A signifier without a signified. A signifier is emptied of any precise content due to 'the sliding of the signifieds under the signifier'. Democracy is an empty signifier as the signifier of democracy is so over-coded that it means everything and nothing.

Epiphenomenalism
An epiphenomenon has no independent value or effectiveness as its form and function is fully determined by another phenomenon. Marxism tends to treat the capitalist state as an epiphenomenon as its role in society is determined by the capitalist economy.

Equivalence (logic of . . .)
The logic of equivalence constructs a chain of equivalential identities among different elements that are seen as expressing a certain sameness. From the point of view of the dominant heterosexual discourse gays and lesbians express the same type of 'deviant sexuality' that seems to undermine the nuclear family.

Floating signifier
A signifier that is overflowed with meaning because it is articulated differently within different discourses.

Hegemony
The achievement of a moral, intellectual and political leadership through the expansion of a discourse that partially fixes meaning around nodal points. Hegemony involves more than a passive consensus and more than legitimate actions. It involves the expansion of a particular discourse of norms, values, views and perceptions through persuasive redescriptions of the world.

Hegemonic agent
A political agency striving for hegemony.

Hegemonic practices
Attempts to articulate a discourse which can bring about a moral, intellectual and political leadership.

Hegemonic project
A political project, including a vision of how state, economy and civil society should be organized, that aspires to become hegemonic.

Ideological fantasy
Ideological fantasy is an illusion on the part of the subjects, which makes it possible for people to act *as if* the totalizing and reductive forms of ideology are true and serious, despite the known fact that they are not.

Ideological state apparatus
The part of the state apparatus that functions primarily through ideology, e.g. the church, the educational system, mass media, etc.

Ideology
A totalizing and reductive aspect of discourse that involves the constitutive non-recognition of the contingent and precarious character of discursively constructed identities. The decidable discursive forms are merely partially fixed meanings that are always overflowed and destabilized by undecidability. However, the ideological aspect of discourse constructs the contingent discursive identities as a part of a totalizing horizon with universalist pretensions (e.g. nationalism, liberalism, etc.).

Interpellation
Ideology interpellates concrete individuals by addressing them in a way which constructs them as particular discursive subjectivities, i.e. as women, consumers, workers, 'trouble-makers', foreigners, etc.

Lack
Lack is another name for the incompleteness of the structure which is a result of structural dislocation. Lack does not refer to a subject's lack of a particular object, but to the failure of the structure to constitute a fully structured objectivity.

Mode of production
A mode of production includes the ensemble of productive forces and relations of production as well as the political and ideological institutions in which the economic relations are imbedded.

Modernity
Modernity involves the rise of modern society (secularized societies with an institutional separation of the state from civil society, a much greater degree of social and technical division of labour, and the formation of nation-states uniting cultural and political borders), a rationalistic epistemology, and an individualistic and objectivistic ontology.

Myth
Myth is defined as a principle of reading of a given situation. The condition of emergence of myth is structural dislocation, and the function of myth is to suture the dislocated space by means of constructing a new space of representation.

Nodal point
An empty signifier that is capable of fixing the content of a range of floating signifiers by articulating them within a chain of equivalence.

Organic intellectuals
A group of intellectuals who are attached to a particular hegemonic project and whose primary function is to organize the masses rather than to practise the acquired skill of thinking.

Overdetermination
Overdetermination gives social identity a symbolic form; identity is conceived as a fusion of a multiplicity of identities. The overdetermined presence of some identities in others prevents their closure.

Particularism
Refers to the claims, interests and demands of a particular group in society which merely aims to preserve its self-enclosed distinctiveness.

Plural democracy
A democratic sentiment that carries a profound respect for plurality and difference. The concept of plural democracy is the result of a disarticulation of the principles of liberalism which aims to get rid of allegedly pro-capitalist principles of private property right and minimal state (economic liberalism), whilst rescuing the respect for plurality and difference (political liberalism). The respect for plurality and difference is then articulated with the democratic idea of equal rights. Hence, the basic thrust of plural democracy is the demand for freedom and equality for all.

Political
The political refers to the institutional order of the state, which provides the primary terrain for the struggle between hegemonic agents who seek to place themselves in a position from where they can 'speak in the name of society' (Easton).

Politics
Politics basically involves taking a decision in an undecidable terrain. As such, politics is simultaneously a constitutive and subversive dimension of the social.

Popular antagonism
A form of antagonism that tends to divide society into two antagonistic camps. The South African Apartheid system tended to divide society into black and white camps.

Populism
The articulation of popular-democratic ideologies into a class discourse that establishes an antagonistic relation to the dominant power bloc.

Postmodernity
Postmodernity should not be seen as involving a rejection of modernity, but rather as involving a recognition of the limits of the modernity. Postmodernity is a movement which at once splits, radicalizes and weakens modernity.

Post-Marxism
An anti-essentialist recasting of Marxism that is inspired by the Marxist problematic, but which moves beyond it, and which, therefore, should not be passed off as Marxism.

Power
Power is neither an effect of subjective capacities nor structural mechanism, but rather a name for a complex strategic situation (Foucault) that constitutes social identity through the exclusion of a constitutive outside.

Productivism
The belief that economic growth is a goal in itself.

Radical plural democracy
A radical plural democracy is the promise that plural democracy, and the struggles for freedom and equality it engenders, should be deepened and extended to all spheres of society.

Reactivation
Over time politically constructed relations become sedimented as they become part of what we take for granted and their political 'origin' is forgotten. The

process of reactivation reveals the political 'origin' of the social relations, which for a time have been repressed, but which have never been completely eliminated.

Regulative idea
The Kantian meaning of the term 'regulative idea' is a transcendental idea that may guide and organize our thoughts and actions, but which has no actual existence and therefore cannot be empirically validated.

Sedimentation
Sedimentation is the process whereby contingent discursive forms are institutionalized into social institutions that exist in oblivion of their political 'origin'. In such institutions 'the government of things' has replaced 'the government of men'. In other words, sedimentation brings us from the political moment of undecidable decision-making to the relatively fixed real of social relations.

Sign
In a sign a signifier (or expression) is conjoined with a signified (or content).

Signified
The concept (or content) that is expressed by a certain signifier.

Signifier
The sound-image (or expression) that signifies a certain signified.

Social
The ensemble of sedimented social relations that establishes a horizon for meaning and action, which is recursively validated by the social agents and thus possesses a relatively enduring character.

Social antagonism
The unity of a discourse is established by social antagonism. Social antagonism is a result of the exclusion of discursive elements, the differential character of which is collapsed through their articulation in a chain of equivalence. The chain of equivalence expresses a certain 'sameness', but the only thing the equivalential elements have in common is that they pose a threat to the discourse in question.

Social imaginary
A social imaginary is a myth in which the fullness of the surface of inscription continues to dominate. As a result, the somewhat limited myth is transformed into an unlimited horizon for the inscription of any social demand.

Statism
The belief that the state is the privileged provider of societal governance.

Strategic essentialism
Strategic essentialism (Spivac) refers to the strategic necessity on the part of the hegemonic agent to essentialize something which cannot be essentialized. Strategic essentialism is a more or less deliberate use of ideological totalization for strategic purposes.

Strong poet
Someone who affirms the undecidability and contingency of the world and knows how to take political advantage of that undecidability and contingency by aiming to imagine and realize a host of new political projects that carry the promise of further emancipation.

Structural Marxism
Started as a structuralist reading of the scientific writings of the mature Marx. Society is viewed as a complexly structured whole, the articulation of which is determined in the last instance by the economy. Within the structuralist view of society, history becomes a 'process without a subject' as the subjects are reduced to mere 'bearers of the structure'.

Structuralism
An intellectual trend that dominated French philosophy in the later 1960s and early 1970s. It emerged out of structural linguistics, which sought to identify the underlying structure ('langue') that governs our spoken and written language ('parole').

Structural superdeterminism
Miliband accused Poulantzas of structural superdeterminism because Poulantzas, in the eyes of Miliband, ended up viewing the form and functions of the state as fully determined by the economic structure.

Subject
Following Lacan the subject is defined as the lack which emerges when the discursive structure is dislocated. The subject is the lack and can only hope to establish itself as a concrete subjectivity in and through acts of identification.

Subjectivity
The traumatized subject might seek to establish itself as a particular subjectivity by means of identifying with the forms of identity that are offered by various discourses. The transition from being merely a traumatized subject to being a concrete discursive subjectivity is guided by an unfulfilled drive to become a fully achieved identity.

The supplement
In discourses guided by western metaphysics of presence the supplement B is conceived as an inferior instance, the function of which is to compensate for the lack of a full presence of the privileged instance A. But since A now owes its fullness to the presence of the supplement B, the relation between A and B

concludes by being more important than A itself. As a result, the constitutive supplement B is turned into a subversive force that blocks the identity of A, which it was meant to complete.

Suture
The concept of suture comes from Lacanian psychoanalysis. Laclau and Mouffe use the concept when referring to the processes whereby the lack in the structure is filled. Hegemonic practices suture the social in so far as they attempt to heal the rift in the structure that has been opened by structural dislocation. A fully sutured society would be one where the filling-in has eliminated the lack and therefore managed to turn society into a closed symbolic order. Social antagonism and structural dislocation prevent such a closure.

Ultra ethics
Refers to the Levinasian ethics that refers neither to a branch of philosophy nor the predominant set of moral conventions, but to an ethics of ethics in the sense of my non-reciprocal and unconditional acceptance of the obligation to respond to the Other's demand.

Undecidability
Deconstruction reveals the undecidable terrain of non-totalizable openness which the decidable inscription of discursive forms must presuppose. Undecidability is the name for the unresolvable dilemmas which occur under wholly determinate circumstances. But undecidabilty refers not only to the fundamental aporias within discourse but also to the call for a constitutive decision that articulates social meaning in one way rather than another.

Universalism
The universal symbolizes the lack of an imaginary fullness, i.e. the lack of community, justice, welfare, etc. The universal has the form of an empty signifier capable of unifying a series of equivalential demands. The universal is the very form of fullness, and its precise content is fixed in and through particularistic political struggles for hegemony.

Further Reading

This list suggests a few key readings to supplement the chapters of this book during a term course on discourse theory.

Chapter 1 A Gramsci-Inspired Critique of Structural Marxism

Althusser, L. 1971 [1969]: Ideology and ideological state apparatuses. In Althusser (ed.), *Lenin and Philosophy*. New York: Monthly Review Press, 158–83.

Mouffe, C. 1981: Hegemony and the integral state in Gramsci: towards a new concept of politics. In Bridges and Brunt (eds), *Silver Linings: some strategies for the eighties*. London: Lawrence & Wishart, 167–87.

Chapter 2 The Advancement of a Neo-Gramscian Theory of Discourse

Geras, N. 1987: Post-marxism? *New Left Review*, 163, 40–82.

Laclau, E. and Mouffe, C. 1987: Post-marxism without apologies. *New Left Review*, 166, 79–106.

Chapter 3 Towards a New Type of Postmodern Theorizing

Best, S. and Kellner, D. 1992: *Postmodern Theory: critical interrogations*. New York: The Guilford Press, 1–33, 192–204.

Laclau, E. 1989: Politics and the limits of modernity. In Ross (ed.), *Universal Abandon?* Minneapolis: University of Minnesota Press, 63–82.

Chapter 4 Discourse

Howarth, D. 1995: Discourse theory. In Marsh and Stoker (eds.), *Theory and Methods in Political Science*. Basingstoke: Macmillan, 115–33.

Laclau, E. and Mouffe, C. 1985: *Hegemony and Socialist Strategy*. London: Verso, 105–14.

Chapter 5 Hegemony

Bocock, R. 1986: *Hegemony*. London: Tavistock, 22–39, 104–19.
Laclau, E. and Mouffe, C. 1985: *Hegemony and Socialist Strategy*. London: Verso, 134–45.

Chapter 6 Social Antagonism

Laclau, E. and Mouffe, C. 1985: *Hegemony and Socialist Strategy*. London: Verso, 122–34.
Laclau, E. 1990: *New Reflections on the Revolution of Our Time*. London: Verso, 3–59.
Žižek, S. 1990: Beyond discourse analysis. In Laclau (ed.), *New Reflections on the Revolution of Our Time*. London: Verso, 249–60.

Chapter 7 Structure and Agency

Laclau, E. and Mouffe, C. 1985: *Hegemony and Socialist Strategy*. London: Verso, 114–22.
Laclau, E. 1990: *New Reflections on the Revolution of Our Time*. London: Verso, 60–85.
Žižek, S. 1990: Beyond discourse analysis. In Laclau (ed.), *New Reflections on the Revolution of Our Time*. London: Verso, 249–60.

Chapter 8 Power and Authority

Clegg, R. 1989: *Frameworks of Power*. London: Sage, 1–20.
Foucault, M. 1990 [1976]: *The History of Sexuality: vol. I*. Harmondsworth: Pelican, 92–102.

Chapter 9 The Universal and the Particular

Laclau, E. 1996 [1994]: Subject of politics, politics of the subject. In Laclau (ed.), *Emancipation(s)*. London: Verso, 47–65.

Chapter 10 The Politics of Nationalism and Racism

Norval, A.J. 1994: Social ambiguity and the crisis of apartheid. In Laclau (ed.), *The Making of Political Identities*. London: Verso, 115–37.
Salecl, R. 1994: The crisis of identity and the struggle for new hegemony in the former Yugoslavia. In Laclau (ed.), *The Making of Political Identities*. London: Verso, 205–32.
Sayyid, B. 1994: Sign O'Times: Kaffirs and infidels fighting for ninth crusade. In Laclau (ed.), *The Making of Political Identities*. London: Verso, 264–86.

Smith, A.M. 1994b: Rastafari as resistance and the ambiguities of essentialism in the 'New Social Movements'. In Laclau (ed.), *The Making of Political Identities*. London: Verso, 171–204.

Chapter 11 The Politics of Mass Media

Fairclough, N. 1995: *Media Discourse*. London: Edward Arnold, 125–49.
See also the many interesting texts collected in Marris, P. and Thornham, S. 1996: *Media Studies: A Reader*. Edinburgh: Edinburgh University Press.

Chapter 12 The Politics of the Modern Welfare State

Torfing, J. 1998: *Politics, Regulation and the Modern Welfare State*. Basingstoke: Macmillan, chs 6, 7, and 9.

Chapter 13 Towards a Radical Plural Democracy

Mouffe, C. 1993 [1989]: Radical democracy: modern or postmodern. In Mouffe (ed.), *The Return of the Political*. London: Verso, 9–22.
—— 1990: Radical Democracy or liberal democracy? *Socialist Review*, May, 57–66.

Chapter 14 Beyond Libertarianism and Communitarianism

Mouffe, C. 1993 [1991]: Democratic citizenship and the political community. In Mouffe (ed.), *The Return of the Political*. London: Verso, 60–73.
Mulhall, S. and Swift, A. 1992: *Liberals and Communitarians*. Oxford: Blackwell, 1–69.

Chapter 15 The Contours of a Postmodern Ethics?

Bauman, Z. 1993: *Postmodern Ethics*. Oxford: Blackwell Publishers, 1–15, 37–61.
Laclau, E. 1996 [1991]: Community and its paradoxes: Richard Rorty's Liberal Utopia. In Laclau (ed.), *Emancipation(s)*. London: Verso, 105–24.
Rorty, R. 1989: *Contingency, Irony, and Solidarity*. Cambridge: Cambridge University Press, 73–95.

Bibliography

The year of publication of the first available edition – English or other – referred to in the edition used is given in square brackets.

Abercrombie, N.H.S. and Turner, B.S. 1980: *The Dominant Ideology Thesis*. London: Allen & Unwin.

Al-Azmeh, A. 1993: *Islams and Modernities*. London: Verso.

Althusser, L. 1971 [1969]: Ideology and ideological state apparatuses. In Althusser (ed.), *Lenin and Philosophy*. New York: Monthly Review Press, 158–83.

—— 1979a [1965]: *For Marx*. London: Verso.

—— 1979b [1968]: The object of capital. In Althusser and Balibar (eds), *Reading Capital*. London: Verso, 71–194.

Anderson, B. 1983: *Imagined Communities: reflections on the orgins and spread of nationalism*. London: Verso.

Applebaum, R. 1979: Born-again functionalism? *The Insurgent Sociologist*, 9: 1, 18–33.

Aquinas, S.T. 1989 [1264]: *Summa Theologiæ: a concise translation*. London: Methuen.

Arendt, H. 1954: *Between Past and Future: eight exercises in political thought*. New York: The Viking Press.

Aristotle 1975 [1933]: *The Metaphysics*. London: William Heinemann.

—— 1988: *The Politics*. Cambridge: Cambridge University Press.

Armstrong, J. 1992: The autonomy of ethnic identity: historic cleavages and nationality relations in the USSR. In Motyl (ed.), *Thinking Theoretically about Soviet Nationalities*. New York: Columbia University Press, 23–43.

Augustine, A. 1988 [1968]: *The City of God against the Pagans: vols I-VII*. London: William Heinemann.

Baldwin, P. 1996: Can we define a European welfare state model? In Greve (ed.), *The Scandinavian Model in a Period of Change*. Basingstoke: Macmillan, 29–44.

311

Balibar, E. 1979a [1968]: Elements for the theory of transition. In Althusser and Balibar (eds), *Reading Capital*. London: Verso, 273–308.

—— 1979b [1968]: On reproduction. In Althusser and Balibar (eds), *Reading Capital*. London: Verso, 254–72.

—— 1979c [1968]: From periodization to the modes of production. In Althusser and Balibar (eds), *Reading Capital*. London: Verso, 209–24.

—— 1985: Marx, the joker in the pack (or the included middle). *Economy and Society*, 14: 1, 1–27.

—— 1991a: Racism and nationalism. In Balibar and Wallerstein (eds), *Race, Nation, Class: Ambiguous Identities*. London: Verso, 37–67.

—— 1991b: Is there a 'neo-racism'? In Balibar and Wallerstein (eds), *Race, Nation, Class: Ambiguous Identities*. London: Verso, 17–28.

—— 1994: Subjection and subjectivation. In Copjec (ed.), *Supposing the Subject*. London: Verso, 1–15.

Ball, T. 1975: Models of power: past and present. *Journal of the History of the Behavioural Sciences*, July, 211–22.

—— 1978: Two concepts of coercion. *Theory and Society*, 5: 1, 97–112.

Barach, P. and Baratz, M.S. 1962: The two faces of power. *American Political Science Review*, 56: 4, 947–52.

—— 1963: Decisions and nondecisions: an analytical framework. *American Political Science Review*, 57: 3, 641–51.

—— 1970: *Power and Poverty: theory and practice*. Oxford: Oxford University Press.

Barthes, R. 1986 [1970]: *S/Z*. New York: Hill & Wang.

—— 1987 [1957]: *Mythologies*. London: Paladin Grafton Books.

Bauman, Z. 1993: *Postmodern Ethics*. Oxford: Blackwell Publishers.

Benton, T. 1977: *The Philosophical Foundations of the Three Sociologies*. London: Routledge and Kegan Paul.

—— 1981: Objective interests and the sociology of power. *Sociology*, 15: 2, 161–84.

—— 1984: *The Rise and Fall of Structural Marxism*. Basingstoke: Macmillan.

Benveniste, E. 1971 [1966]: *Problems in General Linguistics*. Miami: University of Miami Press.

Berlin, I. 1975 [1969]: *Four Essays on Liberty*. Oxford: Oxford University Press.

Best, S. and Kellner, D. 1992: *Postmodern Theory: critical interrogations*. New York: The Guilford Press.

Beveridge, W.H. 1942: *Social Insurance and Allied Services*. London: HMSO.

Bhaskar, R. 1978 [1975]: *A Realist Theory of Science*. Brighton: Harvester.

Blumenberg, H. 1986 [1966]: *The Legitimacy of the Modern Age 4*. London: MIT Press.

Bobbio, N. 1987: *The Future of Democracy*. Cambridge: Polity Press.

Bowles, S. and Gintis, H. 1980: Structure and practice in the labour theory of value. *Review of Political Economics*, 12: 4, 1–26.

—— 1986: *Democracy and Capitalism*. London: Routledge & Kegan Paul.

Brown, G. and Yule, G. 1983: *Discourse Analysis*. Cambridge: Cambridge University Press.

Callon, M. 1987: Society in the making: the study of technology as a tool for sociological analysis. In Bijker, Hughes and Pinch (eds), *The Social Construction of Technological Systems: new directions in the sociology and history of technology*. Cambridge, MA: MIT Press, 83–103.

Castles, F.G. and Mitchell, D. 1990: Three welfare worlds – or four. *Working Paper*, 21, The Australian National University.

Clegg, R. 1989: *Frameworks of Power*. London: Sage.

Cohen, G.A. 1978: *Karl Marx's Theory of History: A Defence*. Oxford: Oxford University Press.

—— 1988: *History, Labour and Freedom*. Oxford: Oxford University Press.

Colletti, C.F.L. 1975: Marxism and the dialectic. *New Left Review*, 93, September/October, 3–29.

Connell, I. and Mills, A. 1985: Text, discourse and mass communication. In Van Dijk (ed.), *Discourse and Communication*. Berlin: Walter de Gruyter, 26–43.

Connolly, W.E. 1974: *The Terms of Political Discourse*. Lexington: D.C. Heath.

Critchley, S. 1992: *The Ethics of Deconstruction: Derrida and Levinas*. Oxford: Blackwell.

—— 1996: Deconstruction and pragmatism: is Derrida a private ironist or a public liberal? In Mouffe (ed.), *Deconstruction and Pragmatism*. London: Routledge, 19–40.

Cutler, A. et al. 1977: *Marx's Capital and Capitalism Today: vol. I*. London: Routledge & Kegan Paul.

Dahl, R. A. 1957: The concept of power. *Behavioral Science*, 2: 2, 201–5.

—— 1958: Critique of the ruling elite model. *American Political Science Review*, 52, 463–9.

—— 1971: A critique of the ruling elite model. In Castles, Murray and Potter (eds), *Decisions, Organizations and Society*. Harmondsworth: Penguin, 354–63.

Dean, M. 1991: *The Constitution of Poverty: toward a genealogy of liberal governance*. London: Routledge.

Derrida, J. 1976 [1967]: *Of Grammatology*. London: Johns Hopkins University Press.

—— 1978 [1967]: *Writing and Difference*. London: Routledge & Kegan Paul.

—— 1981 [1972]: *Positions*. London: The Athlone Press.

—— 1986a [1972]: *Margins of Philosophy*. Brighton: Harvester.

—— 1986b [1974]: *Glas*. Lincoln: University of Nebraska Press.

—— 1986c [1967]: *Speech and Phenomena*. New York: Northwestern University Press.

—— 1987 [1980]: *The Post Card from Socrates to Freud and Beyond*. Chicago: University of Chicago Press.

—— 1988a [1977]: *Limited Inc*. Evanston: Northwestern University Press.

—— 1988b: Letter to a Japanese friend. In Wood and Bernasconi (eds), *Derrida and Différence*. Evanston: Northwestern University Press, 1–5.

—— 1992: Force of law: the mystical foundation of authority. In Cornell, Rosenfeld and Carlson (eds), *Deconstruction and the Possibility of Justice*. London: Routledge, 3–67.

—— 1994: *Specters of Marx: the State of the debt, the work of mourning, & the new international*. New York: Routledge.

—— 1997: *The Politics of Friendship*. London: Verso, forthcoming.

Donzelot, J. 1994 [1984]: *L'invention du Social: essai sur le déclin des passions politiques*. Paris: Fayard.

Downs, A. 1957: *An Economic Theory of Democracy*. New York: Harper & Row.

—— 1960: Why government budget is too small in a democracy. *World Politics*, 12: 4, 541–64.

Dreyfus, H.L. and Rabinow, P. 1986 [1982]: *Michel Foucault: beyond structuralism and hermeneutics*. Brighton: Harvester.

Ducrot, O. and Todorov, T. 1981: Glossematics. In Ducrot and Todorov (eds), *Encylopedic Dictionary of the Sciences of Language*. Oxford: Basil Blackwell, 20–4.

Dyrberg, T.B. 1997: *The Circular Structure of Power: politics, identity, community*. London: Verso.

Easton, D. 1971 [1953]: *The Political System: an inquiry into the state of political science*. New York: Alfred A. Knopf.

Edelman, M. 1988: *Constructing the Political Spectacle*. Chicago: University of Chicago Press.

Edwards, R. 1979: *Contested Terrain: the transformation of the workplace in the twentieth century*. New York: Basic Books.

Einhorn, E. and Logue, J. 1989: *Modern Welfare States: politics and policies in social democratic Scandinavia*. New York: Praeger.

Elster, J. 1982: Marxism, functionalism and game theory. *Theory and Society*, 11: 4, 453–82.

—— 1983: Reply to comments. *Theory and Society*, 12: 1, 111–20.

—— 1985: *Making Sense of Marx*. Cambridge: Cambridge University Press.

—— 1986: Further thoughts on Marxism, functionalism, and game theory. In Roemer (ed.), *Analytical Marxism*. Cambridge: Cambridge University Press, 202–20.

Esping-Andersen, G. 1985: *Politics Against Markets*. Princeton: Princeton University Press.

—— 1990: *The Three Worlds of Welfare Capitalism*. Princeton: Princeton University Press.

—— 1993: *Life Cycles, Work and Welfare*. Unpublished Paper.

Fairclough, N. 1993: *Discourse and Social Change*. Oxford: Blackwell.

—— 1995: *Media Discourse*. London: Edward Arnold.

Fine, B. and Harris, L. 1979: *Rereading Capital*. Basingstoke: Macmillan.

Fishman, J. 1980: Social theory and ethnography: neglected perspectives on language and ethnicity in Eastern Europe. In Sugar (ed.), *Ethnic Diversity and Conflict in Eastern Europe*. Santa Barbara: ABC-Clio, 69–99.

Flora, P. and Alber, J. 1982: Modernization, democratization, and the development of welfare states in Western Europe. In Flora and Heidenheimer (eds), *The Development of Welfare States in Europe and America*. London: Transaction Books, 37–80.

Fonsmark, H. 1990: *Historien om den Danske Utopi*. København: Gyldendal.

Ford, H. 1926: Mass production. In *Encyclopaedia Britannica*, 13th edition, suppl. II, 821–3.

Foucault, M. 1985 [1969]: *The Archaeology of Knowledge*. London: Tavistock.

—— 1986a [1971]: What is enlightenment? In Rabinow (ed.), *The Foucault Reader: an introduction to Foucault's thought, with major new unpublished material*. Harmondsworth: Penguin Books, 32–75.

—— 1986b [1971]: Nietzsche, genealogy, history. In Rabinow (ed.), *The Foucault Reader: an introduction to Foucault's thought, with major new unpublished material*. Harmondsworth: Penguin, 76–100.

—— 1986c [1976]: *Power/Knowledge*. Brighton: Harvester.

—— 1986d [1982]: The Subject and power. In Dreyfus and Rabinow (eds), *Michel Foucault: Beyond Structuralism and Hermeneutics*. Brighton: Harvester, 208–26.

—— 1990 [1976]: *The History of Sexuality: vol. I*. Harmondsworth: Pelican.

—— 1991: Politics and the study of discourse. In Burchell, Gordon and Miller (eds), *The Foucault Effect*. London: Harvester, 53–72.

Freud, S. 1986 [1900]: *The Interpretation of Dreams*. Harmondsworth: Penguin.

Fukuyama, F. 1989: The end of history. *The National Interest*, 16, summer, 3–18.

—— 1992: *The End of History and the Last Man*. Harmondsworth: Penguin.

Furet, F. 1978: *Penser la Révolution Française*. Paris: Gallimard.

Gamble, A. 1988: *The Free Economy and the Strong State*. Basingstoke: Macmillan.

Gane, M. 1983: On the ISAs episode. *Economy and Society*, 12: 4, 431–67.

Gasché, R. 1986: *The Tain of the Mirror*. London: Harvard University Press.

Gaudemar, J. P. 1982: *L'ordre et la production: naissance et formes de la discipline d'usine*. Paris: DUNOD.

Gellner, E. 1983: *Nations and Nationalism*. Ithaca: Cornell University Press.

Geras, N. 1987: Post-Marxism? *New Left Review*, 163, 40–82.

Giddens, A. 1976: *New Rules of Sociological Method*. London: Hutchinson.

—— 1979: *Central Problems in Social Theory*. Basingstoke: Macmillan.

—— 1981: *A Contemporary Critique of Historical Materialism*. Basingstoke: Macmillan.

—— 1982: Commentary to the debate. *Theory and Society*, 11: 4, 527–39.

—— 1984: *The Constitution of Society*. Basingstoke: Macmillan.

Girvetz, H.K. 1968: Welfare state. In Sills (ed.), *International Encyclopedia of the Social Sciences: vol. XVI*. New York: Macmillan and The Free Press, 512–21.

Gissurarson, H.H. 1993: Authority. In Outhwaite and Bottomore (eds), *The Blackwell Dictionary of Twentieth-Century Social Thought*. Oxford: Blackwell, 37–9.

Gough, I. 1979: *The Political Economy of the Welfare State*. Basingstoke: Macmillan.

Grafenauer, N. 1991: Foreword. In Grafenauer (ed.), *The case of Slovenia*. Lublljana: Nova Revija, 1–3.

Gramsci, A. 1971 [1948–51]: *Selections from Prison Notebooks*. London: Lawrence & Wishart.

Greenfeld, L. 1992: *Nationalism: five roads to modernity*. Cambridge, MA: Harvard University Press.

Habermas, J. 1984–1987: *The Theory of Communicative Action: vols I–II*. Cambridge: Polity Press.

—— 1990 [1985]: *The Philosophical Discourse of Modernity: twelve lectures*. Cambridge: Polity Press.

—— 1992: *Faktizität und Geltung: beiträge zur diskurstheorie des rechts und des demokratischen rechtsstaats*. Frankfurt am Main: Suhrkamp Verlag.

Hacker, K.L. 1996: Missing links in the evolution of electronic democratization. *Media, Culture & Society*, 18, 213–23.

Hall, S. 1977: The hinterland of science: ideology and the sociology of knowledge. In Coffey et al. (eds), *On Ideology*. London: Centre for Contemporary Cultural Studies, 9–32.

—— 1980: Encoding/decoding. In Hall et al. (eds), *Culture, Media, Language*. London: Hutchinson, 128–38.

—— 1988: *Thatcherism and the Crisis of the Left: the hard road to renewal*. London: Verso.

Hansen, L 1996: Slovenian identity: state building on the Balkan border. *Alternatives*, 21: 4, 473–95.

Hay, C. 1995: Structure and agency. In Marsh and Stoker (eds), *Theory and Methods in Political Science*. Basingstoke: Macmillan Press, 89–206.

Hegel, G.W.F. 1967 [1821]: *Philosophy of Right*. Oxford: Clarendon Press.

Hindess, B. and Hirst, P. 1977: *Mode of Production and Social Formation*. London: Macmillan.

Hirst, P. 1976: Althusser and the theory of ideology. *Economy and Society*, 5: 4, 385–412.

—— 1988: Associational socialism in a pluralist state. *Journal of Law and Society*, 15: 1, spring, 134–50.

—— 1994: *Associative Democracy: new forms of economic and social governance*. Cambridge: Polity Press.

Hjelmslev, L. 1963: *Prolegomena to a Theory of Language*. Madison: University of Wisconsin Press.

Hobbes, T. 1839: *The English Works of Thomas Hobbes: vols I–II*. London: J. Bohn.

—— 1986 [1651]: *Leviathan*. Harmondsworth: Penguin.

Hobsbawm, E. 1990: *Nations and Nationalism Since 1780*. Cambridge: Cambridge University Press.

Holsti, O. 1969: *Content Analysis for the Social Sciences and the Humanities*. Reading: Addison-Wesley.

Howard, D. 1989: *Defining the Political*. Basingstoke: Macmillan.

Hunter, F. 1953: *Community Power Structure*. Chapel Hill: University of North Carolina Press.

Huntington, S.P. 1996: *The Clash of Civilizations and the Remaking of World Order*. New York: Simon and Schuster.

Ifversen, J. 1989: Den franske revolution mellem demokrati og ideologi. *Slagmark*, 13, summer, 31–52.

Isaac, J.C. 1987: *Power and Marxist Theory: a realist view*. London: Cornell University Press.

Jessop, B. 1990: *State Theory*. Cambridge: Polity Press.

—— 1992: Regulation und politik: integraler ökonomie und integraler staat. In Demirovic, Krebs and Sablowski (eds), *Hegemonie und Staat*. Münster: Westphalisches Dampfboot Verlag, 232–62.

—— 1993: Towards a Schumpeterian workfare state? Preliminary remarks on post-Fordist political economy, *Studies in Political Economy*, 40: 1, 7–39.

—— 1994a: The transition to post-Fordism and the Schumpeterian workfare state. In Burrows and Loader (eds), *Towards a Post-Fordist Welfare State*. London: Routledge, 13–37.

—— 1994b: Post-fordism and the state. In Amin (ed.), *Post-Fordism: a reader*. Oxford: Blackwell, 251–79.

Jessop, B. et al. 1988: *Thatcherism*. Cambridge: Polity Press.

Jones, C. 1993: The pacific challenge. In Jones (ed.), *New Perspectives on the Welfare State in Europe*. London: Routledge, 198–217.

Katznelson, I. 1988: The welfare state as a contested institutional idea. *Politics and Society*, 16: 4, 517–31.

Kavanagh, D. 1987: *Thatcherism and British Politics: the end of consensus?* Oxford: Oxford University Press.

Kellner, D. 1995: *Media Culture: cultural studies, identity and politics between the modern and the postmodern*. London: Routledge.

Kersbergen, K.V. 1991: *Social Capitalism: a study of Christian democracy and the welfare state*. London: Routledge.

Keynes, J.M. 1971 [1933]: *The Means To Prosperity: collected works of John Maynard Keynes: vol. IX*. Basingstoke: Macmillan, 335–65.

—— 1977 [1936]: *The General Theory of Employment, Interest and Money*. Basingstoke: Macmillan.

Kolb, D. 1986: *The Critique of Pure Modernity*. London: University of Chicago Press.

Korpi, W. 1983: *The Democratic Class Struggle*. London: Routledge & Kegan Paul.

Kripke, S. 1980: *Naming and Necessity*. Oxford: Basil Blackwell.

Krippendorff, K. 1980: *Content Analysis: an introduction to its methodology.* London: Sage.

Kristensen, O.P. 1987: *Væksten i den Offentlige Sektor:* København: Jurist-og Økonomforbundets Forlag.

Kristeva, J. 1970: *Le Texte du Roman.* The Hague: Mouton.

Laclau, E. 1977: *Politics and Ideology in Marxist Theory.* London: Verso.

—— 1980a: Democratic antagonisms and the capitalist state. In Freeman and Robertson (eds), *The Frontiers of Political Theory.* Brighton: Harvester, 101–39.

—— 1980b: Populist rupture and discourse. *Screen Education,* 34, spring, 87–93.

—— 1980c: Togliatti and politics. *Politics and Power,* 2, October, 251–8.

—— 1981: Teorias marxistas des estado: debates y perspectivas. In Lechner (ed.), *Estado y Politica en America Latina.* Mexico: Siglo XXI, 25–59.

—— 1983a: Transformations of advanced industrial societies and the theory of the subject. In Hänninen and Paldán (eds), *Rethinking Ideology: a Marxist debate.* Berlin: Argument-Verlag, 39–44.

—— 1983b: Socialisme et transformation des logiques hégémoniques. In Buci-Glucksmann (ed.), *La Gauche, Le Pouvoir, Le Socialisme.* Paris: Presses Universitaires de France, 331–8.

—— 1985: New social movements and the plurality of the social. In Slater (ed.), *New Social Movements and the State in Latin America.* Amsterdam: CEDLA, 27–42.

—— 1987a: Class war and after. *Marxism Today,* April, 30–3.

—— 1987b: Psychoanalysis and marxism. *Critical Inquiry,* winter, 330–3.

—— 1988: Metaphor and social antagonisms. In Nelson and Grossberg (eds), *Marxism and the Interpretation of Culture.* Basingstoke: Macmillan Education, 249–57.

—— 1989: Politics and the limits of modernity. In Ross (ed.), *Universal Abandon?* Minneapolis: University of Minnesota Press, 63–82.

—— 1990a: *New Reflections on the Revolution of Our Time.* London: Verso.

—— 1990b: Totalitarianism and moral indignation. *Diacritics,* 20: 1, spring, 88–95.

—— 1991: Community and its paradoxes: Richard Rorty's Liberal Utopia. In Miami Theory Collective (eds), *Community at Loose Ends.* Minneapolis: Minnesota University Press, 83–98.

—— 1992a: Beyond emancipation. In Pieterse (ed.), *Emancipations: Modern and Postmodern.* Sage: London, 121–37.

—— 1992b: Universalism, particularism, and the question of identity. *October,* 61, summer, 83–90.

—— 1993a: *Discourse.* In Gooding and Pettit (eds), *The Blackwell Companion to Contemporary Political Philosophy.* Oxford: Blackwell, 431–7.

—— 1993b: Power and representation. In Foster (ed.), *Politics, Theory and Contemporary Culture.* New York: Columbia University Press, 277–96.

—— 1993c: The signifiers of democracy. In Carens (ed.), *Democracy and*

Possessive Individualism. New York: State University of New York Press, 221–31.

——— 1994a: Georges Sorel, objectivity and the logic of violence. Paper prepared for Oxford Conference, *Politique et Passion*, June.

——— 1994b: Why do empty signifiers matter to politics? In Weeks (ed.), *The Lesser Evil and the Greater Good*. London: Rivers Oram Press, 167–78.

——— 1995a: Subject of politics, politics of the subject. *Differences*, 7: 1, 145–64.

——— 1995b: The time is out of joint. *Diacritics*, 25: 2, summer, 86–96.

——— 1996a: The death and resurrection of the theory of ideology. *Journal of Political Ideologies*, 1: 3, 201–20.

——— 1996b: Deconstruction, pragmatism, hegemony. In Mouffe (ed.), *Deconstruction and Pragmatism*. London: Routledge, 47–67.

——— 1997: On the names of God. *Working Papers*, 16, Centre for Theoretical Studies in the Humanities and the Social Sciences, University of Essex.

Laclau, E. and Mouffe, C. 1982: Recasting marxism: hegemony and new political movements. *Socialist Review*, 12, November, 91–113.

——— 1985: *Hegemony and Socialist Strategy*. London: Verso.

——— 1987: Post-marxism without apologies. *New Left Review*, 166, 79–106.

Laclau, E. and Zac, L. 1994: Minding the gap: the subject of politics. In Laclau (ed.), *The Making of Political Identities*. London: Verso, 11–37.

Larmore, C. 1987: *Patterns of Moral Complexity*. Cambridge: Cambridge University Press.

Lefort, C. 1986: *The Political Forms of Modern Society*. Cambridge: Polity Press.

——— 1988: *Democracy and Political Theory*. Cambridge: Polity Press.

Leibfried, S. 1993: Towards a European welfare state. In Jones (ed.), *New Perspectives on the Welfare State in Europe*. London: Routledge, 133–56.

Lenin, V.I. 1981 [1916]: Imperialism and the split in socialism. In Lenin (ed.), *Collected Works: vol. XXIII*, 105–20.

Levinas, E. 1969: *Totality and Infinity*. Pittsburgh: Duquesne University Press.

Lübcke, P. 1983: Kant. In Lübcke (ed.), *Politikens Filosofi Leksikon*. København: Politikens Forlag, 227–34.

Luhmann, N. 1993: Deconstruction as second-order observing. *New Literary History*, 763–82.

Lukacs, G. 1971 [1923]: *History and Class Consciousness: Studies in Marxist Dialectics*. Cambridge, MA: MIT Press.

Lukes, S. 1984 [1974]: *Power: a radical view*. Basingstoke: Macmillan.

Lyotard, J.F. 1984 [1979]: *The Postmodern Condition: a report of knowledge*. Manchester: Manchester University Press.

Macdonell, D. 1986: *Theories of Discourse: an introduction*. Oxford: Basil Blackwell.

Machiavelli, N. 1988 [1961]: *The Prince*. London: Penguin.

MacIntyre, A. 1984: *After Virtue: a study in moral theory*. London: Duckworth.

MacPherson, C.B 1962: *The Political Theory of Possessive Individualism: Hobbes to Locke*. London: Oxford University Press.

—— 1972 [1965]: *The Real World of Democracy*. New York: Oxford University Press.

—— 1973 [1964]: Post-liberal-democracy. In MacPherson (ed.), *Democratic Theory: essays in retrieval*. Oxford: Clarendon Press, 170–84.

—— 1977: *The Life and Times of Liberal Democracy*. Oxford: Oxford University Press.

Malthus, T.R. 1798: *An Essay on the Principle of Population as it affects the future improvement of society*. London: Johnson.

Manzin, M. 1994–95: Weary eyes on a new neighbour. *Balkan War Report*, 30, December 1994/January 1995.

March, J. and Olsen J.P. 1989: *Rediscovering Institutions: the organizational basis of politics*. New York: The Free Press.

Marglin, S. 1974: What do bosses do? *Review of Radical Political Economics*, 6: 2, 60–112.

Marshall, T.H. 1965: *Class, Citizenship, and Social Development*. Garden City: Anchor Books.

Marx, K. 1977 [1867–94]: *Capital: vols I–III*. London: Lawrence & Wishart.

—— 1987a [1843]: On the Jewish question. In McLellan (ed.), *Karl Marx: selected writings*, Oxford: Oxford University Press, 39–57.

—— 1987b [1848]: The communist manifesto. In McLellan (ed.), *Karl Marx: selected writings*, Oxford: Oxford University Press, 219–47.

—— 1987c [1859]: Preface to a critique of political economy. In McLellan (ed.), *Karl Marx: selected writings*, Oxford: Oxford University Press, 388–92.

Mastnak, T. 1989: No rationale for the survival of Yugoslavia. *East European Reporter*, 3: 4, 46–8.

—— 1991: From the new social movements to political parties. In Simmie and Dekleva (eds), *Yugoslavia in Turmoil: after self-management?* London: Printer, 45–64.

May, T. 1994: *The Political Philosophy of Poststructuralist Anarchism*. Pennsylvania: The Pennsylvania State University Press.

Mcquail, D. 1975: *Social Processes: communication*. London: Longman.

Miliband, R. 1970: Reply to Nicos Poulantzas. *New Left Review*, 59, 53–60.

—— 1973: Poulantzas and the capitalist state. *New Left Review*, 82, 83–92.

Mills, C.W. 1956: *The Power Elite*. Oxford: Oxford University Press.

Mishra, R. 1984: *The Welfare State in Crisis*. Brighton: Wheatsheaf Books.

Mouffe, C. 1979: Hegemony and ideology in Gramsci. In Mouffe (ed.), *Gramsci and Marxist Theory*. London: Routledge & Kegan Paul, 168–205.

—— 1981: Hegemony and the integral state in Gramsci: towards a new concept of politics. In Bridges and Brunt (eds), *Silver Linings: some strategies for the eighties*. London: Lawrence & Wishart, 167–87.

—— 1987: Rawls: political philosophy without politics. *Philosophy and Social Criticism*, 13: 2, 105–23.

—— 1988a: Hegemony and new political subjects: towards a new concept of democracy. In Nelson and Grossberg (eds), *Marxism and the Interpretation of Culture*. Basingstoke: Macmillan, 89–101.

—— 1988b: The civics lesson. *New Statesman and Society*, 7, 29–31.

—— 1988c: American liberalism and its critics: Rawls, Taylor, Sandel and Walzer. *Praxis International*, 8: 2, 193–206.

—— 1989: Radical democracy: modern or postmodern. In Ross (ed.), *Universal Abandon?* Edinburgh: Edinburgh University Press, 31–45.

—— 1990: Radical democracy or liberal democracy? *Socialist Review*, May, 57–66.

—— 1991a: Pluralism and modern democracy: around Carl Schmitt. *New Formations*, 14, summer, 1–16.

—— 1991b: Democratic citizenship and the political community. In the Miami Theory Collective (ed.), *Community at Loose Ends*, Minneapolis: University of Minnesota Press, 70–82.

—— 1992a: Preface: democratic politics today. In Mouffe (ed.), *Dimensions of Radical Democracy: pluralism, citizenship, community*. London: Verso, 1–14.

—— 1992b: Citizenship and political identity. *October*, 61, 28–32.

—— 1993a: Introduction: for an agonistic pluralism. In Mouffe (ed.), *The Return of the Political*. London: Verso, 1–8.

—— 1993b: Towards a liberal socialism. In Mouffe (ed.), *The Return of the Political*. London: Verso, 90–101.

—— 1993c: On the articulation between liberalism and democracy. In Mouffe (ed.), *The Return of the Political*. London: Verso, 102–16.

—— 1993d: The return of the political. *New Times*, 48, 27 November, 8–9.

—— 1993e: Politics and the limits of liberalism: In Mouffe (ed.), *The Return of the Political*. London:Verso, 135–54.

—— 1993f: Feminism, citizenship and radical democratic politics. In Mouffe (ed.), *The Return of the Political*. London: Verso, 74–89.

—— 1994a: Political liberalism, neutrality and the political. *Ratio Juris*, 7:3, 314–24.

—— 1994b: For a politics of nomadic identity. In Robertson et al. (eds), *Travellers' Tales*. Routledge: London, 105–13.

—— 1995: The end of politics and the rise of the radical right. *Dissent*, fall, 498–502.

—— 1996a: Democracy, power and the 'political'. In Benhabib (ed.), *Democracy and Difference*. Princeton: Princeton University Press, 245–56.

—— 1996b: Deconstruction, pragmatism and the politics of democracy. In Mouffe (ed.), *Deconstruction and Pragmatism*. New York: Routledge, 1–11.

—— 1996c: The parodox of political liberalism. Personally circulated paper.

Nisbet, R.A. 1966: *The Sociological Tradition*. London: Basic Books.

Norval, A.J. 1996: *Deconstructing Apartheid Discourse*. London: Verso.

Oakeshott, M. 1975: *On Human Conduct*. Oxford: Clarendon Press.

O'Connor, J. 1973: *The Fiscal Crisis of the State*. New York: St. Martin's Press.

321

Offe, C. 1974: Structural problems of the capitalist state. In von Beyme (ed.), *German Political Studies*. London: Sage, 31–59.

Outhwaite, W. 1990: Agency and structure. In Clark, Modgil and Modgil (eds), *Anthony Giddens: consensus and controversy*. London: Falmer, 63–72.

Parsons T. 1986 [1963]: Power and social system. In Lukes (ed.), *Power*. Oxford: Basil Blackwell, 94–144.

Pateman, C. 1988: *The Sexual Contract*. Cambridge: Polity Press.

—— 1989: *The Disorder of Women*. Cambridge: Polity Press.

Perelman, C. and Olbrechts, L. 1969 [1958]: *The New Rhetoric: a treatise on argumentation*. London: University of Notre Dame Press.

Poster, M. 1990: *The Mode of Information: poststructuralism and social context*. Chicago: University of Chicago Press.

Poulantzas, N. 1969: The problem of the capitalist state. *New Left Review*, 58, 67–78.

—— 1976: The capitalist state: reply to Miliband and Laclau. *New Left Review*, 95, 62–83.

—— 1978 [1974]: *Classes in Contemporary Capitalism*. London: Verso.

—— 1979 [1970]: *Fascism and Dictatorship*. London: Verso.

—— 1980 [1978]: *State, Power, Socialism*. London: Verso.

—— 1987 [1968]: *Political Power and Social Classes*. London: Verso.

Poulsen, B. 1960: *Ideernes krise i åndsliv og politik*. Copenhagen: Gyldendal.

Rawls, J. 1971: *A Theory of Justice*. Cambridge, MA: The Belknap Press of Harvard University.

—— 1985: Justice as fairness: political and metaphysical. *Philosophy and Public Affairs*, 14: 3, summer, 223–51.

—— 1987: The idea of an overlapping consensus. *Oxford Journal of Legal Studies*, 7: 1, spring, 1–25.

—— 1993: *Political Liberalism*. New York: Columbia University Press.

Rorty, R. 1989: *Contingency, Irony, and Solidarity*. Cambridge: Cambridge University Press.

Rosenau, I.R. 1992: *Post-modernism and the Social Sciences: insights, inroads, and intrusions*. Princeton: Princeton University Press.

Salecl, R. 1994: The crisis of identity and the struggle for new hegemony in the former Yugoslavia. In Laclau (ed.), *The Making of Political Identities*. London: Verso, 205–32.

Sandel, M. 1982: *Liberalism and the Limits of Justice*. Cambridge: Cambridge University Press.

Sassoon, A.S. 1982: State and political strategy. In Sassoon (ed.), *Approaches to Gramsci*. London: Writers and Readers Publishing Cooperative Ltd.

—— 1987: *Gramsci's Politics*. London: Hutchinson.

Saussure, F. 1981 [1959]: *Course in General Linguistics*. Suffolk: Fontana.

Sayyid, B. 1994: Sign O'Times: Kaffirs and infidels fighting for ninth crusade. In Laclau (ed.), *The Making of Political Identities*. London: Verso, 264–86.

Schmidt, L.H. 1995: Velfærd til forhandling: om barmhjertighed, solidaritet og overbærenhed. *Social Forskning*. August, 99–107.

Schmitt, C. 1976 [1927]: *The Concept of the Political*. New Brunswick: Rutgers University Press.

—— 1985 [1923]: *The Crisis of Parliamentary Democracy*. Baskerville: MIT Press.

Searle, J. 1984: *Intentionality*. Cambridge: Cambridge University Press.

Skinner, Q. 1991: The paradoxes of political liberty. In Miller (ed.), *Liberty*. Oxford: Oxford University Press, 183–205.

Sklair, L. 1991: *Sociology of the Global System*. Baltimore: Johns Hopkins University Press.

Sloterdijk, P. 1983: *Kritik der Zynischen Vernuft*. Frankfurt am Main: Suhrkamp.

Smith, A.D. 1995: *Nations and Nationalism in a Global Era*. Oxford: Basil Blackwell.

Smith, A.M. 1994a: *New Right Discourse on Race and Sexuality*. Cambridge: Cambridge University Press.

—— 1994b: Rastafari as resistance and the ambiguities of essentialism in the 'New Social Movements'. In Laclau (ed.), *The Making of Political Identities*. London: Verso, 171–204.

Staten, H. 1985 [1984]: *Wittgenstein and Derrida*. Oxford: Basil Blackwell.

Stedman Jones, G. 1983: *Languages of Class*. Cambridge: Cambridge University Press.

Stone, K. 1974: The origins of job structure in the steel industry. *Review of Radical Political Economics*, 6: 2, 113–73.

Sumic, J. and Riha, R. 1994: The reinvention of democracy in Eastern Europe. *Angelaki*, 1: 3, 143–56.

Taylor, 1985: Philosophy and the Human Sciences. *Philosophical Papers 2*, Cambridge: Cambridge University Press.

Therborn, G. 1989: States, populations and productivity: towards a political theory of welfare states. In Lassman (ed.), *Politics and Social Theory*. London: Routledge, 62–84.

Titmuss, R. 1974: *Social Policy*. London: George Allen & Unwin.

Torfing, J. 1991: A hegemony approach to capitalist regulation. In Bertramsen, Thomsen and Torfing (eds), *State, Economy and Society*. London: Unwin Hyman, 35–93.

—— 1998: *Politics, Regulation and the Modern Welfare State*. Basingstoke: Macmillan.

Tronti, M. 1977: *Ouvriers et Capital*. Paris: C. Bourgeois.

Van Dijk, T.A. 1985: Introduction: discourse analysis in (mass) communication research. In Van Dijk (ed.), *Discourse and Communication*. Berlin: Walter de Gruyter, 1–93.

Walzer, M. 1983: *Spheres of Justice*. New York: Basic Books.

—— 1989: Citizenship. In Ball et al. (eds), *Political Innovation and Conceptual Changes*. Cambridge: Cambridge University Press, 211–19.

Weber, M. 1978 [1968]: *Economy and Society: an outline of interpretative sociology*. New York: Bedminister Press Incorporated.

Wilensky, H.L. 1975: *The Welfare State and Equality*. Los Angeles: University of California Press.

Winch, P. 1967: Authority. In Quinton (ed.), *Political Philosophy*. Glasgow: Oxford University Press, 97–111.

Wolin, S.S. 1960: *Politics and Vision*. London: George Allen & Unwin.

Žižek, S. 1989: *The Sublime Object of Ideology*. London: Verso.

—— 1990a: Beyond discourse analysis. In Laclau (ed.), *New Reflections on the Revolution of Our Time*. London: Verso, 249–60.

—— 1990b: Eastern Europe's republics of Gilead. *New Left Review*, 183, September/October, 51–62.

—— 1991: *For They Know not what They Do: enjoyment as a political factor*. Verso: London.

Index

Index

Index

330

341

MNO = . the McGuffin is a ??? ?
of/for what? About what?
, About itself / About a future
, About something different
for each character
, About nothing / Death / the Void
, About the Other.